The
Holy Days
Code

The
Holy Days
Code

How the Law and the Gospel are an Encryption/Decryption Messaging System

Mark Stading

Table of Contents

Preface

Between the mid 1990's and early 2000's, there were a handful of sources claiming the discovery of concealed information within the Scripture text. It was as if the Scripture was being made out to be a "Crystal Ball", or worse yet, an "Ouija Board" of sorts. It was akin to asking the Bible a question and then extracting an answer by way of a formula. The formula was a technique of letter counting, better known as Equidistant Letter Sequencing, or ELS. By collecting letters from passages taken from the Hebrew Torah, a search was made for the existence of "hidden" messages imbedded within the text. This method counted off letters sequentially by some fixed number and joined them together to see if it would form words and phrases. For example, say the count is the number 7. The simplest method would be to take every 7th letter of a given passage and join together the resulting letters and analyze it for any "hidden message" emerging from the newly formed text. The actual method used included a "framing" box to contain rows of a certain number of letters in which to bound the problem and make it consistent. This would allow the experiment to be conducted over and over again by sliding the box frame-by-frame.

A 13th Century Rabbi is believed to have been the earliest recorded person proposing an ELS code as a means of discovering hidden information within the Scripture. But more generally speaking, Judaism's mysticism of Kabbalah has long proposed all sorts of forms of hidden messages too within the Hebrew Bible and so the thinking on this subject is nothing historically new. What inspired an entirely new modern day search for such hidden messages was the development of computers. With such a tool available it effectively would allow endless searches in a far shorter time and with minimal human toil. It created a curious anticipation for seekers anxious to see what could be found. Would something astonishing jump out of the ancient text after a thousand years or more of existing? (This is somewhat reminiscent of the movie **2001: A Space Odyssey** where a higher form of intelligence plants a beacon on the moon to inform them when human evolution would advance far enough for them to discover it and uncover it.)

The first major claim to be made by using ELS on Scripture, with the aid of computers, was published in a Statistics Science journal by three Israeli Mathematicians in 1994. The article pointed out that famous rabbis and relevant dates relating to them were discovered and that probability theory suggested this was not to be considered a "random" chance possibility occurrence. Through this demonstration the proponents were making the case that the Hebrew Torah was unique in communicating information on a hidden level via a form of Code and not by random coincidence. Furthermore, the implication was that this was also evidence pointing to a Divine Inspiration to the Hebrew Torah in a roundabout way.

Later, in 1998, the book entitled "The Bible Code" written by Michael Drosnin brought this subject out into the much broader public community for inspection and evaluation. But the book was far less technical in merit and was widely panned by critics as sensational and bordering on pure fantasy because of Drosnin's claims of Bible Codes having the ability to predict the future. Drosnin argued that certain modern day events relating to the nation Israel had been "foretold" in Scripture such as Yitzhak Rabin's assassination in 1995 and a terrorist bombing of a bus in Jerusalem in 1996. He further asserted the Code predicted an apocalyptic Third World War event was to occur between 1998 and 2006. Drosnin wrote a second book, "The Bible Code II" in 2002 and there made specific predictions about the future. For example, he predicted that Yasser Arafat would be assassinated and that it would be an inside job. (Arafat did die in 2004 in what was first considered to be "natural causes" although later theories arose of him being poisoned.) Most sensational of all claims however was Drosnin's assertion that the underlying Biblical Code was written by extraterrestrial life and brought to Earth by an alien who left a key to unlock the Code! A final Part III also came out in 2010 wherein Drosnin attempts to explain why his prediction of an Apocalypse had not come as predicted. But by now Drosnin's audience had long left the building.

This naturally led other Scripture "enthusiasts" to get in on the frenzy of activity and do some of their own kind of "searching" for "hidden messages". And this kind of snowballed into a greater and greater sized community of those "searching" for what could be found. Christians in the United States especially were perceiving that should such communication be found existing in the pages of the Hebrew Scripture, certainly the topic of "Jesus" being declared Israel's Messiah would be a prominent message amongst these messages.

There is an old adage amongst scientists and engineers that if one "tortures" the "data" long enough, you can get the data to say anything you want it to say. And so, one thing led to another, and indeed this adage came to take on a whole new meaning. For not only were Christians touting the Gospel message being "encoded" in the Hebrew Bible, but also new groups of skeptics began to join in on the exercise of "torturing the data". And lo and behold, through similar sorts of methods, it was possible to form words and phrases that were essentially blasphemous to all things holy in Scripture! Not only that but someone even claimed to show that the book **Moby Dick** could be extracted of information relating to relatively recent current events such as Martin Luther King's assassination! It wasn't long thereafter that this whole energized community of Biblical "Hackers" came to lose the general public's interest in the subject of Codes existing in Scripture for obvious reasons. The original intent of providing credence to a "Divine" inspiration to Scripture came to backfire in an embarrassing way. Needless to say, this whole exercise perhaps created more skeptics then it did "believers" after the whole affair ran its course.

What is so ironic about these searches for hidden messages in the Scripture is that no one seems to be interested in solving the many openly visible mysteries the text witnesses when reading it in a straight forward fashion. These "out in the open" mysteries continue to prove that readers cannot even grasp the more readily visible message of Scripture, let alone perceive that a hidden one exists and know its meaning. Intuitively it would seem that these mysteries should be of far more concern to resolve than for an inquisitive reader to spend time in looking for hidden messages in Scripture that requires the aid of a computer to find.

The mysteries of the Holy Days certainly represents one very good example of this problem. For those familiar with the Law, these mysteries have existed from time immemorial. Yet many Christians no doubt argue ignorance of these mysteries given the traditional stance of the Law's irrelevancy in a post Cross world. But Christians beware. Modern day translations of the Gospel effectively "hide" the open Holy Days mysteries the Gospel itself testifies to in the original Greek Koine it was written in. Nevertheless, the most indicative mystery in the Gospel accounts remains strikingly out in the open in all the translations. For how many readers are aware that John's Gospel account appears to contradict those of the Synoptic Writers' Matthew, Mark, and Luke? That is, John argues, decades after the Synoptic Writers wrote, that the Holy Day observance of Passover as he recollected came on the very day Jesus was crucified. This is in stark contrast with Matthew, Mark and Luke who unanimously argue that the Last Supper was the occasion for the Passover, coming on the day before Jesus' Crucifixion. (For sure, all the Writers are testifying to a mysterious, and far more suspicious and conspicuous, coincidence between Passover and the Gospel. This single fact, more than any other, forever binds together these two greatest occasions of Scripture, the liberation of Ancient Israel from Egyptian Bondage prompted by the Passover occasion with that of the Crucifixion of Jesus Christ. Christians of all types have always recognized the obvious parallelisms of the sacrificial Passover Lamb with that of the Crucifixion.)

Given that the Gospel account begins with a disagreement over the reckoning of the Last Supper and the subsequent Day of the Crucifixion, this then enshrouds the entire Gospel Chronology with uncertainty. And if that is not enough controversy, it turns out that the testimonies of the Burial Period and the Day of Resurrection are found compounding the reckoning problem even further. Of course, Traditional Christianity has espoused a Friday Crucifixion, a Saturday Burial Period and a Sunday Resurrection for most of the Church Age. But this is disturbingly found to be amiss outrightly by Jesus' own predictions regarding his period of death (e.g., Matt12:40). This Tradition has thus been in error ever since it was first established. Finally, what is discovered regarding the reckoning of the Day of Resurrection is undoubtedly the greatest mystery of all. Indeed, it is a passage so cryptic translators have unanimously deferred to Tradition to describe its reckoning, to the disservice of countless readers who have been left in the dark as to what the original testimony states.

So whether one is a student of the Law or the Gospel, there remains the unresolved mysteries of the Holy Days that ultimately every reader of Scripture, whether knowingly or unknowingly, stumbles over! No student of Scripture should feel comfortable with this situation. It is a gaping hole of unresolved Gospel matters that should drive any serious Scripture student into a vigilante search for truth, day and night, until the truth can be uncovered. Those who suffered under this condition before the Gospel appeared are permitted a pass for having not resolved these mysteries. But for those who have possessed the entirety of the Scripture over the past 2,000 years, no such pass can be granted. It should rank as one of the great embarrassments of the Christian World along with the reality of there being so many other mysteries which continue to languish in darkness too, all casting a pale of shame upon the faith itself.

This book is dedicated to unveiling the meanings of the unresolved mysteries of the Holy Days. What the Gospel accounts will be shown witnessing is the existence of a Holy Days Code. With the Gospels supplying testimonies of the Last Supper, the Crucifixion, the Burial Period, and the Day of Resurrection, the records act as a form of "decoding" of the encoded messages imbedded within the Law's Holy Days testimony. Hence, this explains the cryptic nature of the testimony of both the Law and the Gospel since the former is an encoding whereas the latter is the decoding of a message shared between them. The Code can be found built with repeated symbolisms, used again and again, of which the Gospel unveils the meaning of these symbolisms. It does this by how it parallels the symbolisms of the first Holy Days surrounding the Passover season, in a sort of one-to-one correspondence between the Holy Day symbolism and an overlapping Gospel occasion, which gives the symbolisms sudden meaning where no meaning had existed before. How the Gospel testimony provides meaning to all the rest of the Holy Days is again based on the repeating nature of the symbolisms. Since the symbolisms repeat across all the Holy Days, the Gospel's decoding of the original symbolisms comes to apply to give meaning to all the rest of the Holy Days.

Writing in Code is thus just yet another form of prophecy. As any good student of Scripture knows, the text is filled with veiled prophecy. One need only go looking for it. It would seem that the very "prophetic" nature of a message is what necessitates the various forms of encryption the Scripture is found using. The obvious case to use for illustration is that of Messianic Prophecy, since nearly everyone is familiar with this form of biblical prophecy.

For example, what would happen if, hypothetically speaking, bona fide prophecy were made crystal clear in all aspects of what it was predicting? In such a case, the prophecy could easily be misconstrued for being something else, like a "call to arms", sort of speak. And certainly the Scripture has texts like this, what can be referred to as "Inspirational Reading". Indeed Jewish history has recorded many self-proclaimed "Messiahs" based on the simple elements of prophecy that clearly identify this prophetic person as being a Jewish male (e.g., a Son of David). But since there are many, many more unexplained prophecies conjectured foretelling what must be the same person in the Messiah, any self-proclaimed Messiah has to necessarily explain all of the prophecies regarding this person, not just the ones that are clearly understandable by all readers. Otherwise, such writings would fail to be considered prophecy since it would be permissive for any aspiring person who "fit the bill" to then "fill the shoes" inspired by such a writing.

Put another way, is Messianic Prophecy to be interpreted merely a "humanly engineered" form of writing designed to be about simply encouraging and inspiring future godly Jewish males to take up the call of ruling over the Nation when a lack of leadership were to prevail over Israel? Or does in fact the testimony of the Messiah suggest a "divinely engineered" form of writing that truly anticipates one single Person who has been predestined to appear at a specific juncture in time and fulfill His destiny? All an honest reader and historian needs to do is appreciate the "concealed" aspects of the Messianic Prophecy to find an answer. Given the nature of what Messianic predictions exist there is more than enough cryptic prophecy surrounding the testimony that no one in antiquity was quite clear on what to expect or believe. And if this is how the text was originally received from the beginning, how would it have been possible for anyone to explain the meaning of these prophecies unless the "code" had been deciphered? Certainly skeptics could have questioned the validity of any real substance to the predictions, that is until if and when the prophecies would eventually become unveiled of their meaning. To put it bluntly, veiled and enshrouded visions are not capable of inspiring a "calling" but are indications that either bona fide prophecy is in the making or it is just pure fantasy by the writer(s). Either skeptics win the argument that it is pure fantasy until Someone comes forward and reveals the hidden nature of bona fide prophecy or skeptics win the argument for all time.

So if writing in Code is just another form of prophecy, the question still remains, why? Why does Scripture communicate this way? The only real good answer to supply is that Scripture needs unprecedented evidence to validate its testimony. It needs this because it testifies to Humanity's greatest, most perplexing questions it asks. What is the origin of all things? What is the reason and purpose for existing? Is there a Creator of all and who is this Person? What is the ultimate fate of everything? In order to accept the Scripture's answers to these questions, the human mind must have some means of weighing this information in the balance to have the ability to arrive at a decision to believe or disbelieve what the Scripture supplies for answers. Otherwise, the testimony of Scripture is left hollow and powerless to gain reception in any rational thinking mind. Given the amount of prophecy found in Scripture, there really is no other good reason for it being there other than to provide the kind of validation needed for Scripture's greatest assertions it makes.

In what way, then, can prophecy convince readers that there is a Supreme Being, a Creator over all? That has to do with the "revelatory" nature of Scripture. Whatever form of communication is used, if the Author is truly who He is revealed to be than it is He who dictates the terms by which He uses to convince the human mind of His reality. Thus, it is the very revelation of Scripture, which in summation, does the convincing. On the other hand, if the Scripture does not possess this revelatory power than again it can be argued that the Scripture can be concluded as being simply the work of the human mind and not a transcendent form of communication.

That skeptics of prophecy have existed from the beginning is evidence in itself that the Scripture boldly prophecies but which some minds simply reject as being prophecy. To these, prophecy appears as if to be the work of writers witnessing something in their day but in actuality making it appear as predictions from years before. That certainly is one plausible explanation for the most ancient of prophecies predicting things for the ancient past. But there is so much more prophecy that cannot be questioned in this way because it has ancient origins but fulfillment that came at a time too recent to legitimately question. These more recently fulfilled prophecies thus provide validity for the more ancient prophecies. And similarly those in antiquity who could validate prophecy fulfilled in their own age but who could not validate prophecies yet in their distance future could lean on the earlier prophecy to gain a confidence in the validity for what was predicted to come later. In the present hour, the advanced tools available to the modern reader (computers) are now capable of hastening study like no other time in the past. The work that this book puts forth simply could not have been performed in a timely fashion until now and thus the astonishing things that are discovered here brings a unique sort of validation to Scripture like no other time in history could have.

Thus, without prophecy, Scripture's testimony would be far less capable of convincing readers of the validity of its message. In the end, it is left to the human mind to weigh the evidence and decide if Scripture is the work of the God it portrays or if it is the work of men who projected their own image of who they thought God should be or wanted others to believe He is to be. The Holy Days Code, as this work unravels it, makes its own powerful and irrefutable case as to why it can only be the work of a transcendent being who is above space and time. It must be Someone who possesses an intelligence vastly beyond that of the human mind in the way it speaks multidimensionally, across multiple authors, and across multiple generations and millennia. That much of the encoded information has gone undetected for thousands of years, even to this very day, is evidence that it has the power of concealment should readers violate the rules of interpretation. What else can be concluded if this work accomplishes such a feat, a feat no one has accomplished to date, when it simply adheres to a basic set of rules of interpretation that insists on giving relevancy to both the Hebrew and the Greek Bible?

The very reason why these things have remained enshrouded from time immemorial has everything to do with a reader's perception. Most, if not all, of these perceptions have been under the powerful influences of tradition for a very, very long time. History records a **bipolar disorder** afflicting the two main traditional views. That is, Traditional Judaism rejects the Gospel's relevancy and consequentially accounts for only half the Scripture's message. Its adherents necessarily stumble when attempting to understand the first half of Scripture without the aid of the second half of Scripture! Likewise, Traditional Christianity has failed to see the relevancy of the Law and consequentially winds up accounting for only the latter half of the Scripture message, not unlike Judaism. Its adherents attempt to understand the latter half of Scripture's message without the proper consultation of the first half of Scripture! Thus its adherents stumble as well for the same reason.

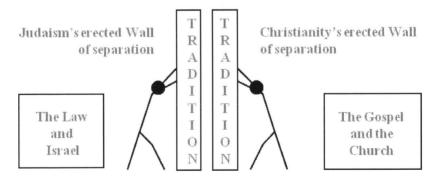

However, if the "Walls of Tradition" can be brought down in one's mind, here is where a revolutionary kind of breakthrough is achieved. The Barrier is simply a figment of the Human Imagination and nothing more. But this figment has been responsible for creating the most historically blinding apparatus to have ever confronted the Human Mind. Far too much time has passed to continue to leave this Wall in place. Each Seeker must demand that the Wall come down today, now. Begin to discover from this book the power of the freedom to read Scripture without any pretext or premonition or prejudice. Come learn what happens when the Barrier is removed! Truly experience that, even in this late hour, Scripture can be shown producing new things that the Mind had previously forbidden itself from knowing!

...in respect to a Holy Day or a New Moon or of Sabbath days...things which are a shadow of _what is to come_...

Colossians 2:16-17

Chapter One

Are the Holy Days Encoded?

The Sabbath. Passover. The 7 Day Feast of Unleavened Bread. The Day of First Fruits. The Counting of 7 Sabbaths. The Feast of Weeks. Yom Teruah. Yom Kippur. The 7 Day Feast of Booths. And last but not least, the last Day, the Day which is given no name, the day which immediately follows the Feast of Booths. Altogether these biblical dates, listed below, have become known as the "Holy Days". According to Scripture, the prophet Moses received these Holy Days from the very voice of God Himself, along with the rest of the Law, on behalf of the Nation of Israel. For thousands of years Jews have observed these Holy Days year in and year out.

List of Holy Days from Leviticus 23

Month	Day	Name of Holy Day(s)
All	Every 7th Day	The Sabbath
1st Month	Twilight of 14th	Passover
	15th	1st Day of the Feast of Unleavened Bread
	16th	2nd Day of the Feast of Unleavened Bread
	17th	3rd Day of the Feast of Unleavened Bread
	18th	4th Day of the Feast of Unleavened Bread
	19th	5th Day of the Feast of Unleavened Bread
	20th	6th Day of the Feast of Unleavened Bread
	21st	7th Day of the Feast of Unleavened Bread
?	Day after Mystery Sabbath	Head 1st Fruits
	1st Sabbath after Mystery Sabbath	Countdown to the Feast of Weeks: Week #1
	2nd Sabbath after Mystery Sabbath	Countdown to the Feast of Weeks: Week#2
	3rd Sabbath after Mystery Sabbath	Countdown to the Feast of Weeks: Week #3
	4th Sabbath after Mystery Sabbath	Countdown to the Feast of Weeks: Week #4
	5th Sabbath after Mystery Sabbath	Countdown to the Feast of Weeks: Week #5
	6th Sabbath after Mystery Sabbath	Countdown to the Feast of Weeks: Week #6
	7th Sabbath after Mystery Sabbath	Countdown to the Feast of Weeks: Week #7
	50 days from Head 1st Fruits	1st Fruits (Feast of Weeks)
7th Month	1st	Yom Teruah
	10th	Yom Kippur
	15th	1st Day of the Feast of Booths
	16th	2nd Day of the Feast of Booths
	17th	3rd Day of the Feast of Booths
	18th	4th Day of the Feast of Booths
	19th	5th Day of the Feast of Booths
	20th	6th Day of the Feast of Booths
	21st	7th Day of the Feast of Booths
	22nd	The Day after the Feast of Booths

Important Dates on the Divine Calendar

The tradition of celebrating certain fixed dates of an annual calendar is nothing new in the annals of human history. Civilizations the world over have commemorated pivotal moments of their histories this way. The United States of America, for example, remembers July 4th (of the Julian-Gregorian Calendar) as its annual Independence Day. So too Passover, falling at the end of the 14th day of the 1st month (of Scripture's Calendar) is to be understood Israel's Independence Day.

Yet Israel's Holy Days must be considered distinguished from all other dates of commemoration given they are written as being Divinely Established dates of commemoration. If hypothetically speaking God is who Israel's God says He is, it would seem that all other reserved dates of human interest from the dawn of time pale in comparison to what significance these Divinely Ordained Dates are to be attributed. Naturally Israel, and later Judaism, developed traditions for the Holy Days, traditions loosely based upon the more easily understood testimony. Unfortunately, these interpretations do not factor in much of the more difficult readings found in the testimony and thus fall short of what ultimate meaning the Scriptures must be assigning to the Holy Days.

For instance, a careful reading of the testimony reveals that the Holy Days (save the Sabbath) are all confined within Israel's annual harvest season. That is, Passover comes at the very beginning of harvest while the last Holy Day comes at the end of the harvest season. Thus, a general consensus within Judaism is that most of the Holy Days are meant to remind Israel that it is God who brings the fruitful bounty of harvest each season. Quite to the point tradition appears to relegate the Holy Days to merely signifying the coming of harvest each year. Perhaps this most simplest reading was all that Israel was meant to know about the Holy Days in the beginning and that the Nation's task was simply to faithfully observe them each year until which time their fuller meaning would become apparent.

For as it turns out the Hebrew Scripture by itself does not provide an adequate explanation as to the meaning of its more difficult readings of the Holy Days testimony. Thus there really was no way for Israel to come to a fuller understanding without the aid of further revelation. And so the passing of time came to reveal something laying hidden within the testimony, to form a sort of expectation that something else must necessarily be on its way to bring Enlightenment.

The Gospel Testimonies Beg the Question

Perhaps for most Christians the Holy Days Testimony is not high on the list of Scripture needing to be understood. But maybe it should have been required reading from the very beginning. For how many of those same Christians realize that the timing of Jesus' Last Supper, the Crucifixion, the Burial Period, and the Day of Resurrection are all mysteriously linked to the Holy Days testimony? And why is this important to know? Because it turns out that the reckoning of these 4 Gospel Occasions, without the aid of the Holy Days testimony, is nearly impossible to determine. Do average Christians realize that Tradition's 3 Day Schedule of a Friday

Crucifixion, Saturday Burial, and a Sunday Resurrection has very little textual support and at the same time outright rejects Jesus' own testimony?:

Matthew 12:40 …for just as Jonah was **three days** and **three** nights in the belly of the sea monster, so will the Son of Man be **three days** and **three** nights in the heart of the earth.

If Jesus' period of death was to be this long, this leaves no traditional time for anything else! But this is only one of several reckoning issues of the Gospel indicating Tradition's woeful lack of regard for the testimony. Here is a brief summary of the difficulties that face honest readers:

1. The Gospel Testimony reveals that Matthew, Mark and Luke all agree together that the Last Supper was a "Passover Meal" as described as such by Jesus himself (Luke22:15). However, John, writing decades later argues that Passover was still a day away in being coincident with the Crucifixion (John13:1;18:28;19:14)! In essence, the Gospels record 2 back-to-back Passovers. So how can this be and what is it to mean?
2. When studying the Burial Period, arguably all 4 Gospel writers reckon just over 2 full days, with the last day being a Sabbath. But Matthew alone strangely reckons "Sabbaths" plural during Jesus' Burial Period. Yet how is it possible to reckon back-to-back Sabbaths and what does it mean?
3. Finally, it turns out that the testimonial reckonings of the Day of the Resurrection are all identical with all 4 writers being in unanimous agreement. The only problem is is that the reading is very difficult to interpret as to its proper meaning when consulting the original text (Matt28:1; Mark16:2; Luke24:1, John20:1). Most translators translate it this way: "on the first day of the week". An accurate rendering from the original Greek would be the following translation: "at the dawning of the first of the Sabbaths". So what does this mean?

An Interdependent Coded/Decoded Message

So as it turns out, the reckoning of the Gospel Testimony is quite "murky" when the testimony itself is solely consulted. Yet for the earliest Jewish readers of the 1st century, those familiar with the Holy Days testimony, these textual difficulties would have been easily resolvable as this book will make apparent to contemporary readers of the 21st century. Not only that, but something far more amazing must have been revealed to those earliest Jewish Believers! What can be discovered is that the Gospel Testimony's reckoning, in all of its "strangeness", is really a form of "decoding" of the Holy Days Testimony.

For the Holy Days Testimony is filled with its own "strange" and mysterious unresolved symbols. And if that's true, then the Holy Days Testimony is a "Coded" Message needing "Decoding". But an even more intelligent conclusion would be to say that the Gospel Testimony itself has now come containing its own "Code" to 21st century readers, which can only become "decoded" by the Holy Days Testimony! So put in another, far more fascinating way, the Law's Holy Days being filled with mystery, and the Gospel's testimony also filled with mystery, can be found working together to solve their respective mysteries! For early Jewish Believers, this meant the Gospel came to decode what Israel had not understood for thousands of years. But now for late Christian readers of the 21st Century, the Gospel Testimony has become itself a Coded Message requiring the Holy Days to decode!

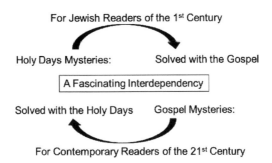

For Jewish Readers of the 1st Century

Holy Days Mysteries: Solved with the Gospel

A Fascinating Interdependency

Solved with the Holy Days   Gospel Mysteries:

For Contemporary Readers of the 21st Century

When Jesus came upon the scene, the Holy Days Testimony had become a countless collection of mysteries to the People of the Law. The Time had become Ripe for Jesus to "crack" the Code left scrambled without him. Take for example, the Seven 7's of the Holy Days as just the beginning of this collection of symbolisms:

The Seven 7's of the Holy Days Testimony

1. Every 7th day, called the Sabbath, is to be a Day of Rest, of No Work and of Holy Assembly

2. Aside from the Sabbath, the Holy Days are confined within a 7 month Harvest Season

3. Aside from the Sabbath, there are 7 Holy Occasions with distinct Offerings by Fire within this Season
   a. Feast of Unleavened Bread
   b. The Day of Head First Fruits
   c. The Feast of Weeks
   d. Yom Teruah (1st day of the 7th month)
   e. Yom Kippur (10th day of the 7th month)
   f. The Feast of Booths
   g. The 22nd Day of the 7th Month

4. The Feast of Unleavened Bread and the Feast of Booths are 7 days long.
5. There are 7 Sabbaths to be counted between the Day of Head First Fruits and the Feast of Weeks

6. Aside from the Sabbath, there are 7 days of "No Work" and of "Holy Assembly"
   a. The 1st day of the Feast of Unleavened Bread
   b. The 7th day of the Feast of Unleavened Bread
   c. The Feast of Weeks
   d. Yom Teruah
   e. Yom Kippur
   f. The 1st day of the Feast of Booths
   g. The 22nd day of the 7th month

7. There are 7 Sabbaths or periods of Sabbaths to account for:
   a. The Sabbath of the Feast of Unleavened Bread
   b. The 7 Sabbaths to be counted (see 4)
   c. The (Lunar) Sabbath of Yom Teruah
   d. The (Lunar) Sabbath of Yom Kippur
   e. The (Lunar) Sabbath of the 1st day of the Feast of Booths
   f. The Sabbath of the Feast of Booths
   g. The (Lunar) Sabbath of the 22nd day of the 7th month

So what can all of these 7's mean? Why are they so prolific? Without a doubt, the greatest singular symbol that binds all of the Holy Days together is the theme of "Harvest" as mentioned in the 2nd 7 of the list above. Again, Passover can be shown as coming at the beginning of the Harvest season in the 1st Month and that the last Holy Days can be shown coming at the end of the Harvest season in the 7th Month.

Every Holy Day Is Filled With Mystery

Depending upon how one counts the Holy Days, different answers can be had. The most instructive and revealing way to do so suggests that there are 28 days as can be counted in the list at the beginning of the chapter. And with these, there can be reckoned 14 "Sabbath" Days and 14 "non-Sabbath" Days in this method of counting. In observing this even split, an interesting thing can be discovered. The very testimony of the Holy Days can be found dividing itself up into two separate paths of testimony just as it begins and just as it ends. One path can be seen being made up of Sabbaths while the other is without Sabbaths. In the very middle of the testimony, the two paths appear to converge for 2 days, on the 1st and on the 10th days of the 7th month:

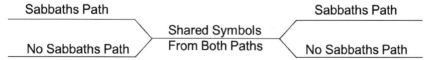

What this can mean is just yet another example of the variety of mysteries needing solving all throughout the Holy Days testimony.

And so, the more the symbolic details of the Holy Days are deciphered, the more questions that arise as to what they must be signifying. And looking at their individual testimonies they each are found having their own peculiar oddities:

The 7th Day Sabbath: This Holy Day is observed all throughout the Year and not just during the Harvest season. It is to remind Israel of God having created the Heavens and the Earth in 6 days and Resting on the 7th. So why then are there 14 specially designated Sabbaths that become part of the Harvest Holy Days testimony? Why is it that there are as many Sabbath Holy Days as there are non-Sabbath Holy Days? Evidently, each must be taking on a unique importance all their own in some way that goes beyond the commemoration of the Creation and Creator. But what? Within their testimony, the Sabbaths have two particular oddities that emerge:

a. The appearance of 4 "Lunar" Sabbaths in the 7th Month: The original Sabbath of Scripture is the one to be observed every 7th day. But in Leviticus 23 (and only here), 4 Holy Days in the 7th Month are defined as Sabbaths yet are clearly fixed days of the month: the 1st (Yom Teruah), the 10th (Yom Kippur), the 15th (first day of the Feast of Booths) and the 22nd (the last Holy Day). Why are these Holy Days designated as Sabbaths? What is this to mean?

b. There are 2 "unmentioned" Sabbaths within the Holy Days and thus appear as if to have some "hidden" or mysterious symbolism. The Feast of Unleavened Bread and the Feast of Booths are each 7 days long. This means there must be one "floating" Sabbath during each of these two Feasts. So what special significance can these "hidden" Sabbaths be telling?

Passover: There are 27 Holy Days to be reckoned in the Law's Holy Harvest Season if the very first Holy Occasion is not to be factored as a "Day". That is because the very first Harvest Season related Holy Occasion comes not as an entire Day but instead as the very "END" of a day. It is the only one of its kind. So why is this and what does it mean?

The Feast of Unleavened Bread: This Holy Feast is a 7 day long occasion of consecutive Holy Days starting on the 15th day of the 1st month . So what could this Feast be signifying? Perhaps its signifies a Divine Era or Age or Epoch, as perhaps do all the consecutive sevens of the Holy Days schedule. So what complete era or age or epoch could this be foretelling? The strangest aspect about this Feast is the testimony of its last day. It will be designated: a) a "Feast" all by itself and b) is given a unique Hebrew term which is shared only with the last Holy Day, the word "Atsarah", a word associated with a woman's womb being "closed". So why is the last day of this Feast given such elevated status and such strange terms?

The Day of Head First Fruits: By far, this day is the most mysterious day of all the Holy Days for one reason. All the other Holy Days unrelated to this one are defined by a fixed day of a given Month either in the 1st Month or in the 7 Month. But not this one and, by default, not the one that is to come exactly 50 days later. In the wording as to how this day is to be reckoned it is most ambiguous and cannot be determined with certainty as a standalone testimony. Furthermore, early Judaism carried 2 traditions as evidence of this fact. The Sadducees and the Pharisees each had their own prescription as to how to reckon this day. It is the reason for why the Synoptic Gospels and John's Gospel appear contradicting one another as to when the Passover was to be reckoned surrounding Jesus' Crucifixion. So why is its reckoning ambiguous? It is one of Scripture's greatest mysteries.

The 7 Sabbaths to be counted until the Feast of Weeks: The Day of Head First Fruits is intimately related to these Sabbaths and the Feast of Weeks because they are all reckoned according to its day of reckoning. And since the Day of Head First Fruits has a mysterious reckoning, so too everything being reckoned by it shares this same attribute by association. Altogether these Holy Days are to be seen as part of a common group of some sort. Since the Feast of Weeks is only a single Holy Day, as opposed to the two other 7 day long Feasts, perhaps these prior 7 Sabbaths are signifying some Age associated with this Feast. So what Age could that be and why is it described in the way it is?

The Feast of Weeks: As was already mentioned, this Feast lasts for only a day whereas the other Feasts last for 7 days each. So why does this Feast last for only a day? The other major oddity of this Holy Day is the description of the Offerings by Fire that are to be presented on this day. It will be shown possessing 3 pairs: 1) There are 2 Offerings by Fire, each defined in a different section of Scripture. 2) There are to be 2 Peace Offerings along with the Offerings by Fire, the only Holy Day which has such a thing. All combined there are 24 separate sacrifices to be offered on this day. 3) There are to be 2 Loaves of Leavened Bread waved before God along with the Offerings. Again, this is something only this Day is to possess. So why and what are these Pairs signifying?

Yom Teruah: This Holy Day begins an entirely new series of Holy Days far removed from the previous Holy Days. So what can this obvious separation signify? It falls on the 1st day of the 7th Month, Israel's Rosh Hashanah (or New Year's Day). It possesses its own peculiar oddities:

    a.   This day happens to be the first Lunar Holy Day of the Divine Calendar to be designated as a day of "Sabbath Rest". So what and why can this be so designated? What does it mean?

    b.   This day will also have 2 Offerings by Fire. Because it is a "New Moon" day (the only Holy Day having this status), it has an Offering being it is the Holy Day of Yom Teruah and another because it is a New Moon day. So does this have any symbolic significance?

Yom Kippur: This Holy Day falls on the 10th day of the 7th Month. And again, this day too possesses 2 Offerings by Fire, one defined in Leviticus 16 and the other in

Numbers 29. It is also a Lunar Sabbath, the 2nd of 4 total. It is to be the day Israel's Sins are to be "atoned" for each Year. As such, it is to be Israel's most solemn day of the year. So out of all of this testimony is this Holy Day representing some sort of solemn occasion in Israel's coming prophetic future?

The Feast of Booths: This is the 3rd of 3 Feasts coming in the 7th Month. It too lasts 7 days between the 15th day and the 21st day just like the Feast of Unleavened Bread in the 1st Month. Its first day is the 3rd Lunar Sabbath of 4 total. So again, is there yet another Age being predicted by these 7 consecutive Holy Days? There are two oddities that can be found within its testimony:

a. The Feast will be described twice, in two sets of passages. After the first description, a closing statement is given making summarizing statements regarding all of the Holy Days. Then, after this closing, the Feast is described yet again only with different symbolisms than what were given in the first description. So why and what can this be meaning?

b. The Feast has a unique prescription for its Offerings by Fire. Whereas the Feast of Unleavened Bread has the same Offerings defined for each of its 7 days, this Feast has a different set of Offerings for each day. So why and what can this be meaning?

The 22nd Day of the 7th Month: Oddly enough, this last Holy Day is not given its own description but is defined as being an "8th day" after the 7 days of the Feast of Booths. It is the 4th and last Lunar Sabbath Day. Since it is given its own separate Offerings by Fire, this seems to imply as if it is to be a standalone Holy Day with its own significance. So then why is it described this way as if to be an extension of the Feast of Booths? Finally, it too is attributed the Hebrew term "Atsarah", the same term the last day of the Feast of Unleavened Bread is given. So why and what could this be meaning? If the Holy Days describe a Divine Timeline, this Holy Day would be representing the "End" to this timeline. Scripture's End is essentially the Future Eternity. So if this Holy Day represents the Future Eternity how does this relate to the last day of the Feast of Unleavened Bread?

Ezekiel's Holy Days Testimony Adds Fuel to Fire

As the previous summary of the Holy Days bears out, the Law's testimony is saturated with all kinds of symbols and peculiarities of witness. It is virtually impossible to come away from all of this without having some sense that there are things being communicated via some sort of Code. Provocatively, the Holy Days testimony does not end in the Law. Some 800 years later, the prophet Ezekiel is found "tinkering" with the Holy Days. What can be discovered within his testimony is perhaps the greatest indications yet that the Holy Days testimony is an encoded message. It too raises many, many questions in search of answers that will not come even after the entire Hebrew Scripture is contemplated.

What Ezekiel's prophecies bring to the Holy Days testimony revolves entirely around the Offerings by Fire. By doing this, Ezekiel is drawing attention to the Offerings by Fire in suggesting they are conveying some sort of encoded message all by themselves in some way. And if a reader is keen to pick up on a most peculiarly consistent theme in all of the Offerings by Fire Ezekiel defines, it becomes yet another gigantic clue as to the idea that the very symbols of the Holy Days are communicating information via code.

Here is a list of 7 peculiar oddities to be found in Ezekiel's testimony:

1. **Ezekiel ADDS 2 and a half new Holy Days**. To the keen observer, it can be discovered that these 3 days actually make the 1st Month and 7th Month Holy Days "mirror" each other as if to form some kind of symmetry between them that does not exist without this testimony. He adds:

   a. The **1st day of the 1st Month**: This happens to be the Divine Calendar's New Year's Day! This comes to parallel the 1st day of the 7th Month, Yom Teruah. And it only makes sense that this day be a part of the Holy Days schedule. But why is it revealed as such by Ezekiel? And what does its signify?

   b. The **7th day of the 1st Month**: This day in the 1st Month makes symmetry with Yom Kippur, the 10th day of the 7th Month. So what is this to signify?

   c. And the **14th day of the 1st Month**: This day is the Law's day in which the Passover is to be observed! But the Law reckons only the end of the Day as Passover. Now Ezekiel makes the entire day a Holy Day on to itself! It comes to parallel the 22nd Day of the 7th Month in being made an "8th day extension" of the 7 Day Feast of Unleavened Bread. So what is this signifying?

2. **Ezekiel ADDS new Offerings by Fire to the Feast** of Unleavened Bread and the same Offerings to the Feast of Booths

3. **Ezekiel ADDS new Offerings by Fire to the Sabbaths**

4. **Ezekiel ADDS new Offerings by Fire to the New Moon days.**

5. **Ezekiel CHANGES the Grain and Oil portions** of the Holy Days Offerings by Fire from what the Law calls out what they are to be.

6. **Ezekiel ELIMINATES the Law's Daily Evening Offering** by Fire!

7. **All of Ezekiel's new Offerings by Fire have NO Drink Offerings**

Once these 7 shocking alterations to the Law's Holy Days testimony become fully grasped a flood of new and disturbing questions come to be raised, on top of all those already being raised from the Law's testimony. What does all of this signify in sum? With so much testimony to consume, it becomes the ELEPHANT in the room that the Holy Days Testimony is PREGNANT with ENCODED information!

This book will go in search of an explanation for what all of these symbolisms are communicating. Its pages produce the evidence that a Code has been found, a Holy Days Code, that is. As will become clear, the Holy Days Code communicates plans for a "Divine Harvest". As it turns out, every symbol and every strange and peculiar piece of testimony represents a form of encoded information regarding a Divine Harvest Plan. What the God of Scripture is planning on Harvesting is of course not literal Barley or literal Wheat or of literal Ripe Things of the Vine but something much greater than these.

Gospel Reveals a 4-Fold Decryption for Code

Christians easily recognize the obvious overlapping of the Passover occasion with the Last Supper, Crucifixion, Death, Burial and Resurrection of Jesus Christ. The main historical problem with this has been the shortsighted interpretation that these connections are a sign that the Gospel has been made the fulfillment of all biblical prophecy, starting with the Holy Days Testimony. In so thinking, Tradition is shown stumbling over what is actually a much deeper level of communication going on between the Holy Days and the Gospel. The shocking unheralded truth, now being unveiled by this book, is that the Gospel is found subtly communicating that the Holy Days Testimony is in fact an encrypted "code" concealing information with its many inexplicable symbols of its testimony. And what the Gospel is found doing is "unlocking" this code with what this work argues are **4 "Decryption Keys"**. These appear designed to unlock the truths hidden within the Holy Days testimony, what this work calls the **"Holy Days Code"**.

What will be identified herein as the 4th and final Key, from a chronological perspective, is the only one historically to be recognized in Christian Theology and then only partially. It boldly professes what profound concealed meaning lay hidden in the Holy Days besides what outward superficial meanings they are attributed with Israel's harvest season. What no tradition seems to have grasped is that the wording describing the Date of the Resurrection is really a form of decoding. That is, the wording implies that the very day in which Jesus was resurrected was in fact the Holy Day when the First Fruits of the Barley Harvest was to be taken into the Holy Place by the High Priest and there waved before God. And so with this single subtle revelation, the most uniting symbol of the Holy Days testimony, the symbol of Harvest, is made connected to a most pivotal event in the Gospel, the Resurrection. Along with this a profound Key materializes to begin unlocking and unraveling the Holy Days Code.

In short, the very first harvest symbol of the Holy Days is being equated with the Resurrection of Jesus Christ, what is being implied as another form of harvest, that of **"Human Reaping"**. Thus, beyond the superficial recognition of this day being the day when the first fruits of Israel's Barley Harvest is to be offered to God, the greater Encrypted information imbedded in this Holy Day, suggested by this Decryption, is that the symbol of crop harvesting is concealing a much more profound Harvest anticipated, the harvesting of human souls. Hence, to apply this newly discovered Key of Decryption to the other remaining Harvest symbolisms of the Holy Days, the implication is that these must be predicting some later scheduled form of Human Harvest. And so the greatest generalization to form from this Decryption is to suggest that some sort of Divine Schedule or Time Table for a "Human Harvest Reaping" is being established by the Holy Days testimony in which Jesus' Resurrection was made the very first. That is, Jesus Christ's Resurrection from the Dead is the first Divine "Human Reaping" of a greater **Divine Harvest Schedule** that the rest of the Holy Days symbolize. In essence, **the Holy Days Code is Scripture's Divine Harvest Schedule** encrypted by the many symbols contained in the Holy Days testimony.

Where Christian Theology has monumentally erred then, if this interpretation is hypothetically true, is in believing the Resurrection of Jesus is somehow the "End" to what all Biblical Prophecy is pointing to, and thus whatever the Holy Days testimony could be symbolizing. In reality however, what the testimony is really suggesting is that Jesus' Resurrection is only the ***beginning*** of a Divine Time Table, not its End! That is, the remaining Holy Days beyond the Day of First Fruits should be interpreted as symbolizing critical Divine milestones or stages or Epochs of what is to become further reaping of the Human Race, a reaping that began with the Reaping of Jesus.

In all, the Holy Days Code is proposed herein as being an Epoch Timetable or Chronology of the Divine Harvesting of the Human Race when all the hidden symbols are accounted for. This book has been written to highlight what complex symbolisms lay at the heart of the Holy Days testimony and to show how, with the aid of the Gospel, these symbolisms come to be unveiled of their meaning. In so doing, the profound significance for what the Holy Days represent is brought out into the light revealing why they are worthy of being made eternal observances in that they first prophetically foretell of, but ultimately memorialize, the Divine Harvest Schedule.

When ancient Israel observed these dates during each harvest season, it was an exercise in mostly prophetic rehearsing and of foreshadow, looking ahead to the time when the things being predicted by the symbolisms would come to pass. But, once the entire Divine Harvest Plan hypothetically comes to fruition in the future, this will cause all of the Holy Days to more or less become memorials thereafter. At that time Israel will be looking back in remembrance to what past monumental events this great Harvest had produced in each of the Holy Days the Nation was asked to observe.

...the LORD said..."this month (Abib) shall be the beginning of months for you; it is to be the first month of the year to you...

Exodus 12:2

Chapter Two

Biblical Timekeeping 101

T he earliest location in Scripture confessing the idea of a Holy Day comes surprisingly early in the very first passages of the Law, indeed, in the very first passages of Scripture itself:

Gen 1:14 Then God said, "Let there be lights in the expanse of the heavens to separate the day from the night, and let them be for signs, and for <u>seasons</u>, and for days and years...

The word "seasons" comes from the transliterated Hebrew word "**moed**" which implies appointment or meeting. This is the word the Law uses again and again when implying the Holy Days. What this earliest passage is stating is that the heavenly bodies are to be the means for determining the timing of the holy appointments:

Ps 104:19 He made the moon for the <u>seasons</u>...

Here again the word "seasons" is the Hebrew word "moed". As will be studied later in this chapter, most of the Holy Days are fixed days of the month, or rather, fixed days of the lunar cycle. Israel is to keep a watchful eye on the moon, as well as the sun, if it is to know **WHEN** the Holy Days appointments are to be observed as commanded by the Law.

So an important aspect in the keeping of the Holy Days is to know when to RECKON them. To do this, one really needs a rudimentary means of telling time, or an acceptable means of "holy" timekeeping. How this comes to be revealed in Scripture is spread across a critical number of passages mainly within the Law. This chapter is reserved in pointing out these passages and to act as an educational "tutorial" into the basic fundamentals of Biblical Timekeeping.

Yom: The Biblical Day

It makes sense to begin this overview of Biblical Timekeeping with the Biblical Day, what transliterated in Hebrew is the word "*<u>Yom</u>*". This will then be followed by the "month" and the "year".

(It should be noted that the frame of reference for Scripture is the Earth's Northern Hemisphere, where the Land of Israel resides. Winter Solstice arrives on December 21st of the Julian-Gregorian Calendar denoting the shortest day of daylight. In this hemisphere the days grow longer from this date until daylight and nighttime become equal on Spring Equinox, March 21st. Summer Solstice arrives on June 21st and signifies the longest day of daylight of the year. Daylight hours then recede again. On the Autumnal Equinox, September 21st, daylight and nighttime are again equal before the daylight hours reduce until Winter Solstice.)

The Scripture's first use of this word suggests the beginning of the day as coming at sundown, or at dusk:

Gen 1:5 And God called the light day, and the darkness He called night. There was evening...there was morning, one day.

Note that the very first cycle of time during Creation is given the term "day". The evening is reckoned as having come first, then the morning. The word "evening" literally infers the "dusk" or at the moment of "sundown". Morning implies a "breaking forth" or the "dawn" or at the moment of "sunrise". This division of the first Day of Creation is consistent with the way the Law later defines the day:

Exo 27:21 "In the tent of meeting, outside the veil which is before the testimony, Aaron and his sons shall keep it in order <u>from evening to morning</u> before the LORD; {it shall be} a perpetual statute throughout their generations for the sons of Israel.

This passage is describing how the High Priest Aaron, Moses' brother, and all his descendants who followed him in that capacity, would be required to have a daily vigilance in their priestly responsibilities. One more passage that explicitly reveals when a holy day is to start and end:

Lev 23:32b "...from evening until evening you shall keep your sabbath."

Thus, the important thing about a biblical day is when it officially begins.

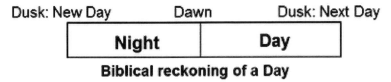

Biblical reckoning of a Day

The simple beauty of this reckoning of a day is in its practical usage. In this way Israel's entire community would be awake to witness the coming of a new day, especially a Holy Day. Whenever the sunset came, this established the coming of a new day. In contrast, the modern reckoning of a day is adopted from the Roman Empire which had its day start at midnight. Yet this posed an ancient challenge of determining exactly when "midnight" arrived each day, being a time when most people are sleeping, thus having no real practical usage.

Chodesh/Yerach: The Biblical Month

The earlier passage of Psalm 104:19 uses the transliterated Hebrew word "**Yerach**" which means "moon". There are only 14 places in the Hebrew Scripture which use this word to infer a period of one month. Below are the 3 places in the Law where it is used this way:

1.   Moses was born and hidden by his mother for 3 "moons" (Exo 2:2)

2.   The Law states that a foreign woman taken in battle was allowed to mourn for 1 "moon" before she could be made an Israelite's wife (Deut 21:13).

3.   Joseph's land was being blessed which included the produce which came during the moon's cycles (Deut 33:14)

What the Hebrew Scripture is found using far more frequently, perhaps between 300-400 times, to depict a period of a month is the transliterated Hebrew word *"chodesh"*. It simply means "new" or "rebirth". The English translators take liberties in using the word "month" where chodesh is used.

TRADITIONAL LUNAR MONTH
(Northern Hemisphere)

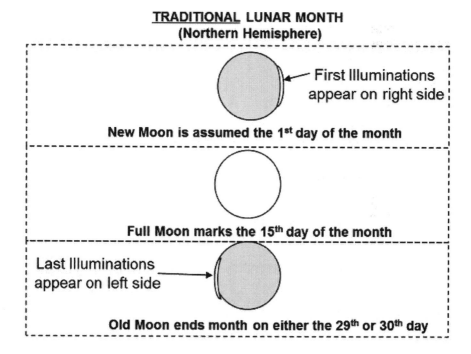

First Illuminations appear on right side

New Moon is assumed the 1ˢᵗ day of the month

Full Moon marks the 15ᵗʰ day of the month

Last Illuminations appear on left side

Old Moon ends month on either the 29ᵗʰ or 30ᵗʰ day

Strangely, the testimony of the Hebrew Scripture provides no crystal clear instruction as to how the beginning of the month is to be determined. But from the frequent usage of *"chodesh"* this seems to be emphasizing the idea of an appearing "new" or "reborn" moon. This makes the most sense for the occasion when the moon passes from being completely enshrouded in darkness to just beginning its cycle of illumination, in the frame of reference of the one witnessing it. Assuming this as the proper reckoning for a coming new month, this means that the middle of the month, or the 15th day, comes coincident with the appearance of a "full" moon, that is, when the moon is fully illuminated.

Being that a month's length is approximately 29.5 days it is not synchronous with the solar day cycle. This means that a rule must be made so as to decide what day is to be the first day of a new month. Judaism's tradition states that if a New Moon appears any time after sundown until noon, that very day is chosen as the first day of the month. But if the New Moon should be noticed coming in the afternoon then the following day is to be made the first day of the month.

What turns out to be unnecessary is keeping track of how long a month should last, whether it should be reckoned as 29 days or 30 days. This is because no lunar Holy Days are observed beyond the 22nd day of any month. Again Scripture's emphasis is placed on reckoning the beginning of a time period, not its end.

So does the Scripture indicate anywhere what an "official" length of a month should be assumed being? The answer happens to be supplied the very first time the word "*chodesh*" appears in Scripture in the Genesis account of Noah and the great flood:

Gen 7:11 In the six hundredth year of Noah's life, in the second month, on the seventeenth day of the month-- on the same all the fountains of the great deep burst open, and the floodgates of the sky were opened.

Gen 7:24 The water prevailed upon the earth one hundred and fifty days.

Gen 8:4 In the seventh month, on the seventeenth day of the month the ark rested...

Here the length of 150 days is given which is the time it took to span from the 17th day of the 2nd month to the 17th day of the 7th month. From here, it can be deduced that the Bible assumes that the length of a "month" is 150/5 = 30 days. (Thousands of years later, in the writing of the last book of the Greek Scripture, this usage remained unchanged, where in the book of the Revelation it describes 1260 days = 42 months = 3.5 years, together inferring a 30 day month.)

Shanah: The Biblical Year

After the month the next biblical period to study is the year, the repeating schedule of the earth's rotation around the sun. The transliterated Hebrew word for year is "**shanah**". From ancient times civilizations have noticed a useful relationship between the lunar cycles and the solar cycle. With a lunar period lasting approximately 29.5 days it turns out that 12 lunar periods is about the length of 354.25 days, roughly 11 days shy of a solar year, what is called a "lunar year" period. So most ancient calendars were composed of a 12 month schedule. But for those civilizations who failed to add some sort of correction to the receding lunar year against the backdrop of the solar year, the months would slowly recede back through the 4 seasons over a 33 year period. Such a calendar would seem to have little utility over time for the most practical needs in life.

For agriculturally based cultures, there was always careful observation of whatever signs existed indicating the coming of spring in order to plant crops at the most optimum time. Hence, it was not uncommon for these cultures to manipulate their lunar based calendars in order to keep the 12 months in sync with the solar seasons. Furthermore, it was also quite common for the beginning of the year to be reckoned coming in the Spring time, aligning it with what was considered the most important time of the year. The Scripture establishes this kind of biblical calendar with the advent of the Passover occasion. But prior to this, Israel's calendar did not follow this convention for some strange reason. And Judaism continues to use this ancient calendar all the while adhering to the new calendar that came with the Passover to honor the Holy Days observances.

Israel's 12 months had names which some are recorded in Scripture. There happen to be two different groups of names, the first set is believed to be Canaanite derived names. After the Nation's Babylonian Captivity the names of the months came to take on Babylonian names. So Scripture identifies a month either by its "numbered" position within the 12 month schedule according to the new calendar arrangement or possibly by one of two names. In a total of 27 places the months are identified by name. The first "half" of these references are listed below and record a Canaanite name depicting a time before Israel was exiled in Babylon:

Abib (6x) is written about in the Torah exclusively, Scripture's "first month" established on the Passover occasion.
  Ziv (2x), identified as the "2nd" month,
Ethanim (1x), as the "7th" month, and
Bul (1x), as the "8th" month.

The last 3, Ziv, Ethanim and Bul, are all recalled during the reign of Solomon in 1 Kings. The last 3 of these 4 references the Hebrew writer chose to use the Hebrew word for moon, "*yerach*", instead of "*chodesh*".

After the exiling of Israel into Babylon, the remaining Hebrew Scripture identifies more names of months. These are the "latter half" of references where Babylonian names are used:

Nisan (2x) used in Nehemiah and Esther. Esther's passage identifies Nisan as the "1st month".
Sivan (1x) identified as the "3rd month" in Esther.
Elul (1x) is in Nehemiah.
Chislev (2x) in Nehemiah and Zechariah where it is identified as the "9th month".
Tebeth (1x) in Esther as the "10th month".
Shebat (1x) in Zechariah as the "11th month".
Adar (9x) is in Ezra and 8 times in Esther where it is said to be the "12 month".

The Hebrew Calendar versus the Holy Calendar

At the leading edge of the Passover testimony, a "new" Calendar, a "Holy Calendar", is introduced. Up until that time, Israel followed its "Hebrew Calendar" which had as Ethanim (or Tishri) as the first month. The difference between the two was that the Holy Calendar would be 6 months removed from the Hebrew Calendar. That is, the "middle" of the original 12 month cycle, at the start of the 7th month, would become the New Holy Year's Month. This 7th Month happens to be "Abib" (or Nisan). And so the difference between the Hebrew Calendar and the rearranged Holy Calendar is that they are 6 months removed from one another as the diagram below denotes:

**Beginning of the
Holy New Year**

1	2	3	4	5	6
Abib	Ziv				
Nisan		Sivan			Elul

**Beginning of
Israel's New Year**

7	8	9	10	11	12
Ethanim	Bul				
		Chislev	Tebeth	Shebat	Adar

The Holy New Year vs Israel's New Year
Canaanite and Babylonian names
shown where Scripture identifies them

But there is strange testimony in the Law describing when the "end of the year" is to be reckoned. The first interesting passage to cite is when God speaks to Moses on Mount Sinai regarding a certain Holy Day that will be reviewed later:

Exo 23:16 (34:22) "...the Feast of Ingathering at the <u>end</u> of the year...

It will be learned that this "feast" begins on the 15th day of the "7th month" of the Holy Calendar. This is the same month Israel's tradition holds to being the first month of the Hebrew Calendar. Note here God calls it the "end" of the year. So how is it possible that the date Ethanim/Tishri 15th, Israel's first month of the year, is being considered here by God the "end" of the year? The only way this could be possible is for the 7th month to be somehow made the last month. But if the 1st month of the Holy Calendar is Abib this would only account for a 7 month period of time. The same conclusions can be drawn about Deut 31:10 where the same thing is communicated.

So it would appear the reader has no other interpretation to make other than to argue there is also an implied "Divine Calendar" to reckon in these passages being 7 months in length. This of course did not mean there was to be no 12 month annual calendar to follow. It simply implies that this is part of a Divine Plan to establish a 7 month reckoning of time that makes no sense unless it is to represent a single timeline, rather than a repeating cycle of time. At the "end" of this Divine 7 Months Year, its "end" is to bring about the things these passages must be prophetically symbolizing for this future time, what is to be considered the "end" of the Divine Schedule or Holy Calendar. It seems that there is no other plausible interpretation to make here. And so these are yet further hints suggesting the idea of a Divine Plan and Schedule that has only one passing from start to end.

The Divine Calendar

Month 1: Abib, The Beginning of the "Divine" Year	Month 2	Month 3	Month 4	Month 5	Month 6	Month 7: Ethanim, The End of the "Divine" Year

Passover   **Final Harvest**

...the fourteenth day (of Abib)...the congregation of Israel is to kill it (the LORD's Passover) at twilight...

Exodus 12:23-24

Chapter Three

Passover: In The Beginning

The study of the testimony of the Holy Days begins with Passover, the first Holy Occasion in the Holy Calendar. Yes, that's correct, a Holy Occasion, not a Holy Day. Strangely enough, this first occasion is not accounted as a "full" Holy Day but only the ending "sliver" of the first Holy Day is to be reckoned. This, in itself, is a **BIG** clue that cannot be ignored. That is, why would the very first event in the Holy Calendar be the coming End of a Day? All of the rest of the Holy Days are full and complete Holy Days so why this very mysterious beginning? Well, if one conjectures the Holy Calendar is to represent quite a long period of time, from beginning to end, then reckoning a fraction of a Day would mean that it represents something that is quite short in duration of time comparatively speaking against the backdrop of the entire Holy Period.

And if this "sliver" of time is the occasion of the Passover that would make perfect sense. That is, Passover lasted for a few hours in the middle of the night! So this is the first HUGE piece of evidence that begins to form indicating that some sort of Divine Timeline is beginning with Passover, with the Passover occasion itself representing what is to be accounted as the very End of the first Holy Day. Thus, Passover begins the timeline!

The very first time Scripture alludes to Passover is when it is part of prophecy foretold to Israel's first great Patriarch Abram/Abraham:

Gen 15:13-14,16 And {God} said to Abram, "Know for certain that your descendants will be strangers in a land that is not theirs, where they will be enslaved and oppressed four hundred years. "But I will also judge the nation whom they will serve; and afterward they will come out with many possessions..."Then in the fourth generation they shall return here, for the iniquity of the Amorite is not yet complete."

Notice the passage says Abram's descendants are to return "here". "Here" would be Canaan, the land of Abram's sojourning. Somehow his Descendants would come to "leave" Canaan for whatever reason and find themselves as "strangers in a land that is not theirs". There they would be enslaved for a period of time that would coincide with a period of time that would cause the indigenous People of Canaan, the Amorites, to give up their right to inhabit the region on account of their prolonged sin. Canaan would then become available territory for Abram's descendants to take as their own which the prophecy predicts that they would.

Abram, later renamed "Abraham", begot Isaac and Isaac begot Jacob who was also named Israel. All 3 of these fathers came to live within the land of Canaan but never living in permanent dwellings there. Near the end of his life Jacob would take his family to live in Egypt, the place where Israel was to become enslaved. How this came about began through envy between Jacob's sons. Jacob's love for his son Joseph, his first by his favored wife Rachel, would cause the rest of his sons to plot to have Joseph sold into slavery. Under Divine Providence Joseph found himself in Egypt, at first as a slave, then a prisoner, then finally ascending to a position of power second only to the Pharaoh himself. Joseph had explained a dream of the Pharaoh's which was predicting 7 years of abundance then 7 years of famine. Under Joseph's lead, Egypt stockpiled food for 7 years in preparing for the coming predicted famine. When the famine eventually arrived, many of the surrounding Nations' Peoples sought food in exchange for whatever they had. Eventually Joseph's brothers would be sent to seek for food in Egypt. There they would be reunited with their long abandoned brother Joseph. In time Joseph invited his father and family to live with him in Egypt thus explaining how this family eventually found itself in Egypt.

But Joseph's place in Egypt would be in time forgotten and Egyptian hospitality towards Israel would turn into a suspicious fear after Joseph died and eventually when the Nation grew in size. A Pharaoh ascended who would decide to put Israel under bondage to prevent the Nation from rising up against Egypt. And so Israel came to suffer under enslavement for centuries thereafter. Near the end of this period another Pharaoh arose and ordered the deaths of Israel's male children in order to halt the Nation's continued growth. One Israelite male infant who escaped this threat of death would go on to become Israel's greatest prophet, the Prophet Moses.

By Divine Providence, Moses' mother and sister Miriam would tactfully see to Moses being adopted by the Pharaoh's daughter after she found him floating in a basket near where she bathed in the Nile. Miriam's act of cunning saw to it that Moses' own mother was arranged to raise him for the Pharaoh's household. And so the Hebrew child would grow up as the Pharaoh's grandson never once seeing a day of slavery. Yet later in Moses' life, he would find himself intervening and killing an Egyptian slave master who he witnessed mistreating a Hebrew slave. But his own People would report him to the Egyptian authorities and Moses had no choice but to flee Egypt to save his life.

So he travelled east and found himself in the land of Midian. There he would marry and have two children. One day, many years later, while he shepherded a flock on Mount Sinai, God spoke to Moses through a burning bush. God told Moses that He heard the cries of the Israelites and was calling Moses to set them free. Moses' brother Aaron would meet him on the way and the two approached Pharaoh together.

What these brothers requested of the Pharaoh was for Israel to be allowed to go into the wilderness and worship God there for 3 days and then return. The repeated response of the Pharaoh was to refuse this request. This would go on for 9 times and each time Moses would mediate a Divine "Plague" to help convince the Pharaoh to change his mind. The various plagues were to demonstrate God humiliating Egypt's various gods it worshipped.

On each and every occasion, what was predicted to take place came to pass. Each succeeding plague became more severe than the previous one. But nothing would persuade the Pharaoh to allow Israel to go free. And so this is what sets the stage for Passover. The coming of this final "10th Plague" would convince the

Pharaoh to set Israel free. What the Pharaoh and all of Egypt were warned of was that death would come to visit all the firstborn of both man and beast. However, provision was given for each household to avoid this calamity, instructions on how to offer up a "Passover" sacrifice. If these instructions were followed, God would "pass over" the house and not bring death to the firstborn.

As will be discovered, Passover is filled with an introduction of symbols and ideas that will set the foundation for the coming Law and its Holy Days. The first important symbolism to identify is what very first divine instruction is given to Israel in preparation for the coming Passover and for all coming time thereafter:

Exo 12:1 3a   Now the LORD said to Moses and Aaron in the land of Egypt, "This month shall be the beginning of months for you; it is to be the first month of the year to you.

What this passage effectively communicates is that a new Holy Calendar was to begin with the coming of Passover. This would be the month of Abib:

Exo 13:4   On this day in the month of Abib...

It is believed the word "Abib" is a Canaanite derived word used to signify the coming of harvest, as it refers to the budding fruit found inside a barley stalk. It necessarily represented the first sign that the harvest period had arrived. Hence, the time when the Passover came was late spring when the initial signs of harvest were appearing. Earlier at the coming of the 7th plague of hail the biblical commentary states this:

Exo 9:31-32 (Now the flax and the barley were ruined, for the barley was in the ear and the flax was in bud. But the wheat and the spelt were not ruined, for they {ripen} late.)

The reader is thus informed that the plague of hail had ruined the flax and barley because these were the crops that appear first, what are the initial signs of harvest season, and that the wheat and spelt mature later and were thus not ruined. At the coming of the 8th plague, the locusts are written to have eaten everything not devastated by the hail. So Egypt's entire crop was ruined in the year of Israel's Exodus. However it should be noted that from the 3rd plague on, the land of Goshen, where Israel lived, was left unharmed so that Israel's crops remained untouched.

Thus Israel's first command related to the Holy Days was to make the month of Abib the beginning of its Holy Year. This so happens to be exactly six months removed from Israel's "Rosh" Ha Shanah, its New Year's Day. It would be like the Gregorian Calendar being given a 2nd New Year's Day on July 1st. Here now is the first great symbol presented. It should not be underestimated. So what is its meaning?

Having Passover come on the first month of the year represents it as being the beginning of a Holy Schedule. This would not become apparent until the rest of the Holy Days would be added to this one. The major hidden sign that was being aligned with this beginning was the coming harvest season in having timed this occasion coming in the month of Abib. What is so odd to discover is that Passover will have no symbols to link it to the initial harvest season even though it has countless other symbols. In other words, that Passover comes at the initial harvest season is a coincidental association for the reader to notice. Thus, the element of harvest is somewhat concealed within the Passover yet undeniably so. Ultimately, this concealed element will take on a major significance in the greater picture.

The other facet that will have symbolic significance is how the Holy Calendar introduced here will go on to be described as 7 months in length in a roundabout way as was described in the previous chapter. It implies that it really is not to be considered a repeating cycle of time but a single passage of time from beginning to end. In this light, the coming of the Passover can be interpreted as the first great Divine Act in a Divine Plan as part of a Divine Chronological Schedule. Since it was an actual historical occasion it thus is a point in time which came once in the past. It saw to Israel's liberation, the coming of its Independence Day. To ensure this would come to pass as planned and that Israel would see to God "passing over" its People on the night of the 10th Plague, Israel would be asked to follow a list of Passover Instructions.

Instructions for Passover

After commanding Israel to begin reckoning the new Holy Calendar, the next important thing to recognize is how Israel begins to be called a "congregation":

Exo 12:3a Speak to all the *congregation* of Israel...

This is the first time this expression appears in Scripture. What it means is that Israel was being "called out" and "set aside" as a distinct "assembly" of people for God. It should be considered as setting the precedent for the later biblical term "church". With Israel following the instructions of Passover, the Nation would be made holy in obedience to them, set aside for God's purposes, given the Nation was obeying Divine Commands. From this point on, the expression "congregation", or "ehad" transliterated from the Hebrew, is used to depict Israel as a Holy Nation set aside for God's purposes. So if Israel's life was changing with the coming of Passover what necessarily should the reader assume has begun here? It is too early to tell in the testimony. But soon after, Passover is seen as having made way for the Nation to receive the Law at Mount Sinai.

There are a number of details and symbols to account for in the analysis of the Passover. To make it easier to digest and remember, the various elements are broken down into 8 different instructions. The first has already been discussed at length:

1.   The month Abib is to be the first month of the Holy Calendar.

Moving on, the next instructions follow:

Exo 12:3-6 "Speak to all the congregation of Israel, saying, 'On the <u>tenth of this month</u> they are each one to take a lamb for themselves...a lamb for each household...'Your lamb shall be an unblemished male a year old; you may take it from the sheep or from the goats. 'And you shall keep it <u>until the fourteenth day of the same month</u>, then the whole assembly of the congregation of Israel is to kill it <u>at twilight</u>.

Here the phrase the "tenth of this month" should be considered Israel's first holy appointment it was being given to keep in its holy existence. It should also be pointed out here that the first references of "lamb" in the above passage is transliterated in the Hebrew as "seh". This simply refers to a smaller animal from the flocks which would be either lambs or goats as the passage eventually spells out. The instructions are clear regarding what to do with the animal.

2. On the 10th day of Abib each household was to take in the Passover animal and domesticate it. It was to be an unblemished year old male from the goats or sheep. The idea of an "unblemished" animal will go on to be repeatedly cited in the Law regarding all of the animal sacrifices permissible to bring to God. There were to be no imperfections to the animal in representing an unacceptable sacrifice. That it was to be a year old also adds further symbolism as does it being a "male". Finally, that it was to be "domesticated" also has implications. Keeping track of which animals were of age would become an important every day task for Israel to reckon from this day on. Not all of the Law's sacrifices would be constrained to these requirements so it should be understood the different sacrifices each had their own worth and merit and were not to be considered equal given they had their own unique distinctions.

3. At the close of the 14th day of Abib the Passover was to be sacrificed.

Recall again that a day begins and ends at dusk. It should also be noted that the close of the 14th day was essentially indicating the arrival of a full moon. Now as to what was to be done with the sacrificed Passover, the reading continues:

Exo 12:7-13 'Moreover, they shall take some of the blood and put it on the two doorposts and on the lintel of the houses in which they eat it. 'And they shall eat the flesh that {same} night, roasted with fire, and they shall eat it with unleavened bread and bitter herbs. 'Do not eat any of it raw or boiled at all with water, but rather roasted with fire, {both} its head and its legs along with its entrails. 'And you shall not leave any of it over until morning, but whatever is left of it until morning, you shall burn with fire...it is the LORD'S Passover. 'For I will go through the land of Egypt on that night, and will strike down all the first-born in the land of Egypt, both man and beast...I am the LORD. 'And the blood shall be a sign for you on the houses where you live; and when I see the blood <u>I will pass over you</u>, and no plague will befall you to destroy {you} when I strike the land of Egypt.

4. Blood from the sacrifice was to be applied to the doorposts and lintel of the house. With this God would see the blood and "pass over" the house refraining from bringing death to any 1st born residing within that household. Thus, here is the first time the principle of "vicarious substitutionary sacrifice" would be demonstrated with Israel. The life of the animal was to go in the place of Israel's 1st born. This will go on to be implied throughout the Law's many later defined sacrifices it would describe.

5. The Passover sacrifice was to be eaten at the beginning of the 15th day. It was to be eaten with unleavened bread and bitter herbs. It was to be roasted with fire, eaten inside the house and none of its bones were to be broken. Whatever remained by morning was to be burned in the fire. Here there are yet even more symbols to ponder as to their meaning. As to why unleavened bread, this was to signify Israel's haste in which it came to leave Egypt, the "bread of affliction". There was no time to allow the bread to rise so it was to be prepared without leaven. As to why bitter herbs, again this is to signify under what conditions Israel would have to leave, escaping in the middle of the night after hundreds of years of slavery. But what is most mysterious is why it was important for the animal's bones not to be broken. If the animal was to be sacrificed, roasted over a fire and then eaten and the rest of it burned, why did this matter? That none of its flesh was to go outside the house suggests it was not to be attempted to try to save another household's 1st born by sharing it with another household. It can be argued that all these symbols have both a superficial meaning and perhaps a deeper one that looks forward to yet another Passover the Law anticipates is to come beyond this initial one.

Exod 12:48 "But if a stranger sojourns with you, and celebrates the Passover to the LORD, let all his males be circumcised, and then let him come near to celebrate it; and he shall be like a native of the land. But no uncircumcised person may eat of it.

6. Israelites and non-Israelites alike were permitted to partake of the Passover as long as male partakers had been circumcised. That such a thing was required perhaps is a sign indicating there were two layers of meanings with all of these symbols, an outward physical one, and an inward spiritual one. Circumcision had earlier been instituted with Abraham and he was commanded to pass along this rite to his descendants. God demanded that Moses' own children be circumcised when Moses was first called to deliver Israel from Egypt revealing that he had failed to do so.

Since it was Israel's 1st born who were to be spared from death, God commanded that *every* first issue of the womb, of both man and beast, would become his, from that point forward from all future offspring Israel would bring forth. More specifically, all 1st born males of Israel's offspring were to become God's possession. Hence, the Passover is to be seen having started something that would go on in perpetuity beyond the Passover. Essentially Israel was being asked to pay for its continued liberty by offering to God its first born from every generation thereafter. Yet provision is given for Israel to "redeem" back its first-born through payment:

Exo 13:12-13 ...you shall devote to the LORD the first offspring of every womb, and the first offspring of every beast that you own; the males belong to the LORD...and every first-born of man among your sons you shall <u>redeem</u>.

7. All Israel's 1st born males were God's possession, of both man and beast.

So what was the purpose of this? What was God to do with a "perpetual" pool of males from one generation to the next? Scripture goes on to reveal that God would create a "perpetual" Priesthood by this command. But first God would "trade" all of Israel's 1st born for the Levites, Moses' tribal origin, once Israel entered the wilderness. It was the Levites who would be made the priestly line. And to encourage them to remain in their priestly duties, various forms of compensation would be made perpetual in nature to them as well. For example, the 1st born livestock and redemption monies for Israel's 1st born would be given to the priesthood. The plunder that Israel took from the Egyptians when they left became part of this too. Much more would develop later regarding the priests but it must be understood Passover was where the elementary building blocks for creating and also sustaining the priesthood were set in motion with this Law of the 1st born. Hence, the Law's Priesthood finds its origin in this first Holy Occasion.

8th Instruction: Make Passover Eternal Memorial

The 8th instruction to be documented here is the command to make Passover a memorial each and every year as an everlasting ordinance:

Exo 12:14-16, 18 'Now this day will be a *memorial* to you, and you shall celebrate it {as} a <u>feast</u> to the LORD; throughout your generations you are to celebrate it {as} <u>a permanent ordinance</u>. 'Seven days you shall eat unleavened bread, but on the first day you shall remove leaven from your houses; for whoever eats anything leavened from the first day until the seventh day, that person shall be cut off from Israel. 'And on the first day you shall have a holy assembly, and {another} holy assembly on the seventh day; no work at all shall be done on them....'In the first {month,} on the fourteenth day of the month at evening, you shall eat unleavened bread, until <u>the twenty-first day of the month</u> at evening.

Three other segments of Scripture close out the instructions for the memorial:

Exo 12:24 "And you shall observe this event as an ordinance for you and your children forever.

Exod 13:6 "For seven days you shall eat unleavened bread, and on <u>the seventh day there shall be a feast</u> to the LORD.

Exo 13:10 "Therefore, you shall keep this ordinance at its appointed time from year to year.

So, summarizing here:

8. The occasion of Passover was to be made an eternally memorialized "feast":

a. Sacrifice the Passover on the twilight of the 14th day.
b. Eat the Passover at the beginning of the 15th day.
c. No uncircumcised person is to eat the Passover.

In addition, there was to be 7 days of eating only unleavened Bread:

d. Remove leaven from the house on the first day
e. Observe 7 days where any bread eaten be unleavened.
f. The 15th and 21st days were to be days of no work and of holy assemblies.

The 21st day was to be made a "feast" to the LORD. This is an odd thing to find and it represents the idea that more things are being concealed here without an explanation. That is, why is there to be yet another distinct Feast to be had on the 21st when that day is already part of a 7 day feast? What this suggests is that this Feast is predicting a future yet to come through its symbolisms.

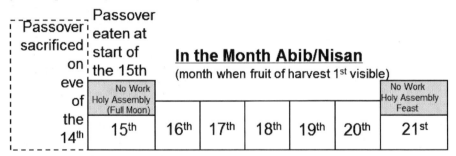

Passover Feast and 7 days of Unleavened Bread

The 1st Feast: A Prophetic Timeline of Israel's Fate

As was argued earlier, with the Passover accounted as being the very end of the 14th Day perhaps suggests the literal fulfillment of Passover was being represented as a "sliver" in time with respect to the 7 Holy Days that were to follow it. That is, if the 7 Days represents some kind of Divine timeline, it would make sense that the Passover appear as a very small piece of this timeline. So why have a timeline of 7 days length? What is this to mean or signify? The only thing in

Scripture prior to this that can shed light on the matter is that of Creation which is recorded having taken place over the same length of time. But many more segments of 7 days will be identified in the Law with this being its first. In sum, the period of time suggests a complete segment of time for whatever it is be associated with. The observant reader has to begin speculating what complete history is being told by these 7 days.

Why a reader should be speculating that this 7 Day period is a timeline has to do with what provocative parallels exist between it and the history that would become Israel's future, from Passover on, as documented in the Word of God. The Prophet Ezekiel especially glaringly supplies the overarching prophetic view of Israel's future that looks an awful like the pattern established in the Feast of Unleavened Bread.

First off, notice that there is no break in time between the Passover and the 1st Day of Unleavened Bread. So one can imagine that the threshold between the end of the 14th Day and the beginning of the 15th Day represents an important transition, a transition that takes place immediately following the Passover. And what transition is that? Well, notice that the 1st Day is to be a day of "Holy Assembly". That is, if one looks at this as a timeline from beginning to end, the 1st Day appears as if to be "Holy" as does the last Day. In other words, with Israel having offered the Passover sacrifice, this was the moment of transition between when Israel was "uncalled" and "common" to that of becoming "called" and made "holy".

Recall that soon after this God manifested Himself as a "Pillar of Fire" by night and a "Cloud" by day. This Epiphany came to lead Israel to the edge of the Red Sea, through the Red Sea, and then eventually on to the very foot of Mount Sinai itself and beyond. Hence, with God in its midst, the Nation was Holy and would remain so until the Day God would depart from its midst. In other words, the 1st Day of Unleavened Bread seems to be representing the time in Israel's early history when God was in its midst. Thus, this moment "began" at the threshold of the Passover between the 14th Day and the 15th Day. If this correlation is further followed, that would mean that the next 5 Days of Unleavened Bread should represent the entire period during which Israel is to be without God in its midst. Finally, the 7th Day of the Feast of Unleavened Bread is then representing the future moment in Remnant Israel's future that anticipates that God is to return to its midst. This would further explain why the last day of Unleavened Bread comes to be made a Feast in and of itself. For the Word of God, Ezekiel especially, states that once God comes into Remnant Israel's Midst in the future, He will never leave the Nation again, forever thereafter.

This brings up an interesting question to ask. What is the symbolic meaning of the "Unleavened Bread"? If it is argued that the entire period of the 7 days represents Israel's prophetic life from Passover on, it must be something that Israel was to "eat" continuously. But what was Israel to "eat" during this whole time, even during the days when God would not be in its midst? The answer can only be regarding the Word of God that Israel would be given. The first piece of this was of course "the Law". And so when God states that "Man does not live on bread alone but by every word that comes forth from the Mouth of God" this is perhaps the prophetic meaning of the "Unleavened Bread". The Unleavened Bread is none other than the Word of God which the Nation would come to "eat" throughout its entire existence.

7 Days of the Feast of Unleavened Bread

Passover	No Work Holy Assembly (Full Moon)						No Work Holy Assembly Feast
	Day 1	Day 2	Day 3	Day 4	Day 5	Day 6	Day 7
	God in Ancient Israel's Midst	God removed from Israel's Midst					God in Remnant Israel's Midst

Still further is the idea of "No Work". What is this symbolically representing? Perhaps those who are familiar with the Sabbath may think this has something to do with the Sabbath. But that cannot be because the Sabbath was not yet given to the Nation as an observance. That comes a few months later. What it must be referring to is that God would be doing the "Work" of looking out for the Nation and seeing it receive "Blessing" as Deuteronomy 28:1-14 spells out. But in contrast, the Law also predicts a time beyond the Blessing when Israel would not adhere to the Law and it would find itself under Divine "Curses" as Deut 28:15-29:29 spells out. Finally however, Deuteronomy chapter 30 speaks of future restoration as the ultimate end of what reads to be a chronological sequence of first Blessing, then Curses and then eventually Eternal Blessing in the End. All of this follows nicely with the pattern of the 7 days of Unleavened Bread!

So with Israel being commanded to memorialize the Feast each year the Nation was and still does and is predicted to "rehearse" its prophetic life from beginning to end forever.

Initial Holy Days Elements: DNA Building Blocks

With a good oversight of what future testimony the Word of God brings regarding Israel's prophetic future, a great deal of "decoding" can be accomplished with the first critical symbols defining the initial Holy Days making up the Feast of Unleavened Bread. This decoding is not only useful for understanding the meaning of the Feast of Unleavened Bread but also the meanings of later Holy Days that become introduced and defined as the rest of the Law is testified to. This is because these earliest of symbols turn out to be "Building Blocks" similar to DNA. That is, the same symbols come to be used repeatedly in defining later Holy Days too. So anything that can be ascertained about these earliest usages of symbols will help to decode later Holy Days as well.

Here is a summary of what has been discovered so far in the deciphering of the Feast of Unleavened Bread:

1. The Passover's unique, one-of-a-kind "End of Day" Symbolism: Suggests that the Passover itself is the beginning of a Divine timeline of some sort.

2. The symbolism of the 7 Day long Feast coming coincident with the end of the Passover: It could arguably be concluded that these 7 days are symbolic of a "complete" Age or Epoch of Israel's Prophetic existence starting from Passover on. What binds all 7 days together is Israel's possession and reverence to the "Word of God" as its dietary "Unleavened Bread" it consumes.

3. The symbols of the 1st Day of the Feast as a Day of No Work and as a Day of Holy Assembly: As the biblical account testifies to, immediately following the Passover, Israel's freedom out of Egyptian Bondage was secured by Divine Intervention void of human work. It marked the beginning of Israel's life with God in its midst which made the entire Nation a Holy Assembly throughout the entire period. That period ultimately came to an end when God left Israel's midst which Ezekiel witnessed with his own eyes (Eze10:18).

4. The beginning of the 2nd Day to the end of the 6th Day of the Feast symbolism: This predicts the period of Israel's existence where God would not reside in its midst.

5. The symbols of the 7th Day of the Feast as a Day of No Work and as a Day of Holy Assembly and as yet another Feast altogether: The Law and the Prophets predict a future day to come when God is to return to Israel and dwell amongst the Nation forever thereafter (Eze43:7). So technically, this day is a future "Eternal" Day of No Work and of Holy Assembly to come.

To Reckon Passover: An Observational Conjunction

One practical question the command to make Passover a memorial raises regards how Israel was to determine the memorial coming each and every year thereafter. Which New Moon was to be selected each New Year so as to properly reckon Passover? The Scripture suggests that the month Israel was to choose for its coming New Year was always to be the one aligned with the coming harvest season.

So the month of Abib has to be considered a "floating" month. As was stated earlier, the moon's phases do not stay aligned to the solar cycle. Because of this requirement the Divine Calendar is to be considered a "lunisolar" calendar. It needs to align the beginning of the lunar year with the signs of the initial harvest season. So whatever moon phase best overlapped with this occasion was to be made the start of the New Year. This ultimately meant the previous year would have been either 12 months long or 13. And as stated before, it was not important as to how long a previous year had actually been.

In this way both the sun and moon play a role where the sun dictates the general time of the beginning of the year and the moon dictates the actual beginning by what moon cycle was best aligned with the start of harvest. This makes the coming of the new Holy Year more or less unknown requiring the community of Israel to be actively looking for the arrival of the year by watching for when the signs of this peculiar conjunction appeared. Hence, the implied biblical method of timekeeping necessary to establish the coming of a New Year is an "observational" one.

This happened to be a tricky thing to determine when later astronomical methods became the preferred method for predicting such dates over the observational technique coming not too far after Jesus' ministry. These so called "calculated" methods were designed to predict when the New Years were coming well in advance through astronomical and mathematical means in order to avoid the need for observation. Of course, the beauty of the observational method is that even a small child can determine the coming of a New Year just so long as the observer has a clear view of the heavens and can visit the crops in the fields in the early spring. What is to be witnessed is a 3 part conjunction:

1) Initial crop of the season signifying the arrival of a new holy year.
2) The new moon as the start of a new month.
3) Dusk as the start of a new day.

In identifying when these 3 occasions converged together each year, this is how Israel, and later the Jewish People, came to establish the Holy New Year and all of its appointments for many years. As will be learned in the coming chapters, a crucial additional command would arise that would help ensure Israel would neither choose a month too earlier nor choose one too late. Altogether, ***Passover's coming is to be reckoned by the first full moon to appear coinciding with the initial barley harvest***.

With the basic requirements and restrictions properly factored in, Israel was given a simple, but elegant means for reckoning each coming New Year. Much later, when institutionalized Christianity had a vested interest in knowing the arrival of Passover too, it decided to use its own methods for determining when the coming Passover season had arrived. But due to the flawed Julian Calendar that was in widespread use at the time, the ancient observational method proved its far superior simplicity in comparison to the manmade methods mathematicians and astronomers concocted at the time. Even in the present hour, there are years when Judaism, the Easter Church and the Western Church all observe the coming season on different dates, as the year 2016 provides a clear example of this (see the chart below). This should not be!

Year	Passover Judaism	Easter Western Church	Eastern Church
2011	April 19	April 24	April 24
2012	April 7	April 8	April 15
2013	March 26	March 31	May 5
2014	April 15	April 20	April 20
2015	April 4	April 5	April 12
2016	**April 23**	**March 27**	**May 1**
2017	April 11	April 16	April 16
2018	March 31	April 1	April 8

See, the LORD has given you the Sabbath...remain every man in his place; let no man go out of his place on the 7th Day. So the people rested on the 7th Day.

Exodus 16:29-30

Chapter Four
The (7ᵗʰ Day) Sabbath

A s the record goes on to tell, the Pharaoh of Egypt would let Israel go free on account of the loss of life Egypt suffered on the eve of the Passover. So in the middle of the night, on the 15th day, Israel would flee into the wilderness. The physical presence of God, the Divine Glory, would lead Israel as a pillar of fire by night and as a cloud by day. Never had such a thing taken place before in biblical history. God dwelling in Israel's midst is to be understood the glaringly obvious thing that began Israel's new holy life beyond the Passover. So was there ever a time when God left the Nation according to Scripture? Yes. And is there a time predicted for God to return to dwell with Israel? Yes. Hence, there are 3 distinct and noticeable phases in Israel's biblically fulfilled and predicted life that correlate nicely with the three phases of the 7 Holy Days of Unleavened Bread. It is the initial evidence of a Holy Days Code being created.

The freed Nation would be deliberately led by God so as to make it look as if it was wandering aimlessly. This was about the time Pharaoh's mourning had turned into a rage and when he decided to take his army and retrieve what he set free. As the army approached Israel, Moses led Israel into the Red Sea where God had split the sea into two with a strong wind. It would blow all night. With the pillar of fire between the Egyptian army and Israel, the army followed Israel into the sea. As dawn approached, the last of Israel came up out of the dry sea floor. Then, Moses lifted his hands and the wall of water came to collapse upon the army while it was standing on the sea floor.

Israel's enemies were instantly destroyed. So one would think that from here on out everything was destined to turn out in favor for Israel. After all God intervened in an unprecedented way both with the coming of the 10 plagues and now at the Red Sea. But in reality, Israel's painful journey had just begun. What the future holds is quite a rude awakening because God was interested in revealing what kind of faithfulness the Nation would return to Him for His good graces. Through this exercise Israel would be found its own worst enemy as the rest of the story unfolds.

After about a month, Israel's food supply dwindled and the Nation began to complain to Moses. Here then is the next relevant topic to highlight. God's response to Israel's hunger was the bringing of the "manna", a bread like substance that would come to form each morning as dew in the wilderness. The Nation was commanded to gather this each day for 5 days, gather a double portion on the 6th day and rest on the 7th day. This 7th day was to be a "holy" Sabbath, or "rest" to the LORD. Later Israel would be taught that God created the heavens and earth in 6 days and rested on the 7th:

Exo 31:16-17 'So the sons of Israel shall observe the sabbath, to celebrate the sabbath throughout their generations as a perpetual covenant.' "It is a sign between Me and the sons of Israel forever; for in six days the LORD made heaven and earth, but on the seventh day He ceased {from labor,} and was refreshed."

And so the Sabbath becomes the next Holy Day to be identified after the Passover. It though is one that is observed year round and not just during the harvest season. So it is a peculiar Holy Day unlike the others that Israel would be commanded to observe. A 7 day span of time is not a natural span to be noticed by anything other than simple accounting. Since the Western world adopted the "week" sequence of time in its own timekeeping it is believed its reckoning is synchronized with when Israel first began to observe it in the wilderness thousands of years ago.

The word "Sabbath" transliterated "*shabaat*" is derived from the Hebrew word for "ceasing" or "*shawbath*". The Sabbath will go on to become the preeminent day of reverence throughout the year simply because of its frequency of occurrence in comparison to all of the other Holy Days. So is there anything relevant here to the Passover memorial? Absolutely. Because the Passover memorial includes a 7 day period of eating unleavened bread, this necessarily makes the occasion have exactly one Sabbath within its lunar 7 day period. And because the lunisolar calendar is not synchronous with a 7 day period, this Sabbath day "floats" within this period.

What it creates are 7 different possible memorial schedules where the Sabbath can fall on each of the days between the 15th day and the 21st day as the diagram below illustrates. And this Sabbath should not be confused with the two days of "no work" on the 15th day and the 21st day. The Passover came before the Sabbath was introduced so these earlier defined days should not be confused with this "7th day" of rest. And depending upon the position of the Sabbath in the 7 days, there could come to be two days of no work back-to-back as schedules 1 and 5 depict below. Although this seems like an unimportant consequence, it plays a major role in matters that will eventually surface in later Scripture testimony.

The 7 "floating" Sabbath schedules for the Passover Memorial

So the question begs to be asked. If the Sabbath was inaugurated after the Passover occasion, should it be assigned as a new symbolism coming to be added to the week of Unleavened Bread? It does not seem that it should. Rather, it appears to be a separate and concealed element. And this is not the only symbolism that will mysteriously come to converge upon the week of Unleavened Bread. What this evolving testimony is a multiple layered form of communication. The first layer is the testimony of the Passover memorial, a rearward looking remembrance. The second layer is the observance of the week of the Unleavened Bread, what has been conjectured as being symbolic of Israel's prophetic future. The third layer is what added and concealed symbolisms come to converge with the week of Unleavened Bread, what is yet something else being predicted coming in the future. These distinct facets of the testimony must be recognized in order to unravel all the aspects of the Holy Days and the Code that is formed by their testimony.

**Three times a year
you shall celebrate a feast to Me.**

Exodus 23:14

Chapter Five

Mount Sinai Testimony

U pon the arrival of the 3rd month from the Exodus (Ex19:1), Israel came to camp at the foot of Mount Sinai also called Mount Horeb. Here Moses would meet God on 8 different occasions. On three of these occasions, a great deal of instruction would be given and documented. It was to be the making of the so called "Sinaitic" Covenant where God and Israel would enter into a conditional covenant agreement. The terms of the covenant were that Israel would obey the commands of the Law and God in turn would bless the Nation and dwell in its midst. Should Israel disobey the commands, God in turn would curse the Nation and turn His face away from it. Although it was the intention for the People to hear directly the instructions from God, after only a short duration of this Law Giving, the People became frightened and requested that Moses mediate the law giving instead. Listed below is a synopsis of what was given on the three noted occasions:

1st giving: Exo20-23. The so called "10 commandments" are given first in chapter 20 up to verse 18 as God directly speaks to the entire Nation. (This expression "10 commandments" is misleading because the original Hebrew reads as "10 words". It misleads Christians to think these specific commandments as separate and ultimately set apart from the rest of the Law's commandments. The best interpretation is to see these 10 commandments as a sort of "Table of Contents" or a consolidation of what the whole of the Law is to represent.) But after this the People become frightened and request Moses hear the words alone and report back to them. What is spoken to Moses is ultimately written down in the "book of the covenant". Moses will later offer a sacrifice and sprinkle its blood on the book and the People after the People agree to the terms of the covenant. This was to establish the covenant agreement between Israel and God, the Sinaitic Covenant. In this section of lawgiving, it is here where it is first learned that there are to be two more feasts to be observed besides the one inaugurated at Passover. Here the Divine Schedule continues to unfold beyond the things predicted by the Passover.

2nd giving: Exo25-31. Moses ascends Mount Sinai for 40 days and nights. Here he receives the blueprints for the tent/tabernacle and instruction for the High Priest service. It is in the tent made from these instructions where God would come to dwell with Israel and where the Priesthood would maintain a holiness to sustain God's presence there. It would also be where Moses would come to receive the latter portions of the Law beyond Sinai. Finally, Moses receives the "10 commandments" on two tablets which God himself is recorded having wrote. But Moses ultimately destroys these tablets upon descending the mountain and seeing Israel worship a golden calf idol the Nation had made while he was gone. Israel's unfaithfulness would continue to be revealed on many more occasions. Thousands of Israelites would be put to death on this occasion. Although it had been God's original plan to make the entire Nation a Priesthood, on account of this great sin, only Levites, those that had not participated in the idolatry and whom were Moses' brethren, would be made priests to God from that day on.

3rd giving: Exo34. Moses ascends again for 40 days and nights. A much smaller portion is received on this occasion but the 3 feasts would again be commanded to be observed. Moses returns with his face glowing and which he must cover as he approaches Israel. He also received a 2nd set of tablets of the "10 commandments", commandments which differ from the first tablets, and comes to eventually place them inside an ark that is made and situated inside the tabernacle which is also constructed and erected.

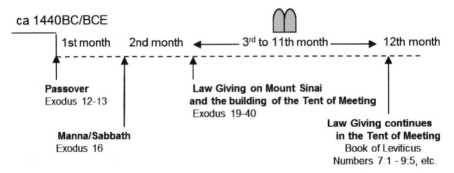

Timeline of the first year from Passover

After these visitations to the Mount, from this point on, any divine instruction to Moses will be given from within the tent of meeting that was constructed. These later occasions are found within the remaining books of the Law: Leviticus, Numbers and Deuteronomy.

Passover made First of 3 Feasts

It is in the 1st giving of the Law that two additional Holy Days are first introduced. The particular excerpt of interest, part of what eventually found its way into the "book of the covenant", is the following:

Exo 23:14-17 "<u>Three times a year</u> you shall celebrate a feast to Me. "You shall observe the <u>Feast of Unleavened Bread</u>; for seven days you are to eat unleavened bread, as I commanded you, at the appointed time in the month Abib, for in it you came out of Egypt. And none shall appear before Me empty-handed. "Also {you shall observe} the <u>Feast of the Harvest</u> {of} the <u>first fruits of your labors</u> {from} what you sow in the field; also the <u>Feast of the Ingathering</u> at the <u>end of</u>

the year when you gather in {the fruit of} your labors from the field." Three times a year all your males shall appear before the Lord GOD.

Here now is the first time that the first feast is given an official name, the "Feast of Unleavened Bread". As for the other 2 new "feasts" there is a limited amount of information supplied for them here in their first revelation. Note the expression "1st fruits of your labors" associated with the "Feast of the Harvest". What this meant was that Israel was required to offer to God the initial harvesting of the crop(s) before taking the rest for itself. Much of this same information is repeated again in the 3rd giving of the Law on Mount Sinai in Exo 34:18-22. But the deviations are to be noted. First, the Feast of the Harvest of chapter 23 is given yet another name, that is, the Feast of Weeks, and the 1st fruits are here specifically identified with the wheat harvest:

Exo 34:22a "And you shall celebrate the Feast of Weeks, {that is,} the first fruits of the wheat harvest

As to what the word "Weeks" is implying must be referring to the delay of the coming of the wheat harvest that follows the initial barley harvest. These are the details provided here and there will need to be more to understand exactly when these Holy Days are to be observed and what was to be done on them.

It should also be noted that here is the first textual evidence that reveals the extent of the Holy Days are to bound the harvest season. That is, Passover comes at the very beginning of the harvest when the barley and flax first appear. This is followed by the Feast of Weeks which comes more toward the middle of the harvest with the wheat and the spelt. The Feast of Ingathering comes at the end of the harvest, a final third wave of gathering including corn, grapes, and other fruits. Finally, it should be recognized that these 2 additional feasts are purely communicating harvest themes and are not signified as being anything historical like Passover was. But then again, if these feasts are portending something, the symbolisms given to them would be the encoded information to have to decode.

It should be clear that these additional feasts are being added as if the occasion of Passover makes a natural connection with them, as if these additional feasts were foreknown at the time of the Passover. Perhaps the suggestion is that the Passover was deliberately chosen to come at the beginning of the harvest season so that these other 2 feasts could be added later to complete the harvest related Holy Day theme being instituted. So "harvest" is really the biggest symbolism that is being presented and which must be "encoding" the most significant concept of the entire Holy Days Code. The oddity of all of this is that the Passover memorial has no harvest theme symbolism other than its annual coming when it does. But the Scripture subtly introduced yet a new harvest offering on Mount Sinai that will eventually be made into its own Holy Day. It will necessarily converge upon the Passover memorial, but only by stealth. Again, this all suggests that the memorial has yet a 3rd purpose in revealing yet a hidden prophetic expectation for the future.

A 2nd First Fruits Offering

As was just mentioned, the topic of "1st fruits" appears here first along with the first Law giving on Mount Sinai. It becomes another relevant subject that arises given it also is associated with the harvest season and is made into more Holy Days. The main idea is that when Israel would come into the Promised Land and grow crops the Nation would be required to offer to God its 1st fruits of its harvest. The 1st fruits noted of in the previous passage regarded the Wheat harvest. But along with this one, there is yet another second offering being implied in the giving of the Law:

Exo 23:19a "You shall bring the <u>choice</u> first fruits of your soil into the house of the LORD your God

Exo 34:26 "You shall bring the <u>very first of the first</u> fruits of your soil into the house of the LORD your God.

Here the word "choice" is the Hebrew word meaning "head", transliterated "Rosh", the same word used for the expression "very first". Given that the very first harvest that appears in the season is barley this is most likely what this head 1st fruits is to be identifying. This then would necessarily have to coincide with the Passover occasion as was mentioned earlier. So it would seem that there is at least two 1st fruits offerings to be distinguished here in the early text, a head 1st fruits offering, of the barley, and a 1st fruits offering of the wheat coming "weeks" later. As an observation, these "pairings" of 1st fruit offerings will come together in 1 more location, in Lev2:12/2:14, before the new Holy Day becomes revealed in Leviticus chapter 23.

Over the next several months, Moses will assign Spirit anointed men to build the furniture and tent in constructing the "tabernacle" where God would establish his presence within Israel's community. Recall that the instructions for this tabernacle came in the 2nd law giving Moses received on Mount Sinai. Nearly a year went by from Passover until the tabernacle came to be completed. The Scripture notes that this important milestone came on the first day of the first month of the second year from Passover. Here is where the book of Exodus closes with Moses completing the assembly and furnishing of the tabernacle. With this, the presence of God is recorded having entered the Holy Place. So just before the first Passover memorial would arrive, over the course of only a few days, Moses would receive a great deal of further law giving namely in the revelations given in the book of Leviticus, while inside the newly constructed tent. It is during this session where the one and only comprehensive detailing of the Holy Days will be given.

These are the appointed times of the LORD, holy convocations which you shall proclaim at the times appointed for them.

Leviticus 23:4

Chapter Six

Testimony of Leviticus

T he book of Leviticus opens by God speaking to Moses from the tent to give him the many laws and ordinances that were to surround the tabernacle in its proper functioning within the community of Israel. In essence, it was the place where Israel would meet God under the provisions of the Law. And because God was to be understood holy, holy provisions would need to be followed to maintain an acceptable presence before Him. Maintaining a holy "cleanliness" before God is the simple idea being conveyed throughout the book of Leviticus:

Lev 15:31 ...you shall keep the sons of Israel separated from their uncleanness, so that they will not die in their uncleanness by their defiling My dwelling place that is among them.

The first 7 chapters of Leviticus define what acceptable offerings were to be presented to God on behalf of the various presenters. These could be for an individual or for the community of Israel. In sum, the offerings were to either provide atonement for sin, a means of reconciling the presenter to God, or they were a means for a freewill act of voluntary worship.

Moses' brother Aaron and his descendants were to be the agents through which the offerings would be made. Leviticus 8 and 9 records Moses conducting the consecration of Aaron and his sons to initiate them to their newly assigned service on behalf of Israel. But soon after, in chapter 10, Aaron's 2 eldest sons, Nadab and Abihu, go astray as they begin serving and are killed in their errant service. This would leave Aaron's 2 youngest sons, Eleazar and Ithamar, to take their deceased brothers' places.

Next, between chapters 11-15, 18-20, and 21-22 the distinction between what is holy and unholy will be defined. Chapters 11-15 will strictly define what is "clean" versus what is "unclean" and what remedy was to be followed to restore someone who would become unclean. After a careful examination of this body of Scripture, it becomes clear that this form of uncleanliness is unrelated to immorality or acts of evil, things that are discussed exclusively in chapters 18-20. In this new section, the root word "defile" is used to identify immorality and forbidden behavior that was not to be tolerated within the community. Chapters 21-22 review the holy standard of conduct to be maintained by Aaron and his sons in their proper execution of their service. Found amidst these chapters, in Leviticus 16, is the unveiling of yet another Holy Day, the Day of Atonement, Yom Kippur.

The Holy Day of Yom Kippur

Yom Kippur, or "Day of Ransom" or more familiarly known as the "Day of Atonement" represents the epitome of everything Leviticus is found communicating. In short, Israel's sins were an unacceptable uncleanliness brought to the community causing a defilement to both Israel and the tabernacle, God's dwelling place in the camp. So reserved for this one day in the year, a cleansing, or an atoning was to be made for all of Israel and the Holy Place:

Lev 16:29,30,33 ...in the seventh month, on the tenth day of the month...on this day atonement shall be made for you to cleanse you; you will be clean from all your sins before the LORD...the priest shall...make atonement for the holy sanctuary...for the tent of meeting and for the altar...for the priests and for all the people of the assembly.

Hence, Yom Kippur comes on the 10th day of the 7th month. (Here now an entirely new month in the Holy Calendar is being assigned a Holy Day. This then is the start of the creation of two general periods of when Holy Days were to be observed. There are the "Spring" Holy Days coming near the beginning of the Harvest Season and there are the "Fall" Holy Days which come near the end of the Harvest Season. Yom Kippur is the first to get assigned to this month in the Fall. The Feast of Ingathering had already been mentioned at Mount Sinai as coming at the end of the Harvest Season but its exact period of observance would not be defined until Leviticus 23.)

The defiling consequences of sin were to be dealt with by the sacrifices offered on Yom Kippur. How the very sins of Israel were to be handled is most peculiar:

Lev 16:22 The goat shall bear on itself all their iniquities to a solitary land...

The High Priest was to lay the sins of Israel upon the so called "scapegoat" and send it away into the wilderness. And this is how the Law deals with Israel's sin, by doing absolutely nothing about them in sending them away! This happens to be ***the main message of Leviticus, that there is to be a means of cleansing for what sin defiles but nowhere does it describe how to deal with the actual sin itself in any of its passages***.

What remains to be discussed are the details surrounding Israel's observance of Yom Kippur as a Holy Day. Interestingly, it was to be a day Israel was to "humble" itself and "do no work". This is the same language that was used for the first and last days of the Feast of Unleavened Bread. But provocatively, it will go on to define this day even more uniquely, by commanding Israel to make this day a "sabbath of solemn rest" (16:31). The word "sabbath" never appeared in Exodus 12 and 13. So here now is a new idea being unveiled for the first time to the reader.

The 10th day of the 7th month happens to be a lunar based day, not fixed to the 7 day Sabbath cycle. What that means is that Yom Kippur can fall on any of the 7 days of the week, making it a unique "Sabbath" day observance. This creates a 2nd form of a Sabbath separate from what is to be now distinguished as the 1st form of a Sabbath, that which falls on every 7th day. What will be studied next is Leviticus chapter 23, the most important chapter in Scripture regarding the Law's Holy Days. In that chapter, 3 more lunar day Sabbath Holy Days will be identified besides Yom Kippur, making a total of 4 lunar Holy Day Sabbaths in the Divine Calendar.

The big mystery here is why a lunar day is to be considered a Sabbath. Why is there a total of 4 lunar based Sabbath days, all in the fall harvest season? In addition, there is nothing in the discussion of Yom Kippur that aligns itself with a harvest theme. Again, the Passover was the same way. It too has no harvest theme, only a sacrificial theme. So the Holy Days seem to be taking on a more subtle purpose other than just strictly harvest. So this is yet another hint of a deeper symbolic message within the Holy Days besides harvest. Here then are yet more symbols the Holy Days Code is adding that will need decoding.

All of the Holy Days Unveiled Together in the Tent

The 23rd chapter of Leviticus will suddenly appear as the book of Leviticus begins to close. It can be discovered that nowhere else in Scripture will all the Holy Days of Israel appear together in one location but here. Before the chapter will close 3 more Holy Days will be added to those already revealed in prior testimony. But, so many more things will come to be added than just this. In fact, the chapter is so filled with new things to identify it will be carefully reviewed in this chapter.

Breaking Down Leviticus Chapter 23 into 12 Parts

The chapter can be broken into 12 parts:

Part I: Opening statement:

Lev23:1-2: The LORD speaks to Moses about the holy appointments the sons of Israel are to observe:

Part II: The Sabbath:

Lev23:3: Every six days is to be for work but every 7th day is to be a "Sabbath rest", a day when no work was to be allowed. Each Sabbath is to be a holy appointment. Hence, this is the most frequent appointment Israel was to observe and the most plausible explanation for why it comes first.

```
┌─────────────────────────┐
│ ░░░░░░░░░░░░░░░░░░░░░░░ │
│    Complete Rest,       │
│     No Work,            │
│    Holy Assembly        │
├─────────────────────────┤
│      7ᵗʰ day            │
│      Sabbath            │
└─────────────────────────┘
```

When the weekly Sabbath was originally given to Israel to observe, the Nation was commanded to gather a double portion of manna for the Sabbath day's meal on the 6th day in order to remain resting on the Sabbath. Exo 16:29 also instructs the Israelites to remain in their place of habitation during this day so as to "rest". And Exo 35:3 also commands that no fire be kindled on the Sabbath. These 3 basic Sabbath "rules" have been adhered to in some form by Jews for thousands of years.

Many readers have speculated that this opening statement is to be seen as representing the lifespan of the present Creation. That is, 7 days are accounted for the Creation being made and in sum, its lifespan is to be divided up into 7 segments of time. But actually the better interpretation is to recognize that the first 6 Days were taken up in the Creation of the World and that the 7th Day has been ongoing. Thus, God is to be understood "resting" ever since. The Significance of the number 7 is thus appropriated in the first chapter of Genesis. Its application comes to be repeated again and again to signify the entirety of something, or its lifespan, The Holy Days themselves will contain their share of "7's".

Part III: Break

Lev23:4: Similar statements as in Part I. That there is a break here means that the remaining harvest Holy Days are yet another kind of Holy Day not to be considered the same as the Sabbath. It will become self-evident that all the rest of the Holy Days will fall within Israel's Harvest Season.

The Spring Holy Days

Part IV:

Passover:

Lev23:5: A simple statement is given that on the 14th day of the 1st month at twilight is the LORD's Passover. In Exodus 12 it was understood that each of Israel's households were to offer such a sacrifice as an everlasting memorial.

In the 1st Month of Abib/Nisan

Close of the 14th day

Passover

Feast of Unleavened Bread:

Lev23:6-8: This Feast is to be celebrated for 7 days starting on the 15th day of the 1st month. Here for the first time the memorial is commanded to have an Offering by Fire to the LORD on each of its days. No specification is given for what they are to be but are later described in Num 28:19-22. It is yet another new element added to the memorial which was not a part of the original Passover occasion.

Holy Assembly, No Work	In the Month of Abib/Nisan Feast of Unleavened Bread					Holy Assembly, No Work Feast
15th	16th	17th	18th	19th	20th	21st

New Element: There is to be an Offering by Fire on each day.

The Holy Days Offerings by Fire

The High Priest is to administer these offerings (unlike how every household is to offer its own Passover sacrifice). By this time many offerings had already been defined in the Law. The daily offerings were defined on Mount Sinai, the most prolific of the offerings. In the early chapters of Leviticus the definitions of the "burnt" offerings, the "sin" offerings, the "meal" offerings and the voluntary "peace" offerings are given. Now the holy appointments will each receive their own offerings. Some are identical to others but most are unique for the given Holy Day or Days.

Oddly, for two of the Holy Days, an Offering by Fire will be defined here in this chapter while all the rest will be defined in Numbers chapters 28 and 29. Finally, 2 Holy Days have 2 Offerings by Fire, not 1. This too is a strange mystery. So what could all of these Offerings by Fire be communicating? Would they have all been the same, perhaps there would be far less mystery surrounding them. But the testimony suggests they contain some deeper symbolic message in them given their uniquenesses. Here is yet more symbols being encoded that will need decoding.

It is repeated here that the 15th and 21st days of the 1st month are to be holy appointments, days of "no work", the same phrase used in the original Passover testimony. Only later, when the "Sabbath" was instituted in the wilderness, did this new Hebrew term bring a distinction of a "sabbath rest", the same term used earlier in the Sabbath description at the opening of this chapter. The great debate this has raised is if these Feast days of "no work" are to be technically considered Sabbaths also. The sect of the Pharisees that would emerge in the 2nd Temple era would carry a tradition arguing that these days did qualify being classified as "Sabbaths" whereas their opposing sect of the Sadducees argued they were not to be so classified.

The Mystery Day(s) of 1st Fruits

As was stated previously, the law giving at Mount Sinai made mention of 1st fruits offerings that Israel was commanded to give, what was conjectured to be two different distinct offerings being defined there. One happens to be simply a first fruits offering while the other is classified as being a "head" first fruits offering. It is at this juncture in the testimony where the details of these two offerings will now be provided by the revelation of one new Holy Day and the crucial details about the Feast of Weeks first mentioned on Mount Sinai.

Note that the head first fruits Day comes immediately after the description of the Feast of Unleavened Bread. And because the timing of this offering appears to converge with the Passover season, it would seem this new Holy Day coincides with these first Holy Days somewhere. But the way it appears here it is written as if to be a separate matter altogether coming after these first Holy Days being defined. This new Holy Day naturally associates itself with a later 2nd first fruits Holy Day as will be discovered. From their reading, Scripture will create a mystery of ambiguity out of both days because not enough information is provided to know with certainty their reckoning. It can be considered the *Law's greatest mystery* it contains because of what impact it came to have down through history and as it came to impact the testimony of the Gospel itself in its two Passovers testimony.

Part V:

Lev23:9: The LORD speaks to Moses again:

The Day of Head 1st Fruits:

Lev23:10-14: When Israel was to enter the Land and reap its harvests there, it was to bring an "**omer's**" worth of the very 1st fruits of the harvest to the priest. The word "omer" was first introduced when the manna appeared to Israel in the wilderness and was described there as being what a single person's daily supply of food is. On this day the priest was to wave an omer's worth of "head" 1st fruits before God in the tabernacle (what was to be from the barley crop as specified from other passages).

Thus this command could not be fulfilled in the wilderness but Israel would have to wait until it entered the Land and gathered its first harvest there. At that time Israel is instructed not to partake of any new grain until this offering was given. So until Israel entered the Land it would remain relying upon the daily appearing manna to sustain it.

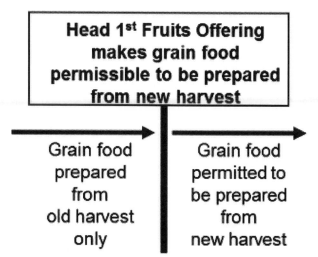

Here is the restriction given to Israel which determines how the coming New Year was to be reckoned. What would prevent Israel from choosing a lunar cycle that was too early was the fact that the Nation had to offer to God a first fruits offering as part of its holy observance, as will become discovered in the coming pages. So if Israel so happened to prematurely begin a year too soon by having no offering to give, it simply postponed the year to start at the next lunar cycle or whenever the initial crops did appear. What prevented Israel from waiting too long to start the new year was the fact that the Nation was forbidden from eating of the new harvest until the first fruits offering had been given to God.

Because this day happens to be the very first harvest related occasion of the holy season its coming necessarily establishes when the coming of the New Year was to be reckoned, and that it be coincident with harvest. This basic principle was ascertained with the subtle details the original Passover occasion communicates in that it was to come in the month of Abib. This means the occasion of the Passover and the giving of the "head" first fruits must necessarily overlap or converge upon one another. Yet none of this is made clear in the text, only inferred.

What makes this day a mystery emerges when instructions are given as to how to reckon this single, specific day. In Leviticus 23:11 it states that **"...*on the day after the Sabbath...*"** *this is to be the day the priest waves the offering*. So just exactly what "Sabbath" is this passage referring to? Because there is a break in the Holy Day instructions between the Feast of Unleavened Bread and this 1st Fruits Holy Day (i.e., Lev23:9) it reads as if this day perhaps is to follow after the Feast of Unleavened Bread. Even with this interpretation though, this still leaves the identity of the Sabbath a mystery. (Notice that all the previous Holy Days were defined expressly by the given numbered days of the 1st month with no mystery. Likewise all the fall Holy Days of the 7th month will be so defined as well.) The best interpretation that can be made contextually is that this Holy Day does not have a numbered day of the month assigned to it because it is defined as coming after a "Sabbath", a day that "floats" within the fixed lunar schedule. It was learned that Yom Kippur was also to be considered a "Sabbath" but at the same time it also happens to be defined as being a fixed lunar day coming on the 10th day of the 7th month. But because of the language used here the mystery Holy Day is not so defined having a fixed lunar date assigned to it. Thus this is indicative of falling after a 7th day Sabbath, that being the 1st day of the week.

And the bigger question still remains, what Sabbath day within the bigger schedule is being inferred as preceding this Holy Day? Because Lev23:9 separates this Holy Day from the Feast of Unleavened Bread it would seem that the Sabbath being defined is to be the 1st Sabbath after the Feast of Unleavened Bread is over. Since the Law provides no further information about this day beyond Lev23:11, *__this is the great mysterious ambiguity of the Law relating to the reckoning of Israel's most important Holy Day.__* It simply must be interpreted as a deliberate ambiguity in the Law, and so perhaps the Law's greatest mystery as to why this Holy Day is reckoned this way. It alone represents yet another symbol encoding something.

Here is how Scripture causes the Law to yield to what must be yet a forthcoming revelation that was to be reserved for specifying what is meant in Lev 23:11. The only revelation in all of Scripture to answer this ambiguity is the Gospel accounting of the Resurrection as will be discussed in a later chapter. Another interesting thing about this day is that its Offering by Fire is fully described here. There has been only one prior appointment Offering by Fire defined in Scripture predating this Holy Day's Offering and that happens to be the Daily Offerings which were specified at Mount Sinai. Here now is the 2nd appointment Offering by Fire to be defined. (Recall that the Feast of Unleavened Bread was also to have such Offerings on each of its 7 days but no details are supplied here.) It is to include "one male lamb a year old" along with "two-tenths ephah of meal" which is to be "mixed with oil" and "one-fourth hin of wine" as a drink offering. These specifications are almost the same as those given for one of the Daily Offerings (Ex 29:39-41) except the grain portion is doubled.

The explanation for why this Offering is defined here instead of in Numbers chapter 28 appears to be because this is to be the only location in Scripture revealing the existence of this mystery Holy Day. It will not be written about again until the Gospel cryptically refers to it in the Resurrection testimony. And still another mystery surrounding this day is that it is neither a holy day of assembly nor a day of "no work". All the other single, standalone Holy Days (4 of them) are each days of holy assembly and days of "no work" as will be examined shortly. So why then is this single mystery day not to be given these symbols?

Mystery Day

(Head) Barley 1st fruits wave offering: Omer sheaf

On the day after the Sabbath

Offering by Fire: 1 year old male lamb w/ grain, oil and wine

One last note to make is that this occasion was to be an everlasting ordinance just as Passover and the Feast of Unleavened Bread were commanded to be in Ex 12:14, 17.

Second 1st fruits:

Lev23:15-21: This occasion is also a single day observance to be reckoned by Israel "counting off 7 Sabbaths and a day", or exactly 50 days, after the giving of the Head 1st fruits offering. So was this segment of time indicative of the coming of the wheat harvest only or does it signify something else? Here again no fixed lunar numbered day is given for this day. This is further indication that the mystery day falls on the 1st day of the week because this new Holy Day is coming exactly 50 days later and it too is not associated with the greater calendar schedule. By defining these two Holy Days in this fashion it gives both of them an aurora of existing detached from anything else, as if not to be part of the monthly schedule. Separating them by a fixed number of days also creates an intimate connection between the two being that they both are 1st fruits offerings as well. Hence, both days are to necessarily fall on the 1st day of the 7 day solar week schedule. But again, what Sabbath is Lev 23:11 referring to so as to reckon this day coming 50 days later?

Given that the Head 1st Fruits Offering is from the barley harvest, this 1st Fruits offering coming 7 weeks later is to be understood being taken from the wheat harvest. Along with this *2 loaves of leavened bread* are to be made as part of a greater Offering waved before God. Bread made from leaven was never to be made part of what was burned on the altar but which the priests themselves were given to eat (Lev2:11-12; 7:13-14). So what is the significance of leaven for this Holy Day?

And again, details for this day's Offering by Fire to the LORD are given here. Here now is the 3rd appointment Offering to be specified in Scripture. On this occasion 7 male year old lambs, a bull and 2 rams are to be for a Burnt Offering along with their meal and drink offerings. Also 1 male goat is to be given for a sin offering and 2 male lambs a year old for peace offerings. The latter lambs along with the loaves of leavened bread are to be waved by the priest before God. These are to be food for the priest to partake of. The strange thing about this day is that it will be

69

assigned yet a 2nd Offering in Numbers 28:26-30. As the totality of witness surrounding this day is accounted for, it suspiciously appears as if to be representing 2 things. That is, there are to be 2 loaves of bread offered as well as 2 Offerings by Fire as well as 2 Peace Offerings. So what do these 3 doublets infer or suggest? The encoded symbols continue to mount as each new Holy Day is unveiled.

Further details provided for this Holy Day is that it too is to be a day of holy assembly and a day of "no work", the 3rd of a total of 7 appointment days having this specification. And yet again, this is commanded to be an everlasting ordinance for Israel to observe.

<u>Since this Holy Day is reckoned coming exactly 50 days from the 1st mystery day, that makes this 2nd Holy Day a mystery day too</u>. Clearly these 2 mystery days are to be a pair of related significance. Oddly, there is no mention here of this being a "Feast" day. The lawgiving at Mount Sinai identified there were to be 3 feasts each year to be observed (Ex23:14). Yet there will only be 1 more feast described in this chapter. But it must be surmised here that this Holy Day is the 2nd feast because Ex34:22 calls the 2nd feast the "Feast of Weeks", a first fruits gathering of the wheat harvest. So why is it not identified here in Leviticus chapter 23 as being the 2nd of 3 feasts? All of these peculiar details make these 2 harvest days appear as being a great mystery.

2nd Mystery Day

Assumed 1st fruits wave offering from the wheat harvest along with 2 loaves of leavened bread; assumed 2nd of 3 feasts

Holy Assembly, No Work

Count 7 Sabbaths & a day from Head 1st Fruits

Offerings by Fire:
7 male year old lambs, 1 bull & 2 rams
w / grain, oil and wine for burnt offering,
1 male goat for sin offering,
2 male year old lambs for peace offerings

Part VI:

In Lev23:22, the text now takes advantage of the previous subject matter of harvest having been just described in the 2 mystery Holy Days. Israel is commanded not to reap its fields to its corners or glean them. These portions were to be left for the alien and the poor. (The greatest history related to this command is the one told of in the book of Ruth. There a Moabite widow by the name of Ruth is described as having gleaned the wheat fields of an Israelite by the name of Boaz. Her and Boaz were later married and bore a son together on behalf of her Jewish mother-in-law Naomi whose sons had died. Here is the Scripture's earliest origin it supplies for the lineage of the later coming King David.) This will now end what are referred to as the "Spring" Holy Days. The remaining Holy Days will all fall within the 7th month and are typically referred to as the "Fall" Holy Days.

The Fall Holy Days

Part VII:

Lev23:23: Again the LORD speaks to Moses:

Yom Teruah:

Lev23:24-25: On the 1st day of the 7th month, this day is to be a day of "Sabbath rest" which is to be remembered by way of "loud clamoring". Here now is a 2nd lunar day also given the classification as being a "Sabbath". Yom Kippur in Leviticus 16 was the only prior day to be given such a classification. So a pattern is developing here regarding lunar days being a different kind of Sabbath. In all, there will be 4 total lunar days given the distinction of also being a "Sabbath'. Nowhere else outside of Leviticus 16 and 23 will such Sabbath days be defined. So why does the Law in these 2 chapters create 4 extra days out of the year that are to be considered Sabbaths but not necessarily falling on a 7th day? What is this to mean? In addition, this day is to be a day of holy assembly and when no work is to be done and also when an Offering by Fire is to be given, later specified in Numbers 29:2-5.

The popular interpretation as to what this day is symbolizing is that of blowing trumpets as an alarm as described in Numbers 10:1-9. This day happens to be a New Moon day as well as Israel's New Year's Day, Rosh HaShanah. This is the first Holy Day that has no direct or indirect connection with the subject of harvest. So is this to infer that there is something fundamentally "new" and different about these latter fall Holy Days in comparison to the spring Holy Days? All of these things further reinforce the suspicion that there is more being communicated with these Holy Days than just strictly harvest related matters. Yom Teruah happens to be the 4th of a total of 7 extra days classified as days of "no work" and the 1st of 4 to be classified as a Sabbath. So this day becomes yet another mystery Holy Day because there is no clear indication or subject to just exactly what this day is to be signifying and why it is to be considered 1 of 4 specially classified Sabbaths.

In the 7th Month of Ethanim/Tishri

Yom Teruah (Rosh HaShanah)

Holy Assembly, No Work, Sabbath, New Moon
The 1st

Offering by Fire (not specified here)

Both Judaism and Christian speculation is that these Fall Holy Days regard the "latter days", or End Times. This first day then is often interpreted as being the day it all begins with the blowing of trumpets to usher it in. The word Teruah does not specifically imply the blowing of trumpets yet because this is a New Moon Day it is specified as being a Day of Blowing Trumpets, none the less. The most familiar reference to cite is when the Israelites went up against the city of Jericho and were told to shout at the City, the word Teruah is used. As will be discovered later on, this expression of Teruah, that of human shouting, will align well with the positioning of this day. Regarding many of the symbolisms presented in the Holy Days testimony, it is a valid and general statement that tradition continues to provide little to no insight as to their meaning.

Part VIII:

Lev23:26: And the LORD spoke to Moses:

Yom Kippur:

Lev23:27-32: This Holy Day was described in the previous chapter. It again falls on the 10th day of the 7th month, a day for when Israel's sins were to be atoned for and the day when Israel was to be humbled. This day was also to be a day when an Offering by Fire was to be given. Leviticus 16 does not describe an Offering by Fire. Only Numbers 29:8-11 designates what offering Lev23:27 is referring to.

Again, this day is to be a "Sabbath of complete rest". Along with Lev 16:3, Lev 23:32 happens to be one of only two places in all of Scripture where a fixed lunar day is directly classified as being a "Sabbath". The other 3 lunar Holy Days to be classified the same are only described as days of "Sabbath rest" (see 23:24; 23:39). Hence, 16:3 and 23:23 provide the impetus to classify the other 3 Holy Days as Sabbaths equal to Yom Kippur's Sabbath classification. Yet although these Days are given a Sabbath classification, the 7th Day Sabbath Offering by Fire is not one that was to be given on these special Sabbath days as Numbers 29 clearly indicates.

In the Month of Ethanim/Tishri

Yom Kippur

Holy Assembly, No Work, Sabbath
The 10th

Offering by Fire (not specified here)

It goes on to be stipulated that if anyone was to work or not humble themselves on this day such a person was to be cut off from Israel. Judaism has interpreted this as meaning the Nation was to "fast" on this day although nothing in the text specifically commands this. This day is also commanded to be an everlasting ordinance. Unlike Yom Teruah, this day has a clear purpose having plenty of explanation given for it in Leviticus 16. Yet it too lacks a harvest related theme. So again, a reader is led to conclude that more is being communicated here than just matters of harvest as Passover and Yom Teruah already suggest.

In sum, Yom Kippur is the 5th of a total of 7 extra days of "no work" out of the year besides the weekly Sabbath. It is also the 2nd of 4 fixed lunar days in the 7th month which are to be considered "Sabbaths", whatever this extra classification means beyond the idea of being a day of "no work". Given the two terminologies of "no work" and "Sabbath rest" between the spring and fall Holy Day classifications, it has been a contentious historical debate as to whether the spring "no work" Holy Days are to be also classified as lunar day "Sabbaths". By the strict construction of the chapter however, there is nothing about the Spring Holy Days that warrants a reader to classify any of them as being Sabbaths since this Hebrew word is not found in the springtime Holy Days as it is so prominently found in the Fall. So why are none of the spring Holy Days given this special classification like Yom Kippur is, as well as 3 other Fall Holy Days? It is yet one more layer of questions that become heaped upon a pile already accumulated from this chapter thus far. There are still several more symbolisms yet to be unveiled.

Part IX:

Lev23:33: And the LORD spoke to Moses:

Strangely, the last Holy Days will be defined twice, once in 23:34-36 and then again in 23:39-43 with verses 37 and 38 acting as a break between the two. So why are these Holy Days revealed in this way?

The Feast of Booths Pt 1:

Lev23:34-36: A 7 day feast is defined starting on the 15th day of the 7th month called the "Feast of Booths". This is the first time this Feast is given this name. Previously it had been called "Feast of Ingathering" (Exo23:16; 34:22), an indication this was the last harvest gathering of that year's harvest season. No explanation will be given here in this section for why it has this new name.

The 15th day is to be a holy appointment, a day of "no work". For 7 days an offering by fire is to be given. Further still, on the "8th day", this day is to be yet another holy appointment, a final day of "no work" and when yet another offering is to be given. (It is at this point that a new and mysterious term is introduced that is typically translated "assembly". The transliterated Hebrew word is "atsarah". It appears here first in Scripture and goes on to be used in 2 more places in the Law. The collective testimony of this word suggests that this 8th day is most unique and different from all the others. Its root meaning can best be described as communicating to "corral" or "confine together" as when a woman's "womb" becomes shut. It appears this day is to suggest a special gathering of Israel unlike any other.) So why does the Scripture point out this final feast as being 7 days in length only to turn around and define yet an 8th day to follow the 7? It reads much like how Passover leads into the 7 days of unleavened bread. That is, it perhaps signifies there is no break in time between the symbolisms of what the first feast signifies and what this last day's symbolisms infer.

Holy Assembly, No Work	In the Month of Ethanim/Tishri						Holy Assembly, No Work
15th	16th	17th	18th	19th	20th	21st	22nd

An Offering by Fire on each of the 8 days   **Special Assembly: "Atsarah"**

←   Feast of Booths: **Part I**   →

The Offerings for these 8 days are specified in Numbers 29:13-38. What is found there is that a great number of Offerings are to be given, the first day having the most and each succeeding day having one less with the 7th day having the least. Finally, the 8th day has its own Offering unrelated to the 7 previous days with their descending order of offerings. In total, there will be more than double the Offerings for these last Holy Days than those offered for the Feast of Unleavened Bread. So what is this to signify?

Part X: First closing

23:37-38: This break reads as if to be a closing statement for all the aforementioned appointed times specified. So a mystery forms here as to why a second description of the final Holy Days are given again after this closing statement.

Part XI: Feast of Booths Pt 2:

23:39-43: This 2nd section opens with this time being described as just after all the crops have been gathered in. And again it is revealed to be a 7 day feast. Yet strangely it identifies the 1st day and 8th days as days of "Sabbath rest".

Next, it is commanded that various leafy branches be gathered together on the 1st day. Then for 7 days there is to be celebration before God. For these 7 days the native-born of Israel were to live in "booths". What is implied is that the leafy branches gathered were to be for making a tent or booth to live in (see Neh8:14-16). The reason for doing this was to remind all succeeding generations that God had made the Exodus Nation live in booths when God delivered them out of Egypt. Clearly this Feast is relating itself back to the occasion of Passover as if the final Holy Days are coming full circle back to where they began in an unusual sense. So these Holy Days have two aspects to them, a harvest aspect and a memorial aspect, akin to the first Holy Days of Passover. Finally, these last days are to be made an everlasting ordinance for Israel to observe.

Sabbath	In the Month of Ethanim/Tishri						Sabbath
15th	16th	17th	18th	19th	20th	21st	22nd

Gather foliage; live in booths

← Feast of Booths: **Part II** →

In comparing the two sections, they each have their own unique elements describing these last Holy Days. The first specifies the holy appointments of the 15th and 22nd days as "no work" days. Also mention is made of Offerings to be given. The second specifies the 15th and 22nd days as "Sabbath rest" days. Further, there is no mention of Offerings here yet the new subject of harvest arises and an explanation for what the meaning of "Booths" is given. So why are there two sections dividing up this last feast occasion into two unique and nonoverlapping halves?

It would seem that the Feast of Booths is taking on the same sort of thing that the Feast of Unleavened Bread does. The first feast comes to have added elements to it by stealth, as if to be something separate. And those added elements happen to be harvest related too. Now here, the last feast is simply described twice as if it were to represent two different things going on at the same time. The first description has no harvest elements just like Passover and the Feast of Unleavened Bread has none. And the second listing does have harvest elements as if paralleling with the First Fruits Holy Days that appear to be overlapping the Passover and the Feast of Unleavened Bread.

Finally, the last Holy Day has similarity to the 1st Holy Occasion of Passover in that both connect directly to an adjacent Holy Day as if no break in time is to be understood existing between them.

Part XII: Last Closing

Lev23:44: So the LORD spoke to Moses regarding all the holy appointments.

And so the mysterious symbolisms added to the Holy Days come to a close. The diligent student must compile all of these details and expect Scripture to come along later to help explain the meaning of all of them. But there will come to be even more details to further complicate the Holy Days as the next few chapters will highlight.

Then the LORD spoke to Moses, saying, "Command the sons of Israel and say to them, 'You shall be careful to present My offering, My food for My offerings by fire, of a soothing aroma to Me, at their appointed time.'

Numbers 28:1-2

Chapter Seven
Numbers and Deuteronomy Testimony

There will be 4 more chapters of divine instruction in Leviticus given to Moses within the tent of meeting. As the book of Numbers follows this in 1:1 it is found to be jumping ahead in time to the 1st day of the 2nd month in the 2nd year (from the Exodus) until the end of its 6th chapter. Then in 7:1, it falls back to a time congruent with what was taking place at the closing of Exodus sometime still in the 1st month of the 2nd year. So somewhere between Numbers chapters 7 and 8 the book of Leviticus is assumed having been given to Moses within the tent. Then, in chapter 9, the time arrives for the first memorial of Passover to be observed, what is the 14th day of the 1st month of the 2nd year from Exodus. Later, Numbers 10:11 will be found picking up again from where chapters 1-6 had first jumped ahead in time to the 2nd month of the 2nd year and continue on from there.

Date	Passage & Occasion
2nd Year 1st Month 1st-14th Day	Exodus 40, Numbers 7-8, Book of Levi (Tent Preparations)
2nd Year 1st Month 14th Day	Numbers 9-10:10 (Passover Memorial)
2nd Year 2nd Month 1st Day	Numbers 1-6 (Census taken, etc.)
2nd Year 2nd Month 20th Day	Numbers 10:11 (Cloud lifts and Israel begins to sojourn)
2nd Year ? ?	Numbers 13 (Spies sent to view the land over 40 day period)
2nd Year ? ?	Numbers 14:33 (Israel's 1st Exodus Gen condemned to die in wilderness, 2nd Gen to wait 40 years to Enter Land)
40 Years Transpire	Between Numbers 15-20:27
42nd Year 5th Month 1st Day	Numbers 20:28; 33:38 (Aaron dies at the age of 123)

Given the interest here is to follow the testimony of the Holy Days wherever it may lead inside the Law, Numbers 9 is the next relevant place. It happens to be the record of Israel's 1st Passover memorial:

Num 9:1-5 Thus the LORD spoke to Moses in the wilderness of Sinai, in the first month of the second year after they had come out of the land of Egypt, saying, "Now, let the sons of Israel observe the Passover at its appointed time." On the fourteenth day of this month, at twilight, you shall observe it at its appointed time; you shall observe it according to all its statutes and according to all its ordinances." So Moses told the sons of Israel to observe the Passover. And they observed the Passover in the first {month,} on the fourteenth day of the month,

at twilight, in the wilderness of Sinai; according to all that the LORD had commanded Moses, so the sons of Israel did.

Further testimony in Numbers 9 discusses the disposition of certain Israelites who became "defiled" because of exposure to a dead person. In the many instructions given in the Law one command was that a person was declared defiled if contact was made with a corpse. This first appears in Leviticus 21:1, then in Numbers 5:1-2 and then later in 19:14-19. Normally, the next of kin would necessarily have to make this contact but nevertheless this caused one to be defiled requiring a cleansing ritual and a period of separation from the rest of the community. On this occasion those who were defiled were requesting how they could partake in the Passover. So Moses approached God and this is the reply that came:

Num 9:9-14: Then the LORD spoke to Moses, saying, "Speak to the sons of Israel, saying, 'If any one of you or of your generations becomes unclean because of a {dead} person, or is on a distant journey, he may, however, observe the Passover to the LORD.' In the second month on the fourteenth day at twilight, they shall observe it; they shall eat it with unleavened bread and bitter herbs.' They shall leave none of it until morning, nor break a bone of it; according to all the statute of the Passover they shall observe it. 'But the man who is clean and is not on a journey, and yet neglects to observe the Passover, that person shall then be cut off from his people, for he did not present the offering of the LORD at its appointed time. That man shall bear his sin. 'And if an alien sojourns among you and observes the Passover to the LORD, according to the statute of the Passover and according to its ordinance, so he shall do; you shall have one statute, both for the alien and for the native of the land.'"

Here another new instruction for the memorial is given. If because of uncleanness or because of absence from the community, a person was to be allowed to celebrate the memorial exactly one month later. But if a person had no excuse and failed to observe the memorial, this person was to be executed. There was to be no leniency for disobedience to the Law.

Numbers 10:11-13 states that on the 2nd year from Passover on the 20th day of the 2nd month Israel broke camp for the first time since the tabernacle was built. Soon they would arrive in the "wilderness of Paran" (Num 12:16). From here God commanded Israel to send spies into the land for 40 days and have them report back to the rest of the nation on their findings. Moses selects twelve men, one from each tribe. Upon their return, only two spies will give a good report and encourage Israel to take possession of the land. These are Joshua and Caleb. The other 10 spies discourage Israel out of fear of the natives whose numbers seem too vast in number, and too large in size and might to overcome. Based on this news the Scripture records that the Nation decided it would not attempt to take the land. The divine response to this unfaithfulness was the condemnation of the first generation of the Exodus to live out its days in the wilderness, a year for each of the days spent spying, or a total of 40 years. God informs Moses that this was the 10th time Israel had grumbled since Passover.

As a consequence, Joshua and Caleb would be the only two of this generation surviving to enter the land after this forty year period. Even Moses would not be allowed to enter on account of disobedience. From Numbers chapter 15 to the end of chapter 19 it is clear that 40 years had passed. In Num 20:1, it states that the Nation Israel arrived at the "wilderness of Zin" in the "first month". Five months later Moses' brother Aaron dies at the age 123 on the first day of the "fifth month" of the fortieth year from Passover (Num 20:28; Num 33:38-39).

Offerings by Fire Enumerated

Israel will now continue to approach the Promised Land. They would confront several Nations/Kingdoms as they went. First was the Canaanite Arads which they defeated (Num21:1-3). The next were the Amorites who attacked them too and were defeated (Num21:21-32). Then they moved and captured Bashan (Num21:33-35). After that were the Moabites, whose king was Balak. There was great fear across the land so Balak hired the prophet Balaam to curse the Nation Israel, but this failed. However Israel's men would eventually be lured into idolatry with the Moabite women. A plague soon broke out in Israel killing 24,000 before Aaron's son Phineas acted with a zeal for God to bring it to an end. After the plague, God called for a 2nd Census of Israel's able bodied men for war in Numbers 26, the number came to 601,730 (Num26:51), the earlier Census of the 1st Gen was 603,550 (Num2:32). At this point God informs Moses that his ministry is coming to an end. Moses then entreats God to choose his successor. God answers by selecting Joshua, one of the two who brought back a good report about the Promised Land.

This then brings the narration to Numbers chapters 28 and 29 where the revelations for the Appointment Offerings by Fire are enumerated to Moses. It was the 23rd chapter of Leviticus that first spoke of these Offerings, two of which become specified there, but of which the rest were not. Prior to this, the Law had discussed various Offerings in various places.

1. Exodus 29 had outlined what offerings would be required for Aaron and his sons for them to be ordained into the priesthood. After this the most frequently offered sacrifice by the priests is defined, the Daily Offerings. It was to be two lambs. One offered at dusk. The other offered at dawn.

2. The first 9 chapters of Leviticus covers the general descriptions for all the Offerings: the burnt offerings, the grain offerings, the peace offerings, the sin offerings, the guilt offerings, the votive offerings and the freewill offerings. It goes on to record the testimony of Aaron and his sons being ordained and consecrated for their work as Priests.

3. Leviticus chapter 16 discusses "Yom Kippur", the Day of Atonement. Here the sin offerings are defined for this occasion in their detail.

Summary of the Holy Days Offerings by Fire: Leviticus 23 & Numbers 28-29

Holy Day	Offering by Fire				Libation?
	bull	ram	1yr old lamb	goat	
Daily: Morning & Evening			2		Yes
Sabbath			2		Yes
New Moon	2	1	7	1	Yes
Feast of ULB: 1st Day	2	1	7	1	No
16th Day 1st Month	2	1	7	1	No
17th Day 1st Month	2	1	7	1	No
18th Day 1st Month	2	1	7	1	No
19th Day 1st Month	2	1	7	1	No
20th Day 1st Month	2	1	7	1	No
Feast of ULB: 7th Day	2	1	7	1	No
Head 1st Fruits (2x Grain)			1		Yes
Feast of Weeks Lev 23	1	2	7	1	Yes
2 leavened loaves of bread					
2 peace offerings			2		
Feast of Weeks Num28	2	1	7	1	Yes
Yom Teruah	1	1	7	1	No
Yom Kippur (Num 29)	1	1	7	1	No
(Leviticus 16)	1	2		2	No
Feast of Booths: 1st Day	13	2	14	1	No
16th Day 7th Month	12	2	14	1	Yes
17th Day 7th Month	11	2	14	1	Yes
18th Day 7th Month	10	2	14	1	Yes
19th Day 7th Month	9	2	14	1	Yes
20th Day 7th Month	8	2	14	1	Yes
Feast of Booths: 7th Day	7	2	14	1	Yes
22nd Day 7th Month	1	1	7	1	Yes

Grain/Oil/Wine Offering portions for Offerings by Fire

	bull	ram	lamb
Ephah of Grain	3/10ths	2/10ths	1/10th
Hin of Oil	1/2	1/3rd	1/4th
Hin of Wine	1/2	1/3rd	1/4th

4. The 23rd chapter of Leviticus 23 outlined peculiar Offerings for the Head 1st Fruits day and the Feast of Weeks.

5. Numbers chapter 6 describes the Nazarite vow and its accompanying Offerings surrounding its ritual.

6. In Numbers chapter 15, a redefining of certain voluntary and sin offerings are established as to regards to when Israel would "enter the Land". These new adjustments to the original Law's provisions in Leviticus are mysterious as to their necessity. But one possible explanation is that certain aspects of the Offerings' components (grain, wine, etc.) would not have been as plentiful in the wilderness as they would be once in the Land.

Now, the 7th and final installment of Offerings by Fire are given in these two chapters. As stated earlier, the Daily Offerings had already been defined in Exodus 29 but are repeated in Numbers chapter 28. Next, a Sabbath Offering is defined, followed by a New Moon Offering, sacrifices to be given on each 7th day and on the 1st day of every month, respectively.

What follows after these are the defined Offerings for the Feast of Unleavened Bread which were mentioned in Leviticus 23 but left undefined there. Next, the Feast of Weeks offering is described here even though there already is another defined for it in Leviticus 23. Hence, this day is to have two sets of Offerings, one derived from Leviticus 23 and the other derived here in Numbers 28. Next, offerings are defined for Yom Teruah, Yom Kippur, and the Feast of Booths, all specified in Leviticus 23 but which were left undefined there. Yom Kippur too has additional Offerings identified for it in the 16th chapter of Leviticus.

Questions surrounding the Offerings by Fire

A noteworthy observation to point out here is that there will be no more definitions of Offerings in the Law beyond Numbers chapter 29. So after surveying all these passages of Scripture defining Offerings there are a few important observations to make regarding them:

1)   The first thing to notice is that most of the harvest Holy Days Offerings consist of 4 different animals: bulls, rams, 1 year old lambs and goats. This is unique to the Holy Day Offerings. Offerings mentioned at the beginning of the book of Leviticus regard specific sins committed by the priests, the elders, the community at large, or individuals. These usually have a single sacrifice for the Burnt Offering and a single sacrifice in an accompanying Sin Offering. Furthermore, there are patterns to notice with the combinations of sacrifices. Several Holy Days have the same pattern. Yet there are several that are unique, especially the Feast of Booths. It has quite a large number of them with each day having something slightly different than the day before. Are these patterns to be considered random and communicating nothing to the reader? It does not seem likely. So why then do the harvest Holy Days possess the most complicated Offerings in Scripture? And what exactly are they for or what do they represent?

2)   Every distinct sacrifice also includes its own supplemental elements to be added to it:

a.   There is the "grain offering" that is mixed with oil. Bulls receive 3/10th of an ephah of grain and a ½ of a hin of oil. Rams receive 2/10th of an ephah of grain and a 1/3rd of a hin of oil. The yearling lambs receive 1/10th of an ephah of grain and a 1/4th of a hin of oil. Goats are for sin offerings and are always offered alone.

b.   There may or may not be a "drink offering" or "libation". This is a cup of wine that was poured out upon the sacrifice as part of what was to be burned. Its measure was the same as that of the oil, if the sacrifice called for one. The mysterious thing about the libation is that it appears to be randomly applied. Why do some Offerings get a libation and others do not? Is this communicating something to the reader?

3)   The Daily Offerings are scheduled for the morning and the evening. At the time of the Daily Morning Offering was to be when all other Offerings were to be given as well. This means that the Evening Offering is isolated from the others being given all by itself. The rare exception was on the one night of the year when the Passover sacrifice was to be offered at this same time as well. So is this to have some significance?

4)   Surprisingly the subject of "atonement" arises in these 2 chapters in Numbers. It would seem that atonement follows the same sort of logic as do the Offerings themselves. That is, atonement is explained as being something necessary to attain to at both a personal and a community level. The personal forms of atonement again come with personal sin and Offerings designated for these specific occasions. At the community level, Yom Kippur presents itself as being when this atonement is to be achieved for the community. Yet, strangely, the subject arises in regards to the harvest Holy Days and only for some of them. The Feast of Unleavened Bread Offering, the Feast of Weeks Offering, and the Offering for Yom Teruah are all given the classification of "making atonement for you" (28:22; 28:30; 29:5). But no such comment is made for the Feast of Booths or the last Holy Day. Is this to mean something?

In putting some of the pieces together, it would seem that the harvest Holy Days are more complex because they are representing the greatest "things" as they somehow relate to the community at large. What all of the details surrounding the Holy Days Offerings by Fire are to be interpreted as meaning will need to be resolved, if possible.

Memorial to be held in a place chosen by God

As the book of Deuteronomy opens, it states in 1:3 that Moses again spoke to Israel one last time on the first day of the 11th month of the 40th year (from the time of the curse put on the 1st Exodus generation). This time he will address the 2nd generation of the Exodus. He happens to be the last surviving member of his generation, besides Joshua and Caleb, the two who were permitted to enter the Land as promised.

There will be two more relevant passage to examine in this final section of the Law in regards to the Holy Days. Surprisingly or not, it will add what final new elements are to be detected being given to the Holy Days testimony. Deuteronomy chapter 16 will remind the reader of the 3 feasts one final time in the Law. With it, the Feast of Unleavened Bread is strangely described in detail while the other feasts are not. The one new thing to discover is the following unusual addition that is being given to the Feast, even at this late point in the text:

Deut 16:8 "Six days you shall eat unleavened bread, and on <u>the seventh day there shall be a solemn assembly</u> to the LORD your God...

The words "solemn assembly" is the single word "atsarah" that appeared first in Leviticus 23:36 assigned to the last Holy Day, the 22nd day of the 7th month. The details for this word were supplied in the description of the Feast of Booths in the review of Leviticus 23. This word pops up here for the 3rd and last time in the Law. The 2 previous places it was assigned to the last Holy Day. So why is the last day of the Feast of Unleavened Bread given this late and new classification?

The final Holy Day testimony detail needing to be pointed out comes only 8 verses after this one:

Deut 16:16 "Three times in a year all your males shall appear before the LORD your God <u>in the place which He chooses</u>, at the Feast of Unleavened Bread and at the Feast of Weeks and at the Feast of Booths."

All 3 feasts are to be celebrated in the same location. But that place remains unidentified by the time the Law closes. It was to be a place where God was to put His Name. This ultimately was revealed to be the city of Jerusalem some 400 years later when King David captured it for his kingdom.

This marks the end of the Holy Days testimony supplied by the Law. The inundation of symbols these Days are assigned beg for explanation as to their meaning. This testimony will continue to be examined as it spills over in the section of the Prophets. It will be discovered there that the Prophet Ezekiel comes to bring yet one final but shocking twist to the Holy Days testimony. Nearly 800 years after the Holy Days instructions had been laid down in the Law Ezekiel brings some very provocative "changes" to the Holy Days. It is the Hebrew Scripture's greatest evidence for the existence of a Code beyond the Holy Days testimony.

Diagram of the Holy Days

7th day
Sabbath

In the Month of Abib/Nisan
(month when barley harvest 1st visible)

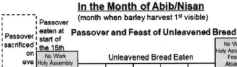

3 Feasts to be held at the Place Where God would put His Name

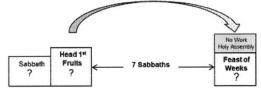

In the 7th Month of Ethanim/Tishri

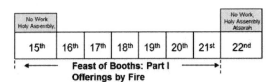

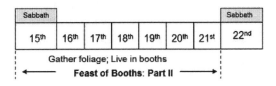

While the sons of Israel camped at Gilgal they observed the Passover on the evening of the fourteenth day of the month on the desert plains of Jericho.

Joshua 5:10

Chapter Eight
Israel's History of Holy Day Observances

Observances of Holy Days are recorded beyond the books of the Law. Each observance has its own special circumstances as to why it is being documented. In total, there will be 4 more Passover observances recorded:

1. 1st Passover memorial observed inside the Promised Land (Joshua 5:10-12)
2. King Hezekiah reinstates Passover memorial after he succeeds his lawless father Ahaz (2Chron 30)
3. King Josiah reinstates Passover memorial after he succeeds his lawless father Manasseh (2Chron35)
4. 1st Passover memorial of the 2nd Temple Era soon after the 2nd Temple is rebuilt (Ezra 6:19-22)

In addition, the Feast of Booths will be recorded being observed on 3 different occasions:

1. King Solomon officiates occasion just after the 1st Temple is built (2Chron7:8-9)
2. Returning Exiles observe just after an Altar is built for its Offerings by Fire (Ezra 3:4)
3. Observance is held just after Nehemiah completes rebuilding the Walls of Jerusalem (Neh8:13-18)

The book of Deuteronomy closed with God informing Moses he would not be allowed to cross over into the Land due to an error of judgment he had made. In his place Moses would commission Joshua to lead the People. Joshua had been Moses' assistant and one of only two people of his generation allowed to enter the Promised Land. Moses would then be told to leave the camp and view the Land from a mountain top. Israel will never see him again, presumably having died there because no one of Israel witnessed it. With this the book of Deuteronomy closes.

The book of Joshua opens with Joshua preparing Israel to take the Land. Crossing the Jordan River would represent the great threshold to pass in order to enter it. In Joshua chapter 3, the nation crosses the river on dry ground as Joshua divides the water in much the same way Moses divided the water at the Red Sea. Joshua 4:19 states this crossing was completed on the "tenth day of the first month" on what was the 43rd year since the original Passover occasion.

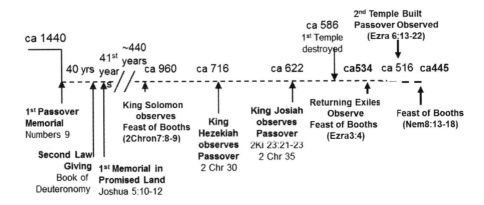

History Timeline of Israel's Observances of Holy Days (BC/BCE)

1st Passover Memorial in the Promised Land

In only 4 days the Passover memorial would arrive. Readers learn here that the offspring of the Exodus generation had not been circumcised in the wilderness. Yet it had been commanded that any male partaking of the memorial observance be circumcised. So God informs Joshua that the community needed to be circumcised and this is what happens next. The Passover memorial arrives and so signifies that the initial harvest had arrived also:

Joshua 5:10-12 While the sons of Israel camped at Gilgal, they observed the Passover on the evening of the fourteenth day of the month on the desert plains of Jericho. And <u>on the day after the Passover</u>, on that very day, they ate <u>some of the produce of the land</u>, unleavened cakes and parched {grain} And the manna ceased <u>on the day after they had eaten</u> some of the produce of the land, so that the sons of Israel no longer had manna, but <u>they ate some of the yield of the land of Canaan during that year</u>.

Notice that the Passover comes and that in two days the manna ceases after Israel had begun eating "produce from the land" on the day after the 14th, what would obviously be the 15th day. Then the writer happens to remind the readers that in that same year Israel began to eat of the "yield of the land", that is, that years harvested crops from the Land.

Breaking Down Joshua 5:10-12

Joshua 5:10	Joshua 5:11	Joshua 5:12
Eve of the 14th Sons of Israel prepare the Passover	**The 15th** Passover meal is eaten with bread made from previous harvest	**From the 16th onward** Manna ceases (A 7th day?)

So is there information supplied in this passage that would help shed light on what Sabbath and mystery day Lev23:11 is reckoning? The answer would have to be no. However, tradition went on to insist that there is information being supplied here but in a hidden sort of way. What the Pharisees attempted to argue was that the 15th day of the month was being identified as the "Sabbath" of Lev 23:11 and most certainly used this passage to help support their view. But the only way one could justifiably argue this is if there was mention of the eating of new grain on the day the manna ceased. But all the writer informs the reader is that sometime in that year new grain came to be eaten. This statement does not appear to be associating with the Passover memorial in any way but is a general statement as to why the manna ceased. The People of Israel had already started to gather old grain for consummation and would then collect from the new harvest when the opportunity came.

The strongest case the Pharisees could make is that the Passover memorial was certainly being described as something which converged with the appearing of the head 1st fruits. But to insist that the 15th day is to be considered the Sabbath of Lev 23:11 does not appear to be supported in this passage. What is perhaps a greater clue is that the manna ceased on the 16th day. What is known is that manna did not form on the 7th day as Exo16:27 infers. So one possible interpretation is that the 16th actually fell on a 7th day Sabbath which would have then ended the cycle of manna on precisely the end of the last Sabbath cycle just as the start of the manna appearing was the 1st day of the 1st Sabbatical cycle.

The general conclusion about this time of year is again that the very 1st fruits were to appear during the month in which Passover was to be observed just as the actual Passover occasion had been observed in reference to Exo 9:31. So as the Law implies, these two occasions, the Passover memorial and the head 1st fruits, are to somehow converge upon one another yet via a mystery in that the latter is to come "after the Sabbath". One other great clue is also the fact that the other 2 feasts that this first feast is associated with are both harvest occasions. By inference, this also seems to suggest that this feast is to have some sort of harvest theme attributed to it. In all of this speculation the obvious question arises. Why so much mystery here?

The Holy Days were things commanded be observed. So how was Israel to fulfill a most important occasion without a sufficient amount of information to properly reckon its observance? Is it to be assumed Moses and Joshua were fully aware of when these mystery Days were to be observed? If so, this information certainly came to be lost because the earliest records to document the opinions about these mystery Days reveal that there was no single tradition being observed. This subject will be discussed further at the end of this chapter.

Holy Day observances during the Kingdom era(s)

The next occasion where the subject of the Holy Days arises is during the time of Israel's Kingdom and Kingdoms. A total of 3 kings will be mentioned having something to do with especially the feasts. These are King Solomon, King Hezekiah and King Josiah.

Between the time of Joshua and the coming of the Kingdom, there was roughly a 300 year period when judges were raised up to lead the nation. Time and time again the Nation would fall into unfaithfulness and God would raise anew a judge to restore it. Fourteen judges are listed by name in the book of Judges. In short it was a most dark time. Yet the parallel story of Ruth as recorded from the book of Ruth during this same period is the hopeful events of this era. The Scripture tells of King David's ancestral lineage and how it came to form through Ruth.

Israel's United Kingdom began with the last mentioned judge, Samuel, anointing Saul as Israel's first king around 1050BC/BCE. David would succeed Saul and then David's son Solomon would succeed his father. It would be during Solomon's reign when the next reference where the Holy Days appear in the witness.

King Solomon: Following in his father's footsteps Solomon had built the first temple and now the prophesied place where God was to put His Name had finally been revealed to Israel. This took 7 years to build. Over the course of the next 13 years Solomon would have his own house built. During this time the king hired a man named Hiram to build the various pieces of bronze work to furnish the temple. Finally, after what had been 20 years, Solomon made arrangements to bring the Ark of the Covenant into the temple.

But interestingly enough, the Scripture records that Solomon chose the time of the Feast of Booths to place the Ark in the temple along with the remnants of the tent of meeting and the holy utensils. Evidently these had been stationed in the city of Gibeon until this moment had come. Surrounding this activity the Scripture records:

1Kings8:2, 6, 11, 65: All the men of Israel assembled themselves to King Solomon at the feast, in the month Ethanim, which is the seventh month…the priests brought the ark of the covenant of the LORD to its place…when the priests came from the holy place, the cloud filled the house of the LORD…So Solomon observed the feast at that time, and all Israel with him, a great assembly…

2 Chr 7:9…And on the eighth day they held a solemn assembly…

So out of the 3 Feasts, the first recorded occasion for any of them to be fulfilled in the way the Law had envisioned came to be the Feast of Booths. Notice there is mention of the last Holy Day being observed as a "solemn assembly", what is a rare word the Hebrew Scripture uses to describe an assembly. Perhaps, the things that were taking place in Solomon's day were to be somehow symbolic of what this Holy Day was to be ultimately predicting for the future.

In a second reference regarding the Holy Days, Solomon is recorded having obeyed the command to fulfill the burnt offerings for the "daily rule, the Sabbaths, the new moons, and the feasts":

2Chr8:12-13 Then Solomon offered burnt offerings to the LORD on the altar of the LORD which he had built before the porch; and did so according to the daily rule, offering them up according to the commandment of Moses, for the sabbaths, the new moons and the three annual feasts – the Feast of Unleavened Bread, the Feast of Weeks and the Feast of Booths.

The prophetic peace that David's Son and his Kingdom were to bring, as promised to David through the prophet Nathan, reads as if it indeed had come with Solomon. And although this aspect of Solomon's reign was short lived relatively speaking, the Scripture indicates his Kingdom was legendary and would never be equaled again in stature and splendor in the record of the Hebrew text. Yet it must be understood that David was promised the coming of an eternal Kingdom which his offspring would reign over so this prophecy could not have been entirely fulfilled with Solomon. Thus the sum total revelation of a coming King to reign in glory is looking beyond Solomon to a future vision which he merely foreshadowed.

And so there is internal evidence within the Hebrew text indicating that perhaps Israel's Holy Days have both a short term fulfillment and a long one. The short term fulfillment being found in Israel's ancient history. The Passover memorial's short term fulfillment looked to Israel's deliverance from bondage and the coming into the Promised Land to enjoy its harvest blessings there. The symbolic short term fulfillment of the Feast of Booths perhaps was Israel coming into the tranquility of Solomon's Kingdom. And yet there are prophetic expectations of a long term fulfillment as envisioned by the prophets Ezekiel and Zechariah which will be examined further in later chapters.

King Jeroboam of the Kingdom of Israel: After Solomon's reign ended in tragedy with his great acts of apostasy, the Kingdom divided into two: 10 tribes from the north joined together and 3 tribes from the south likewise. The Northern Kingdom was known as the Kingdom of Israel. Its first king was Jeroboam. He decided to establish his home and throne in the hill country of Ephraim by building the city of Shechem. He immediately feared that the People of his Kingdom would travel to Jerusalem to offer sacrifices there and would then decide to turn against him and return and make Rehoboam, the King of Judah, be their king. So he decided to set up his own religious worship places for the people to worship inside the Kingdom. He also made Priests of his own people, none of them being from the Tribe of Levi. Furthermore, he also decided to establish a "Feast" in the eighth month:

1Kings12:32 Jeroboam instituted a feast in the eighth month on the fifteenth day of the month, like the feast which is in Judah

Of course, the entire affair was a complete act of apostasy and was condemned soon thereafter by a Prophet sent from God.]

The Southern Kingdom was known as the Kingdom of Judah. The kings of this kingdom continued to be David's descendants and also retained the throne in Jerusalem, the Temple and the Levitical priesthood. Two kings from this kingdom will be recorded calling the Nation to observe the Passover memorial on two notable occasions. These kings are King Hezekiah and King Josiah.

King Hezekiah: The next time the occasion of the Passover memorial would arise on record is during King Hezekiah's reign:

2 Chr 30:1-26 Now Hezekiah sent to all Israel and Judah and wrote letters also to Ephraim and Manasseh, that they should come to the house of the LORD at Jerusalem to celebrate the Passover to the LORD God of Israel. For the king and his princes and all the assembly in Jerusalem had decided to celebrate the Passover in the second month, since they could not celebrate it at that time, because the priests had not consecrated themselves in sufficient numbers, nor had the people been gathered to Jerusalem. Thus the thing was right in the sight of the king and all the assembly. So they established a decree to circulate a proclamation throughout all Israel from Beersheba even to Dan, that they should come to celebrate the Passover to the LORD God of Israel at Jerusalem. For they had not celebrated {it} in great numbers as it was prescribed...Then they slaughtered the Passover {lambs} on the fourteenth of the second month...The sons of Israel present in Jerusalem celebrated the Feast of Unleavened Bread {for} seven days with great joy, and the Levites and the priests praised the LORD day after day with loud instruments to the LORD...

At the time of King Hezekiah's reign, the Northern Kingdom had just suffered being dismantled by the Assyrian Empire. But this did not stop Hezekiah from sending out an invitation to all of Israel throughout the land. The text will record that some northern tribesmen responded and came to celebrate the Passover. But the witness also speaks that the King was unprepared in dealing with the masses who did respond. Why was this so?

For starters, Hezekiah's father King Ahaz is ranked as one of the most ungodly of Judah's kings and so it is best to conclude that no assembly of the Passover was held with large numbers during his 16 years reign. 2Chr28:24 even states that Ahaz had the doors of the temple closed thus suspending its services until

Hezekiah could restore them later. This required that the priests and the temple would need to be again consecrated for service.

Eventually Hezekiah would attempt to have this Passover observance after what must have been a very long hiatus. A great deal of those who had assembled were far from being compliant with the regulations of the Law. The northern tribesmen had been part of another kingdom that had not adhered to the Law but followed a counterfeit law that its first king, king Jeroboam, had established. He was fearful his subjects would remain loyal to the southern kingdom in continuing to assemble in Jerusalem as prescribed so he created another place of worship, priesthood and laws for his own kingdom.

Essentially the Law of Moses required a maintenance of "holy" cleanliness. As was studied from the very first memorial observed, there were those who had come into contact with a dead person and were instructed to wait out the Passover and memorialize it one month later. This was one way a person already within the community could come to be defiled or unclean. There were other ways to become unclean that everyday life could bring upon the members of the community.

But besides the need for a continuous maintenance of cleanliness, there first had to be an initial consecration for those who were coming into the community for the first time or who had been removed from it for some time for whatever reason. For example, when the entire Exodus generation came to the foot of Mount Sinai, God instructed Moses to have the people "consecrated" so as to prepare them for the receiving of the Law. This was the washing of the clothes and a 3 day period of purification during which no sexual relations were to be had. Thus many of those who had come upon king Hezekiah's invitation were simply not consecrated to begin with and were most certainly unclean by the standards of the Law.

So to remedy the situation it was first decided that the actual beginning of the Feast begin a month later. This would allow time for a greater quantity of priests to ready themselves for service. The reason being was that it was decided that the priests themselves would offer the Passover lambs on behalf of the People who were not prepared. The king then prayed that God overlook the unprepared state and the unorthodox means of offering the sacrifice on behalf of the People so that the Feast could go forward.

As this record closes the following is mentioned:

2Chr30:26 So there was great joy in Jerusalem, because there was nothing like this in Jerusalem <u>since the days of Solomon</u> the son of David, king of Israel

And so the reader can conclude that yes indeed during Solomon's reign there must have been the assemblies of Israel during the 3 Feast times as was earlier speculated. But that since the time of Solomon no such significant assemblies are to be understood having taken place until Hezekiah's reign.

King Josiah: Whereas Hezekiah had succeeded his evil father Ahaz, king Josiah would succeed an even more evil and notorious father and grandfather, kings Amon and Manasseh. What made it worse was that Manasseh had the longest reign of any king in either of Israel's kingdoms, a length of 55 years. Actually Manasseh was

Hezekiah's son, who succeeded him. Things had been allowed to deteriorate so bad that Josiah ordered the temple to be refurbished. While rummaging through the neglected temple precinct a priest stumbled across a scroll of the Law!

How unusual it is for a reader to discover that the king was so ignorant of the Law, indeed the entire Nation, that upon having it read to him he tore his clothes upon learning what curses were to come upon Israel should it come to be noncompliant with the Law. After the king summoned a prophetess by the name of Huldah, she informed Josiah that because of his humble and contrite heart God would allow him to live out his days without seeing the fulfillment of the curses but which would eventually come upon Israel after his life was over.

So as part of Josiah's being moved to act upon the words of the Law, the following is recorded:

2 Chr 35:1-19 Then Josiah celebrated the Passover to the LORD in Jerusalem, and they slaughtered the Passover {animals} on the fourteenth {day} of the first month…And Josiah contributed to the lay people, to all who were present, flocks of lambs and kids, all for the Passover offerings, numbering 30,000 plus 3,000 bulls; these were from the king's possessions. …Thus the sons of Israel who were present celebrated the Passover at that time, and the Feast of Unleavened Bread seven days. And <u>there had not been celebrated a Passover like it in Israel since the days of Samuel the prophet; nor had any of the kings of Israel celebrated such a Passover as Josiah did</u> with the priests, the Levites, all Judah and Israel who were present, and the inhabitants of Jerusalem. In the eighteenth year of Josiah's reign this Passover was celebrated.

Based on what is being said in this passage, it must be concluded that this is the first recorded Passover memorial to have been fulfilled per every last detail of instruction that was commanded. Josiah had allowed enough time to prepare for the occasion and so it was held on the very day it was instructed to be on, the fourteenth day of the first month. Inhabitants from both Israel and Judah were present. Furthermore, the priests offered the sacrifices that the king himself supplied on behalf of all of Israel and even had them cook the Passovers and distribute to all the People. Finally, the chronicler notes that this was the greatest Passover memorial ever observed in the history of ancient Israel's existence even going back as far as the time of Samuel the prophet before the united kingdom was established.

But the days of the Nation's autonomy were numbered. The curse of the Law was soon to come down upon the Nation as promised. The prophets Isaiah (1:14), Amos (5:21; 8:21) and Hosea (2:11) write of the Holy Days as times God had come to hate because of the idolatry and false worship Israel had infused with them. Within less than 100 years, the Babylonian Empire would begin to bear down on the kingdom and slowly over 20 years the kingdom would come to crumble. Three waves of exile would materialize, one in ca606, another in ca596 and then the final and most destructive exile in ca586BC/BCE.

Returning Exiles observe Feast of Booths,Passover

After 70 years of Israel's exile, the Babylonian Empire would fall to the ascending Persian Empire. Subsequently the Persian Empire's king Cyrus granted permission for Judah's Exiles to return and rebuild a 2nd temple in the Land of Israel as Isaiah the prophet had predicted in Isaiah 45. Some 42,000 would be documented deciding to return with leaders Zerubbabel the "governor of Judah and Joshua the High Priest. It represented only a fraction of the people of Judah that were displaced to Babylon. Those that would remain in Babylon would become part of the first great body to form a distinct populace of the so called "Diaspora" as they would spread far and wide over the many centuries.

The rebuilding would begin in ca535BC/BCE. But the peoples of mixed races formed by the Assyrian Empire living in the region would interfere and ultimately succeed in having the building suspended for about 18 years, after the foundation was first laid, under the orders of the Persian Empire. They were successful in building and installing a burnt offering altar. This coincided with the coming of the Feast of Booths. It states that the People observed the Feast but the only details provided is that they presented the Feast's prescribed Offerings by Fire as the priest Ezra documents:

Ezra 3:3-6 ...So they set up the altar on its foundation... and they offered burnt offerings on it to the LORD, burnt offerings morning and evening. And they celebrated the Feast of Booths, as it is written, and {offered} the fixed number of burnt offerings daily, according to the ordinance, as each day required; and afterward {there was} a continual burnt offering, also for the new moons and for all the fixed festivals of the LORD that were consecrated, and from everyone who offered a freewill offering to the LORD. From the first day of the seventh month they began to offer burnt offerings to the LORD...

Eventually, a second attempt at finishing the temple would be tried and succeeded in ca521 with the encouragement of the prophets Haggai and Zechariah. Haggai stirred up the people by stating that they had built their own houses but left God's house in ruins. By ca516BC/BCE, some five years later, the second temple would be completed. Ezra would record that it became completed on the 3rd day of the 12th month. The time of the Passover was approaching. And for the first time in the so called "2nd Temple Era", the Passover memorial came to be observed documented by the priest Ezra:

Ezra 6:19-22 And the exiles observed the Passover on the fourteenth of the first month. For the priests and the Levites had purified themselves together; all of them were pure. Then they slaughtered the Passover {lamb} for all the exiles, both for their brothers the priests and for themselves. And the sons of Israel who returned from exile and all those who had separated themselves from the impurity of the nations of the land to {join} them, to seek the LORD God of Israel, ate {the Passover.} And they observed the Feast of Unleavened Bread seven days with joy, for the LORD had caused them to rejoice, and had turned

the heart of the king of Assyria toward them to encourage them in the work of the house of God, the God of Israel.

And so the beginning of the 2nd Temple era began with the observance of Passover. It is believed that from here on in never would there be a time when the Feast would not be observed in large numbers either within the land of Israel proper or in the Diaspora. The effects of the exile had essentially encouraged an unprecedented discipline to emerge amongst the Jewish People in keeping observant with the Law.

Historically Jews would successfully retain their identity by continuing to observe the Law outside the Land. Those who did not were susceptible of becoming assimilated into the greater gentile communities they lived within. It would be very difficult from this point on for Jews to retain their identity without adhering to the Law, the one element that proved vital in preserving the Jewish People as a distinct People wherever they would become scattered.

Those who returned from the exile to rebuild were clearly evidencing their desire to make observance of the Law priority one. This is how history remembers the reality of post-exile Jewish life. Idol worship would really never surface again in the community, the one major thing that had been so destructive to Israel's and Judah's adhesion as an autonomous nation and people before the exile.

Feast of Booths observed recorded by Nehemiah

Yet one final testimony from the Hebrew Scripture referring to yet another Holy Day observance would come from Nehemiah, a Jewish man who coordinated the building of Jerusalem's walls some 75 years after the rebuilding of the temple around 450BC/BCE. What Nehemiah records is an unusual tradition begun for the Feast of Booths based on an interesting interpretation on what Leviticus 23 implies be done with the vegetation that was to be gathered during this feast:

Neh 8:14-18 And they found written in the law how the LORD had commanded through Moses that the sons of Israel should live in booths during the feast of the seventh month. So they proclaimed and circulated a proclamation in all their cities and in Jerusalem, saying, "Go out to the hills, and bring olive branches, and wild olive branches, myrtle branches, palm branches, and branches of {other} leafy trees, to make booths, as it is written." So the people went out and brought {them} and made booths for themselves, each on his roof, and in their courts, and in the courts of the house of God, and in the square at the Water Gate, and in the square at the Gate of Ephraim. And the entire assembly of those who had returned from the captivity made booths and lived in them. The <u>sons of Israel had indeed not done so from the days of Joshua the son of Nun to that day</u>...And he (Ezra) read from the book of the law of God daily, from the first day to the last day. And they celebrated the feast seven days, and on the eighth day {there was} a solemn assembly according to the ordinance.

Passover Traditions emerge in the 2nd Temple Era

The Persian Empire would eventually be crushed by the Greek warrior Alexander the Great and his armies around 333BC/BCE. Within 10 years Alexander would sweep as far east as India. But quite suddenly he died and left his vast empire to his generals. Eventually Israel found itself sandwiched between two empires formed by two of his generals, the Ptolemaic Empire to the south and the Seleucid Empire to the north. These two empires would vie for domination for centuries. Eventually the Seleucid Empire would gain supremacy and bring a pagan hegemony to bear upon the Jewish Nation. At the height of the campaign to "Hellenize" the Nation, the 2nd temple came to be seized and defiled by the Seleucid king Antiochus IV Epiphanies in ca167BC/BCE. He also forbid practice of the Torah and thus brought great oppression to the religiously fervent followers of Judaism.

This came to incite what is known as the Maccabean Revolt. In time, those revolting would regain possession of the temple. The extra-biblical sources that record this ominous time reveal the emerging religious sects within the community. Most importantly, the Pharisees and Sadducees become prominent in the record.

What is so relevant about these two prevailing sects is that these were the sects that held sway within the Jewish community until the end of the 2nd Temple era. Essentially history records Lev 23:11 caused two interpretations to emerge. The phrase "after the Sabbath" of Lev23:11 came to mean either the day "after the 15th day of the 1st month" OR the day after "the Sabbath" of the Feast of Unleavened Bread. The way the mystery Holy Day is defined even these interpretations appear quite speculative. Yet the Law commanded the Day to be observed so Israel had no choice but to "guess" at the best interpretation. And so tradition records that the Pharisees sided with the first interpretation while the Sadducees sided with the latter:

The Pharisees' Interpretation of Leviticus 23:11:

To the Pharisees the "Sabbath" of Leviticus 23:11 came to be understood being the 15th day of the 1st month. This was the 1st day defined as being a day of "no work" amongst the harvest Holy Days listed in Leviticus 23. Thus, the 16th day of the 1st month is always the Day of Head 1st Fruits in this interpretation. This also means the Feast of Weeks falls exactly 50 days after the 16th day of the 1st month in this interpretation:

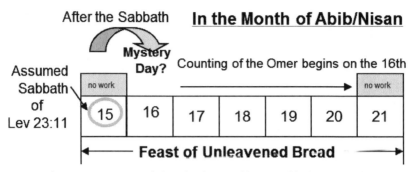

The consequences of the Pharisees taking on this interpretation meant that the Holy Days described as days of "no work" were to be classified as "Sabbaths". There were 3 total of these, the 15th and 21st days of the 1st month and the Feast of Weeks. The Fall Holy Days which were described as "no work" days are also defined there as "Sabbath" days. There are 4 total of these, the 1st, the 10th, the 15th and the 22nd. In sum, this would create 7 fixed lunar days being classified as Sabbaths if this interpretation is the correct one.

The Sadducees' Interpretation of Leviticus 23:11:

To the Sadducees, they interpreted the "Sabbath" of Leviticus 23:11 as being the 7th day Sabbath within the Feast of Unleavened Bread. The mystery Head 1st Fruits Day could thus fall anywhere between the 16th and 22nd days of the month given the Sabbath could fall anywhere between the 15th and 21st days of the 1st month:

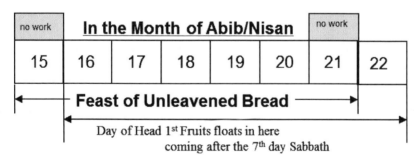

What is clear from the traditions is that both sides believed that the two occasions of the Passover memorial and the mystery Day were convergent disagreeing only on the identity of the Sabbath of Leviticus 23:11. In entertaining this convergence theory, this idea essentially divides the Feast of Unleavened Bread into two portions. Since there are 7 total days of eating of unleavened bread, the Head 1st Fruits offering would come and divide this 7 day period into two segments. The first segment is that period when only bread made from the old harvest could be eaten. This would always mean that the Passover meal itself was to be eaten with bread made from the previous harvest. This seems rather odd that an initial celebration of the harvest season would require the eating of old grain. This would then continue until the "day after the Sabbath", what is the fixed lunar day of the 16th according to the Pharisees or the floating 1st day of the week of the feast according to the Sadducees. The latter days of the feast after this is to allow the eating of the new harvest.

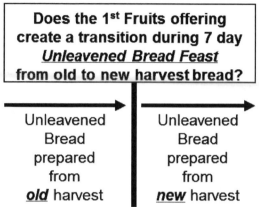

Does the 1st Fruits offering create a transition during 7 day _Unleavened Bread Feast_ from old to new harvest bread?

| Unleavened Bread prepared from **old** harvest | Unleavened Bread prepared from **new** harvest |

Hence, Judaism's traditions had established that the Feast of Unleavened Bread is to be a transitional celebration with eating of old grain ending with the Head 1st Fruits Offering and the remaining days of the feast left for eating new grain. It represents a fascinating synthesis for the Passover Memorial and the mystery Holy Day if this theory of convergence is correct.

The Counting of the Omer

It is also important to remember that 50 days, or 7 "Sabbaths" and a day, were to be counted leading up to the Feast of Weeks starting from the Holy Day of Head 1st Fruits. Judaism calls this the "Counting of the Omer". The word "omer" is the transliterated Hebrew word for the amount of barley that was to be waved by the priest. Because the 7 "Sabbaths" were to begin being counted from the day the omer of barley was to be waved by the priest. These 7 Sabbaths have been recognized as an important passage of time within Judaism.

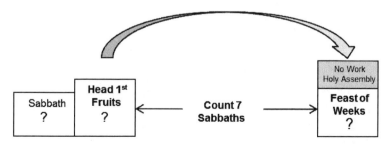

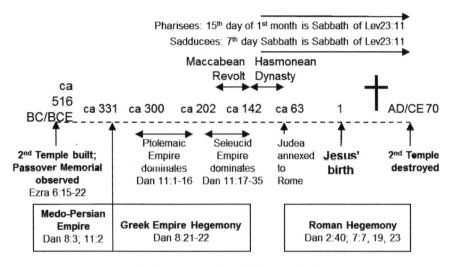

Timeline of the 2nd Temple Era

Sadly, history records how bitterly opposing brothers from the Maccabean line would fight over the seat of High Priest only to have the Roman Empire enter the feud and annex the land of Israel to the empire in 63BC/BCE. Malachi's predictions, briefly reviewed in the following chapter, appear to have 20/20 vision looking into the future. In time a rebellious Jewish element would rise up and revolt under the oppression this brought to the Jewish People. Eventually this would lead nearly every Jew scattered to the wind never to return for thousands of years. And so Malachi's words predicting the decay of the priesthood would bring about Israel's demise came to pass exactly as history remembers.

But just before all of this loss came, the testimony of Jesus would appear and bring the most shocking but enlightening revelation to ever bear upon the Law and the Prophets. It was the Roman Empire that would facilitate Jesus' Crucifixion. But through these events, the Holy Days themselves would come with the Gospel's decoding to unlock their meanings. But perhaps only a few believing Jews could see the astonishing Holy Days Code as it became unraveled before their eyes.

The next chapter will review how the Gospel testimony came to overlap with the Passover memorial in the year of the Gospel. In several critical places, the testimony will become cryptic and difficult to interpret. Tradition has glossed over these difficulties and has paid a monumental price. Fascinatingly, only those familiar with the Law can come to "decode" what the Gospel testimony is communicating. The authors can be found using the language of the Law to describe the chronology of the Gospel events. In this very intriguing way, the Law and the Gospel events come to "decode" each other.

Beyond the Law and the history of Israel, there comes the testimony of the Prophets. Here additional crucial information will be supplied by a handful of them, namely Ezekiel, Haggai and Zechariah.

It shall be the prince's part to provide...at all the appointed feasts of the house of Israel...the sin offering, the grain offering, the burnt offering and the peace offerings, to make atonement for the house of Israel.

Ezekiel 45:17-18

Chapter Nine

The Testimony of the Latter Prophets

In the first wave of Israel's Babylonian exile, the prophet Daniel is written to have been one of those led away. Based on his opening remarks, Ezekiel appears to have been taken in the second wave of exile. Hence Daniel's and Ezekiel's writings were penned while they lived in exile. Ezekiel's initial passages were written while Judah's Kingdom was still standing, albeit teetering. There would be yet a third and final destructive phase of the exiling of Israel. A little more than half way through Ezekiel's writing Jerusalem is recorded as having fallen by the hands of the Babylonians in this 3rd wave (33:21) sometime around 586BC/BCE.

Ezekiel's writings are relevant here because he provides additional Holy Days testimony beyond what the prophet Moses establishes in the Law. Along with the Gospel, Ezekiel's testimony is the most suggestive in indicating the Holy Days are encoded with concealed information. Even a general knowledge of Ezekiel has the power to decode the symbolic pattern set down by the Feast of Unleavened Bread. That is, the Prophet is first found being an eyewitness to God's Glory departing from Solomon's Temple in his 10th Chapter. Then later he has a prophetic vision witnessing God's Glory returning to inhabit the prophetic Temple he describes in his 43rd Chapter. Thus, Israel at first had enjoyed God's Glory in its midst in its early years starting from Passover. But then the day came in Ezekiel's life when this Presence left. This then created a new era where Israel's life would exist without the Glory of God in its midst. Yet Ezekiel foresees a Day coming when this situation will be reversed forever thereafter. All of this follows the simple pattern set down by the symbols of the Feast of Unleavened Bread as pointed out in an earlier chapter.

Unfortunately, there is far more of the Prophet's writing that remains enigmatic for both Judaism and traditional Christianity than there are simple ideas being conveyed. The greatest difficulty posed has been in the interpretation of Ezekiel's vision of a Kingdom he was made to see recorded in his last 9 chapters. Is this vision to be construed as Israel's literal Kingdom Come that was first prophesied to king David and then also to the other Prophets? Or is it to be interpreted as merely figurative?

For Judaism, the institution has had its own peculiar reasons why it has difficulty interpreting Ezekiel's Kingdom as being a literal kingdom to come. As part of Ezekiel's testimony, it would appear that Ezekiel calls for change to come to the Law. These changes are what are at the heart of his Holy Days testimony. Ezekiel anticipates that there will be more Holy Days Offerings for this Kingdom than what the Law prescribes. He also foresees changes to the Law's Offerings and even the elimination of one of the Law's most frequent Offerings. It is these alterations that disturb Judaism. So the question begs to be asked. Why does Ezekiel expect change to come to the Law for his prophetic kingdom he sees? It is the most obvious question posed to the reader in need of an answer. Upon closer inspection however, many more questions emerge out of this vision. All in all, Ezekiel's writings represent a very big pill for Judaism to have to swallow. As such, Judaism has never embraced Ezekiel's Kingdom as being Israel's expected prophetic kingdom to come.

For most Christians Ezekiel's Kingdom comes to be a difficult pill to swallow as well but for a fundamentally different reason. That Ezekiel envisions the vast majority of the Law to remain intact, especially the Levitical Priesthood and the Offerings by Fire, this is most difficult for traditional Christian doctrine to reconcile in a post Cross world (if indeed Ezekiel's Kingdom is a vision looking from a reference point beyond the Gospel). What is popularly believed by Christians about Ezekiel's Kingdom falls under two major views. The first view simply rejects the kingdom as literal arguing it is a physical representation of Jesus' spiritual kingdom. The second view believes it is prophetic of a literal Messianic Kingdom of finite duration, what is John's "Millennial Kingdom" he foresees in his book of Revelation.

The problem with these two views is that Ezekiel provides just enough testimony to rule out that this kingdom is to be ruled by Jesus Christ, whether figuratively or literally. That's because Ezekiel's "Prince David" of 37:25 is predicted to offer up a Sin Offering for himself at a critical juncture in this prophetic kingdom (45:22). Hence, the Gospel's sinless Messiah cannot be interpreted as being this Prince even though many Christians argue for this viewpoint. Where an argument can be made that the Messiah is in view is in 34:23-24. This will be explored more in chapter 15.

So whether Ezekiel's Kingdom is perceived purely figuratively or literally, no traditional position has ever formed explaining just exactly what purpose Ezekiel's testimony of a kingdom is to serve. The same goes for Ezekiel's Holy Days testimony. Judaism rejects the idea the Law is to be altered so it has no explanation to offer as to why Ezekiel foresees change to it. Traditional Christianity believes the kingdom is either a figurative or literal kingdom which Jesus rules over or will rule over even though these interpretations are not Scripturally permissible. These traditional positions have been in place from time immemorial and represent meaningless interpretations. What this means is, that whatever Ezekiel's message is, it has been left in a state of unexplored limbo for thousands of years!

Many minimalists, skeptics and detractors have attempted to make Ezekiel's entire message as an inspiration for Israel's Babylonian exiled People to return and rebuild once the Nation was allowed to return to the Land. But there is one lone passage in Ezekiel that not only flies in the face of this interpretation it actually happens to be the very heart and soul of everything Ezekiel is communicating:

Eze37:24,25 My servant David will be _king_ over them...David my prince will be their prince forever...

Many things did come to be restored once Israel was allowed to return and rebuild. But the one thing that never was restored was Israel's kingdom. Yet this theme of a coming King and Kingdom is the one central prophetic pulsating message running through the veins of nearly all the Hebrew Prophets. It is reiterated time and time again as being the climatic end the text is anticipating. If the post-exile rebuilding of Israel is what readers see Ezekiel envisioning in his greatest prophecies, this is simply evidence of a great disconnect between writer and reader with there being no fault of the writer for this misinterpretation. Certainly Ezekiel does envision a post-exile rebuilding but his more monumental message sees way beyond that.

In chapters 40 through 48 specifically, Ezekiel essentially provides a textual blueprint for the kingdom. There is to be a City, a King, a Temple, a Priesthood, an "altered" Law, and apportionments for tribal land inheritance in the Land surrounding the City. There is just enough testimony indicating Ezekiel is seeing this kingdom in the present world yet inferring it is on the very threshold of a coming Future Eternity. For example, after describing the architectural details of the Temple situated at the heart of this envisioned kingdom, and after Ezekiel envisions the glory of God entering this Temple, God is recorded speaking the following to Ezekiel:

Eze43:7 He said to me, "Son of man, this is the place of My throne and the place of My feet, <u>where I will dwell among the sons of Israel forever</u>…

Why traditional Christianity argues against this kingdom as becoming a literal "eternal" one is because the Greek Scripture appears not to communicate of its existence. And this, it seems, to be enough reason to declare it isn't to exist. Evidently the Hebrew Prophets are not to be consulted when attempting to understand the Scripture's vision for the future. Hence the conclusion is made that there will be no distinct Israel or Law in place in the end since the Testimony of Jesus does not seem to corroborate the Prophets, only the Church and its Gospel are assumed to be eternal.

Why Does Ezekiel's Vision Have Alterations to Law?

As part of the Kingdom the Prophet witnesses, Ezekiel is given Holy Days testimony that is reminiscent of the Law's own Holy Days testimony. Yet this just raises a very mysteriously disturbing question. Why is Ezekiel's Kingdom expected to need more Holy Days ordinances than those already defined in the Law? And why is a major Offering by Fire to be eliminated altogether for this same Kingdom? To sufficiently answer this question will require reserving 2 later chapters to explore this Prophet's enigmatic writings. But before Ezekiel's Holy Days testimony can come to be unveiled of their concealed messages, the Law's Holy Days Code will have come to be unraveled first for its meaning with the help of the Gospel testimony.

Libationless Offerings are for Atonement

The major aspect of the Holy Days that Ezekiel reveals needs altering for the coming Kingdom are the Offerings by Fire. By making this subject of the Offerings the primary focus, Ezekiel confines his testimony to just one aspect of the Holy Days' symbolisms. This allows a reader's attention to narrow and be sensitive to the peculiar details of the Offerings. What is discovered is that Ezekiel is found throwing more fuel on to the fire that suggests the Holy Days are encoded with all kinds of prophetic expectation. To the keen observer, Ezekiel's Holy Days testimony can be broken down into 3 sections. Each focuses upon a certain type of "alteration" to be made to the Law with the least altering ordinances coming first and the most altering coming last:

A summary of Ezekiel's "alterations" to the Law:

1. Ezekiel "Adds" Holy Days and Offerings the Law does not have. —*Drinks vs. no drinks*
2. Ezekiel "Changes" Holy Days and Offerings the Law has.
3. Ezekiel "Eliminates" one Offering the Law has and portions of another.

Where to begin unraveling Ezekiel's Holy Days testimony is in 45:17, where it begins. Its importance cannot be overstated here. It comes in two parts. But since the two parts read as if to be redundant, translations have difficulty distinguishing the parts as separate ideas. Here it will be carefully parsed as it was meant to be understood:

Statement 1: Ezekiel 45:17a: All Offerings which have <u>Libations are segregated to this first half passage</u>:

"And it shall be the prince's part {to provide} the burnt offerings, the grain offerings, *and the libations*, at the <u>feasts</u>, on the <u>new moons</u>, and on the <u>sabbaths</u>:

Here it states that the "Prince", who is to be the King of this Kingdom, is to be the one providing the elements for all the Holy Days Offerings that Ezekiel identifies here in this first statement. One could question that this statement is referring to the Law instead of to Ezekiel's Holy Days he is about to introduce in the immediate passages after this one. In other words, one could entertain the idea that Ezekiel is seeking to "replace" the Law's Holy Days' Offerings with the ones he will outline in his own writing. Here is where the details of the passage however insist that the Offerings it has in view are of the Law specifically. It happens to be the most important detail in helping to unravel Ezekiel's Holy Days testimony.

    The main reason why 45:17a can be concluded as pointing out that the Prince is expected to present the Offerings of the Law that are specified (that is, those for the Feasts, New Moons and Sabbaths) is because Ezekiel points out that "libations" are an integral part of these Offerings by Fire. And why is this peculiarly distinguishing and important to notice? Because a reader needs to be aware that ALL of Ezekiel's new Offerings by Fire he introduces are WITHOUT libations. That is, 45:17a is essentially pointing out those Offerings of the Law that come with a Libation and which the Prince will present. Again, 45:17a points out the 3 groups of Offerings in view:

    1. The Feasts: Weeks and Booths both have Libation Offerings. The Feast of Unleavened Bread however does not. But perhaps this is a subtle clue that the Head First Fruits Offering falls within this first Feast.

2. The New Moon
3. The Sabbaths

Thus, Ezekiel is to be interpreted as first pointing out those Offerings of the Law's Holy Days that are to remain unchanged. The role the Prince is to play is reminiscent of what the previously mentioned kings of Israel are remembered acting as when they fulfilled the Holy Days celebrations that they organized and administered. That is, he supplies all the components of the Offerings, the animals, the grain, the oil and the wine. However, lambs specifically are to be collected from the pastures of the People as 45:15-16 details to provide for the People's atonement.

What is conspicuously missing from Ezekiel's first list in 45:17a is the Law's "Daily Offerings" which also have Libations with them. Notice he makes no mention of them. This can only mean that Ezekiel's later Daily Offering testimony is not to be interpreted as an "addition" to those of the Law's Offerings but is in fact to "take the place of" the Law's Daily Offerings. This happens to be Ezekiel's greatest alteration he prophecies for the Law's Offerings as they are to apply to the Kingdom the Prophet envisions. More discussion follows on this topic in the order it comes.

After having pointed out what Offerings by Fire of the Law will remain unchanged (those having a libation with the exception of the Daily Offering), part 2 of Ezekiel 45:17 will now discuss yet a second group of Offerings that will include those that Ezekiel will describe subsequently after this passage.

Statement 2: Ezekiel 45:17b

"...at all the appointed feasts of the house of Israel he shall provide the sin offering, the grain offering, the burnt offering, and the peace offerings, to make atonement for the house of Israel."

This second part may read as appearing somewhat redundant with the first part because both mention burnt offerings and grain offerings. But what is really going on is that the Offerings by Fire are being partitioned between two kinds. The first kind are those that come with a Libation whereas the second kind are those that come without a Libation.

The phrase "appointed feasts" is the word "moed", or appointments. This is a blanket statement that represents ALL of the Holy Days, not only those of the Law but the new Holy Days and Offerings Ezekiel will now outline beyond this passage. The major distinction to be noticed is that there is no mention of Libations in this second part of 45:17. This will become more clear as Ezekiel's new Offerings are revealed, which none of them will have a Libation. He will add 7 total and then, for the 8th, he will alter the Daily Morning Offering so that it is defined to be without a Libation even though the Law specifies it is to have a Libation (at the same time he eliminates the Daily Evening Offering altogether).

Once this critical distinction is perceived a huge revelation is discovered just as the second half of the passage comes to an end: ***The latter Offerings are to act to MAKE ATONEMENT for Israel whereas the former listed Offerings having***

Libations are NOT to be interpreted as providing atonement yet are to continue to be presented nevertheless.

As Ezekiel's testimony continues from 45:17, he will introduce entirely **_new_** additional Offerings that suspiciously lack libations between 45:18 and 46:12. Hence, all of Ezekiel's Holy Days testimony that follows this passage, in 45:18-46:15, are to be specifically for "atoning" the house of Israel. So who is being predicted here making up the "house of Israel"? In the context of Ezekiel's writing, this would be Remnant Israel.

The first huge question that Eze45:17 raises is: If the Offerings by Fire that do not come with a Libation are to be for atonement, what then are Offerings by Fire that come with a Libation for? The Gospel message will come with its own Decryption Key to explain the significance and meaning of these distinct Offerings.

The second huge question raised is: Why does Ezekiel add Offerings above and beyond those called out in the Law and eliminate another? It can be readily noticed that all of Ezekiel's new Offerings provide "additional" atonement from what the Law prescribes. Between the lines, it would seem as if the interpretation is that the Law's Atonement Offerings had been sufficient in providing atonement for Ancient Israel but are not expected to be so for Remnant Israel, hence the need for the addition of Ezekiel's Offerings.

In an obvious sort of way, needing more atonement simply implies there is more of Israel expected to need atoning for in its Remnant than what was needed for in Ancient Israel. So do the Prophets foresee the Remnant Nation as becoming greater in size than ancient Israel? The simple answer is yes. In fact, Abraham was promised that his descendants would become as the "sand on the seashore" and as the "stars in the heavens" (Gen22:17). As will be discovered, Ezekiel's Offerings mimic the Law's Offerings in that they become assigned to certain Holy Days. But there are oddities in the testimony that lends to the idea that the Holy Days themselves are representing a certain segment of time and are being assigned for a certain group of People or Saints living in that segment of time. The original analysis of the Feast of Unleavened Bread in an early chapter established this basic idea. Now again, in all of Ezekiel's Holy Days testimony he is found not only creating his own encoded message but is also reinforcing the Law's Holy Days testimony as being encoded itself at the same time.

Ezekiel's additional ordinances

As the table below lists, there are 7 "additional" Offerings anticipated to be needed for the House of Israel in Ezekiel's coming kingdom. The first 2 Offerings are to be given on 2 new Holy Days which the Law does not testify to. The other 5 Offerings are to be Offerings given in addition to those the Law already prescribes on existing Holy Days. The Law's original Offerings are listed in the same table just below each of Ezekiel's last 5 Offerings for comparison sake. What is made apparent in comparing the Law's Offerings with those of Ezekiel's Offerings is that none of Ezekiel's Offerings contain libations whereas the Law's Offerings for the Feast of Booths, Sabbaths and New Moons all have libations.

Ezekiel's 7 Added Offerings for the House of Israel's Atonement

summary

Ezekiel's Holy Day	Offering by Fire				Libation?
	bull	ram	lamb	goat	
1. 1st day 1st month	1				No
2. 7th day 1st month	1				No
3. 14th day 1st month	1				No
4. Feast of ULB: All 7 days	7	7		1	No
(Law's ULB Offerings) ✖	2	1	7	1	No →
5. Feast of Booths; All 7 days	7	7		1	No
(Law's Booths Offerings) ✖	13-7	2	14	1	No on 15th; Yes on 16th-21st
6. Sabbath		1	6		No
(Law's Sabbath Offerings) ✖			2		Yes
7. New Moon	1	1	6		No
(Law's New Moon Offerings) ✖	2	1	7	1	Yes

Each of these 7 "additional" Offerings will be briefly examined here for the peculiarities they can be noticed possessing:

Summary of Ezekiel's Additional Offerings

1.   **A new Sin Offering on The 1st Day of the 1st Month** to "cleanse the sanctuary": This is the 1st of 3 consecutive Sin Offerings to be added to what the Law already prescribes. These 3 days are the only Holy Days in Scripture which contain a single Sin Offering and nothing else. Starting with this first new Holy Day, there is an immediate sign of something monumental being communicated here. Notice that this day is essentially the Divine Calendar's Rosh HaShanah. If this is not a monumental clue as to the Holy Days being encoded with Divine Symbolisms, than one does not exist. *Jewish New Year*

What is being implied here is that this very special day must have been reserved from the very beginning so that it could later be designated the very first date in the Divine Calendar. Recall that this calendar was first introduced at Passover in Exodus 12:1. Passover itself was an historical occasion hinting to the idea that this Divine Calendar is to contain Epoch Dates of which Passover was to be made the first. But here now, when Ezekiel's Temple is to become prophetically cleansed for the very first time, this occasion is to be noted coming on the very first day of the first month, prior to the Passover, even though it necessarily must come much later in real time! So what is this communicating? It would seem that Ezekiel argues the reserved Dates for this Calendar are not necessarily to be in so much of a chronological order as they are to follow some greater "theological" order. So why and how is the 1st day of Ezekiel's Kingdom to be taking preeminence over the date of the Passover itself?

Another thing to point out is that there is no mention of a veil in the Temple upon which to sprinkle the blood of these 3 Sin Offerings. The Law specifically requires that blood be brought into the Holy Place and be sprinkled upon the veil that separates the Holy Place from the Most Holy Place (see Lev16). Here only the outside of the Temple and the altar are to receive blood. Furthermore, in Ezekiel's description of the Temple and its furnishings a veil is not mentioned. So what has happened to the veil? It seems to be gone here. Why is the veil not accounted for here?

2.   Another new Sin Offering on the 7th Day of the 1st Month to "cleanse the sanctuary": *Naïve* Following the first Holy Day in its enormous suggestive date of coming, here is yet another Day taking on more symbolic meaning than possible direct meaning. For why, only after 6 days, should it be deemed important to have yet another Sin Offering for those who are "naïve" and whom bring defilement to the Temple? What more obvious evidence is needed to suggest that this "7th Day" is part of a greater chronological sequence of important dates Ezekiel compiles here, a list of Holy Days which are meant to symbolize a sequence of events for some schedule Ezekiel is communicating? It is these kind of hints that make the reader ever more suspecting that the Law's original Holy Days should be interpreted under a similar light.

3.   Another new Sin Offering on the 14th day of the 1st Month for the Prince and all the People of the Land: And if the first 2 days were not suggestive enough, perhaps Ezekiel's Holy Days testimony should be seen climaxing in its suggestive power when the 3rd and final Sin Offering is to fall on, of all days, the day of Passover! Furthermore, it is on this occasion in the unveiling of this 3rd New Holy Day, when the reader learns that the Prince and King of Ezekiel's Kingdom is a fallible, sin committing son of David! It would seem that Ezekiel's testimony finally seems suggestive enough here at this juncture to declare that what he is anticipating in all of his prophesies is what came 600 years later in the coming Gospel. Essentially the Gospel disallows Ezekiel's king from being its revelation of the Messiah in Jesus. Yet if Ezekiel's Kingdom is not Messianic then how can it be argued that this passage is anticipating the Gospel? *Passover = Prince Sacrifice*

Essentially what Ezekiel is doing is making the Passover have to "share" the date of the 14th Day of the 1st Month with something else! In Ezekiel's Kingdom, Passover is anticipated to be observed in addition to yet something else on the very same day, that is, atonement for the Remnant! So too the Gospel will come and proclaim the Messiah's own death on the day of Passover too! Ezekiel has thus given precedent for the Passover taking on more than Ancient Israel's date of Passover before the Gospel appears and does the same thing! This represents yet another "transforming" element to be added to the "testimony" of the Passover, a testimony that is transforming into looking as much into the future as it does in the past! Recall that this transformation first develops in the Law as the previous chapters pointed out. Here now both the Law and the Prophet Ezekiel are found working together to reveal that the date of Passover is becoming a multifaceted one of importance in the Divine Schedule, one that not only looks back but also prophetically forward as well.

Sin Offerings Bring symmetry to asymmetrical Law

[handwritten: balance] *[handwritten: Not balance]*

In sum, these first 3 days can be noticed doing something interesting when joined with the rest of the Law's Holy Days. An unusual symmetry forms between the 1st and 7th months:

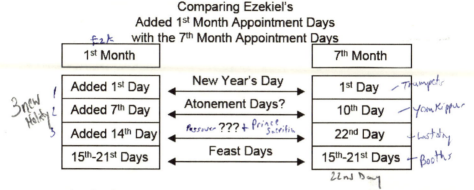

Comparing Ezekiel's
Added 1st Month Appointment Days
[handwritten: Ezk] **with the 7th Month Appointment Days**

1st Month		7th Month
Added 1st Day	New Year's Day	1st Day *[Trumpets]*
Added 7th Day	Atonement Days?	10th Day *[Yom Kippur]*
Added 14th Day	*[Passover ??? + Prince Sacrifice]*	22nd Day *[Last day]*
15th-21st Days	Feast Days	15th-21st Days *[Booths]*

[handwritten left margin: 3 new Holy 1 2 3]

[handwritten: 22nd Day]

That is, the 1st day of the 1st month compliments the 1st day of the 7th month. The first day can be considered the Holy New Year's Day and the latter Israel's original New Year's Day. The 7th day of the 1st month compliments the 10th day of the 7th month. The 14th day of the 1st month compliments the 22nd day of the 7th month. And of course, the two Feasts' lunar days always matched each other.

Perhaps Ezekiel is communicating something in a hidden sort of way. Before these alterations are made, the Law can be seen as being "asymmetrical". With these new additions, these come to make the Law "symmetrical" in the coming New Covenant Kingdom. The message seems to be that the Law is out of balance in its original state and is being "corrected" with Ezekiel's alterations. It is a rather trivial form of "correction" though. But perhaps it should be interpreted as being symbolically precedent setting in the same way the Passover is being expanded. It perhaps is paving the way for allowing something much more substantive to come in Ezekiel's future that will "supplement" the Law in a much deeper sense. This is very similar as to how the Prophet adds new benign prophecy regarding the Passover so as to argue the Passover is to "share" the date of the 14th with yet something else. Altogether, in what Ezekiel writes, it appears the Prophet is effectively blazing some kind of foreshadowing trail for something that is to appear and make similar kinds of revelations regarding the Law in it being inadequate in its original form. The very obvious revelation that Ezekiel is adding Offerings is the greater overarching message that is establishing this sort of precedence for suggesting the inadequacy of the Law.

4&5. Additional Offerings by Fire for the Feast of Unleavened Bread and the Feast of Booths: Here a natural break is made with these Offerings by Fire from the first 3 Offerings being exclusively Sin Offerings. The two 7 day feasts of Unleavened Bread and Booths are to have additional Offerings by Fire. These same Offerings are to be given for all 14 days. Notice too that all the other harvest Holy Days are skipped over in Ezekiel's testimony: the Feast of Weeks, Yom Teruah, Yom Kippur, and the 22nd day of the 7th month. So why is Passover and these 2 feasts the only part of Ezekiel's Holy Days schedule for his Offerings?

Again, given that these Offerings are for "atoning the house of Israel", these 2 additional feast Offerings must suffice for that purpose. Here more than anywhere else, the idea of "additional" atonement above and beyond what the Law prescribes seems to particularly stand out. That is, Ezekiel's first 3 Holy Days were for cleansing the sanctuary, a new sanctuary the Law did not know. So these first 3 apply more to the new Temple's cleansing than atoning. But now the feast Offerings are not particularly ascribed to the Temple and given they are multifaceted in nature and are for 7 day periods, this seems to symbolize something much greater akin to an era of some kind. And an era associates with a certain population of People/Saints who exist during that era. Hence, the Offerings of the Feasts perhaps are accounting for a specified population of Israel's People that represent more people than what ancient Israel was represented by in the Law's original Feast Offerings.

In addition, here is where the Ezekiel's missing libations begin to become particularly noteworthy. Since no Sin Offering is to have a grain or drink offering, the first 3 Offerings being without libations is simply being consistent with the Law's Sin Offering ordinance. But starting with the Feast of Booths here is where the Law has a great number of Offerings with libations. With Ezekiel he records none for his additional Offerings for Booths. So what does it mean that the Law's Booth Offerings have libations whereas Ezekiel's Offerings for the same feast do not have any? The same situation is true for Ezekiel's last 3 Offerings as well.

6&7. Additional Offerings by Fire for the Sabbaths and the New Moons: Interestingly, the New Moon becomes a new day upon which the People are predicted to come to worship at the Temple along with the Sabbath. The Law prescribes Offerings by Fire for the New Moons but makes no mention of it being a day of worship. Num 10:10 perhaps hints at the idea. But here in Ezekiel it is made official for Ezekiel's Kingdom. Isaiah also predicts the same only he envisions the Nations, plural, are expected to come and worship God on these days (Isa66:23). The context of Isaiah's passage implies that this prophecy is to be fulfilled in the coming Future Eternity and why Ezekiel's Kingdom should be seen as being consistent with this expectation.

On the days of the Sabbaths and New Moons, the East Gate to the Temple is to be opened all day. There the Prince and the People are to worship. If the Prince wishes to offer other voluntary Offerings on an arbitrary day, the same gate is to be opened for this Offering and shut after the Offering is given. In the same context, it is pointed out that at all the other appointed Holy Days besides these, the North and South Gates are to be opened and the People are to walk through the Temple grounds as they worship but are commanded not to turn around and go out the same way they came in. In this telling, it would seem that the Holy Days are reserved for special celebration and for promoting the trafficking of the People perhaps to allow larger numbers of worshippers to be allowed access to the Temple than what is to be allowed on the Sabbaths and New Moons.

Appointment Offerings: The Law versus Ezekiel

Title	Day of Reckoning	The Law	Ezekiel	Status
New Year's Day?	1st Day 1st Month		45:18-19 No Libation	Add
???	7th Day 1st Month		45:18-20 No Libation	Add
Passover?	14th Day 1st Month		45:21-22 No Libation	Add
Feast of ULB	15th – 21st Days 1st Month	Num28:19-24 No Libation	45:23-24 No Libation	Add
Head 1st Fruits	After the Sabbath	Lev23:12-13 Libation		No Change
Feast of Weeks	50 days after Head 1st Fruits	Lev 23:18-19 Libation Num28:26-30 No Libation		No Change
Yom Teruah	1st Day 7th Month	Num29:2-5 No Libation		No Change
Yom Kippur	10th Day 7th Month	Lev16:5-10 No Libation Num29:8-11		No Change
Feast of Booths	15th – 21st Days 7th Month	Num29:13-34 16th-21st Libation	45:23-25 No Libation	Add
Last Day	22nd Day 7th Month	Num29:36-38 Libation		No Change
Sabbath	Every 7th Day	Num28:9-10 Libation	46:4-5 No Libation	Add
New Moon	Every 29/30 Days	Num28:11-15 Libation	46:6-7 No Libation	Add

And once again, there are no libations for either Offerings of the two days. So what does it mean that the Law's Offerings for the Sabbaths and New Moons contain libations but Ezekiel's do not?

Ezekiel's Ordinances which change the Law's

The observant reader should recognize that Ezekiel is progressing from least altering ordinances to more altering ordinances with respect to the Law as the Holy Days testimony moves along. He first introduces those things that are to be "added" to the Law's Offerings. Now Ezekiel will identify what "changes" are to be had in comparison to the Law in Ezekiel's Kingdom:

Ezek 46:11 "And at the festivals and the appointed feasts the grain offering shall be an <u>ephah</u> with a bull and an <u>ephah</u> with a ram, and with the lambs <u>as much as one is able to give</u>, and <u>a hin of oil</u> with an ephah.

What the Law commands for the Grain Offerings in Numbers 15 is 3/10th of an ephah for a bull, 2/10th of an ephah for a ram and 1/10th of an ephah for a lamb. The oil portions are to be a ½ of a hin of oil for a bull, a 1/3rd of a hin of oil for a ram and a 1/4th of a hin of oil for a lamb. It should be obvious that the new portions Ezekiel specifies are much larger than those of the Law:

Ezekiel's Grain/Oil Offering portions altered from Law

	bull		ram		lamb	
	Law	Ezekiel	Law	Ezekiel	Law	Ezekiel (not Daily)
Ephah of Grain	3/10th	1	2/10th	1	1/10th	As much as can give
Hin of Oil	½	1	1/3rd	1	1/4th	1 per ephah
Hin of Wine	½		1/3rd		1/4th	

So just as there is found more Atonement Offerings predicted for the House of Israel, so too the Grain Offering portions are to be much larger. This further suggests Remnant Israel is expected to be comparatively larger in size than that of Ancient Israel and hence the reason for why there are to be more Offerings and greater portions of Offerings. Thus, this is the reason why more ordinances need to be added for Ezekiel's Kingdom above those the Law prescribes. It appears that simple.

Ezekiel's Ordinance which ends a Law's Offering

The basic conclusion so far is that Ezekiel's additional Libationless Offerings seem to imply that the House of Israel is to be relatively larger and hence the reason why there are more atoning Offerings than what the Law prescribes. Ezekiel's last and 8th Offering he testifies to reinforces this same idea but in its own unique way. It happens to be the most provocative ordinance Ezekiel proposes. Contextually, the reader has been led to this point by first being presented with the lesser difficult testimony of the "additional" Offerings and then the more difficult testimony of the "changes" to be made to the Grain Offerings. Now the reader is being presented with the most difficult testimony which communicates an elimination of an Offering.

And not just any Offering. Ezekiel's testimony brings an end to the Daily Evening Offering for Ezekiel's Kingdom! Recall that Eze 45:17 opened Ezekiel's Holy Days testimony by first identifying what Offerings were to remain being given from the Law. Strangely, the Daily Offerings are not listed there. Hence, the reader is to come to the realization that Ezekiel's Daily Morning Offering is in fact to take the place of the Daily Morning and Evening Offerings the Law prescribes. The entire context of the Scripture disallows any other form of interpretation.

Ezekiel's Daily Offering(s) removed/altered from Law

Title	Day of Reckoning	The Law	Ezekiel	Affect to Law
Daily	Every Day	Morning & Evening Num28:3-8 Libation	Morning Only 46:13-15 No Libation	Replaces

Furthermore, this Daily Morning Offering is to have a unique Grain Offering. And again it happens to be larger than the Law's Grain Offering as well:

Ezekiel's Grain Offering portions for the Daily Offering

	Lamb for Daily Offering(s)	
	Law	Ezekiel
Ephah of Grain	1/10th	1/6th
Hin of Oil	1/4th	1/3rd
Hin of Wine	1/4th	

And thus the reader is left with the most difficult thing to try to comprehend just as Ezekiel's Holy Days testimony comes to an end. Presumably, if there are more People to atone for in Remnant Israel in comparison to Ancient Israel, as has been conjectured thus far, by making the previous Daily Morning Offering having a Libation now be without one, follows this basic prescription of more Atonement Offerings for Ezekiel's Kingdom. But what permits these changes to be made? What significance do the original Daily Offerings have and why can one be eliminated altogether and the other have its Libation removed?

It further reinforces the basic implied message that Offerings with Libations have no Atonement efficacy for their existence but have some other purpose. What is also being implied is that whatever these Daily Offerings were representing, or symbolic of, has passed in needing representation by the time Ezekiel's Kingdom is to be established. Here again is a huge clue that each Holy Day and Occasion is symbolic of something beyond itself.

The Daily Evening Offering has always been mysterious because it is the only Offering to be presented at twilight, except for one twilight in the year. And here is where perhaps Ezekiel is again hinting to the Gospel message. The Daily Evening Offering comes to be presented at the same time the Passover is to be offered, only the Passover is not offered by the High Priest but by each Household of Israel. It would seem as if this particular Offering is being brought under the Lamp of inspection here and identified as some kind of Offering that will not be needed later on. So in some sense ***the Daily Evening Offering seems to be an ELEMENT OF FORESHADOW that is to go away when its symbolism it foresees comes to pass and is fulfilled***. Since no other elements of the Holy Days are to see an elimination of this kind, it seems to suggest that this is the only Symbol of its Kind in all of the Holy Days testimony in it being an ELEMENT OF FORESHADOW. As to why the Daily Morning Offering is permissible to have its Libation removed will require more study and analysis of the Holy Days Code.

7 Final Transformations of the Passover Memorial

For the observant reader, the Passover and Feast of Unleavened Bread takes on a transforming kind of embellishment as Scripture's testimony proceeds beyond Exodus 12 and 13. With Ezekiel's testimony, this will bring the final metamorphosis to this Holy Occasion some 800 years beyond the Law. There are basically 7 new things that will change the Passover memorial in Ezekiel's Kingdom:

The final 7 Transforming Elements the Passover Memorial is to acquire:

1.   Ezekiel's City will be the place where the memorial will be observed forever by Ezekiel's House of Israel.

2.   Ezekiel's "Prince" is to administer the elements of the Offerings.

3.   Since the Morning Offering is to change in Ezekiel's Kingdom according to Ezekiel's ordinance, then on the morning of the 14th Day the Morning Offering is to change from what the Law prescribes. Along with the Morning Offering, a Sin Offering is to be given for the Prince and the House of Israel. In addition, now this same day will also have the Law's 1st ULB offering on this day instead of on the 15th.

Unleaven Bread

4.   Since the Evening Offering is to be eliminated in Ezekiel's Kingdom according to Ezekiel's ordinance, on the close of the 14th Day the Passover sacrifice is to be given alone without the Evening Offering.

5.   Ezekiel's ordinances calls for additional Offerings for each of the 7 days of the Feast of Unleavened Bread. But he accounts the first day to fall on the 14th, not the 15th. Hence, the Law's ULB offerings will start on the 14th and end on the 20th day in Ezekiel's Kingdom.

6.   Since one of Ezekiel's ordinances calls for additional Sabbath Offerings this means on the Sabbath of the Feast of Unleavened Bread there will be more Offerings to give.

7.   Ezekiel's ordinances calls for the Grain Offerings to change for Ezekiel's kingdom. Hence, all of the Memorial's Offerings will have a changed Grain Offering to go with them.

Eze46:14: The Last of the Everlasting Ordinances

Imbedded within Ezekiel's last and provocative piece of Holy Days testimony, there is yet another subtle but profound message being communicated in the original Hebrew text. The Law comes to point out at least 20 ordinances which are each defined as an "everlasting ordinance". Mysteriously, the Daily Offerings, established on Mount Sinai, are not defined as being an "everlasting ordinance"! But now here, suddenly in the middle of this last ordinance of Ezekiel's, in establishing a Daily Morning Libationless Offering, a form of this familiar phrase appears here in Ezekiel's Daily Offering testimony for the very first time and the very last time in Scripture!

English translations have completely missed the significance of what is being communicated here. It would be enough to declare Ezekiel's Daily Morning Offering as an "everlasting ordinance". But the Prophet goes one GIANT step further. The declaration is made of the "everlasting ordinances", plural! It is the only place in all of Scripture where this phrase comes in its PLURAL FORM. In other words, the moment had finally arrived when the "LAST everlasting ordinance" of the Law had come to be revealed and so immediately upon this revelation, the total summation of the "everlasting ordinances" had been given! The Law was forbidden in making such an announcement since it is left in a state of incompleteness without Ezekiel's additional ordinances!

What this means is that upon Ezekiel's Kingdom being established, and with the additional fulfillment of Ezekiel's ordinances, the entirety of the everlasting divine ordinances are to first become fulfilled. It is yet one more profound witness to the idea that the Law, and Ezekiel's alterations to it, are to be carried out forever thereafter, time without end! What else can "everlasting ordinances" be interpreted as being?

Diagram of Ezekiel's Holy Days and Offerings

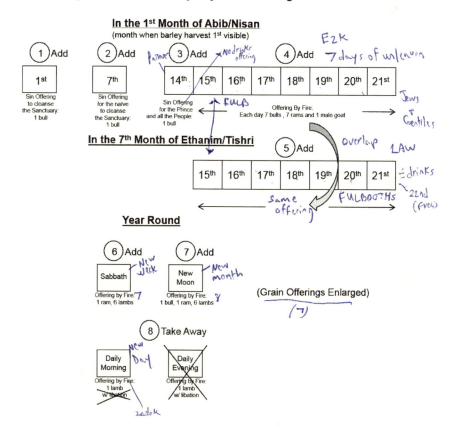

The Law and Ezekiel are pregnant with prophecy

In closing, Ezekiel's Holy Days testimony brings sudden and provocative new revelations to the Holy Days testimony. At the heart of this testimony is the additional Offerings that are to bring atonement to the House of Israel. Suspiciously, Passover comes to be at the heart of what is to change. These changes, along with all the other ones the Law brings to the occasion, are just too many hints suggesting that the date of Passover is prophetically pregnant awaiting a future birth to reveal what these symbolisms are pointing to. And the very Holy Days events the Prophet chronicles are too suspicious not to recognize that they are communicating their own symbolically encoded message. Ezekiel, more than any other prophet after Moses, clearly suggests there is a Code to be decoded within the Holy Days testimony.

Haggai's Prophecy of 21st day of the 7th Month

It was King Cyrus of Persia who gave the permission for the Jewish Exiles to return to the Land of Israel from Babylonia in and around 535BC/BCE. He also gave permission for the Temple to be rebuilt. Zerubbabel, the "governor of Judah" and Joshua, the High Priest, were the two leaders who led some 42,000 Exiles and their 7,000 servants back to their fathers' Homeland. The rebuilding began soon after the Exiles had arrived. But shortly thereafter, the surrounding peoples of Samaria were successful in convincing the Persian authorities to halt the rebuilding while they also confounded the Exiles and their efforts.

These halted conditions remained this way for approximately 18 years. It was at that time when the prophet Haggai along with the prophet Zechariah arose with a Word from God for the returned Exiles. By then the People had taken up permanent residence within homes they had built. So through Haggai God would complain to them that the Peoples' houses had been built but His House was left in ruins!

Haggai speaks to Zerubbabel and Joshua on the 1st day of the 6th month in telling them to restart the rebuilding(Hag1:1-11). They and the rest of the Remnant of Israel obey and begin anew on the 24th day of the 6th month (Hag1:12-15).

Then some 27 days later, on the 21st Day of the 7th Month, what happens to be the last day of the Feast of Booths, Haggai receives an amazing prophecy:

Hag2:6-9 "...Once more in a little while, I am going to shake the heavens and the earth, the sea also and the dry land. I will shake all the nations; and they will come with the wealth of all nations, and I will fill this house with glory...the latter glory of this house will be greater than the former...and in this place I will give peace, ' declares the LORD of hosts."

Many interpreters have had difficulty understanding this prophecy in imagining how the 2nd Temple and its history could ever measure up to what is being predicted. But then several days later more prophecy comes that is meant to further clarify what was first said...

Hag2:21-22 "I am going to shake the heavens and the earth. I will overthrow the thrones of kingdoms and destroy the power of the kingdoms of the nations; and I will overthrow the chariots and their riders, and the horses and their riders will go down, everyone by the sword of another...

Hence, the "shaking" is actually a very literal and unique cataclysmic event followed by a great reformation, something that never came to be true surrounding the 2nd Temple. So the best interpretation is that the circumstances of Haggai's day are acting to be a foreshadow, and not a literal fulfillment, of what must become similar future circumstances surrounding an ultimate Temple, arguably Ezekiel's Temple to be exact. When all the pieces are assembled it will be discovered that the last day of the Feast of Booths, the day on which this prophecy was first given, is yet another mystery day of huge significance within the Holy Days Code.

Zechariah's Feast of Booths Prophecy

To feed fuel upon this fire regarding the Feast of Booths, and upon Haggai's "shaking" prophecy, his prophet companion Zechariah adds what must be an inferno. Here is Zechariah's telling revelation regarding the Feast of Booths:

Zech 14:16 Then it will come about that any who are left of all the nations that went against Jerusalem will go up from year to year to worship the King, the LORD of hosts, and to celebrate the Feast of Booths.

The context of Zechariah's prophecy is visions for Israel's coming Kingdom. Zechariah predicts that the "nations" are to come up against Jerusalem in the latter day and be annihilated by the Wrath of God. Of course, this all ties in with the great "shaking" that Haggai was told about. Out of his prophecy comes the same result, the Nations respond and come with their wealth. So here too it is predicted that those that "survive" the confrontation will be convinced to come to Jerusalem to worship God during the Feast of Booths.

The main question this raises is why is the Feast of Booths, in particular, to be the period of Holy Days when all the Latter Day Nations are to be observant along with Israel? Why do they not have to go up for the Feast of Unleavened Bread? Here is yet another very powerful clue indicating that the Divine Plan has made the Feast of Booths representative of the coming Kingdom. With these clues of especially Ezekiel, Haggai and now Zechariah, the evidence is simply too much to ignore and should give the reader all the initial clues needed to go in search of answers to what all the Holy Days symbols are depicting on a deeper level, to search for what can be found decoding the Holy Days Code.

The Passover of the Jews was near, and Jesus went up to Jerusalem

John 2:13

Chapter Ten

Gospel Testimony of the Holy Days

Having studied the Hebrew Scripture's testimony of the Holy Days, the student is now prepared to turn attention to the Holy Days testimony of the Gospel accounts. The reader who is familiar with the Law is most prepared to take in all that what is being presented. Having the capacity to read the Gospel in the original Greek has its advantages as well as will be shown in this chapter.

Given that there are 4 accounts to consult, various angles are provided for the reader in which to witness the life of Jesus. John' Gospel is especially noteworthy here because he uses the Holy Days as a means of telling time as it transpires through Jesus' ministry. But of course, the greatest connection that the Gospel testimony will make with the Holy Days will be the noticeable overlap of Jesus' final mortal days with the Passover Season. Given that the Gospels spend nearly a third of the text on these final days it is a monumental convergence with Passover that has escaped virtually no one's attention.

However, there has been a great traditional interpretative blunder that has since prevailed over the text. Its outcome has been most tragic. Christian Doctrine argues for Jesus' Crucifixion, Death, Burial and Resurrection as being the culminated "End" to all things prophetic. But let the eye take a much more closer look into these occasions to discover that just the exact opposite can be concluded. Rather than these occasions bringing an "End" to matters, it becomes instructive as to how it actually is a monumental "Beginning" to the great Divine Harvest that began with the Resurrection of Jesus Christ.

Take an even closer look, and a reader can find that the text contains the means for unraveling a Code that is to be found imbedded within the Holy Days testimony. What will be presented in chapters to come will be the discovery of 4 basic "Decryption Keys" that will unlock the hidden meanings behind the treasure trove of symbolisms that inundate the Holy Days testimony. This chapter will come to document the various places where the Holy Days testimony is both relatively visible and invisible within the Gospel testimony.

What will become discovered is that reckoning of time will become especially tricky the closer a reader approaches the final events of the Gospel. Most shocking of all is to find that the crucial moments, those of the Last Supper, the Crucifixion, the Burial Period, and the Resurrection are each as if to be mystifying pieces of a Brain Teaser of a Puzzle to solve. But lo and behold, here is where the greatest connections are being made with the hidden realities of the Holy Days mysteries, mysteries that have come to be pointed out in previous chapters. As it turns out, Scripture creates a paradoxical testimony. In a nutshell, the Holy Days testimony will come to solve the Gospel mysteries while the Gospel testimony will come to solve the Holy Days mysteries. But none of this takes place unless both testimonies and mysteries are solved together. It is a sort of Grand Interdependent Revelation that is not solvable unless both sides of the testimonies are put on the table and grappled with together. Take either testimony off the table and nothing is resolvable.

What it appears that this textual testimony is witnessing is the Divine Mind creating a message that mesmerizingly and paradoxically cannot be solved unless both testimonies are intertwined with one another, each reinforcing the other in a self-closed loop of revelation that the Human Mind has a hard time wrapping itself around. The only explanation for why this is done is so that neither the Law nor the Gospel can be made to be a standalone revelation without the aid of the other. The two are eternally interlocked within each other in a most mindboggling way. What this first initial message represents is a "crack" in the Holy Days Code, an initial "breaking of the Code" which leads the curious reader to sift through the testimony for further clues to solving the riddles of the Holy Days Code.

This intertwining intimacy that the Gospel forms so happens to be with the mystery First Fruits testimony and how traditional Jewish interpretations of the mystery passages created dueling interpretations of the Passover that prevailed in that day. Alongside this testimony there will also be an unlocking of the meaning behind the building blocks of the Code as they come to be used in the initial Holy Days testimony. How the Gospel "decodes" these building blocks becomes applicable in unlocking the meaning of these same building blocks where they are used in later Holy Days testimony. That is, the Gospel gives meaning to the first usage of the building blocks as they overlap with the initial Holy Days testimony which then indicates what these building blocks are communicating regarding the later Holy Days testimony as well.

Jesus' Ministry thru John's Holy Days Testimony

It is John who interleaves his Gospel with Holy Day observances to help establish when things were taking place in general. But it turns out that it is also possible to determine the length of Jesus' entire ministry if it can be argued John made these recordings for the express purpose of helping the reader determine the passage of time. Whether this is a proper interpretation or not, the number of distinct harvest seasons recorded in John are the following:

Season 1: Passover in Jerusalem: John 2:23

Between harvests: Four months before harvest: John 4:35

Season 2: Unnamed feast (Feast of Weeks?): John 5:1

Season 3: Passover in Galilee, feeding of the 5000: John 6:4

6 months later: Feast of Booths in Jerusalem: John 7:2

Between harvests, 3 months later: Hanukkah in Jerusalem: John 10:22

Season 4: 3 months later: Passover in Jerusalem: John 11:55

Season 1: Jesus' 1st Post-Baptism Passover

John opens his Gospel with an ominous proclamation that Jesus not only became the Son of God but that he has always been one of three persons of God. John will go on to recall many other occasions that reinforce the idea of Jesus' divinity. This was something the earlier Gospel accounts had only indirectly inferred and which John specifically emphasizes.

From here, John will introduce John the Baptist and recollect how he declared Jesus as the "Lamb of God who takes away the sins of the world". After this, John recalls the incident of Jesus turning water into wine at the wedding at Cana. Then John informs his audience:

John 2:13 And the Passover of the Jews was at hand, and Jesus went up to Jerusalem.

Passover is identified here for the first time in John and there is no explanation given for what Passover is. Because three other accounts had preceded his own, John perhaps sees no reason to provide details of what Passover is at this late stage.

It is at this occasion that Jesus, for the first time recorded, overturns the moneychangers' tables and turns loose the cattle which were used for the sojourning pilgrims to buy and use for sacrifices at the temple. (The Synoptic writers record something similar occurring but in Jesus' last week of life.) What is implied is that many people came to Jerusalem without bringing animals for sacrifice. These would be needed for the Passover and also volunteer offerings since the opportunity was greatest for the People to offer them on these mandatory feast days.

As was learned in the previous chapter, there were a few occasions where the king of Israel provided Passover sacrifices for all the feast goers. So what had progressed along these lines up to the time of Jesus was that arrangements were in place to simply have sojourners "buy" sacrifices for the sake of convenience. Because people came from many different places there was further business opportunities availed where money would need to be exchanged for the "accepted" temple currency in order to buy the needed sacrifices. So this whole affair turned into being an opportunity to make money which Jesus highly objected against.

In his anger, he explained that his Father's house was not to be a place for business. So the temple authorities approached Jesus and asked him by what authority he was saying and doing these things. He responded by telling them that if they were to destroy "this temple" he would raise it up in 3 days. The authorities remind Jesus that it had taken 46 years to bring the temple to the refurbished condition it was in at

125

that time. John lets the reader know that Jesus was not talking about Herod's temple but was referring to his own body.

Season 2: John's unidentified feast occasion

To make sure the next recognizable season is properly reckoned, a reader must be aware of the clue provided in the following passage of John recording a certain statement Jesus made:

John 4:35 "Do you not say, 'There are yet four months, and {then} comes the harvest'?...

When time is described falling outside the harvest season, this means that should a later passage come along making note of any Holy Day or feast this necessarily means a new harvest season has come. This is what actually happens between verses John 4:35 and John 5:1:

John 5:1 After these things there was a feast of the Jews, and Jesus went up to Jerusalem.

So between 4:35 and 5:1 a new harvest season has come, what is the second distinct season in John's accounting.

Since John does not identify this feast, one can only speculate. First of all, John will go on to identify 3 distinct Passovers in all within his Gospel along with one reference to the occasion of the Feast of Booths. Because of this it is unlikely John was speaking of any of these feasts and is perhaps referring to the third unmentioned feast, that is, the Feast of Weeks. Recall that this feast lasts for a single day and is also a day when no work was to be done. So it is also interesting to note that in verse 9 John states that the day being witnessed in chapter 5 was a Sabbath.

Furthermore, after healing the lame man on this day Jesus will later bring up the topic of the resurrection, an event he states that he will initiate with his own voice. Nothing about this occasion particularly warrants this discussion so it seems out of place. One clue may be that this feast day is to be prophetic of this great moment. And since Jesus' own resurrection will come on the Day of Head 1st Fruits, it would seem to correlate that this 2nd first fruits occasion also regards a resurrection that is to follow Jesus' own resurrection.

There may be more than one reason why John does not identify this feast day. Another is that he perhaps does not want this day compared with the day of Pentecost recorded in Acts 2:1, the date recorded when the first believers were empowered with the Holy Spirit. Yet another reason may be because this feast day is a mystery and it is understood that Pharisees and Sadducees had different interpretations on when this day was to be observed. For only 1 out of 7 years would the two interpretations agree upon the same day for the Feast of Weeks.

Season 3: Jesus spends Passover in Galilee

The next time a feast is identified is in the following:

John 6:4 Now the Passover, the feast of the Jews, was at hand.

Since Passover is the beginning of a harvest season then nearly a year has passed between John 5:1 and John 6:4 if John is in fact using the seasons to reveal the passage of time. On this particular Passover memorial Jesus is recorded having fed 5,000 men (women and children would make it more) upon a hill top where he taught them in the region of Galilee. It is interesting to note that all 4 Gospel writers recall this occasion. So here is where all 4 accounts converge and where John's recollection of time can be synchronized with the other Gospels when framing Jesus' ministry.

Jesus in Jerusalem on the Feast of Booths

Continuing, John's next place for identifying a feast is the following:

John 7:2 Now the feast of the Jews, the Feast of Booths, was at hand.

Here John recalls Jesus' brothers mocking him telling him to go to Jerusalem and reveal himself as the Messiah there. Eventually, Jesus goes and on the last day of the feast openly speaks declaring himself as the mediator for the eternal springs of living water, an inference of the Holy Spirit. It is believed Judaism had formed a tradition surrounding this day where pitchers of water were drawn from the pool of Siloam and poured out near the altar at the temple. Is this also suggestive of a greater meaning behind this feast, or at least the last day of this feast, in which an outpouring of the Spirit is to come to Israel?

This date, if assuming coming after the Passover of John 6:4, would be six months later. During this time Jesus is written to have taught in Capernaum. So again, this kind of passing of time is altogether reasonable.

Jesus in Jerusalem at the time of Hanukkah

Continuing with John's chronicling, the next passage identifies yet another important date in Jewish history:

John 10:22-23 At that time the Feast of the Dedication took place at Jerusalem; it was winter...

In the original Greek, "Feast" is not in this passage. Notice the passage refers to the fact it is winter, a time when no Holy Day exists, again a time between harvests. The word "Dedication" refers to the dedication the 2nd Temple had underwent due to its defilement under the Greek Seleucid ruler Antiochus IV Epiphanies. The Maccabean revolt had dislodged this hegemony and brought a temporary Jewish autonomy in the Hasmonean Dynasty. From this occasion the celebration of Hanukkah arose.

The speculation can be made that between John 7:2 and John 10:22 three months have passed if again the writer is conveying the passage of time. The entire passage between these two endpoints has Jesus teaching in and around the temple area. It could be that John is indicating Jesus stayed in or around Jerusalem from the time of the Feast of Booths to Hanukkah three months later.

The particular occasion has the Jews insisting that Jesus is blaspheming since he declares himself equal to God. Right after this passage, John writes of the incident of Lazarus dying whom Jesus later resurrects after having been entombed for four days. This event enrages the leaders even further so Jesus then decides to spend his time in a region called Ephraim until Passover arrived. In some respects then it was Jesus who was helping to arrange the timing of his death in order that it come coincident with Passover.

Season 4: Jesus' Final Passover

And so again the time of Passover was nearing:

John 11:55 Now the Passover of the Jews was at hand, and many went up to Jerusalem out of the country before the Passover, to purify themselves.

Here John informs the readers that the people would leave early for the Passover in order to have time for purification. As learned in an earlier chapter it was necessary to be undefiled in order to partake. The text around this passage mentions the fact that many people had heard of what happened to Lazarus and that many came anticipating Jesus to be in Jerusalem. But they knew that the authorities wanted to seize him if he were to appear so they were not sure if Jesus would appear. So, from Hanukkah of John 10:22 to John 11:55, roughly 3-4 months had transpired. Within a week Jesus would be crucified.

Chronology and Dissection of Passion week

This study now continues to follow the chronology leading up to and including the Last Supper, Crucifixion, Death, Burial and Resurrection of Jesus. All four Gospel accounts will need to be consulted to put all the pieces together.

Six days before Passover, 8th day of 1st month

To begin, it is critical to find the very first passage of the Gospels which directly links to the Passion week. This happens to be John 12:1.

John 12:1 <u>Six days before the Passover</u>, Jesus arrived at Bethany, where Lazarus lived, whom Jesus had raised from the dead.

Recall that the Passover comes at the twilight of the 14th of the 1st month, the month Abib or Nisan. Therefore, 1 day before Passover would be the 13th of the 1st month, 2 days the 12th, 3 days the 11th, 4 days the 10th, 5 days the 9th and 6 days the 8th. Thus, John 12:1's reference to "six days before Passover" is best understood to be the 8th day of the 1st month. Jesus approaches Jerusalem by way of Bethany from the east. He dines with Lazarus and his family that evening. There is no indication as to what possible day of the week it is here and it will not be possible to do so until further information is supplied. (As an aside, the Synoptic accounts, i.e. Matthew, Mark and Luke, convey that Jesus returns to Bethany each night beginning here and ending the night before his betrayal. John 12 reveals why. This is where Lazarus and his two sisters lived. This family was apparently very close to Jesus and is the reason he returns here each night.)

Five days before Passover, 9th day of 1st month

Further in John 12, it is stated:

John 12:12 <u>The next day</u> the great crowd that had come for the Feast heard that Jesus was on his way to Jerusalem.

The phrase "the next day" is once again the indicator of time. Recall that every nightfall brings a new day to Israel. Therefore, John 12:12 occurs on the 9th day of the first month determined from John 12:1 and Mark 14:12. Because Jesus had raised Lazarus not long before this, many people were seeking to see Jesus. This occasion came to be known traditionally as "Palm Sunday".

John 12 goes on to reveal the following:

John 12:13 They took palm branches and went out to meet him, shouting, "Hosanna!" "Blessed is he who comes in the name of the Lord!" "Blessed is the King of Israel!"

Time wise, this is now what brings all the Gospel accounts to the same moment since all 4 accounts mention this day. All 4 Gospel accounts discuss this Palm Sunday bridging John's account in time with the Synoptic's here. So is it in fact a "Sunday" as tradition asserts? The chronology must be continued so as to find the first day which would indicate a particular day of the week and then extrapolate back to this day.

Four days before Passover, 10th day of 1st month

Many have suggested that Palm Sunday took place on the "10th day" so that Jesus fulfills the symbol of the lamb that was to be taken in by Israel to be domesticated on the same day and then sacrificed on the twilight of the 14th as what happened in the original Passover (Exo12:3). Up to this point, the reader is inclined to believe that this day is the 9th day by John's account. But there happens to be a very small detail that only Mark's account contains that reveals the passage of a day not included in the other accounts. After describing the excitement of the people in declaring Jesus the Messiah, Mark follows with a rather anti-climactic statement that Matthew and Luke will not do in their accounts:

Mark 11:11 Jesus entered Jerusalem and went to the temple. He looked around at everything, but <u>since it was already late</u>, he went out to Bethany with the Twelve.

Since this would mean the end of the 9th day and the beginning of the 10th day, it appears that Jesus entered Jerusalem being hailed Messiah just as the 10th day was dawning. Matthew and Luke describe that other things went on after this occasion as if on the same day (see Matthew 21:1-16 and Luke 19:30-46). Hence Mark alone inserts the transition of a day coming upon the heels of the "Palm Sunday" incident.

Close of the 4th day from Passover: Mark 11:12-19

It will be discovered that between here and the Last Supper Mark will distinguish the most amount of time having passed compared to the others. John will not even account for these days leading up to Passover:

Mark 11:12,19 And <u>on the next day</u>, when they had departed from Bethany…<u>And whenever evening came</u>, they would go out of the city.

On this particular day, Jesus curses a fig tree for having bore no fruit for him to eat in his hunger. Later, Jesus enters the temple area and drives out the profiteers in the temple, cleansing it, now a second time (given John recorded a similar thing early in Jesus' ministry). This display of anger upsets the leaders who no doubt profited immensely from this business. So Jesus' death becomes imminent with his provocations. Notice that Mark recounts much of what Matthew and Luke do but reckons it a day after Palm Sunday instead of on the same day. Finally, nightfall approaches and it is now the beginning of the 11th day of the 1st month.

The 3rd day from Passover, 11th day of 1st month

Mark 11:20 <u>In the morning</u>, as they went along, they saw the fig tree withered from the roots.

Mark 13:1 <u>As he was leaving the temple</u>, one of his disciples said to him, "Look, Teacher! What massive stones! What magnificent buildings!"

      The above passages bound the day portion of the 11th day of the first month beginning in chapter 11. When Jesus leaves the temple area as it states in Mark 13:1, this suggests that the day's end was approaching and he was starting to make his way back to Bethany. Throughout this day this would be the time when Jesus would especially debate his adversaries. Matthew supplies the most Scriptural content as to the teaching of this day but there is some in all the Synoptic accounts with John not including any. An outline like format is provided below to describe the conversations Jesus had with those who tested him.

      Jesus is approached with 4 questions from Israel's leaders IQ1-4 (IQ=Israel's Questions for the Messiah), He ultimately answers with JA1-4 (JA=Jesus' Answers to Israel) and also asks them 3 questions, JQ1-3 (JQ=Jesus' Questions to Israel), and their answers IA1-3 (IA=Israel's Answers), and Jesus' teaching of 5 parables (P1-P5):

IQ1: By what authority do you come?

JA1: Jesus replies with his own question.

      JQ1: By what authority did John the Baptist come?

      IA1: No answer. (Jesus then tells 3 parables.)

      P1: Two sons are sent to the vineyard but only 1 actually goes to work. Meaning: Israel's prostitutes and tax-collectors became workers of the Gospel but the "religious" had not accepted the call.

      P2: The Vineyard owner sends his Son to his vineyard to collect the harvest but comes to be killed instead: Meaning: Israel's leaders would be guilty of killing God's Son the assigned Gospel harvester.

      P3: Wedding feast for the Son ends up with "outsiders" attending. Meaning: The Nation is invited to be a part of the Gospel but few respond so the Nations are also welcomed to receive.

IQ2: Should one pay Caesar's taxes?

JA2: Give Caesar what is due him; give to God what is due him.

IQ3: To what deceased husband is the 7 time widow married to in the resurrection?

JA3: No one. All become like angels, not entering into marriage. And, the physically dead are to be assumed yet living according to Exodus 3:16.

IQ4: What is the greatest commandment of the Law of Moses?

JA4: Quotes Deut 6:4, 5 (Love God) and Lev 19:18b (Love Your Neighbor)

(Jesus then baits them with a question.)

    JQ2: Whose Son is the Christ?

        IA2: The Son of David. (Jesus reels them in with another question.)

        JQ3: How can He be David's Son if He is David's Lord as Ps 110:1 implies?

        IA3: No reply.

    To summarize what is happening Jesus is being examined by the chief priests, the elders, the scribes, the Pharisees, the Sadducees and the Herodians. This comes during a time when all of Israel was invited to Jerusalem as it was a feast occasion to witness it. Jesus answers without flaw and sends his debaters scratching their heads. Thus he is found as a spotless yearling lamb of God ready for slaughter as witnessed by all Israel. His debating also proves that he was a literalist of the Scriptures and what literal conclusions can be drawn from them Jesus argues to his advantage. After he silences all of his foes, Matthew 23 has Jesus delivering a scathing message of 8 woes to all the leaders of Israel warning the greater Nation of Israel of them as everyone listens on. Just like the prophets of old, like Isaiah, Jeremiah, Ezekiel and Habakkuk, who came to warn Israel of pending judgment for forsaking the obvious, Jesus became a prophet of doom to the Nation of Israel as he delivers the Woes to Israel. Because he would be put to death without just cause, he predicted the destruction of his enemies who would arrange for his execution. And because these same ones would go on to persecute Jesus' followers, for this Jerusalem would be destroyed within that generation's lifetime (coming true around 40 years later in AD/CE70).

    Jesus then notices a widow putting in her small offering into the Temple Treasury and points out that she gave more than those who gave much. He then leaves the temple when his disciples turn and make mention of the splendor of Herod's temple grounds. Jesus unexpectedly replies to them that not one stone would be left upon another. As Jesus comes to sit on the Mount of Olives just east of the city, Peter, James, John and Andrew approach Jesus inquiring further about what Jesus had said regarding the temple. What Jesus tells them has come to be called the Olivet

Discourse. There he foretells the predicted signs of his Second Coming. Jesus essentially recounts the Hebrew Scripture's depiction of the cataclysmic Latter Days only now places himself to be in the center of what is to transpire.

In closing he teaches two more parables that day:

P4: 10 virgins and their oil lamps

P5: The Master distributes talents to His servants.

The message here moves away from predicting Israel's rejecting its Messiah to one that focuses on the calling of a people who will eventually receive him as their Bridegroom and Master who he admonishes to remain persevering until he comes.

After this, there will be no more public speaking that Jesus will do that the Gospel accounts reveal. What Jesus had done was seal his own fate. The end of this 11th day brought a close to the 2nd and most scathing public rebuke Jesus gave the leaders of Israel. The 1st was his entering the temple and overturning the moneychanger's tables and rebuking them the day earlier. Jesus had irrevocably humiliated and infuriated all the leaders of Israel into ensuring his own death on this second day.

From this point on, the leaders of Israel are in preparation looking for the right moment to seize him. But since during the day he was surrounded by so many admirers, it would become necessary to take him at the cover of night. As has been stated, each night he predictably passed through the Mount of Olives and then went off to Bethany to sleep. It was Jesus who here had provided the motivation for his execution. It was Jesus who was revealing the place and time of day to seize him with minimal restriction by repeating his nightly course for his betrayer to observe. Jesus was carefully planning the way in which his arrest and execution would come about unencumbered.

Two Days before Passover, 12th day of 1st month

The close of this day meant the approaching day was the 12th day of the 1st month as has been reckoned thus far starting from John 12:1. It is at this juncture that the text once again provides another indication as to what time it is:

Mark 14:1 Now the Passover and the Feast of Unleavened Bread were <u>only two days away</u>...

This provides a check to the chronology underway here and it does correlate with this passage.

The Synoptic account's next occasion is the visitation of Jesus to Simon the leper's house. This probably took place just as the 11th day was ending and the 12th day began. This entire day is basically a quiet day while Jesus allows his enemies to plan his death. During this visit, Matthew 26 and Mark 14 recollect a woman pouring expensive perfume on Jesus' head. Earlier in John 12, a similar incident took place where Mary, Lazarus' sister, anointed Jesus' feet with perfume using her hair to wipe them. There it stated that Judas was in charge of the money for Jesus and his disciples' affairs and that he was a thief who skimmed from this money. He complains there that the perfume could have been sold and the money given to the poor. On this occasion some of the disciples also complain that the woman could have given of her wealth to the poor. On both occasions Jesus rebukes them saying that the poor will always be among them but not him.

No accounting for the day before the Passover

Now what is quite odd is that there will be no direct accounting for the day before the Passover. The 13th day of the 1st month is not reckoned in the testimony. How come? Did nothing happen on this day worth noting? Or is there something being communicated between the lines here?

Preparing for the Passover meal

The week has now progressed to the preparing of Jesus' Last Supper, certainly unbeknownst to his disciples that it would be his last. This becomes apparent as the night approaches for Jesus' betrayal. Before another night falls, Jesus will be dead. After reviewing the Scripture accounts of these last hours of Jesus' life, it is evident that the Synoptic Gospels make a departure with John's Gospel with respect to WHEN this meal was eaten. But between the time when the people laid down their palm branches for Jesus at the beginning of the 10th day and up to this meal, John is silent while it is the Synoptic writers providing all the details. From here on in though, John's account reappears. And it is here that he deviates in a most shocking way with that of the Synoptic accounts. Furthermore, he recollects much more being spoken during the Last Supper comparatively with all the others.

John's account has been traditionally dated as being the last to have been written. He thus knew the content these earlier Gospel accounts had and undoubtedly saw need to add critically missing pieces of information. He mainly addresses two newly developing and antithetical problems of that day: those questioning Jesus' divinity and those questioning Jesus' humanity, in the rise of Gnosticism.

Here his accounting of the Last Supper deviates sharply from the other accounts. Whereas the Synoptic accounts appear to reveal that this Last Supper is THE Passover Memorial meal eaten on the 15th day of the 1st month, John's account can be deduced to insist on it being eaten a day earlier, at the close of the missing day, or what would be the beginning of the 14th day. Thus, for John, there is no missing day to account for. That is, his testimony supports the recollection that this meal indeed was prepared on the 13th day of the 1st month as the rest of his account corroborates this. Yet for the Synoptic writers it appears there is a day missing although they soon share a testimony that appears to reinforce John's testimony starting from the day of the Crucifixion.

Regardless of when the meal was eaten, the Synoptic accounts reveal the following:

Luke 22:7-13 Then came the day of Unleavened Bread on which the Passover lamb had to be sacrificed. Jesus sent Peter and John, saying, "Go and make preparations for us to eat the Passover." "Where do you want us to prepare for it?" they asked. He replied, "As you enter the city, a man carrying a jar of water will meet you. Follow him to the house that he enters, and say to the owner of the house, 'The Teacher asks: Where is the guest room, where I may eat the Passover with my disciples?' He will show you a large upper room, all furnished. Make preparations there." They left and found things just as Jesus had told them. So they prepared the Passover.

Mark and then Matthew reveal less then what Luke records. Regardless, they all insist it is the day on which the Passover lamb was to be sacrificed, which occurs at the end of the 14th day, and that the meal is the Passover meal, which is to be eaten at the beginning of the 15th day. The Passover meal was to be eaten in Jerusalem and in that day upper rooms were usually rented out for nonresident feast keepers according to Josephus, the 1st Century Jewish historian. In conclusion, all Synoptic implications point to the obvious exegesis that this is the Passover meal and this coming from Jesus' own mouth.

1st Mystery Part 1:
Why does John disagree about the Last Supper?

John's account now provides details that are unique to itself and necessary for this study. The following statement is made in John's Gospel with respect to when this meal took place:

John 13:1a It was just before the Passover Feast...

In other words, John writes that it is not the Passover meal but prior to the meal when the Last Supper was eaten. This reads as if to be a clear contradiction from what the Synoptic writers convey. Because John's account is later and more reflective and provides some interesting details left out by the others, along with further evidences that will be explored here, how can it be concluded that his accounting is not the more accurate of all of the previous ones?

Many have argued that John is insisting there is a theological importance for this meal having been something other than the Passover meal. Early on in John's Gospel, John recalls John the Baptist declaring Jesus as the Lamb of God. Therefore, John disallows Jesus EATING the Passover lamb and rather has Him BECOMING the Passover lamb. Besides John 13:1a, there are 3 more particular passages in John which INSIST that the day of Jesus' death is coincidental with Passover at the end of the 14th day which will be discussed shortly.

Bread and Wine prefigure Jesus

Much commentary has been provided for what Jesus came to say during his Last Supper with his disciples. But one passage that will be pointed out here relevant for the discussion at hand is found in Luke's Gospel:

Luke 22:15-16 And He (Jesus) said to them, "I have earnestly desired to eat this Passover with you before I suffer; for I say to you, <u>I shall never again eat it until it is fulfilled in the kingdom of God.</u>"

This is quite an interesting statement Jesus makes here. He acknowledges that the Passover will be "fulfilled" in the kingdom of God and that he would partake of it at that time when it would be.

Then, during the meal, he instructs the disciples to do the following:

Matt 26:26-28 And while they were eating, Jesus took {some} bread, and after a blessing, He broke {it} and gave {it} to the disciples, and said, "Take, eat; this is My body." And when He had taken a cup and given thanks, He gave {it} to them, saying, "Drink from it, all of you; for this is My blood of the covenant, which is poured out for many for forgiveness of sins.

Notice that Jesus does not associate himself symbolically with the meal of the lamb but of the bread and wine. Hence, he argues that the unleavened bread and the wine symbolize his sacrificial body. The unleavened bread signifies sinlessness. But wine was not a part of the original Passover occasion. This will be looked at more closely in a later chapter as it actually creates one of the Gospel's Decryption Keys that help decode the Holy Days Code.

The Betrayals and Trials throughout the night

During the Last Supper Jesus tells disciple Judas to leave and do what he must. Judas had planned to betray Jesus and now the time has come. Later that night, in the Garden of Gethsemane, Judas arrives with guards and betrays Jesus with a kiss.

All throughout the coming night, Jesus is put on trial. But what is so odd about this is if the Passover meal was eaten earlier that night this would imply that this was the 15th day of the 1st month, what was to be a day of "no work". Why do the religious leaders find it acceptable to put Jesus on trial if this is to be a day of no work? Many commentators suggest that this was done in the cover of night so that only they would know they were violating the command. This seems unlikely that this would be done. So the reader must make this one more piece of the puzzle to help unravel the two Passovers of the Gospel. One other thing to note is that the Pharisees do not appear again in the testimony until the day after the Crucifixion.

The Law requires that on the testimony of two or more witnesses a party was to be found guilty as charged. For the trial there came to be rounded up various witnesses, apparently bribed, in order that they speak against Jesus. But they cannot form a consistent testimony evidencing the effectiveness of the Law's decree for how to obtain truthful testimony. So the high priest resorts to directly questioning Jesus:

Matt 26:63-66 But Jesus kept silent. And the high priest said to Him, "I adjure You by the living God, that You tell us whether You are the Christ, the Son of God." Jesus said to him, "You have said it {yourself} nevertheless I tell you, hereafter you shall see the Son of Man sitting at the right hand of Power, and coming on the clouds of heaven." Then the high priest tore his robes, saying, "He has blasphemed! What further need do we have of witnesses? Behold, <u>you have now heard the blasphemy</u>; what do you think? "They answered and said," He is deserving of death! "

Clearly this guilty verdict is not based on any testimony of witnesses revealing Jesus had committed any crime. Rather it is based on how the Law finds it acceptable to put to death one that blasphemes or speaks as a false prophet. In short, because Jesus was declaring himself to be the one who was to one day fulfill Daniel's vision of the Messiah coming on the clouds of heaven it was this that the leaders equated with blasphemy. That is, on account of Jesus having made himself equal to God this was what the elders find worthy as to why Jesus should be put to death.

1st Mystery Part II:
Why do Gospels record back-to-back Passovers?

Because the Romans ruled the land, the Nation needed to seek Rome's approval of an execution of someone as popular as Jesus had become. The elders of the Sanhedrin, what was Israel's highest court, would have to approach the Roman Procurator Pontius Pilate to get his consent. It is here where John notes that they did not want to defile themselves so as to be forbidden from eating the Passover meal.

John 18:28 Then the Jews led Jesus from Caiaphas to the palace of the Roman governor. By now it was early morning, and to avoid ceremonial uncleanness the Jews did not enter the palace; <u>they wanted to be able to eat the Passover</u>.

The idea being that if gentiles did not abstain from being defiled according to the Law then Law abiders would necessarily become defiled coming into contact with them. This is the Law's basic concept of remaining purified through separation. Since Israel's community had become infiltrated by a Roman presence, remaining undefiled became a difficult task. So they do not enter Pilate's quarters and instead asked that he come out to them to hear their case. So once again, John is making the fundamental case that Passover was arriving just as Jesus was being arranged for Crucifixion. (Hence, there can be accounted 2 Passovers coming back-to-back. Jesus accounted his Last Supper as the first of two and John declares the next day as the second. How can this be? This is now a 2nd part to the 1st Mystery identified already. Solve one of the two parts of the same mystery and the other should automatically be resolved too.)

Pilate sought a way to appease the Jews while avoiding putting Jesus to death. So he had the guards beat him and then presented him to the Jews. But they sought Jesus' death even more arguing Jesus was a threat to Rome. Eventually Pilate reluctantly agreed to have Jesus crucified. Here John will mention what day it is:

John 19:14a Now it was the day of preparation for the Passover

Again, according to John Passover had not yet arrived. Soon Jesus would be led away made to carry his own cross to his death. He would falter on the way and another man, Simon the Cyrene, would bear his cross to the place of Golgotha, the place of the Skull, where he would be crucified at about 9am. Two others would be crucified with him. Jesus would utter 7 statements throughout his Crucifixion. From noon to 3pm, the sky went dark. So after having been crucified for about 6 hours, near his death, Matthew recalls Jesus uttering:

Matt 27:45,46 ..."Eloi, Eloi, lama sabachthani?" (translated: My God, my God, why have you forsaken me?")

This happens to be a direct quote of Psalm 22:1. It implies that the content of this Psalm of David was fulfilled in Jesus' Crucifixion. Soon after Jesus breathes his last.

John next communicates uniquely that the execution was hastened so as to prevent the crucified from hanging during the Sabbath that was coming:

John 19:31 The Jews therefore, because it was the day of preparation, so that the bodies should not remain on the cross on the Sabbath (for that Sabbath was a high {day}, asked Pilate that their legs might be broken, and {that} they might be taken away.

The testimony will go on to state that Jesus had already died and the Roman guard subsequently took his spear and pierced through his heart so as to ensure he was dead. John witnesses he was there seeing water and blood pour out. This was a sign that the blood had already separated meaning Jesus' heart had stopped beating for quite some time, indicating Jesus had died. The rest of Jesus' disciples were not particularly concerned with Jesus' body because they themselves were in hiding fearing for their own lives.

Joseph of Arimathea, a member of the Sanhedrin who did not agree to have Jesus put to death, came to Pilate seeking permission to take the body for burial. Matthew (27:57) and Mark distinctly recall this moment is having taken place in the evening. Mark and Luke corroborate John 19:3 in declaring it was a preparation day for the approaching Sabbath:

Mark 15:42 And when evening had already come, because it was the preparation day, that is, the day before the Sabbath...

Luke 23:54 And it was the preparation day, and the Sabbath was about to begin.

Now with Matthew and Mark mentioning that "evening had already come", this should alert the reader that this signifies a new day having arrived. It can be shown that all 4 Gospel writers designate this new day as the "preparation day" or the "day before the Sabbath". Thus everyone agrees that Jesus' Crucifixion came before the preparation day for the Sabbath. This means the Crucifixion fell on Thursday.

2rd Mystery: How can/Why does Matthew say Jesus was buried during back-to-back Sabbaths?

Matthew, Mark and Luke all recall Joseph of Arimathea taking responsibility of Jesus' body and preparing it for burial. John further states that Nicodemus, another elder that had approached Jesus earlier and became a secret believer amongst the elders, assisted Joseph in the burial. The ministering women who had followed Jesus would now shadow these men to see where they were placing Jesus' body. Joseph had purchased a tomb quarried from the rock nearby and there is where Jesus' body would be entombed. A large rock was positioned so that once the body was secured the stone would be easily rolled in place and left there. Luke recalls that the women went home and prepared spices and perfumes with the intention of returning and further anointing the body of Jesus after the Sabbath was over even though they must have known it would be impossible for them to roll away the stone (Luke23:56).

Matthew's account will now record the next major development:

Matt 27:62 Now on the next day, which is {the one} after the preparation, the chief priests and the Pharisees gathered together with Pilate…

Here Matthew mysteriously reckons the given day as "the next day, which is after the Preparation". This is a rather odd way of identifying the Sabbath day. So it seems there is something the reader is being alerted to with such an odd expression. On this day the chief priests and Pharisees would approach Pilate to get his permission to allow the tomb of Jesus to be sealed and guarded. It should be noted here that the Pharisees have not been accounted for since Jesus had debated them in the days leading up to his Crucifixion. They are not accounted for in his betrayal (only officers sent by them according to John 18:3), nor in his trials with the Sanhedrin throughout the night, nor the trials before Pilate and Herod, nor at his Crucifixion. But here suddenly they reappear. Where have the Pharisees been all this time? It is another clue to take in.

What they and the chief priests remember on this day is that Jesus prophesied he would rise from the dead on the third day. Also, recall that it is Matthew who quotes Jesus predicting that he would lay buried for three days and three nights just as Jonah remained in the belly of the fish (Matt12:40). So exactly what day is it? What Matthew is implying is that this day was "Day2" since the Crucifixion. The following day would then be "Day 3", the day Jesus predicted he would rise and the reason why these religious leaders plot with Pilate to seal the tomb. Mark, Luke and John too can be shown all agreeing to this 2+ days of burial as the

Crucifixion was identified coming on a Thursday, meaning that Jesus lay buried for a full day on Friday and a full day on the Sabbath so as to rise on Sunday.

Where the 3rd Mystery arises surrounding the Gospel though is when Matthew reckons the Burial Period uniquely, different from Mark and Luke (John has no equivalent reckoning). The following text provides the original Greek and a translation below it since Matthew's phrase in particular is never translated correctly:

Matthew28:1a	οψε	δε	σαββατων			
	after	but	the Sabbaths			

Mark 16:1a	και	διαγενομενου	του	σαββατου		
	And	passing	the	Sabbath		

Luke 24:1a	και	το	μεν	σαββατον	ησυχασαν	κατα	τη	νεντολην
	And	on	the	Sabbath	they rested	according to the	command

In first examining Mark and Luke, these provide the simplest testimony. They state a "Sabbath" had passed from the last point they had provided testimony. Recall this was the Sabbath that followed the preparation day. So really they are simply stating that the day before the Resurrection was a Sabbath. But when examining Matthew, his passage is mindbending, to say the least, when he testifies that "Sabbaths", plural, had transpired. Recall that Matthew had already made a strange statement in rephrasing the Sabbath as being the "day after the preparation". Hence, it would seem as if Matthew is accounting the preparation day and the Sabbath that all the writers witness as a plurality of Sabbaths, or, more to the point, back-to-back Sabbaths.

Yet how is that possible? This is yet a 3rd Mystery surrounding the reckoning of the Gospel Events. So what is going on here? John indicates that the approaching Sabbath was a "Great Day" or "High Day", as stated in John 19:31 quoted previously. So it would appear as if there is some religious terminology being used here in more than one place, either inspired by the Law or Tradition, that readers need to become educated about in order to understand what is being communicated.

Mark (16:1) will specifically recall Mary Magdalene, Mary (mother of James and John) and Salome buying spices after the Sabbath was over (instead of before the Sabbath as Luke had recalled in Luke 23:56). This means they bought the spices in the evening after the Sabbath and would bring them to the tomb on Sunday morning. (Markets most certainly were opened just as soon as the Sabbath ended as nightfall came because of them being closed for a full day as Amos 8:5 implies.)

3rd Mystery:
How to reconcile Jesus' 3 Days/Nights Prophecy?

If the Gospel writers all agree that the Burial Period began some time on Thursday night and lasted until some time until Sunday Morning that would account for 3 Nights but only 2 Days. Yet how is this to be reconciled to Jesus' Prophecy that

He would be in the heart of the earth for 3 days and 3 nights? He also said that he would arise on the 3rd Day. How do these statements reconcile with what actual time transpired during the Burial Period?

4th Mystery: Why is Resurrection Day reckoned as following and preceding Sabbaths?

What comes next of course is the reckoning of the day when the Empty Tomb was witnessed. Mark, Luke and John note specifically that the women came early in the morning seeking to tend to the body with the spices and perfumes. Mark even mentions the women were wondering who would roll the stone away for them. But upon their arrival they found the stone had been rolled away with the tomb empty inside. This means Jesus had already been resurrected sometime prior to their arrival. Matthew 28:2-4 states that an angel had caused an earthquake which rolled away the stone and frightened the guards sometime during the night prior to the women having come.

Now in reckoning the testimony regarding when the women came to the tomb, the original Greek text must again be consulted because the English translations are so misleading none of them are useful for understanding what is being communicated. How this visitation is reckoned first is by Matthew and Mark looking back from this moment, what was already studied earlier in Matthew recording Sabbaths having passed during Jesus' Burial Period.

What testimony follows after Matthew's and Mark's looking back from the Resurrection is what all 4 writers see unanimously looking forward beyond the Day of the Resurrection in reckoning the very Day of the Resurrection:

Matthew28:1b	τα	επιφωσκουση	εις	μιαν	σαββατων
	at the	dawning	into the	first	of the sabbaths

Mark 16:2a	και	λιαν	πρωι	της	μιας	σαββατων
	and	very	early	on the	first	sabbaths

Luke 24:1a	τη	δε	μια	των	σαββατων
	on the		one	of the	sabbaths

John 20:1a (&19)	τη	δε	μια	σαββατων
	on	the	one	sabbaths

So what could these strange statements be saying? Why do all the writers agree that the Resurrection Day is the beginning of a plurality of Sabbaths looking into the future? This is similar as to how Matthew sees a plurality of Sabbaths looking back into the past from the Resurrection in reckoning the Burial Period. So are these 2 mystery statements related? And why does tradition, evidenced in all of the English translations, assume that these passages are simply reckoning the Resurrection Day

141

coming on a Sunday? Is that all these writers are communicating with these strange statements? It does not seem so. So although, finally, all the writers come to agree unanimously on something, it turns out that what they do agree on is most cryptic and difficult to interpret. Here now is the final mystery surrounding the reckoning of the Gospel.

Altogether, the Gospel Events of the Last Supper, the Crucifixion, the Burial Period and the Resurrection create basically four reckoning mysteries to resolve:

1) How can it be and what does it mean that the Gospel testimony records back-to-back Passovers, one assigned to the Last Supper and the other assigned to the Day of the Crucifixion?

2) How can it be and what does Matthew mean when he records back-to-back Sabbaths as reckoning the length of Jesus' Burial Period?

3) How can the Burial Period be reconciled with Jesus' prophecy that he would be in the heart of the earth for 3 Days and 3 Nights while at the same time also stating he would rise on the 3rd Day?

4) What do all the Gospel writers mean when they see a plurality of Sabbaths looking into the future beyond the Day of the Resurrection? How does this help reckon the Resurrection?

Thus, just as the Hebrew Scripture comes with its many mysteries surrounding the Holy Days so too the Gospel testimony is found having similar mysteries regarding how it overlaps with the initial Holy Days starting with Passover. It would seem that what originally plagued Israel in its ambiguous testimony of the mystery Holy Day has now spilled over into the Gospel testimony. In order to ultimately resolve these mysteries, both the Law and the Gospel have to be consulted together as if needing to assume they were two revelations meant to be united together. The next 4 chapters will reveal how the Law and the Gospel consort in creating a Holy Days Code where a Divine Plan is imbedded in its many symbols, and a means in which to decode this message.

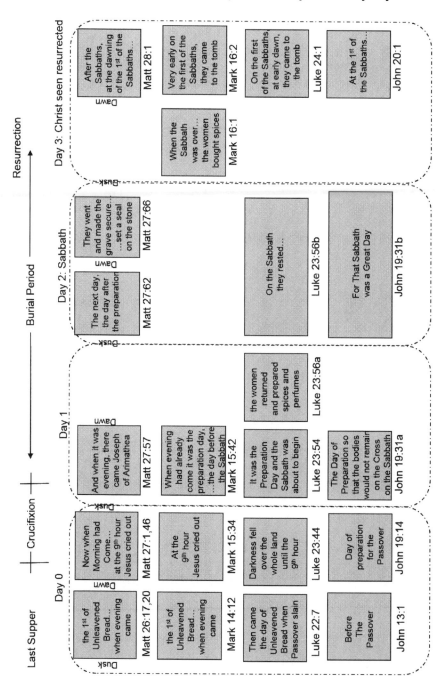

And (Jesus) said to them, "I have earnestly desired to eat this Passover with you...

Luke 22:15-16

"This is My body, which is for you..

This cup is the new covenant in My blood

(eat and drink) in remembrance of Me."

1Cor 11:24-25

Chapter Eleven

The Last Supper Decryption Key

A As the previous chapters have pointed out, both the Law and the Gospel contain mysteries that tradition has not been able to resolve. Thousands of years have passed with no solution in sight. Perhaps the problem is not the Scripture's form of communication but the human mind which cannot seem to conform to what is being communicated.

Starting from this chapter and over the next three that follow this one, the Holy Days Code will be dissected, one symbol at a time, to discover a rich and textured Divine Plan that emerges. The tragic news is that tradition stumbles before it can even begin to contemplate this Code. That's because it fell into and continues to remain held captive in its own trap when it interprets the Gospel testimony as if "replacing" or "fulfilling" the Passover of old. The argument made is that there are simply too many coincidences between the Passover memorial and the Gospel events overlapping them to think any other way.

But in fact there is a far superior way to understand these "coincidences" because of what can be discovered when thinking another way. Where the mind needs to naturally roam with these "coincidences" is back to the source where these originally came from. Should anyone take the time to compare notes between the Law and the Gospel, it would be found that the Gospel follows the trail the Law blazed for it. In short, what the Gospel is found doing is "mapping" or "pairing up" certain symbols of the Law with aspects of the Gospel, as if the Gospel were providing a "decoding" as to what meaning these original symbols are now taking on with the testimony of the Gospel.

Not all of the symbols make connection to the Gospel because some are reserved for Israel. Hence, Passover serves two purposes. What the testimony indicates is that this first symbol is shared between two things. Or another way to put it is that the Scripture teaches there are to be 2 Passovers in the Divine Plan, not 1! How this can be extracted from the testimony will be the main body of what this chapter is to review and provide evidence for. This evidence began in the Word of God, as has been reviewed in an earlier chapter, revealed as a morphing Passover Memorial testimony.

And again, this is where traditional Christianity stumbles, at the very beginning, when it insists the Gospel is replacing the original Passover. Thus, if it stumbles here, how can it go on and discover all the rest of the things that await to be found in the Holy Days Code? It tragically has never gone down the trail the Scripture has made for those capable of discerning the reality of 2 Passovers. Not surprisingly, this will only be the beginning of what challenges there are to be faced. Thus, one careful but bold step at a time is the only way to successfully make it down this trail.

So why should the Gospel share an idea emanating from Israel's Past? The most fundamental reason why is that it implies an identical Source from which both things emanate from, that being God Himself. But look closer to recognize the Divine Wisdom in how many symbols of the 1st Passover have mysterious parallels to the Gospel's New Passover without the need to argue one has "replaced" the other:

Elements of Passover	Parallel Elements in the Gospel
Israel's domestication of an unblemished lamb or goat	Jesus is tested in Jerusalem in his last week of mortal life
Israel's Passover	Crucifixion of Jesus
Israel's eating of the sacrifice and of unleavened bread	A believer's spiritual sustenance in partaking of Jesus
Redemption of Israel's 1st born for priesthood	Believers made as spiritual priests
Israel's Red Sea passage	A believer's baptism of the Spirit
Death of Israel's enemies	Satan's Dominion comes to an end for believers
Coincided with early harvest season	Jesus the first of those to be resurrected from the dead
Passover Memorialized	Jesus institutes the Lord's Supper as a memorial of His death
Male Participants must be circumcised	Believer is inwardly circumcised

So what evidence is there in the Holy Days Code that there is to be 2 Passovers? What will be discovered is that the Law creates 2 Paths of Holy Days. The first Path is the one created by the Feast of Unleavened Bread argued as being prophetically symbolic of Israel's Life starting from Passover on. Next, the Law also establishes yet another Path, a Mystery Path, composed of Sabbaths and Harvest Holy Days whose reckoning is left ambiguous. As the Gospel Decryption Keys come to unlock the Holy Days Code it will be shown that this Mystery Path is actually symbolic of the Church Age, what is to be understood as being a Mystery Age.

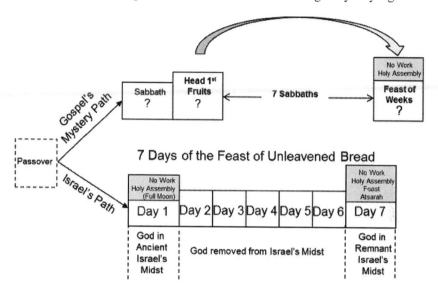

So the original path follows Israel's Life and Destiny. Now a new path will follow the Church's Life and Destiny. That there is a common origin of the Passover is the expression of God who implanted concepts that both can share in the symbols of the Passover, the latter coming a thousand years and more after the former. But the symbols Israel and the Church share through the Passover immediately end at the Passover. Indeed, Passover is the leading edge of the Holy Days Code. So beyond the Passover, as the rest of the Holy Days follow after, the two symbolic Paths will go their separate ways, at least in the testimony of the Spring Holy Days. This chapter is meant to understand how these 2 Paths come to share Passover as their common beginnings.

Passover & Harvest: First Clue of a Code

The strongest evidence that the Passover was symbolizing more than just the occasion of Passover, and something Israel had the capacity to recognize, is the fact that it coincided with the coming of harvest. Granted, the occasion had to come somewhere in the year. But that it came when it did, this is what interjects into the story of the Passover another element that had nothing to do with the events of the Passover. And when the final Holy Day is revealed in the Law it coincidentally comes at the end of the harvest. Again, there is way too much coincidence. Since not all of the Holy Days signify something to do with harvest, harvest simply is made the primary uniting theme and not its only theme. The fact that Passover and Yom Kippur are also made as part of the Holy Days interjects the theme of vicarious sacrifice into the greater harvest theme.

And the nature of how this interjection is made happens to be exactly the same nature as to how the 2nd Passover lurks in the testimony, by stealth and mystery. For starters, there are no harvest symbolisms being observed or instituted in the original Passover or its memorial. Yet, the very date of WHEN to observe Passover leads back to the approaching harvest. And by stealth, the Great Mystery Holy Day came later and its reckoning is entirely uncertain, and made deliberately so. Yet because it is THE symbol of the initial harvest, it interjects itself into the Passover by the simple fact that both occasions converge upon the same time of the year. The Sabbath is the other addition the memorial gains by a similar sort of stealth. Because the Spring feast was defined being 7 days long, at a time before the Sabbath was instituted, this occasion came to adopt a Sabbath once the Sabbath came to be instituted. And here again, the subject of the Sabbath plays a central key role in the Gospel.

Why this work classifies the mystery Holy Day as THE Great Mystery Holy Day is because of how it ultimately caused the Gospel testimony to witness there being 2 Passovers observed surrounding the Gospel. It is the very reason why there appears to be a confusing reckoning between the Synoptic writers and John. The reader is not directly told this but with meticulous attention to detail this truth can be deciphered. Thus this outcome implies why the ambiguity was put in the Law in the first place. It was so central to the establishment of how each New Holy Year was to be reckoned Israel was reminded of this mystery each and every harvest season. No doubt the question "Why?" was one that was asked from generation to generation.

That the Nation carried along 2 traditions as to how to interpret the Great Mystery Day is the greatest historical evidence of the sheer power and genius of this ambiguity. And so when the Gospel came along, the lingering effect of the mystery is found prevalent in the testimony. With 4 Gospel accounts to consult the writers became divided between themselves over this issue, with Jesus himself steering 3 writers in one direction while John was compelled to go the other way. Combined together they appear contradicting one another as the power of the ambiguity evidences it was capable of doing. And as history proceeded forward, Christianity adopted one reckoning while Judaism retained the other, as it is to this day. It is quite a shocking thing to behold.

Now the time has come to forever reconcile the mysteries if only because the Law and the Gospel are given the opportunity to speak as a unified witness in the pages to come. Put simply, the Law and the Gospel are found working together through the mysteries of the Holy Days Code to bring about a communication that can only be rendered by joint consultation between the two. Leave only one to consult and there is no resolution.

How the Law and the Gospel speak 2 Passovers

What this chapter will put forth is that the Last Supper, as the Synoptic Gospel writers have recorded it, is symbolic of 2 Passovers being put forth, not 1. And with John coming later, his point of view is that he is telling of another Passover that came on the next day. So the arguments proposed here are fourfold:

1) The Synoptic Gospel accounts communicate that Jesus observed Israel's Passover and thus the occasion is to remain independently relevant as the Law stipulates it being an everlasting ordinance. That Jesus ate the Passover makes it impossible for it to have symbolized himself. Thus Jesus kept the Law by partaking in the meal as all members of Israel are to do. Yet,

2) because Jesus took bread and wine and gave it to his disciples to eat and drink, things he did not partake of himself, this was symbolic of yet another Passover he was to become the next day, what was a new Path of the Divine Plan unfolding.

3) And because John's testimony offers circumstantial evidence for a 2nd Passover being observed the next day, this argues for the fact that there were actually 2 Passover observances in that year. Thus, there is to be understood 2 theological Passovers in the Divine Plan and that in the year of the Gospel there happened to be 2 actual Passover observances designed to communicate this as the Law and history helped to create.

4) This in turn implies that the Law and the Gospel worked together to create a 2 Passover observance for the main purpose of communicating there is to be two distinct Passovers henceforth. If the latter was to be interpreted as replacing the former, there would have been no Last Supper Passover meal for which Jesus himself would have partaken in. Instead he would have served the Passover to his disciples, refrained from eating it himself, and declared it represented his own body. What did actually happen was that he did eat the meal but later set aside bread and wine to serve the 2nd purpose. What this implies is that the Divine Plan uses the Passover as a shared launching point for two distinct callings creating two different Holy Days Paths.

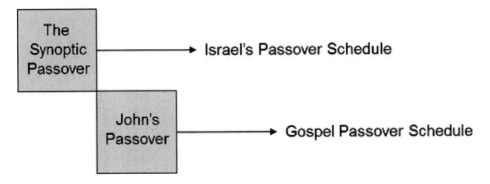

With these points summarized, they collectively create the first Decryption Key that helps resolve the mysteries imbedded in the Scripture. As the rest of this chapter will reveal, mysteries prevail in both the Law and the Gospel because the two were deliberately created this way to help resolve one another. This is the great harmonizing architecture constructed in Scripture that argues for the relevancy of the testimony from both halves of Scripture. That is, if the Gospel is not included in resolving the Law's mysteries, those mysteries will never be resolved. And likewise, if the Law is thrown out and not consulted in helping resolve the Gospel mysteries, then the Gospel's mysteries will never be resolved either. So if the two have to always remain relevant to solve each other mysteries neither one can ever be abandoned. This is the first great essential message that emanates from the combined testimony of the first Holy Days.

That is, the Law and the Gospel are to remain forever relevant. Before the Gospel appeared the Law was left in a state of incompleteness. As traditional Christianity has now shown over thousands of years, when the Gospel abandons the Law it remains in a state of incompleteness too. But bring the two together and a message appears that is greater than the sum of its parts as the rest of this book will reveal to its readers who boldly prepare themselves to read it. The first great challenge is the following: There were always 2 Passovers represented in the Holy Days Code and always will be. Judaism fails to recognize the prediction of the 2nd Passover and institutionalized Christianity fails to recognize the eternal relevancy of the 1st Passover.

How Law & Gospel created 2 observances

In order to fully communicate this theological point in the Scripture, it was deemed necessary to actually witness there being 2 Passover observances surrounding the Gospel. How this is done is by the Law creating the ambiguous reckoning of the Great Mystery Holy Day as was described in chapter 3. The key passage is Leviticus 23:11 where it states that "after the Sabbath" is when the Head First Fruits is to be waved by the High Priest. The barley was the first harvest of the season so its First Fruits were to be gathered as soon as they appeared and brought to the High Priest. No one of Israel was to eat any new harvest until this offering was given.

Where this day is defined is right after the description of the Feast of Unleavened Bread is given. Since "after the Sabbath" is not a sufficient amount of information to know for certain what Sabbath is being referred to, this is an ambiguous command. But since Israel was refrained from eating any new harvest until this command was obeyed, it was forced upon the Nation to decide what Sabbath was being referred to. That is, it was impossible to ignore this command if Israel did not want to violate the Law's injunctions. But since there was no certain date all Israel could do is "guess" at what date this was to be.

What is implied by this is that something in the future would ultimately come along and decipher this command, if the ambiguity had a purpose to begin with. In the meantime, Israel would move forward with some kind of tradition or traditions and wait until confirmation came along that what was being observed was the right date or it wasn't. An "educated" guess would thus entail careful analysis of all relevant testimony. Noticeably, Head First Fruits comes at the initial harvest season but so does the Passover memorial. Because of this, Judaism's earliest record reveals that two religious sects, the Pharisees and the Sadducees, each believed the Sabbath of Leviticus 23:11 revolved around the Passover occasion.

The Pharisees chose to believe the Sabbath of Leviticus 23:11 was the 15th day of the 1st month. It was this day that the Law stipulated the Passover meal was to be eaten on as well as be a day of "no work". Given the 15th day of the 1st month is a fixed lunar day so is the next day, the Pharisees' Day of Head First Fruits. This interpretation made the Passover occasion have a 3 day "fixed" schedule every year.

The Sadducees disagreed with the Pharisees interpretation of the Sabbath of Leviticus 23:11. They believed it was the 7th day Sabbath that fell within the Feast of Unleavened Bread. Hence, the Sadducees had no 3 day "fixed" schedule. In the illustration below, the two traditions are compared with the 7 possible scenarios for the memorial given a "floating" Sabbath day. In each of the 7 schedules, the 7th day Sabbath is the darker background day running down the center of the illustration. The dotted triangle in each schedule highlights the 16th day, the day the Pharisees' tradition interprets as the Day of Head First Fruits. The dotted circle in each schedule shows where the same Holy Day falls according to the Sadducee's tradition, falling after the Sabbath. Notice that only Schedule 6 is where the two traditions converge upon the same date of the 16th. Everywhere else the two are not in agreement.

Passover	Pharisees' interpreted Sabbath of Lev 23:11	Pharisees' interpreted Day of Head 1st Fruits
Abib/Nisan	Abib/Nisan	Abib/Nisan
14th	15th	16th

The Pharisees' (fixed) Holy Days Schedule

151

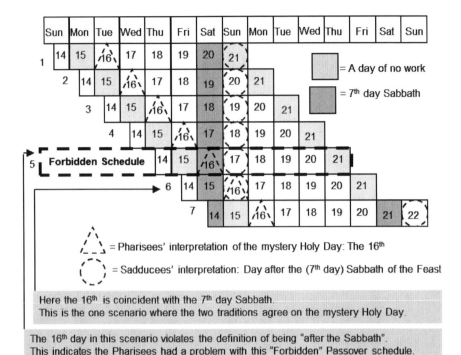

= Pharisees' interpretation of the mystery Holy Day: The 16th

= Sadducees' interpretation: Day after the (7th day) Sabbath of the Feast

Here the 16th is coincident with the 7th day Sabbath.
This is the one scenario where the two traditions agree on the mystery Holy Day.

The 16th day in this scenario violates the definition of being "after the Sabbath".
This indicates the Pharisees had a problem with this "Forbidden" Passover schedule.

The 7 "floating" Sabbath schedules for the Passover Memorial

But more importantly, Schedule 5 reveals where a problem arises for the Pharisees in their interpretation. It is called here the "Forbidden Schedule". Why this particular scenario should be considered forbidden is because the 16th day falls on the 7th day Sabbath. So why is this a problem? Leviticus 23:11 states that this mystery Holy Day is to fall "after the Sabbath". How can a day defined to fall "after the Sabbath" be found falling on a Sabbath? Because the Pharisees interpret the Sabbath of Leviticus 23:11 to be the fixed lunar day of the 15th day, sooner or later the 16th day itself will fall on the 7th day Sabbath and violate Leviticus 23:11. Although it should have been the greatest form of evidence to the Pharisees that this interpretation was not the correct interpretation, it did not deter the Pharisees from maintaining it as their tradition.

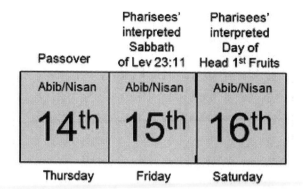

The Pharisees' "Forbidden" Holy Days Schedule

What is even more intriguing is that the Pharisees' interpretation is the one that continues to survive in modern day Orthodox Judaism! Since post temple Judaism essentially came to adopt the Pharisees' traditions, necessarily the competing tradition of the Sadducees was essentially abandoned. So this makes for an intriguing piece of modern day evidence suggesting this interpretation was in existence at the time of Jesus and even before his birth. And this is extremely illuminating, to say the least. Why? Because it supplies the perfect explanation for why the Gospel accounts can be found containing 2 Passover observances.

Gospel coincided with Forbidden Schedule

So how is this to be understood possible? Suppose the "Forbidden Passover Schedule" happened to be the very one that the Gospel events coincided with. What did the Pharisees do when encountering this predicament? They certainly would not have observed this Schedule without artificially doing something to "fix" the problem. But given this tradition lives on in modern Orthodox Judaism, perhaps it is just easier to consult modern day Judaism as to what it does in the years this "Forbidden Schedule" arises. So what does modern day Judaism do in the years the "Forbidden Schedule" arises? Few, if any, Jews or Christians realize that Judaism must be doing something similar as to what the Pharisees were led to do. What is done is that the appointment of Passover is "moved". Provocatively, it "postpones" the arrival of the month of Abib/Nisan by 1 day in its so called "Postponement Rules" tradition.

Why this practice is so hidden from view is because most understand these rules as being simply a calendar "adjustment". Everyone realizes that even the most modern calendars have adjustments made to them. For example, there is the leap year day in the modern Gregorian Calendar added every 4 years. There just is no perfect calendar that exists that does not need some form of correction. So too post temple Judaism has put into place subtle manipulations of their Hebrew calendar that appear to be necessary "tweaks" to keep the calendar synchronized with the solar year.

But take a closer look at these calendar "manipulations" and one discovers that the activity has nothing to do with making "corrections" to lunar-solar misalignments. They have everything to do with simply rearranging what days of the week the Holy Days come to fall on during the 7 month period that would otherwise be objectionable to tradition for one reason or another. And one of the "forbidden" days of the week that cannot be made a New Year's Day is specifically to prevent the Forbidden Passover Schedule from arising. That is, the Pharisees, and post temple Judaism, have never observed a Passover coming on a Thursday at sundown even though this schedule should arise on average once every 7 years. And since there is really no modern day competing tradition arguing against such a practice, as there was in the days of Jesus, there is no real opposition from the religiously devout Jewish community objecting to such a practice. With no one really objecting to this practice, the practice has become virtually invisible to nearly everyone.

But, in the days of Jesus however, the surviving tradition did compete with another tradition. This meant that the community would have been divided. One portion would have agreed with the Pharisees and observed Passover according to their traditions. The other portion would have agreed with the Sadducees and observed Passover according to their traditions. And in the peculiar years when Passover happened to fall on Thursday at sundown, the Passover would have been observed on two different days. But what the Gospel record implies is that the Pharisees did not "postpone" the Passover by a day but instead moved it up a day earlier. Perhaps this direction was more beneficial for those days when another competing tradition existed alongside it. Once the competing tradition faded however, the day could have been moved in either direction with little consequence and it appears there was more benefit in postponing the day rather than moving it forward.

Based on what all the reasons there are for why the Postponement Rules exist, it is very possible that avoiding the Forbidden Passover Schedule was the original most important reason for putting them into practice. The very provocative outcome this has created is that Judaism has never observed the Passover Schedule that reflects the original Gospel Passover schedule since it has now become "forbidden"! And traditional Christianity has not either! Thus, no tradition has ever followed the true Gospel Schedule. It is as if the Gospel was reserved its own Passover Schedule which tradition wants nothing to do with!

It must be recognized that the Law and its ambiguous reckoning of the Day of Head First Fruits is what caused all of this to come about in the first place. It was a deliberate thing that was done in order that the Gospel might be able to testify to there being 2 Passovers in the Divine Plan, not 1. It required the testimony to be written in such a way to encourage the 2 traditions to prevail within temple Judaism. Both the Law and the Gospel can clearly be seen working together to ensure this testimony came to be communicated the way it did. The confusion and bizarre nature of the testimony is certainly designed to motivate the truth seeker to find a resolution to this strange form of witness and eventually come to the conclusion, through perseverance, to discover that 2 Paths were built into the original Divine Harvest Plan.

Jesus uses 1st Passover to unveil 2nd

How all of the Gospel testimony begins to unfold a 2 Passover witness starts with the Last Supper. It is Jesus who directs his disciples to prepare for what was to be his last Passover meal. Nothing at first in the Synoptic witness suggests there is anything peculiar about this Passover other than the fact that the 13th day of the month is not accounted for. Why it isn't accounted for is because it happens to be the day this first Passover is being observed on!

Since his crucifixion would come on the next day Jesus would be prevented from observing the latter Passover. Thus, the earlier Passover appears to have made a convenient extra Passover for Jesus to use to accomplish 2 things:

1.   Observe his last mortal Passover Meal

                 and

2.   Usher himself in as a new Passover symbolized by the bread and wine of the latter part of the Supper.

Since Jesus partook of the Passover meal it is impossible for readers to interpret the meal as symbolic of his own sacrificial life. Thus it is to be considered an observance of the memorial. If this memorial was to be interpreted done away with and replaced by the Gospel then the Last Supper's Passover observance would not have been a part of the meal as John's testimony is seen doing. That is, the Synoptic writers remember the earlier Passover while John only remembers the latter Passover. The Synoptic writers however testify to the 2 distinguishable Passovers in the Last Supper while John never sees the early Passover at all.

During the meal, as the Synoptic writers remember, after Judas departs to betray Jesus, Jesus takes a specific piece of bread and a cup of wine and serves it to his disciples. He asks them to eat and drink of these things as a community so as to symbolize them ingesting Jesus' body and blood as if it were a spiritual 2nd Passover meal they were partaking of. Note specifically Jesus does not partake of it since it represents himself. Oddly, it is John who recalls Jesus teaching on the previous Passover from this one, in John chapter 6, how his followers must eat his flesh and drink his blood if they are to inherit eternal life. But he again emphasizes however that his words are spiritual and not to be taken physically literal. So the two realms of the Divine Plan retain their distinctions. Israel's Passover is physical and regards mortal life whereas Jesus as a new Passover is spiritual and regards spiritual life:

John 6:49-50 "Your fathers ate the manna in the wilderness, and they died. "This is the bread which comes down out of heaven, so that one may eat of it and not die.

2 Passover schedules complicate Gospel

Until the following day at sundown, the present day that began with the Last Supper was considered the 15th day of "no work" according to the early schedule for the Passover. As to the unaltered Passover schedule, it was the 14th day, a day which was only considered a "preparation" day having no special restrictions. And as can be noticed within the testimony, there is no mention of Pharisees anywhere related to the arrest and trials and actual crucifixion itself. These will only reappear again two days later in seeking to have the tomb sealed as Matthew records. So it would seem that the Pharisees are indeed remaining quiet on this earlier 15th day observance.

And as the Crucifixion testimony reveals, there are two opinions as to what was coming next in the timeline. Mark and Luke see a preparation day coming followed by a Sabbath day. Given that the earlier schedule's 15th day was ending here this meant the 16th day was coming, a day which had no special significance other than the Pharisees having made this the Day of Head First Fruits, a day where no special restrictions were to be imposed. Yet the Synoptic writers do not convey the idea the following day was to be interpreted this harvest occasion. So in this respect, Mark and Luke begin to deviate from the earlier Passover tradition starting here. It must be reiterated it was Jesus who recognized the earlier Passover and this did not mean the writers themselves were continuing to agree with the rest of its schedule.

John however sees a "high" day coming on as the Crucifixion ends. To him it is both the coming of Passover and a "Sabbath". With John's schedule, he does recognize the unaltered day of the 15th as being considered a Sabbath. But he is following the interpretation of the Sadducees who did not consider the 15th as the Sabbath of Leviticus 23:11. Yet because it is classified as a day of "no work", it would seem that both John and Matthew reveal that Jews in general had been considering the 15th day as a "Sabbath" nonetheless. Matthew is the Synoptic writer who conforms to John's schedule but in his own unique way when he calls the day of the Sabbath as the "day after the preparation". Here he is avoiding the use of the word Sabbath because he soon classifies both days of Jesus' burial as 2 Sabbath days back-to-back in 28:1. So this strange wording is just to prevent further confusion.

Finally, all 4 writers will end their testimony of the Gospel agreeing to the idea that the Day of Head First Fruits came after the 7th day Sabbath. So although they start out following two different Passover schedules, all of them in the end agree that Jesus' resurrection came on this first holy harvest occasion. Thus, all 4 eventually concur with the latter Passover schedule.

The two Passover schedules
of the Gospel testimony

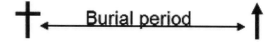

Schedule 1: Sadducees unaltered calendar

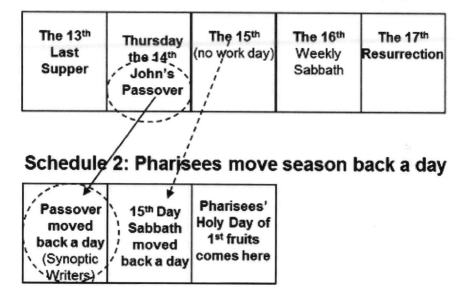

The 13th Last Supper	Thursday the 14th John's Passover	The 15th (no work day)	The 16th Weekly Sabbath	The 17th Resurrection

Schedule 2: Pharisees move season back a day

Passover moved back a day (Synoptic Writers)	15th Day Sabbath moved back a day	Pharisees' Holy Day of 1st fruits comes here

What Last Supper symbol is not part of Passover?

For the keen observer, there is a symbol Jesus used in his Last Supper which the Passover memorial did not have. That would be the cup of wine Jesus said symbolized his blood that would be poured out for the forgiveness of sin:

Luke 22:20 "This cup…poured out…is the new covenant in My blood.

Even though the symbol is not part of Passover it certainly creates interesting connections to the Law nonetheless. It happens to make up part of the 2nd Decryption Key for the Holy Days Code discussed in the next chapter.

Jesus' Death, Burial and Resurrection:
3 More Decryption Keys for the Holy Days

As was previously discussed, the Gospel testimony can be broken down into a 5 day schedule:

Gospel Schedule

1. Meal	2. Sacrifice	3. Sabbath Rest		4. Resurrection
Last Supper	**John's Passover**	**Day of no work**	**7ᵗʰ day Sabbath**	**Head 1ˢᵗ Fruits**
13	**14**	**15**	**16**	**17**

Here the Gospel chronology is understood being composed of 4 basic elements: Supper, Sacrifice, Sabbath Rest, and Resurrection. As can be observed each of the days beginning with the 15th day are unique building blocks which all the succeeding Holy Days after them are built out of. The 14th day happens to be a unique day amongst all of the Holy Days. The 15th day is the first Holy Day to be considered a day of "Holy Assembly" and a day of "no work". There will be more like it to follow. The 16th day is a Sabbath day, the first Sabbath of the Holy Season. There will be more to follow. Finally, the 17th day is the first harvest related day of the Holy Season. There will be more to follow. Every Holy Day that follows these first 3 Holy Days will be composed of these 3 things cited.

What the Gospel appears to be doing is providing what symbolic meaning is to be given to these building blocks based on what was coincidentally happening to Jesus as the very 1st Holy Days composed of these blocks were transpiring. And if these same blocks appear on successive Holy Days does this not suggest that the Gospel testimony is acting as a decryption code to what the later Holy Days are prophetically to signify as well?

The coinciding Crucifixion falling upon John's Passover has been recognized universally. Less so has Jesus' burial been recognized correlating with the 1st Sabbath "rest" of the Holy Season. And the Resurrection has also been readily correlated with the initial harvest season quite universally. With so much obvious connections being made between the Law and the Gospel these signs indicate that they are only the beginning of a correlation, they are only the leading edge, the tip of what iceberg of correlation is being established. Tragically, this whole connectedness has been traditionally interpreted as meaning the latter Gospel testimony was to be understood "replacing" the former Law and its Passover testimony. But nothing could be further from what is being communicated.

That is to say, if the Crucifixion is to be understood a Divine Offering should not a reader attempt to connect this in some way with all the Offerings by Fire that follow for each and every Holy Day thereafter?

And what about the Sabbath? Was Jesus' body lying buried during the very 1st Sabbath rest period of the holy season a mere coincidence or is there some greater correlation going on here? Are the later Sabbaths of the holy season to make some sort of correlation with Jesus' burial rest in some way? The evidence falls in favor of a deeper correlation existing.

Finally there comes the day Jesus is recorded having resurrected from the dead on the very first occasion of harvest in the holy season. It was the Day of Head 1st Fruits. It is a Day which can claim being the most mysterious and important of all the Holy Days. It was the telling moment for how Israel was to reckon the beginning of the holy season. So was the day chosen for Jesus' resurrection merely a coincidence of history in it falling on the very first harvest occasion? Or is it the evidence of evidences that points the way to the reality of the Gospel forming a great connectedness with the Law?

Indeed these 3 key elements of the Gospel, Jesus' Sacrificial Offering, his Burial Period and his Resurrection create an unmistakable correlation with the 3 common elements making up all of the Holy Days:

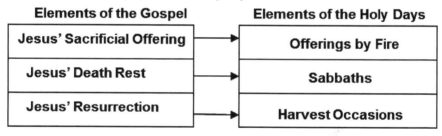

Elements of the Gospel	Elements of the Holy Days
Jesus' Sacrificial Offering	Offerings by Fire
Jesus' Death Rest	Sabbaths
Jesus' Resurrection	Harvest Occasions

In essence, this connection suggests the Gospel creates a set of 3 more Decryption Keys which are designed to unlock or decode messages hidden within the Law's Holy Days. Each key is designed to unlock the encoded messages for which it is assigned. That is, the Decryption Key of Jesus' Sacrificial Offering will be found unlocking or decoding an encoded message hidden within the Offerings by Fire for all the Holy Days. The Decryption Key of Jesus' Burial will be found unlocking or decoding an encoded message hidden within all of the Sabbath Holy Days. The Decryption Key of Jesus' Resurrection will be found unlocking or decoding an encoded message hidden within all the Holy Day harvest occasions.

The next 3 chapters will examine each of these 3 Gospel Decryption Keys one at a time. Each one will present a unique form of unveiling to the Holy Days Code. The message lying hidden within this code is a Divine Harvest Plan on a scale so grand it will span from Passover to the Future Eternity!

...you shall pour out a drink offering of strong drink to the LORD.

Numbers 28:7

...He poured out Himself to death...

Isaiah 53:12

And in the same way {Jesus took} the cup after they had eaten, saying, "This cup which is poured out for you is the new covenant in My blood.

Luke 22:20

Chapter Twelve

The Crucifixion Decryption Key

As the close of the previous chapter revealed, Jesus introduced a symbol into the Last Supper that the Passover memorial does not have. He used a cup of wine to represent his blood. The most suggestive aspect of this symbol is Jesus speaking of it being "poured out". What this harkens back to in the Law is Leviticus 17:11:

Lev 17:11 'For the life of the flesh is in the blood, and I have given it to you on the altar to make atonement for your souls; for it is the blood by reason of the life that makes atonement.'

Any life that was to be offered up as a sacrifice would necessarily fulfill its purpose once the life's blood was made to "pour out" of the body. That is, the blood signifies the life that the body holds within it. Pour out the blood from the body and the life becomes removed from the body bringing death. So Jesus' blood "poured out" was to be the sign of his life having been made a sacrifice.

And the worth of a given sacrifice, explained in Leviticus 17:11, is to be based upon the life sacrificed. Given that Jesus declared himself the Son of God, then the idea is that a divine sacrifice was offered up. It is to be considered an offering free of sin and thus capable of redeeming a life having committed sin. Indeed, John writes that Jesus' sacrifice was effectual to pay for the sins of the whole world (1John 2:2).

There are two good passages from the Hebrew Scripture that prophetically associate with Jesus' declaring himself being "poured out". In perhaps the first location in Scripture that pertains to the Messiah's tortured death is the famous 22nd Psalm written by David. It begins with the famed phrase "My God, My God why have you forsaken Me?", the same words Jesus is quoted uttering during the Crucifixion. It would seem that David is made a prophetic medium throughout this Psalm as it pertains to what the suffering Messiah would both see, hear and feel while being crucified. As part of what David was given the sense to feel is the following:

Ps 22:14   I am poured out like water...

Another passage that communicates very much what Psalm 22 does is the prophet Isaiah's 53rd chapter. He too also describes a similar idea:

Isa 53:12   ...He poured out himself to death...

The Law's many Offerings are not created equal

There are of course more symbols relating Jesus to being made a sacrifice for sin. John declared Jesus the "Lamb of God" while more explicitly Paul declared Jesus "our Passover". What this led traditional Christianity to conclude was that **_all_** the Law's blood sacrifices were to be interpreted more or less "foreshadowing" the Crucifixion as some have interpreted Heb10:11-14, and similar passages, as meaning. This ubiquitous theology is quick to dismiss any form of ongoing relevancy for the Law's Offerings. By making such a universal assessment however tradition greatly errs because the Law's sacrifices are not all the same and thus are not created equal.

Once a doctrine lumps all of the Offerings together in this fashion there is little incentive for the mind to entertain what the distinctions that make each sacrifice a little different than another could mean. What the body of this chapter will hopefully convey is that no part of God's Word should be trivialized and sent out to pasture in any time, in any frame of reference, or in any place. The wisdom of God is revealed in how things uttered from God's mouth never become irrelevant if only it is God who keeps them from becoming irrelevant and how.

Upon closer inspection to what new symbol Jesus introduced at the Last Supper the emphasis needs to be placed on the aspect of the "cup". It becomes much more telling when the mind uses the image Jesus provided in his illustration of his blood being symbolically in a "cup" and from there being "poured out" (e.g., Matt26:27-28). But even more to the point is for the mind to see Jesus' cup of "wine" he served to his Disciples being poured out. Here is where traditional Christianity has failed to see the provocative connection being made with the Law, a different connection with the Law apart from the Passover memorial.

In an earlier chapter the matters of the Holy Days "Offerings by Fire" were discussed. Why this subject arose there is because each Holy Day or groups of Holy Days came to acquire an "Offering by Fire". A few are defined in Leviticus chapter 23 while most are described in Numbers chapters 28 and 29. Since it was noticed that the Offerings are not all the same, and indeed, most are not, it became one more clue suggesting that a Holy Day or related group of Holy Days are being given some sort of distinction along with whatever other symbols make them distinct.

Atonement Misappropriated in Christian Theology

Furthermore, in analyzing the nature and make-up of these Offerings by Fire, it was also brought to the reader's attention that there was something mysterious about one particular aspect of the Offerings. That happened to be the libations or drink offerings as they are also known:

Num 28:7 ...you shall pour out a libation of strong drink...

Whereas the Offerings always come to include an animal sacrifice along with a grain offering mixed with oil, not every Offering however has a libation. Where the libation was added, and where it was not, appears to be somewhat random. In chapter 9, it was discovered that the Prophet Ezekiel reveals that Offerings by Fire that are without libations were to be understood as those that make "atonement". He does not however explain what those Offerings by Fire having a libation are to be for.

In what has to be the most intriguing clue to help solve the mystery surrounding the libation offerings is the apostle Paul's statement he makes in his last letter when he realizes his time of death is near in prison:

2 Tim 4:6 For I am already being <u>poured out as a drink offering</u>, and the time of my departure has come.

(He uses this metaphor in Phil 2:17 in a slightly different and more positive tone.)

In joining all of these suggestive dots together to form a message, it should be clear at this juncture that the Libation Offerings are in some way symbolic of Jesus' Cup being poured out. So whereas the Prophet Ezekiel communicates that Offerings without Libations are for the purposes of Atoning for the House of Israel this 2nd Crucifixion Decryption Key explains that those Offerings with Libations are for the purposes of identifying Prophetic Gospel Saints:

Crucifixion Decryption Key:

Offerings by Fire w/o Libations: Flesh Atonement (Eze45:17b)
Offerings by Fire with Libations: Memorializes Gospel Saints

This basic interpretation, of course, is something entirely new being presented here. It is one of the main reasons why this book has been written. What this means is that Classical Christian Theology has effectively misappropriated the Law's concept behind what is most often translated "Atonement" to the Cross of Christ. The transliterated Hebrew root words are "kaphar", "kopher" or the more familiar word "kippur", all of which have as a base meaning "to cover". When Christian Theology argues that all of the Law's animal sacrifices are symbolic of the Gospel Sacrifice this is basically an erroneous conclusion. So what this 2nd Gospel Decryption Key communicates is essentially 2 ideas at once:

1. ONLY THOSE OFFERINGS CONTAINING A LIBATION OFFERING ARE PROPHETICALLY LINKED TO THE CROSS, HENCE…

2. ALL REMAINING LIBATIONLESS OFFERINGS THEREFORE ARE FOR THE PURPOSES OF ATONEMENT WHICH MEANS TO "CLEANSE THE FLESH".

Hebrews 9:13 …the blood of goats and bulls and the ashes of a heifer…sanctify for the _cleansing of the flesh_.

Applying the Crucifixion Decryption Key

A decoding exercise was begun in the previous chapter. It now carries over into this chapter by applying this new 2nd Decryption Key. Not everything will be made clear even here because there are still 2 more Keys to discover and exercise. Hence, some things will be solved while others will need further resolution from the remaining Keys to be studied in the next two chapters.

The primary decoding of the 2nd Gospel Decryption Key is to unlock the meaning behind any given Holy Day's Offerings by Fire. Hence, each Day will be examined and deciphered for whether the Offering is Gospel related or if it points to the cleansing of mortal flesh and also to whom a given Offering is to be appropriated for. So, how this simple but extraordinary decoding works is summarized in the following way:

1) Atonement Offerings are prophetically assigned to certain mortal Saints who are to appear in the general timeframe of the Divine Harvest Schedule where the Offering is defined. As such, this means they are to be accounted for in their mortal flesh. Thus, these Offerings do not apply to the dead, nor do they foreshadow the dead, but solely identify the mortally alive.

2) Libation Offerings are prophetically assigned to certain Gospel Saints who are to appear in the general timeframe of the Divine Harvest Schedule where the Offering is defined. As such, Libation Offerings could be logically assigned to both the living and/or the dead since the Gospel transcends those mortally alive or dead.

Given that traditional theology has never attempted to "decode" the meaning behind the various differences between the Offerings by Fire, these ideas put forth here will seem strange and alien at first. But these things will naturally become more familiar as more and more exposure is gained while studying how they are to be applied repeatedly to the various Holy Days in the pages to come. There are critically fascinating things to discover awaiting the curious seeker who employs this decoding method when contemplating the meaning behind the Holy Days Offerings. It would appear as if by Divine Design the Early Holy Days are simpler to decipher and help build confidence for attempting to solve the more challenging encodings of the Latter Holy Days.

As the revelation of this Decryption Key suggests a great historical error of Classical Christian Theology regarding the Law, it should come as no surprise that there are more shocking things to discover because of the reality of this new Key. These long neglected and darkened passages from the Law are given the due attention they deserve in the pages to come and are allowed to come out into the light where they can be illuminated of the secrets they symbolize, all because of the help of the Gospel.

The Great Mystery: Remnant Israel's Fate

For the Early Holy Days testimony, this 2nd Key will decode simple but profound things to be known regarding the "First Fruits" of the Divine Harvest. But, when turning to the Latter Holy Days testimony, things immediately become much more complicated. What will become self-evident is that a Great Mystery hovers over this testimony given the simple fact that Remnant Israel must emerge as part of the symbolisms of the "Last Fruits". This Great Mystery has always hung over the more direct and unencoded message of the Latter Hebrew Prophets in their prophecies regarding Remnant Israel.

The main Mystery Question that has dogged every honest reader of Scripture from time immemorial goes something like this: "What is the fate of Remnant Israel?" Jews and Christians have been debating this question for a very, very long time. Both sides have inhibited the truth from being discovered. And so the potential here with the Holy Days Code is that with the aid of the 4 Gospel Keys perhaps this Great Mystery can be solved! Indeed, if the Holy Days Code symbolizes even the Future Eternity, does it not seem plausible that the fate of Israel would be predicted by the time the Holy Days Code is entirely decoded? May the reader be convinced here that the mind cannot cleave to Tradition if it wants to be liberated to resolve Mysteries that no Tradition has been able to solve to date.

Deciphering The Daily, Weekly, Monthly Offerings

To begin the analysis of the Offerings, it makes sense to analyze the most frequent Offerings even though most of them do not actually become part of the Holy Days Code. This is because these Offerings provide their own clues as to how Offerings are to be interpreted symbolizing. These are those Offerings provided Daily, Weekly, and Monthly. Although the Daily Offerings permeate all Holy Days, it will be argued here that they communicate a separate message unto themselves apart from the Holy Days. As for the Weekly Offerings, there are 13 Sabbath Days that come to be included within the Holy Days schedule whereas only 1 New Moon Day does.

As it turns out, the Daily, the Sabbath, and the New Moon Offerings are all Libation Offerings. Using the simple idea of decoding Libations postulated earlier, this means the Gospel and Gospel Saints are to be considered in view:

Year Round Offerings by Fire

Holy Day	Offering by Fire				Libation ?
	bull	ram	lamb	goat	
Daily: Morning (Exo29:39)			1		Yes
Daily Evening (Exo29:39)			1		Yes
Sabbath (Num28:9)			2		Yes
New Moon (Num28:11-15)	2	1	7	1	Yes

So what could the Libations for these particular Offerings communicate about the Holy Days Code? First, the Daily Offerings of Morning and Evening will be pondered. It should be somewhat intuitive to argue that these perpetual Daily Offerings suggest that the Gospel of Jesus Christ has always been the source of God's Forbearance long before the actual Cross of Christ appeared. Indeed, when contemplating Ancient Israel and there being no Libation Offering as part of the Feast of Unleavened Bread, it would appear that Ancient Israel is to be seen nevertheless symbolically "covered" in the Blood of Christ by its symbolism. This is not an argument for "Universal Salvation" to all but merely the teaching that the repentant Sinner, no matter what span of time such a one comes to live in this Present Creation, will indeed find Salvation.

Provocatively however, the Prophet Ezekiel looks into the Future and prophecies that the Daily Libation Offerings will be eliminated there as if to say that God's Grace comes to an End after this present Creation is replaced with the New Creation. The Window of Opportunity is to be considered shuttered in the New Creation. Therefore, it suggests that only a finite number of Saints are to be called, not an infinite number. And so Ezekiel seems to be predicting a Future Day when Salvation will be applicable to the "Last Saint" and then it will cease to be applicable to any future Human Beings, hence the meaning behind the cessation of these Daily Libations. Furthermore, every Saint is to have at least one Libation Offering assigned to them within the Holy Days schedule to symbolize the eternal nature of God's Salvation for each one, what is to be a reminder and a memorial when the Offering is provided for each and every Year during the Holy Days Schedule throughout eternity.

The Sabbath and the New Moon Offerings can perhaps be interpreted slightly differently but along the same vein of thought. The Holy Days themselves help to illuminate the meaning of these Offerings because some of them are included within its schedule as cited earlier. What is discovered is that, instead of the concept of perpetually available Salvation portended in the Daily Offerings, time is captured into segments with these Offerings. That is, a Sabbath Offering covers 7 symbolic Days what is perhaps to be seen a factoring of certain generations of Saints. Likewise, a New Moon Offering covers 30 Days representing a greater amount of time like an Epoch or Era of time worth of Saints. Hence, Saints emerging in either of these time segments are identified by the Offerings provided in their own generation or era, sort of speak.

One interpretation of how this idea could be employed goes something like this: Imagine that the Future Eternity retains the time cycles of Weeks, Months and Years as the prophet Isaiah predicts (Isaiah 66:23) as well as Revelation (Rev22:2). As each Year transpires then, each Holy Day and Offering could be arranged to memorialize those Saints that were saved at any given time of the Year. By the time the Year is over every Saint would conceivably have been remembered, some more than once depending upon their place in history. Those Offerings falling in the very 7 Month Divine Calendar, and especially on the monumental Harvest Holy Days, would signify the largest number of Saints being recognized, which will be discussed next.

Partitioning of the Harvest Holy Days Offerings

Moving now to examine the Harvest Holy Days, below is a list of the Holy Days and the nature of their Offerings. They have been partitioned into 8 Libation Offerings groups and 5 Atonement Offerings groups, each reviewed in this chapter.

Month	Day	Name of Holy Day(s)	Libation	
	Twilight of 14th	Eve of Passover	No	**Atonement 1**
	15th	1st Day of Feast of Unleavened Bread	No	⌐
	16th	2nd Day of Feast of Unleavened Bread	No	
	17th	3rd Day of Feast of Unleavened Bread	No	
1st Month	18th	4th Day of Feast of Unleavened Bread	No	**Atonement 2**
	19th	5th Day of Feast of Unleavened Bread	No	
	20th	6th Day of Feast of Unleavened Bread	No	
	21st	7th Day of Feast of Unleavened Bread	No	⌐
	Mystery Sabbath	(Day before Head 1st Fruits)	Yes	**Libation 1**
	Day after Mystery Sabbath	Head 1st Fruits	Yes	**Libation 2**
	1st Sabbath after Mystery Sabbath	Countdown to Feast of Weeks: Week#1	Yes	⌐
	2nd Sabbath after Mystery Sabbath	Countdown to Feast of Weeks: Week#2	Yes	
Mystery Month	3rd Sabbath after Mystery Sabbath	Countdown to Feast of Weeks: Week#3	Yes	
	4th Sabbath after Mystery Sabbath	Countdown to Feast of Weeks: Week#4	Yes	**Libation 3**
	5th Sabbath after Mystery Sabbath	Countdown to Feast of Weeks: Week#5	Yes	
	6th Sabbath after Mystery Sabbath	Countdown to Feast of Weeks: Week#6	Yes	
	7th Sabbath after Mystery Sabbath	Countdown to Feast of Weeks: Week#7	Yes	⌐
	50 days after Head 1st Fruits	1st Fruits (Feast of Weeks/Pentecost)	Yes	**Libation 4**
			No	**Atonement 3**
	1st	Yom Teruah (New Moon)	(Yes)	**(Libation 5)**
	10th	Yom Kippur	No	**Atonement 4**
	15th	1st Day of Feast of Booths	No	**Atonement 5**
7th Month	16th	2nd Day of Feast of Booths	Yes	⌐
	17th	3rd Day of Feast of Booths	Yes	
	18th	4th Day of Feast of Booths	Yes	
	19th	5th Day of Feast of Booths	Yes	**Libation 6**
	20th	6th Day of Feast of Booths	Yes	
	21st	7th Day of Feast of Booths	Yes	**Libation 7**
	22nd	Day After the Feast of Booths	Yes	**Libation 8**

Notice that the 8 Libation groupings can be further consolidated into 3 contiguous Libation Groups. This important observation will be a momentous one when the subject of discernible Divine Harvest phases are discussed two chapters from this one. It should also be mentioned here that Ezekiel will add 2 more very important Holy Days Atonement Offerings in his prophecies as chapter 9 has already pointed out. This brings the Atonement Offerings Groups to a total of 7. The symbolic interpretation of these last 2 Offerings will be described in the closing chapter and pages of this work so as to bring a climatic end to this incredible Holy Days Code.

Early Harvest Holy Days Offerings

As the previous chapter went to great lengths to argue, Passover is a shared symbolism between the Law and the Gospel.

Atonement 1: The memorial of Passover comes without a libation in the offering of the Passover Lamb which each household of Israel is to offer each year. But of course, the Gospel Passover saw the shedding of the Lamb of God's Blood on the Cross at Golgotha for whom all the Libation Offerings symbolize.

Atonement Path	
Holy Day	Libation?
Original Passover	No: Exodus 12

Libation Path	
Holy Day	Libation?
Gospel Passover	Yes: Christ's Blood Poured Out

FULB Offerings: Atonement for Mortal Israel

Immediately following Israel's Passover Memorial comes the Feast of Unleavened Bread. Since it was proposed in chapter 3 that this 7 day Feast was symbolic of Israel's Prophetic Life, it should be somewhat intuitive to conclude that the Feast's Offerings by Fire without Libations are for the purpose of atoning for Israel's mortal community.

Atonement 2: All 7 days of the FULB have Offerings by Fire without libations.

Holy Day	Offering by Fire				Libation?
(Num28:19-22)	bull	ram	lamb	goat	
Feast of ULB: 1st Day	2	1	7	1	No
16th Day 1st Month	2	1	7	1	No
17th Day 1st Month	2	1	7	1	No
18th Day 1st Month	2	1	7	1	No
19th Day 1st Month	2	1	7	1	No
20th Day 1st Month	2	1	7	1	No
Feast of ULB: 7th Day	2	1	7	1	No

Again, the best way to interpret this schedule is what has been proposed in chapter 3. The idea is that Day 1 symbolizes the Generations spanning from Moses' generation of Israel who witnessed the very Theophany of God come into its midst and ending with Ezekiel's generation that suffered God's Theophany departing Solomon's Temple just prior to the Babylonian Siege as described in Ezekiel 10.

Then, Days 2-6 depict all the generations of Israel starting from Ezekiel all the way up to when God's Theophany once again is expected to return, only this time to Ezekiel's City and Temple he envisioned described in Ezekiel 43. Certainly Remnant Israel will have also materialized somewhere along the transpiring of these prophetic days too.

Just exactly when the Feast's 7th and final day comes is a subject beyond the scope of this chapter and is reserved for discussion in chapter 16 of this same book. What the majority of Day 7 then is portending by default is of course the coming Future Eternity. The prophetic vision suggested by this interpretation of the Feast of Unleavened Bread is that Mortal Israel will be in the presence of God's Theophany forever thereafter. Hence, the definition of Atonement 2 is really the making of a Mortal Path that began at Passover and reaches out into the Future Eternity.

Now if the mind concedes that this is what this first Feast portends then one cannot help but be confronted with the Great Mystery as was mentioned earlier. And so this Mystery is noticeable even at this early stage of the Code: How is a Mortal Nation to exist forever? It is a Great Mystery as well as a Great Paradox. Now with the unveiling of the 2nd Gospel Decryption Key this Great Mystery will be brought out into the open to visibly contemplate as will be seen shortly.

In explaining how the Atonement Offerings might work is perhaps logically understandable yet likewise creating a Great Mystery dilemma when it comes to the End of Time. It is proposed that all 7 Offerings for all 7 Days are efficacious for any given living mortal population of Israel which comprises of effectively 3 generations. That is, in any given period of Israel's past there was an elderly generation, a primary generation and a young generation. As time moves forward, one dies, the primary then becomes elderly while the young becomes primary and finally yet another is born. So it makes sense to conclude that the Offerings maintain efficacy for this constant 3 generation window as it moves through time. Hence, the Offerings effectively end up applying for all generations of Israel as mortality prevails. But again, this interpretation lacks an explanation as to how this is to work as time reaches into the Future Eternity.

The First Fruits Libations Path

The "Path" created by Libations 1-4: What is described after the Feast of Unleavened Bread is essentially a span of related Holy Days spanning 50 days, what is called herein the "50 Day Mystery Path". It is given this distinction because the way in which it is described to be reckoned as starting is ambiguous as has been discussed at length in previous chapters. In short, it is to begin the "day after" the Mystery Sabbath. The previous chapter identified the Mystery Sabbath as the Sabbath of the 1st Feast and which coincided with the Burial Period of Jesus Christ. Hence, this Burial Period's Libation Offerings define what is identified in the earlier Offerings list as **Libation 1**. This and all related subjects dealing with the Holy Days Sabbaths will be discussed in the next chapter.

Libation 2 then happens to be offered on the Day of the Resurrection, coming on the Day of Head First Fruits, the first Harvest Occasion of the Harvest Period. This will be examined further two chapters from this one.

Libation 3 is a series of 7 Sabbath Libation Offerings that are obviously symbolic of something related to the events of the Gospel. This will become quite obvious as to its meaning when the subject of the Sabbath symbol is studied at length in the next chapter as is central to the 3rd Gospel Decryption Key.

Libation 4 is an Offering that comes 50 days after Libation 2. It is the Holy Day defined as the Feast of First Fruits/Weeks/Pentecost. And again it must be symbolic of yet another great event related to the Gospel Events that it mimics. This too will become clear when the 4th Gospel Decryption Key is examined at length two chapters from here.

In examining the Path that is created across Libations 1-4, what is a 50 Day Mystery Period, it becomes apparent it creates its own Path of Mystery Time along the Divine Timeline apart from the 1st Feast's timeline of Mortal Israel's Prophetic Life. Altogether then, there are 9 consecutive Holy Days spanning 50 Days all with Libation Offerings. It is the first and longest streak of Libation Offerings in a row that the Holy Days Schedule contains. So this 2nd Path is composed of 3 symbolisms that are NOT found at all in the 1st Feast Path: Libations, Sabbaths, and Harvest Occasions:

First Fruits Libations Path

Mystery Sabbath	Head 1st Fruits	Sabbath #1	Sabbath #2	Sabbath #3	Sabbath #4	Sabbath #5	Sabbath #6	Sabbath #7	Feast of 1st Fruits

← ———————————————————— **Libations** ———————————————————— →

Holy Day	Offering by Fire				Libation?
	bull	ram	lamb	goat	
Sabbath of FULB			2		Yes
Head 1st Fruits			1		Yes
Sabbath #1			2		Yes
Sabbath #2			2		Yes
Sabbath #3			2		Yes
Sabbath #4			2		Yes
Sabbath #5			2		Yes
Sabbath #6			2		Yes
Sabbath #7			2		Yes
Feast of Weeks (Lev 23:18-19)	1	2	7	1	Yes
(Lev23:17)	2 leavened loaves of bread				
2 Peace Offerings (Lev23:19b)			2		?
Feast of Weeks (Num28:27-30)	2	1	7	1	Yes

So the distinctions of the 2 Paths become quite noticeable if a reader is aware of the symbolisms attributed to the Holy Days. One Path possesses no Libation Offerings and no Sabbaths while the 2nd Path has all the Libation Offerings and

Sabbaths in this Early Harvest Season! Hence, the 1st Path is best identified as being an "Atonement" Path while the other is a "Gospel" Path when applying the 2nd Decryption Key decoding defined earlier that denotes Libations as Gospel related.

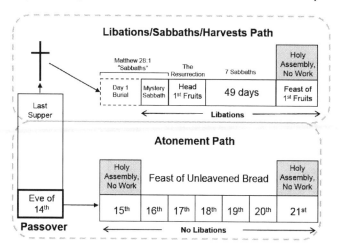

That this Libations Path also contains Sabbaths and Harvest Dates simply means these are additional symbolisms that will need to be decoded. The incredible observation is again how the Gospel Events came to overlap with the initial days of this First Libations Path. Christ's Crucifixion overlapped with Passover. Next, Christ's Burial Period overlapped with the Sabbath Period of the Feast of Unleavened Bread. Next, Christ was witnessed as raised from the Dead on the Day of Head First Fruits. Because of this astonishing overlap of Holy Days symbolisms with major Gospel Events, this is what makes the 4 Gospel Decryption Keys observable.

All of these initial symbolisms will require one or more of these Gospel Decryption Keys to decode them. But since these Keys must be introduced one at a time, some symbolisms are not possible to decipher until the other 2 Keys are unveiled. Thus what conclusions will be drawn in this chapter will be an abridged interpretation given the reader is assumed unaware of any impact of what remaining Keys make on this subject of the Offerings by Fire. This means later chapters will have to revisit open-ended items that will be left here from this chapter. Eventually, as all the Keys are made known, many decodings become trivial to see as these Keys can be found working together to communicate a common theme.

The Counting of 7 Sabbaths & the Feast of Weeks

Notice that the number 7 is found enjoining Head First Fruits with that of the Feast of Weeks. This is similar to the 7 Days of the Feast of Unleavened Bread which was argued as being symbolic of Israel's Prophetic Timeline. Hence, this implies that the 7 Sabbaths span may also be portending yet another timeline or Age. So what Age could this be? It should becoming more and more clear that this can only be symbolizing the Church Age, in contrast to that of Israel's Age. This will become more clear in the chapters to come.

One of the big clues to help unravel the meaning of the Feast of First Fruits/Weeks/Pentecost is within the various odd characteristics found in the details of the Offerings by Fire:

Holy Day	Offering by Fire				Libation?
	bull	ram	lamb	goat	
Feast of Weeks (Lev 23:18-19)	1	2	7	1	Yes
(Lev23:17)	2 leavened loaves of bread				
2 Peace Offerings (Lev23:19b)			2		?
Feast of Weeks (Num28:27-30)	2	1	7	1	Yes

Notice there happens to be three "pairs" of testimony being created. First off, there are 2 separate Libation Offerings allotted to this Day, one defined in Leviticus 23 and the other in Numbers 28. Furthermore, there are 2 "Peace Offerings" to be given along with these 2 Libation Offerings. Finally, there are 2 "Leavened" Loaves of Bread the High Priest is to wave before God in the Tabernacle/Temple. These additional Offerings are all unique, with no other Holy Day Offering including these additional elements. So what do all of these "Pairs" mean? That the Bread is to be Leavened is quite a striking clue too. One last interesting thing to discover is that if all of the separate Offerings are counted the number comes to 24 or, in other words, 2 groups of 12. As will be seen later, the number 24 has very special significance in the book of Revelation.

Another big question moving forward is whether or not the 2 Paths, Israel's timeline and the Church's timeline, are to continue growing in length in having association with the rest of the Holy Days or if they are to abruptly end here.

Early Holy Days Schedule

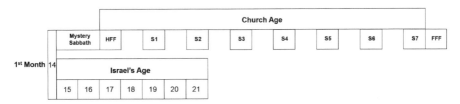

Certainly these 2 Paths by themselves are to be understood overlapping each other given the Sabbath of the Feast of Unleavened Bread is in fact the Mystery Sabbath that begins the 50 Day Mystery Path. These questions will have to wait to be confidently answered one way or another. This then brings an end to the discussion of the Early Holy Days Offerings by Fire.

The Latter Holy Days: Encoding the Remnant

The analysis continues with the examination of the Offerings by Fire for the Last Holy Days. Given these Holy Days come in the 7th and last month of the Divine Calendar, this suggests these Holy Days are representing the final chronology of the Divine Plan, things that converge upon the "Latter Day" or the "End Times", as they are known in Christian Eschatological circles. Since the 7th Month is far removed from the Early Holy Days, it should be perceived that something entirely new is being introduced beyond the life and times of Ancient Israel or the Church or even the Messiah himself since all of these things have already been encoded symbolically in the Early Holy Days.

Hence, by the process of elimination, the only thing prophetically remaining in Scripture to unveil with the Holy Days Code is Remnant Israel. Thus, the 7th Month's Holy Days testimony should really be understood to be the encoding of Remnant Israel and everything prophetically significant about the Remnant in its use of symbols. For example, the Early Holy Days have Passover and how it gave birth to Ancient Israel whereas the Latter Holy Days have Yom Kippur and how it is yet to give birth and sustain Remnant Israel forever. How that is to come about is what solving the Mysteries of the 7th Month is all about.

Yet, it should be clear that the prophetic Remnant cannot appear in a vacuum. Recall that the Feast of Unleavened Bread symbolized Israel's Prophetic Life, ALL of Israel's Prophetic Life, and not just Ancient Israel's. Technically speaking then, this means the 7th Month can be considered occupying the same space in time as the last Days of the Feast of Unleavened Bread. And, as far as the Last Day of either schedule is concerned, it has been shown that both share the symbolism of "Atsarah", what will later be argued signifies the Future Eternity. So perhaps all the 7th Month Holy Days, save the Last Day, can be considered overlapping with the 6th Day of the 1st Feast while the very Last Day aligns with the 7th Day of the 1st Feast:

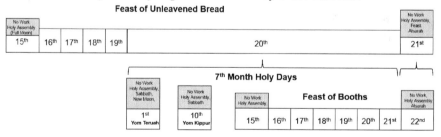

In proposing this relationship it begs the next question: Is there a relationship to be proposed between the 50 day Mystery Period symbolizing the Church Age and the 7th Month and thus creating a possible convergence of all the Holy Days? Indeed there is. The book of Revelation alludes to the Latter Days as a transitional era where the Church Age is to come to an End while at the same time a New Remnant Age is to Begin! In other words, these two major things transitioning are to happen at the same time. While the former is to come to an End, the other is to be simultaneously beginning. Hence, what the first portion of the 7th Month Holy Days is symbolizing is a transitional era. The book of Revelation dedicates a good portion of its passages to defining and describing this very unusual period of time and greatly aids the decoding process of these Holy Days. How exactly the two portions of Holy Days are to overlap one another will need the aid of the 3rd Decryption Key developed in the next chapter to reveal. For now, a simple pictorial of the idea is provided here:

Early 7ᵗʰ Month Transitional Era

End of the Church Age

Beginning of the Remnant Age

In various locations in this chapter and in chapters to come, the reader may be unfamiliar with the topic of Eschatology being discussed. Because of this, it is highly recommended that another book (or Website) be consulted regarding many topics that will be raised here in regards to End Times Prophecy. The book is entitled "Alpha Kai Omega: Explaining Scripture's Climatic Ending" (the Website can be found at alphakaiomega.info). The work reviews the book of Revelation, chapter by chapter and so study of the Holy Days Code can be aided by seeing how Revelation helps solve the riddles of the Fall Holy Days portion of the Code.

Christian Eschatological doctrine will be put to the test in light of what this decoding process will illuminate. In short, long held beliefs will be uprooted. Whole concepts like Post Millennialism (and Amillennialism) will be proven Scripturally untenable and even Pre-Millennialism will need serious overhauling. And room will have to be made for even a new "ism" to be formed. But not only in the study of Eschatology the greater theological teachings of a great deal of traditional thinking will need fundamental reform and purging. Replacement Theology will fall like a House of Cards as even the ideas of this 2nd Decryption Key obviously concur. Thus, the Holy Days Code brings a whole new angle in which to look upon matters of Scripture, an angle that has not been previously available for consultation because of how Tradition has forbidden its discovery.

Yom Teruah: A Time for the Law and the Gospel

To Judaism, the first 2 Holy Days of the 7th Month, Yom Teruah and Yom Kippur, are considered the "High Holy Days". They each stand alone unlike all the other Holy Days. What this must be communicating is that these days are not to be considered part of an Epoch or Age but as something much shorter in duration. Given the most important span of time in End Times Prophecy is the 7 year period of Daniel's final 70th Week, speculation must contend that Yom Teruah and Yom Kippur fall within this 7 year period.

In particular, Yom Teruah should be considered the beginning of Daniel's 70th Week. And in examining the Day's symbolisms, it certainly suggests that it is. It comes with few words but communicates a great deal with them. Perhaps there are 7 symbols to find as part of Yom Teruah's description as was pointed out in an earlier chapter: 1) It is to have a holy assembly. 2) It is to be a day of no work. 3) It is a new Sabbath rest day unlike the normal Sabbath previously defined. 4) It has Offerings by Fire without libations, 5) it is the day of "Teruah" and "Zikrown", Hebrew words meaning loud, clamoring noise and remembrance, respectively. The last 2 symbols are consequential in nature and are without mention. 6) By definition, it is a New Moon day which comes with Libation Offerings. And also, 7) it is Israel's Rosh HaShanah, or New Year's Day.

To understand what contextual meaning the words Teruah and Zikrown are communicating for this Holy Day, it so happens these words are used very similarly in one other location coming later in the Law. It is found in the book that follows Leviticus, that would be Numbers, and in its 10th chapter. There the general description is given as to how 2 Silver Trumpets are to be fashioned and used for the purposes of summoning Israel on various occasions. In particular, they are to be blown on all the Holy Appointments including the New Moon. But this is not where the words of interest are used. Where they occur is in the description of when the Trumpets were to be "blasted" (Teruah) so as to be an "alarm", on the occasion when Israel would be called to war against its enemies. Ironically, it wasn't so that the People were to hear the alarm but that God would hear it and "remember" (Zikrown) Israel and save it from its enemy.

So it would seem the "encoded" message here is that Israel is prophetically expected to come into a Period of Epoch Distress in the Latter Days as it confronts a tumultuous Enemy arrayed against it. The Nation is to then "alarm" God and God is expected to hear the Nation and protect it. Those of Israel who would survive this End Time Distress are none other than Remnant Israel, or the very first of the Remnant.

Another unique symbolism is that this day has two groups of Offerings, one with and one without a libation. There is no other Holy Day that shares this attribute, none. By being a New Moon Day it receives this hidden Libation Offering.

Holy Day	Offering by Fire				Libation ?
	bull	ram	lamb	goat	
New Moon (Num28:11-15)	2	1	7	1	Yes
Yom Teruah (Num29:2-6)	1	1	7	1	No

And so, this gives the Day yet more uniqueness which turns out to introduce a new kind of symbolism not seen in the Early Holy Days symbolisms. As was previously mentioned, the distinction of the Offerings by Fire which have no libations was that these act as providing "atonement" for the living according to Ezekiel and that those containing libations point out some new emerging group of Saints that require being identified. So what then can a Holy Day be communicating if it has Offerings by Fire of each kind? What does it mean when both the subject of Atonement and the Gospel are shared symbolisms for Yom Teruah?

And if that was not enough, there is yet another new element introduced here for the first time to add to the mix. It is the first day of a newly emerging Sabbath not

175

seen before and which will be discussed in the next chapter for its unique meaning. Because of these many symbolisms assigned to Yom Teruah, this Holy Day is the most complex of them all and will need very careful analysis to understand the total breadth of testimony it is putting forth.

To start to unravel this Day's Offerings symbolisms, it has to be contemplated as to what it could mean that there is to be both an Atonement Offering and a Libation Offering attributed to a group or groups of Saints in this Prophetic Day. This situation invokes a very unique set of circumstances from which to draw from the Scripture's testimony to identify what is a very unusual situation it must be symbolizing. The book of Revelation does not disappoint and glaringly has plenty to offer as far as an explanation is needed for what these two Offerings together symbolize.

Essentially the Atonement Offering is an idea emanating from the Law whereas the Libation Offerings are explained by the Gospel. So it would seem that this time era is being described as a period when both the Law and the Gospel are predicted to be coexisting together. This is how it was in the early days of the Church Age before the 2nd Temple was destroyed. Symbolically, this can be seen by the first Libation Offerings of the 50 day Mystery Period overlapping with the Feast of Unleavened Bread's Atonement Offerings. So, just as was in the early Church Age so it is to be again just as the Church Age comes to an end!

It is a very powerful suggestion that perhaps Israel's Path and the Church's Path are being made to converge upon this period of time so as to *__share__* the day of Yom Teruah together in their schedules! The book of Revelation also communicates this same message in its own unique way. A primary premise of the Book and a foundational teaching it puts forth is the vision of the Law and the Gospel coming to be fulfilled by Latter Day Saints:

Rev 14:12 (and 12:17) Here is the perseverance of the Saints who keep the Commandments of God and their Faith in Jesus

At the same time Revelation will also go on to imply that a (Third) Temple will be existing in the Latter Day and is to have "worshippers" in it (Rev11:1). Hence, things are symbolized as if imitating those days when the Church and the 2nd Temple coexisted together before the Temple was destroyed by the Romans in AD/CE70. Assuming this is what is being implied, then very conceivably both the Commandments of God and a Faith in Jesus are anticipated to be fulfilled together in the Latter Day. And so it would seem that the symbolism of Yom Teruah evokes the very heart and soul of the book of Revelation. This becomes a huge clue that will help in proposing what the symbolisms of Yom Teruah are prophetically revealing.

New Moon: Intersection of Saints, Old with New

Recall that there are 3 Groups of Libation Offerings within the Holy Days testimony shown earlier in this chapter. In the general context, this New Moon Libation happens to be the 2nd appearance of Libation Offerings and here standing alone on this one day. There will be yet a 3rd and final appearance of Libation

Offerings spanning the last 7 Holy Days in the schedule. So in total, there are basically 3 groups of Libation Offerings with this one coming in the middle.

So then what is the meaning behind Yom Teruah's New Moon Libation Offerings designated **Libation 5** in the table provided earlier? As was proposed at the very start of the analysis of Libation Offerings, New Moon Offerings can be considered as symbolizing all the Gospel Saints that the given month anticipates prophetically. And because it comes to overlap with Yom Teruah, the best interpretation to offer is to argue that all the 7th Month Gospel Saints are somehow to be accounted for during the prophetic time Yom Teruah portends in some fundamental way. So this provides the hint to the Puzzle Solver to conduct a mental exercise in surveying the Latter Day landscape and consider who are to be considered all the Latter Day Saints looking as far into the future as possible.

In conducting this inventory, there are perhaps 4 different Groups being foreseen by Yom Teruah's Libation Offerings. Each of them will be discussed here in the chronological order they perhaps appear:

1. The Rapture Mortals of the Church: The idea behind this group of Saints is mainly put forth by the Apostle Paul's famous passage suggesting there is to be a sudden snatching of Mortal Church Saints into heaven, and event popularly referred to as the "Rapture":

1Thes 4:16-17 For the Lord Himself will descend from heaven with a shout, with the voice of {the} archangel, and with <u>the trumpet of God</u>; and the dead in Christ shall rise first. Then we who are alive and remain shall be caught up together with them in the clouds to meet the Lord in the air...

After all the Holy Days symbolisms are accounted for, it will turn out that no other symbolism of the Holy Days makes sense other than this one. The next chapter will explain why these unique Saints (those who escape Mortal Death and go straight from mortally alive to immortal upon the Resurrection) are not symbolized in the 50 day Mystery Period. A popular 20th century position has been to argue that the Rapture and Resurrection are one and the same event. But this is untenable because all Church Saints are to go before Christ to be judged *__before__* the Resurrection (see 1Cor3:15 and 2Cor5:10).

That leaves one big question being exactly when the Rapture Saints will be raptured. It appears that from the Holy Days Code it is to occur inside the 70th Week but perhaps very early on. Again, this seems to be intentional in order to replicate the overlapping early Church Age coexistence with the 2nd Temple&Offerings up until AD70. This then makes it appear as if Daniel's 69th and 70th Week's seamlessly join together as if they had never been severed by the Church Age, what is a Divine Mystery.

2. The Appearance of Revelation's Two Witnesses: These Witnesses of Revelation's 11th chapter are to appear probably just before the 70th Week begins and who are to then minister for half of it. Then they are to be killed by the Antichrist somewhere in the middle who will then reign for the latter half, more or less. Perhaps

177

Elijah and Moses are these 2 Witnesses, Saints from long, long ago. Hence, these Saints need new accounting in the Holy Days Code. With the idea of Israel sounding off an alarm to God, perhaps these Two Witnesses are God's remembering Israel in sending them. These Two Witnesses are to effectively "call" the "first fruits" of Remnant Israel, similarly as John the Baptist (said to have come in the "spirit" of Elijah) called 1st Century Israel to repentance to prepare them to meet the Messiah.

3. **The 144,000 of Israel**. The very first fruits of Remnant Israel are identified in the book of Revelation as these, 12,000 called from each tribe save Dan. No doubt this is to signify them being the "firstborn", being a possession of God for His Purposes as was established on Passover. Because of this, they so happen to represent the entire Remnant that will eventually emerge as to what the remainder of the Remnant Harvest is to become. Revelation goes on to declare that these will "follow" Jesus wherever he goes. This is code in establishing these will do similarly as Jesus' original 12 Apostles. Only they will preach both the Law and the Gospel from around the world and call forth the so called "Tribulation Saints" discussed next. What is so conspicuously different between the 144,000 and the Tribulation Saints is that the 144,000 are expected to be preserved in Mortal Life whereas the Tribulation Saints are not.

4. The Elect

4. **The Tribulation Saints/Martyrs.**: The book of Revelation envisions "countless" Martyrs to lay down their lives at the hands of the Antichrist. They are to represent all Nations, Tongues and Peoples. These 2nd Chance Saints are false Saints who make up the apostate section of the Church that is to emerge in the Latter Days. Subsequently, they are not called in the Rapture and thus are "Left Behind". They are given a unique opportunity to become true Saints in voluntarily offering up their own lives to the Antichrist for slaughter (including the 2 Witnesses). Hence, these sacrificial Lambs lay down their lives in order that Remnant of Israel might escape harm in this becoming a sort of replay of the original Gospel story. Why they are convinced to do this is because the 144,000 will call them into repentance and the Spirit of God will move those who heed that call to do so. These Tribulation Saints are prophesied to observe both the Law and the Gospel and most likely are to congregate to the 3rd Temple to worship God there. Because of this, these Saints are not considered members of the Church but who nevertheless are also predicted to be part of the First Resurrection.

Hence, perhaps the use of the word "Teruah" is also prophetic for all that is expected to happen throughout the breaking of the Seals. Few, if any, commentators have speculated that Teruah could also imply the Shouting of the Human Voice. Yet in the day Ancient Israel was called to destroy the city of Jericho, the entire Nation was commanded to Shout:

Joshua 6:5 ...when you hear the sound of the trumpet, all the people shall <u>shout</u> with a <u>great shout</u>; and the wall of the city will fall down...

The Hebrew word for "shout" here, used twice, is the word "Teruah". Likewise, the initial Martyrs who die at the hands of the Antichrist are to stand under the Heavenly Temple's Altar in Heaven and Cry Out to God seeking vengeance for their spilled blood as Revelation points out:

Rev 6:9-11 ...I saw underneath the altar <u>the souls of those who had been slain</u> ...and <u>they cried out with a loud voice</u>, saying, "How long, O Lord, holy and true, wilt Thou refrain from judging and avenging our blood on those who dwell on the earth?"

What must be kept in mind is that of these 4 groups of Saints, only the 144,000 of Israel escape death (and possibly the 2 Witnesses). Hence, only these go on to become part of the Remnant Age whereas Deceased Saints become part of the First Resurrection. But up until the day of these Saints' deaths, all 4 groups come to live mortal lives overlapping with one another. As such, Yom Teruah's Libations Offerings anticipate both old and new Saints appearing, hence these earlier days are again transitional in nature.

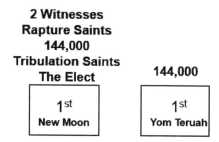

3 Roadblocks Ahead!: The Great Mystery

What Offerings remain for Yom Teruah are its Atonement Offerings and what information these encode (**Atonement 3**). Recall that Atonement Offerings symbolize living mortal Saints. The previous Atonement Offerings presented, those of the Feast of Unleavened Bread, were somewhat manageable to understand. The argument was put forth that these Offerings applied to any period of Mortal Israel's Life. Hence, as aging generations died the Offerings would simply transpose on to new arising generations in a continuous, uninterrupted fashion. As such, this basic concept works well when the time scale of history is immense. But when the time scale is small, this concept no longer works and an entirely new and provocative idea must hold true. This so happens to be the case for Yom Teruah as well as the next 2 Holy Days that follow it.

In all 3 of these cases, the Puzzle Solver is presented head on with the Roadblock that is the Great Mystery. The Great Mystery is the very definition of Remnant Israel and how it is to be understood eternal in scope as the Prophets foresee it to become. So either the Great Mystery is solved here once and for all or these Atonement Offerings will have to remain unresolved. Yet the Holy Days Code, and this 2nd Crucifixion Decryption Key in particular, provide an implied answer that begs for the Great Mystery to be solved if the Puzzle Solver is bold enough to accept what is being communicated in these 3 Offerings.

Why and How a huge problem becomes posed over the next 3 Holy Days' Atonement Offerings is because these Holy Days are not representing Epochs or Ages but instead a relatively short period of prophetic time. So if this is the case then Whoever the Atonement Offerings are for, these cannot be transposed on to someone else for a later time as was proposed for the Feast of Unleavened Bread's Atonement Offerings. In this new case, the only way to resolve the problem at hand is to insist that the given Offerings always apply to the one group of Saints it is designed for, and no one else, for all eternity. In other words, these Atonement Offerings can never be transferred to some other Mortals at a later time because they are assigned for Saints that are to appear in the very small prophetic window these 3 Days portend.

For the sake of further explanation, it will help to establish just what Groups of Saints are best interpreted as being assigned to the 7th Month Atonement Offerings in general. All of them must be assigned to Mortal Saints given they are Atonement Offerings designated to purify the Flesh of Mortal Saints. The one group that was defined earlier and qualifies here to be the 1st of 3 Groups being identified by these Offerings are the 144,000 of Israel (two more will be identified later in Matthew 24 and another in Matthew 25).

Now here is the problem. If Yom Teruah's Atonement Offering is to be assigned as providing Atonement for the 144,000 of Israel then it cannot be assigned to anyone else for all of time. For who else could these Offerings be assigned to? The Offering is locked in time prophetically representing the early years of Daniel's End Times. There are no other qualifying candidates who can take the place of those who it was originally accounting for. If hypothetically the 144,000 were to eventually die then this Offering will come to have no efficacy beyond their death since they would no longer need to be purified. Yet the Law implies that every Offering retain its efficacy otherwise it would not exist in the first place.

Here the Great Mystery is confronted head on. What the 2nd Crucifixion Decryption Key is implying is that ***ATONEMENT OFFERINGS OF THE 7th MONTH PORTEND A MORTAL REMNANT WHO WILL NEVER SUCCUMB TO MORTAL DEATH LEST THE OFFERINGS BECOME USELESS***! And so the Great Mystery, if it is accepted for what this Decryption Key is saying about the coming Remnant, is finally solved once and for all! And these Atonement Offerings are only the beginning of symbolisms that address the Great Mystery. After the entire 7th Month Holy Days are studied it can be concluded that they all play a part in communicating this repeating theme in various ways as will be discovered in the pages to come. And that is, the Remnant accounted for by the 7th Month's 3 Atonement Offerings can never succumb to death for whoever in particular they are assigned for.

Yet this should not be a surprise given that the straightforward message of the Latter Prophets regarding Remnant Israel, especially Ezekiel, prophecy the same thing right out in the open. Why Classical Christian Theology continues to ignore this basic message is because it is steeped in Replacement Theology which cannot accept it. Because of this mindset this is why Modern Day Eschatology is a vast wilderness incapable of putting together the End Times Puzzle.

Yom Kippur: A Libationless Day

In Jewish religious circles, the days counting down to Yom Kippur are known as the "Days of Awe" what has become a time of seeking repentance of sins. The reason for this sacred time is because the belief is that the Righteous of Israel are to be chosen by God on this most holiest day of the year. Tradition mandates fasting on Yom Kippur along with other forms of prohibition and abstinence in its interpretation of what the command to "afflict the soul" means for this day.

Yom Kippur is first defined in Leviticus 16 as the annual date for when the Nation was to seek to be cleansed of its Sins. There is where the details of how its Atonement Offerings are to be given, nowhere is there a sign of any libation whatsoever. In fully understanding the dichotomy of Atonement versus Libation, the very Day of Atonement must be completely devoid of Libation if its own day is to be about the epitome of Atonement Offerings. When Yom Kippur is made as part of the other Holy Days in Leviticus 23, it gets yet another Atonement Offering later defined in Numbers 29. This is the clear sign that Yom Kippur also signifies an ominous prophetic day in Israel's future placed in the Divine Calendar as it is now understood to be. Christians have long argued that this must be the moment when Israel is confronted with the long awaited appearing of Jesus and in that moment repentant Israel receives forgiveness of its Sin for having rejected Him. Unfortunately, Christian Eschatology is in such a state of confusion it has no good place to offer as to where and when this is to take place. That the very day is signified by the word Atonement means it cannot be considered the day of Israel's spiritual salvation but most certainly is to be understood its salvation from impending Mortal Death.

Yom Kippur and the next Holy Day after it, the 15th Day of the 7th Month, creates the only period in the 7th Month where no Libations are recorded. This perhaps communicates the idea that the Gospel goes into hiding during the darkest portion of Daniel's 70th Week. Other indications suggests the same thing as the next chapter will disclose. This should help determine just exactly when this moment is to come in Daniel's 70th Week. At the same time however the Atonement Offerings argue for the idea that Mortal Life is being preserved on both these dates.

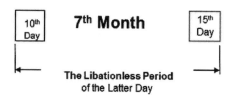

Yom Kippur: The Gathering Together of the Elect

One way to become convinced that Yom Kippur must be revolving around the Appearing of the Messiah is to argue how such an occasion would NOT be included in the Divine Calendar. What other occasion could trump this one? Yet why believe this ominous occasion comes on Yom Kippur? Recall that Passover and Yom Kippur are the 2 dates in the Calendar whose sacrificial themes are similar and which stand apart from the other Dates. Each is made central in their respective portions of the Calendar. What this is encoding is that the Messiah has 2 different roles in each half of the Calendar. With Passover Jesus came as the Lamb of God suffering Mortal Death in order to secure Humanity's spiritual salvation. In the Latter Days Jesus is to come as Israel's Mighty Messiah and save it from certain Mortal Death, what is the epitome of Atonement.

So through the process of elimination, Yom Kippur's Atonement Offering, designated **Atonement 4**, must be symbolizing the so called "Elect" that Jesus spoke of when He said "He will send His Angels... (who) will gather together His "Elect" from the four winds, from one end of heaven to the other" (Matt24:31). That period of time is to be so tumultuous that if things were allowed to naturally progress without interruption no Mortal Life would remain on Earth. And so, for the sake of the very "Elect", there will be Divine Intervention to prevent this human annihilation from happening (Matt24:22).

Why this Day is not to see repentance to spiritual salvation is because by this time a Great Tribulation has already come over the world. The greatest slaughter of Saints will have just transpired. Thus, hearts and minds will already have been forcibly committed to take a stand either for God or for the Antichrist by the time this moment comes. So it would seem the fate of every Israelite soul will be determined leading up to this prophetic Day just as Judaism's traditions believe.

In firmly establishing Yom Kippur's symbolic representation as the future fulfillment of Jesus' Appearing to Gather the Elect, this pins Yom Kippur down in the Chronology of the End Times. However, Christian Eschatology cannot place this date because it has no real understanding of how Daniel's 70th Week is to be broken down so as to pinpoint this moment. For most, Christ's 2nd Coming is a one time and done event. This is a most preposterous assertion.

As to where to place Yom Kippur in the greater timeline, this will be more convincingly proposed in the next chapter once the understanding of the symbolism of the Sabbath makes its impact. Certainly, if Matt24:31 fulfills Yom Kippur's symbolisms, this means, at the very least, that the Great Tribulation has just transpired. So what is the next event after the Great Tribulation? For Christian Eschatology it is the 2nd Coming of Christ. If this is so then Yom Kippur comes far too early and hence is the wrong interpretation.

The Elect

```
┌─────────────────────┐
│   ┌─────────────┐   │
│   │             │   │
│   │  No Work    │   │
│   │ Holy Assembly│  │
│   │             │   │
│   └─────────────┘   │
│                     │
│        10ᵗʰ         │
│     Yom Kippur      │
└─────────────────────┘
```

1st Day of the Feast of Booths: No Libations

The next Holy Day of the Fall is the first day of the Feast of Booths. It is readily recognizable that this Feast is very similar to the Feast of Unleavened Bread. Namely, it is 7 days long and falls on the same days of the month. Again, this must be conveying the idea that the Feast's 7 days are some kind of "Age". And there happens to be only one other major prophecy noticeably visible in Scripture that could be considered an "Age" besides the Future Eternity. That would be the Messianic Kingdom Age of course. But at the same time, this "Age" cannot be interpreted stretching out into the Future Eternity. This is because its last day, the 21st day of the 7th month, is not the last Holy Day but is immediately followed by the last unnamed Holy Day, the 22nd day of the 7th month. And indeed, according to Revelation, the Kingdom Age is not to be understood an eternal age, but specifically a thousand years according to John.

But strangely enough, the very first day of the last Feast observably separates itself from the remaining Feast Days on account of its Offerings by Fire:

Holy Day	Offering by Fire				Libation?
	bull	ram	lamb	goat	
Feast of Booths: 1st Day	13	2	14	1	No

All the remaining Holy Days after this will be found to have Libation Offerings. So this happens to be the last noticeable Offerings transition taking place amongst the Holy Days. Again, there is no sign of Gospel Saints appearing on this day. What then could the first day of the Feast of Booths be envisioning? Perhaps a passage in Deuteronomy can shed more light on the matter:

Deut16:13 You shall celebrate the Feast of Booths...after you have gathered in from your threshing floor and your wine vat; and you shall rejoice...you and your son and your daughter and your male and female servants and the Levite and the stranger and the orphan and the widow who are in your towns...

The book of Revelation will use these exact harvest symbols, that of a threshing event and a wine vat event, in its 14th Chapter in prophesying of the

Resurrection of the Saints and of the Slaughter at Armageddon, coming in succession respectively. Therefore the symbolism of the Feast of Booths is to follow these 2 great occasions. What Armageddon equates to is the 2nd Coming of Christ to destroy the Antichrist and to subsequently establish His Kingdom on Earth. Hence, Christ gathering together the Elect must be an earlier occasion taking place. So what then is happening between Yom Kippur and the 1st Day of the Feast of Booths? In the next chapter, this framework for Daniel's 70th Week will be proposed once the 3rd Gospel Decryption Key helps break down the Week in noticeable segments.

In analyzing the nature of the Offerings by Fire of the Feast of Booths in general, and in the Offerings of the 15th Day in particular, it would make sense to conclude that the non-Libation Offerings signify all those End Time Mortals who Survive the Latter Day by Divine Providence. As the passage of Deuteronomy above supports, there are several different "parties" to be invited to celebrate the Feast including "the stranger". It would seem that this is illustrating the plurality of the Gentiles that are expected to be a part of the Surviving Citizenry of the End Times.

So who could be in view here? Again, a reader can turn to Matthew, this time shortly after Matt24:31, in chapter 25, to discover that Jesus prophecies of the Sheep and Goats that presumably survive the carnage of the Latter Days. Here is now a third party to assign to the 3rd Atonement of the 7th Month, **Atonement 5**. The first Party is to be the 144,000, the second Party is to be the "Elect", and now the third Party is to be the Sheep and Goats given they survive as Mortals to appear before Jesus after Daniel's 70th Week is over. The Sheep and Goats represent the Nations of the World. Jesus is expected to separate the Sheep from the Goats, sending the Sheep who had compassion on the Martyred Saints into the Kingdom but casting the Goats out of the Kingdom, those who are expected to show no compassion. But, perhaps lurking in Jesus' Prophetic vision for the Goats, it makes perfect sense to simply include the Antichrist and the False Prophet in with this crowd because Revelation later predicts the identical fate as those of Jesus' Goats, eternal punishment

13th Offering:
Antichrist
False Prophet
Goats

15th

Last 6 Days of Booths:Libations = Millennial Saints

The final 6 days of the Feast of Booths all record Offerings with Libations:

Holy Day	Offering by Fire				Libation?
	bull	ram	lamb	goat	
Feast of Booths: 1st Day	13	2	14	1	No
16th Day 7th Month	12	2	14	1	Yes
17th Day 7th Month	11	2	14	1	Yes
18th Day 7th Month	10	2	14	1	Yes
19th Day 7th Month	9	2	14	1	Yes
20th Day 7th Month	8	2	14	1	Yes
Feast of Booths: 7th Day	7	2	14	1	Yes

It should be immediately noticeable that the number of "Bull" Offerings is descending throughout the Days of the Feast of Booths starting with a count of 13 on the first day and ending with a count of 7 on the 7th day. The first Day of Libations has the Bull count at 12. Since the other Offerings remain unchanged throughout the Feast Days, it must be understood that the changing count of the Bulls is communicating something of significance to the reader. The second symbol of communication is the non-libations for the first day and the libation Offerings for the rest of the Feast Days.

It was speculated earlier that the number 13 communicates the idea that this is representing the Surviving Population of the Latter Days, those that come out mortally alive. By these not having a Libation associated with them perhaps means that the Survivors are not necessarily to be presumed members of the coming Kingdom, necessarily those who did not receive the Mark of the Beast and yet mortally survive. Certainly the number 13 has a notoriety in Scripture and suggests that some members of this group are indeed not to be considered welcome into the Kingdom. What then is an interesting proposition is the whole telling of Jesus' Prophecy of the Sheep and Goats in Matthew 25:31-46. There Jesus predicted that when He Comes to sit in his "Glorious Throne" He would separate the Survivors of the Latter Day between "Sheep" and "Goats". The Sheep would be given "eternal life" and be welcomed into the Kingdom of God whereas the Goats would be sent to eternal punishment.

So if the number of Survivors of the Latter Day are to be depicted by the "13" Bull Offerings of the first day of the Feast of Booths this then suggests that the "12" Bull Offerings that the next Day possesses perhaps signifies the Righteous Saints of the original population symbolized by "13". That is, the 12 Libation Offerings represent those that Jesus chose amongst the 13 Atonement offerings. Hence, the beginning of the first Day of the Feast of Booths seems to include some portion of Daniel's 70th Week. Then, later in the same 1st Day, Christ is to judge in separating the Sheep from the Goats. Indeed, the entire Day seems to be set aside for Judgement. Since the greater portion of the 7 Day Feast of Booths is to be considered the Messianic Kingdom Age lasting 1,000 years, an entire Day set aside for Judgment means this is no small occasion.

Libation 6. The remaining Days of the Feast and their respective Offerings must be then signifying something about the nature of the Count of Saints as the Messianic Kingdom proceeds. Recall that the book of Revelation quantifies the length of the Messianic Kingdom as 1,000 years. So then each of the Days of the

Feast, perhaps starting with the 16th Day, represents a certain amount of time transpiring throughout this so called "Millennial Kingdom" Age. If this is an accurate interpretation, why then are the number of Bull Offerings descending throughout the Feast Days? What is this communicating? Is this signifying a dwindling Count of Saints as time passes or an accumulation of Saints that has diminishing returns as time moves forward?

The best interpretation, based on Revelation's depiction of the number of Mortals existing on the Earth at the End of the Millennial Kingdom being like the "sand on the seashore", is that the number of Bull Offerings must be representing the incrementally growing number of Saints being added to the Kingdom as time passes. How these additional "Millennial Kingdom" Saints materialize must be by way of Procreation. The Surviving Righteous Mortals (the Sheep) entering the Kingdom along with the Elect continue to procreate and out of the new generation come both Saints and Rebels. The ratio of Rebels to Saints must grow continually throughout this Kingdom era and is indirectly represented by the dwindling number of Bull Offerings as the Days transpire.

Perhaps one could conjecture that the number is falling because the number represents what Mortal Saints remain alive as time moves on with the falling number suggesting the reality of Mortal death throughout this Age and thus reducing the Count of the Saints of this Age. But this cannot be the case as once again the observer is faced with the reality of the Great Mystery, as is the case for all the Holy Days of the 7th Month. Since the Resurrection has already taken place during the Latter Day, any Mortal Saints that appear after the Resurrection must be understood living forever and not dying. Without the existence of another Resurrection for Saints, which the Scripture does not teach, this disallows any Mortal Saints to succumb to Mortal Death. How Mortal Saints of the Latter Day can be expected to live forever is discussed further in the book entitled "Lifes, Deaths, and Immortalities: Scripture's fate for the Human Race".

At the end of this Kingdom era, Satan is to be unbound from the Abyss where he will have been temporarily detained throughout the Kingdom Age according to Revelation. He will then be allowed to gather the Mortal Rebels of that time together. This "horde" is to then instigate an Invasion on Jerusalem by its leader Gog and the ethnic peoples of Magog as the lead Nation as both the Prophet Ezekiel, and several other Prophets, as well as the Apostle John, foretell. During that confrontation God is to send fire down from Heaven and destroy all the Rebels before even entering the City. At that time Satan is to be caught, bound and permanently thrown into the Lake of Fire. And for a second time, there will again be Survivors for this occasion as well, as there are expected to be for the Latter Day. These will then be added into the fold of Mortal Saints at the end of this Kingdom. So as the last day of the Feast comes, the final Bull Offering Count will come to "7", what is to represent the "Fullness" of Mortal Saints that are to be brought into the Kingdom at the close of this Feast.

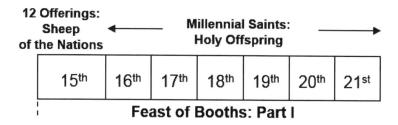

Feast of Booths: Part I

The Sabbath of the Feast of Booths:
A Hidden Libations Day of Unknown Significance

Libation 7: What extra significance this final Day of Ingathering could have above and beyond the narrative of the Messianic Kingdom Age, based on its 7 Bull Libation Offerings, is hidden inside the Feast of Booths testimony. It sneaks up to the unsuspecting student who knows something about the nature of a 7 Day Feast period as well as a major prophecy that remains unfulfilled even in this late hour of the Divine Harvest Plan. The surprise is that there happens to be one more important symbol of the Feast of Booths to take into account that is not readily noticeable. Because the Feast is 7 days long, there happens to be one 7th day Sabbath somewhere within this period of time. The Feast of Unleavened Bread shares this same hidden symbolism which the Gospel testimony reveals was coincident with the Burial Period. So now similar questions come to be raised about the Feast of Booth's 7th Day Sabbath. For one, on what Day of the Feast of Booths is the 7th Day Sabbath to be reckoned falling upon?

By the power of suggestion of certain prophecies, and as Tradition would argue for it as well, this Sabbath should be positioned coming as the last Day of the Feast of Booths. That is why the earlier table shows Libation 7 as being placed on this Day. Hence, it adds Sabbath Libation Offerings to those that are already assigned for the Day. What this special day appears to be aligning itself with is the Gog/Magog events. Since the symbolisms of the Sabbath are to be unveiled in the next chapter, what exactly its association with the Gog-Magog Prophecy is will have to be examined there. Yet its Libation Offerings are already known to convey the anticipation of Gospel Saints. So what new and noteworthy Gospel Saints are being predicted to emerge as part of the Gog-Magog Prophecy above and beyond what are referred to here as "Millennial" Saints? What immense surprise that this hidden Sabbath brings to the Holy Days Code cannot be overestimated. At this juncture however there is not enough information to figure this out. The latter chapters of this book will turn to the examination of especially Ezekiel to help chip away at what secrets lie hidden here. To the curious and persistent student there will indeed be a colossal find awaiting.

Now before moving on to the final Holy Day another observation needs to be made regarding the Feast of Booths. With 6 out of 7 Days having Libation Offerings, the major question arises regarding the prophetic Mortal Saints they anticipate. Do not all these Saints require accompanying Atonement Offerings since they are not expected to die? The subtle affirmative answer to this question goes back to an earlier discussion regarding the efficaciousness of the Offerings of the Feast of Unleavened Bread. It would appear as if all 7 Days of its Atonement Offerings are to become transposed upon the Saints who are to appear during the last 7 Holy Days in the schedule!

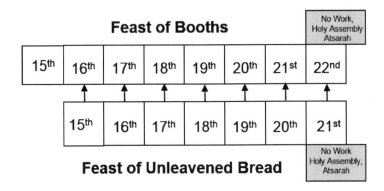

22nd Day of 7th Month: Future Eternity Libation

Libation 8. The last Holy Day must be reserved for the Future Eternity, representing what the Divine Plan's prophecies see in the furthest point into the future. That this final day is immediately following the last day of the Feast of Booths simply conveys the idea that there is to be no break in time to be accounted for between the end of the Kingdom Age and the beginning of the Future Eternity.

The last and final Day of the Holy Days, the 22nd Day of the 7th Month is a day having Offerings by Fire which have Libations!:

Holy Day	Offering by Fire				Libation?
(Num29:35-38)	bull	ram	lamb	goat	
22nd Day 7th Month	1	1	7	1	Yes

Last Fruits

No Work, Holy Assembly Atsarah
22nd

This last Holy Day must be representing whatever the furthest point End Times prophecy can see into the future. This would have to be the prophet Isaiah's prediction of the coming New Heavens and Earth which are to be ushered in for the Future Eternity. Likewise, John argues for the very same thing after he envisions the "Millennial Kingdom". Indeed, this resonates with the Scripture's illustration of Booths which represent "temporary housing" throughout the Kingdom Age. Booths were to be constructed and lived within for the 7 days of the Feast just as Exodus Israel had lived. This then would leave the 8th Day, the last Holy Day, to be the transitional moment when "temporary housing" would be replaced with an eternal "permanent dwelling place" for the Saints of God to live within in the New Heavens and Earth.

But John also mentions that God is "among men" and that death is no more (21:3-4) in the coming Future Eternity. These statements cannot be applicable to those who have been resurrected for over a 1,000 years by the time this moment arrives. This only makes sense if it applies to all the mortal righteous of the Millennial Kingdom who are now brought into the Future Eternity as Mortals! It reads as if these are to live forever as Mortals yet more confirmation of the Great Mystery. This idea will become further explored and reinforced as the Holy Days Code continues to be unraveled in the pages to come.

That this final Day has a Libation suggests that the Future Eternity will acquire new Gospel Saints which its Libations symbolize! Recall that there are 2 Holy Days that share the symbolism of "Atsarah". This Day and the last day of the Feast of Unleavened Bread, that is the 21st Day of the 1st Month (See Deut16:8).

Holy Day	Offering by Fire				Libation?
(Num28:19-22)	bull	ram	lamb	goat	
Feast of ULB: 7th Day	2	1	7	1	No

Holy Day	Offering by Fire				Libation?
(Num29:35-38)	bull	ram	lamb	goat	
22nd Day 7th Month	1	1	7	1	Yes

What this must be telling the reader is that these 2 Days must be representing the same general Time on the Divine Timeline, that is, the Future Eternity itself. And again, it is made up of Atonement Offerings as well as Libation Offerings when interpreted in this way. Thus, the Atonement Offerings of the last day of the Feast of Unleavened Bread must be accounting for Israel's Mortal Saints of the coming Future Eternity! And the Libation Offerings of the last Holy Day must thus be symbolizing their Gospel Saint status! Indeed, in surveying what all the Atonement Offerings come to signify from beginning to end is ultimately an assignment to Mortal Saints who are never expected to die for all Future Eternity. And that all of the Libation Offerings of the Feast of Booths represent the Godly Offspring of these same Mortal Saints!

Summary of the Holy Days Offerings by Fire: Leviticus 23 & Numbers 28-29

Holy Day	Offering by Fire				Libation?
	bull	ram	1yr old lamb	goat	
New Moon	2	1	7	1	Yes
Yom Teruah	1	1	7	1	No
Yom Kippur (Num 29)	1	1	7	1	No
(Leviticus 16)	1	2		2	No
Feast of Booths: 1st Day	13	2	14	1	No
16th Day 7th Month	12	2	14	1	Yes
17th Day 7th Month	11	2	14	1	Yes
18th Day 7th Month	10	2	14	1	Yes
19th Day 7th Month	9	2	14	1	Yes
20th Day 7th Month	8	2	14	1	Yes
Feast of Booths: 7th Day	7	2	14	1	Yes
22nd Day 7th Month	1	1	7	1	Yes

Latter Holy Days Schedule

	Daniel's 70th Week		Messianic Kingdom Age							Future Eternity
7th Month	1	10	15	16	17	18	19	20	21	22

As was discussed previously, there are still things left unanswered. Some will be resolved by the remaining 2 Decryption Keys but some will remain as hidden secrets. For example, who exactly are the Saints represented by the Sabbath Libation Offerings in the Feast of Booths? And now, who are the Saints to appear in the Future Eternity as symbolized by the Libation Offerings of the last Holy Day? To resolve these questions requires an in depth study of Ezekiel's prophecies, some of which were summarized in chapter 9. The final three chapters of this book, chapters 15-17, will be set aside to unveil the meanings of these most hidden and profound symbolisms found within the Holy Days Code.

**For the Son of Man is
Lord of the Sabbath**

Matthew 12:8

**Now the women...saw the tomb and
how His body was laid...And on the
Sabbath they rested according to the
commandment.**

Luke 23:55-56

Chapter Thirteen

The Death Rest Decryption Key

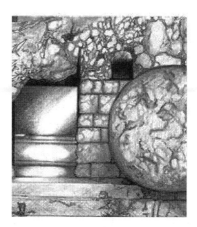

So far, the chronology of the Gospel testimony has offered up 2 Decryption Keys which have begun to expose the reality of a Holy Days Code. Both Keys appear within the Last Supper testimony. The 1st Key is found when it is noticed the Supper unveils 2 Passovers. With Jesus eating the meal himself, he is found honoring Israel's Passover memorial. But when he set aside a piece of bread and a cup of wine to serve to his disciples, a new Passover in Jesus' own blood was being symbolized. Each of these 2 Passovers can be shown to usher in their own separate paths. Israel's Atonement path began on the night the Nation fled from Egyptian bondage. The 7 day Feast of Unleavened Bread immediately following the Passover symbolizes this path which continues on into the Future Eternity. The Gospel's Libation path began on the day of Jesus' Crucifixion and also must continue on into the Future Eternity.

The 2nd Decryption Key comes to be recognized specifically with the Cup of Wine Jesus served to his disciples in the Supper. He said it symbolized his blood and life which was to be poured out for many for the forgiveness of sins. But since the Passover testimony makes no mention of wine in its symbolisms, Jesus is found introducing a new symbol for the new Passover. To readers who understand the elements of the Offerings by Fire, there is a fascinating correlation between the Law's wine libations that are poured out over some of the Offerings and Jesus' Cup. And it is just the fact that some Offerings have libations while others do not that a form of communication seems to be imbedded within the Holy Days Offerings. At first the Holy Days testimony appears as if this form of decryption suggests that the 2 Divine Paths follow different Offerings by Fire, one made up of Atonement Offerings whereas the other contains Libation Offerings. But as will be shown, this early division of paths does not remain this way through the Fall Schedule. Rather, the 2 Paths can be found divided along another theme of Life and Death. That is, One Path follows Israel's Prophetic Mortal Life whereas the other follows Mortal Death.

What comes next in the chronological unfolding of the Gospel testimony is the discovery of a 3rd Decryption Key associated with Jesus' Burial Period. That is, the Supper Key suggests 2 Passovers, the Crucifixion Key suggests 2 kinds of Offerings, and now Jesus' Burial Period comes to coincide with the Sabbath. In an earlier chapter, it was learned that the Gospel accounts have a divided testimony over what kind of days transpired during Jesus' Burial. Mark and Luke record Jesus' body having laid in the tomb starting on a Preparation day for the Sabbath and then followed by the second day being a Sabbath. But Matthew specifically recalls "Sabbaths" plural having transpired during the Burial Period. This appears to reflect the opinion of what the sect of the Pharisees believed was to constitute a Sabbath. Finally, John simply accounts a Sabbath coming coincident with Jesus' burial and noting it was a "high day". Regardless of what testimony is consulted, all 4 writers witness Jesus' burial period coming coincident with a Sabbath, whether it be reckoned as one long Sabbath period made up of 2 days of Burial or 2 separate Sabbath days of Burial.

Hence, the Gospel Burial Period and the Sabbath come coincident. But wait, Sabbath means "Rest" while the idea of burial epitomizes "Rest". So is it a coincidental fluke that Jesus "rested" in Death Rest during a Sabbath Rest? Or was it preplanned for more than a thousand years in advance (or even before time began)? The Holy Days Code argues for the latter. And so the 3rd Gospel Decryption Key is born:

Burial Decryption Key:

Sabbath Holy Day = Death Rest of (?)

How to use this 3rd Decryption Key then is to locate a given Sabbath in the schedule and understand that some person or group is being identified as suffering Death at some prophetic time on the Divine Calendar. It begins with the very first Sabbath of the Holy Days schedule coinciding with Christ's Death Rest. Hence, all the Sabbaths are key places on the Divine Timeline where notable Deaths are expected to occur.

The First 7th Day Sabbath of the Holy Season

The most noteworthy thing to recognize about the first Holy Season's Sabbath is the same noteworthy thing that can be recognized for all of the things the Gospel is found overlapping with the Holy Days. Each Gospel occasion comes to overlap with the very first elements of the Holy Days as if it were the DNA of the Holy Days Code.

That is, the Passover is the very first Holy Occasion of the season. The day after the Passover is Israel's first day of holy assembly and the first day which Israel is not to work in the season. This was the first day of Jesus' burial. The next day after this came to be the Sabbath, the 1st Sabbath Holy Day of the entire holy season. On the following day Jesus would be seen resurrected on the first harvest related Holy Day of the holy season.

With the Gospel coinciding with these initial Holy Days building blocks, here is where the obvious clues of decryption are being shown to the observant reader. The Gospel testimony is simply "pairing up" an aspect of itself with the Holy Days building blocks. By whatever connection is being made to Jesus this is what the original symbol is to be understood the Law had at first encoded into the Holy Day:

The DNA of the Holy Days Code

1. Memorial	2. Sacrifice	3. Sabbath Rest		4. Resurrection
Last Supper	John's Passover	No work Holy Assembly	7th day Sabbath	Head 1st Fruits
13	**14**	**15**	**16**	**17**
1st Holy Memorial	1st Holy Occasion	1st "No Work" "Holy Assembly" Holy Day	1st 7th Day Sabbath Holy Day	1st Harvest Related Holy Day

With Jesus' "Burial" coming to be paired up with the "Sabbath", the Scripture is subtly introducing a new take on the original Sabbath meaning of "Rest". That is, it is God who "Rests" on the present ongoing 7th Day after having created the Heavens and the Earth in "6 days". So too Jesus also "Rested" on the Sabbath. Yet, most importantly, it was a new form of "Rest", it was a Bodily "Death Rest".

Tragically, traditional Christianity came to read into the Gospel testimony as if it were suggesting the demise of the importance of the Sabbath. Why? Because it perceived there was a new emphasis being placed on the first day of the week, the day of the Resurrection, as if suggesting the importance of the Sabbath had now been replaced. However the Law communicates the Sabbath is to be an eternal observance for Israel to honor. And when examining the symbolisms surrounding the Day of Head First Fruits, the day representing the Resurrection, surprisingly it has no special attributes that should indicate it as an elevated day of observance. For example, it is not a day of holy assembly nor is it a day of no work and it certainly is not to be considered a Sabbath.

Furthermore, Jesus never told his disciples to make the day of His Resurrection a day of special significance but did tell them to make his "Death" something to periodically remember until he was to "come", a remembrance traditionally coined as the "Lord's Supper" (e.g., 1Cor11:26) now called "communion". However, institutionalized Christianity was only too eager to promote the demise of the Sabbath and elevate the first day of the week so that it could distance itself from the Law.

But in reality, it can be seen that the Divine Plan gave Christianity its own unique reasons for keeping the Sabbath sacred since it was during a Sabbath, the first

Sabbath of the holy season, that Jesus' body lay buried. Arguably, the Sabbath can only be interpreted as having acquired additional sacredness with the coming of the Gospel, not having become demoted by it. For it now represents a resting period not only for the Father but also for the Son too! It is yet another fascinating example of how the Gospel is made to seamlessly coexist with the Law. This simple observation should motivate any reader to look further into matters where the Law and the Gospel cross paths.

The 1st Sabbath symbolizes the 1st Death

At this point, a reader has to take a step back from this first Sabbath of the Holy Season and be reminded of how Leviticus 23 opens discussion of the Holy Days by introducing the 7th Day Sabbath in Lev23:3. In recalling the chronological history, the Sabbath was inaugurated after the Passover. Yet it comes first in Leviticus 23. So why is this? In having reviewed this earlier, it was suggested that this is perhaps to represent the greater timeline of human history in that the "7th Day" symbolizes all of the Present Creation.

Now however, in understanding that the Sabbath is taking on a new symbolism of Death with Jesus' testimony, the interpretation of Lev23:3 can take on an even more provocative one. That is, what "Death" can Lev23:3 be signifying, if in fact the symbolism of the Sabbath in the Holy Days testimony is to be decoded as representing Death? It should become immediately clear that this must be the Death suffered in Eden forewarned of God in Gen2:17. It was a Death that came to be universal according to the Apostle Paul in Rom5:17. A spiritual death to God came over the entire Human Race. Thus, the "7th Day" of this present Creation was corrupted with Adam's Sin and Death has since enveloped the entire "7th Day" Sabbath of God's Rest. The book of Revelation implies that this Death is to be called the "1st Death" in that it predicts a coming "2nd Death" in Rev20:14-15.

In summary, the 1st Death is to be understood temporary and existing during the present 7th Day. It will be replaced by the 2nd Death at the end of this present Creation, an eternal Death away from the life of God for all those who do not escape the 1st Death. (It will be proposed later, near the end of this chapter, that the 14th and last Sabbath of the Holy Days is in fact symbolic of this 2nd Death!) It is to be one's personal faith in the Good News of Jesus Christ having died for Sin that causes one to be "Born Again" out of this Death and into Eternal Life (e.g., John3:3-7).

The "1st Sabbath" of Leviticus 23:3 symbolizes the "1st Death"

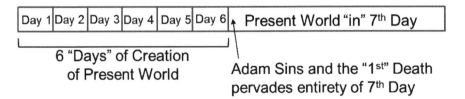

196

The 13 Sabbath Holy Days

So if the 1st Sabbath of Leviticus 23 represents the 1st Death, a reader discovers that the 2nd Sabbath of Leviticus 23 represents the Messiah's Death to conquer this 1st Death! But this is only the beginning of the Holy Sabbath Days. In the opening chapter of this book, there was mentioned to be 14 total Sabbaths to be counted amongst all the Holy Days. If the first Sabbath is not counted since it does not identify a given Holy Day but just the definition of a Sabbath, then there actually 13 Holy Day Sabbaths within the Divine Schedule

13 Sabbath Holy Days to be reckoned in Leviticus 23

1: The 7th Day Sabbath within Feast of Unleavened Bread (hidden, unmentioned)
2-8: The 7 7th Day Sabbaths between Head First Fruits & Feast of First Fruits/Weeks
9: The 1st day of the 7th month: Yom Teruah (A "Lunar" Sabbath)
10: The 10th day of the 7th month: Yom Kippur (A "Lunar" Sabbath)
11: The 15th day of the 7th month: 1st day of Booths (A "Lunar" Sabbath)
12: The 7th day Sabbath within the Feast of Booths (Hidden, unmentioned)
13: The 22nd day of the 7th month (A "Lunar" Sabbath)

So what then do the remaining 12 Sabbaths of the Holy Season symbolize? Each will be carefully examined in the remainder of this chapter. The list below creates a new "alphanumerical" assignment for these Sabbaths by which the remainder of this book will use to recall them.

S0   = 7th Day of Creation: Humanity's Ongoing 1st Death Period
MS1   = Mystery Sabbath of the Feast of Unleavened Bread (Jesus' Burial Period)
S1-S7 = 49 Day Sabbath Period between the Harvest First Fruits Ingathering
LS1   = Yom Teruah's Lunar Sabbath
LS2   = Yom Kippur's Lunar Sabbath
LS3   = Lunar Sabbath of the 1st Day of the Feast of Booths
MS2   = Mystery Sabbath of the Feast of Booths
LS4   = Lunar Sabbath of the Last Holy Day

The first important observation to make is that 4 of these Sabbaths are Lunar based meaning that they are fixed days of the month and are not 7th Day Sabbaths most of the time. These all come in the 7th month and are unique Sabbaths unlike the 7th day Sabbath and is why they are labelled LS1-4. Leviticus chapters 16 and 23 are the only locations in Scripture where Lunar days are given such a "Sabbath" distinction. Whereas the 7th day Sabbath is designated an Offering by Fire in the Law, these Lunar Sabbaths do not share this same distinction as Numbers 28 and 29 confirm. What major difference this makes between the 2 different kinds of Sabbaths is that a 7th day Sabbath is to be understood possessing 2 symbols while the lunar Sabbaths possess only 1 symbol:

Sabbath Symbolisms

7th day Sabbath	Lunar Sabbath Holy Days: 1st, 10th, 15th, 22nd days of 7th Month
- Death Rest	- Death Rest
-Libation Offering (Gospel element)	- No Offering

Hence, the 7th day Sabbath brings an additional symbol of the Gospel to its Death Rest symbolism whereas the Lunar Sabbath does not. Intuitively, this means a 7th Day Sabbath not only communicates Death but also brings an element of the Gospel. The simplest application for a 7th Day Sabbath is that it signify the Death of a Saint. Clearly, Jesus' Burial is the epitome of this. In contrast, a Lunar Sabbath appears to communicate Death absent the Gospel as if to suggest the Death of someone damned. So a corollary to the Burial Decryption Key is that 7th Day Sabbaths seem to communicate Death and Saints while Lunar Sabbaths identify the Death of the Damned only. This leads to the following observations in review of the Holy Days:

1. All mentioned 7th Day Sabbaths are in the Early Holy Days
2. All Lunar Sabbath Holy Days appear in the 7th Month.

From this, 4 more observations can be concluded:

1. Early Holy Day Sabbaths appear to be accounting for ALL DECEASED SAINTS
2. There are no Deceased Saints associated with the 7th Month (the Great Mystery)
3. The Damned Dead are only accounted for within the 7th Month period.
4. Two distinct Paths emerge across the entire breadth of the Holy Days Code:
   a. One accounts for all the Sabbaths thus accounting for all the dead
   b. The other must then be accounting for only the living

What this implies is that the 2 Holy Days Paths can be found dividing up the Holy Days Code between the Mortal Living and the Mortal Dead.

Counting of 7 Sabbaths: The Saints' Death Rest

The next Sabbath Holy Day after the Mystery Sabbath of the Feast of Unleavened Bread is actually the first of 7 that Israel was asked to "count" between the Day of Head First Fruits and the Feast of First Fruits/Weeks/Pentecost signified by S1-S7. In all, they represent a 49 day period of separation between the Day of Head First Fruits and the Feast of First Fruits/Weeks/Pentecost. This was discussed in the previous chapter. The Jews have long called this counting of Sabbaths as the "Count of the Omer". An "omer" was the Law's definition of a person's daily portion of grain one could eat, that is, a person's daily bread. It was an omer of barley that the

High Priest was commanded he Wave before God as an Offering on the Day of Head First Fruits.

These 7 Sabbaths can either be accounted for individually as 7 total or the entire period can be seen as one long Sabbath as the context suggests. Regardless of how they are counted, the Divine Plan is seen creating a pattern that is formed over the 51 day period linking the two First Fruits Holy Days together. It appears to be a game of pattern recognition:

**Play the Code's Game of Pattern Recognition:
What comes next?**

As the diagram indicates, there are two pairs of Holy Days to recognize as being composed of the same symbols. The first pair is the Sabbath Holy Days associated with Jesus' Death Rest followed by the Harvest Day of Head First Fruits, the day Jesus was resurrected. This pattern is now noticed to repeat itself. That is, there is another Sabbath period which immediately follows the Resurrection which is then followed by yet another Harvest Day of First Fruits. The observant reader should be able to recognize the pattern and speculate as to what the second pair is symbolizing given what decoding is provided by the first pair through the Gospel message.

That is, if the first Sabbath Period represented Jesus' Death Rest then by association the second Sabbath Period should also suggest yet another Death Rest. But of whom? And if the Day of Head First Fruits symbolized the Resurrection of Jesus so by pattern recognition the very similar First Fruits day of the Feast of First Fruits/Weeks/Pentecost should also be symbolizing the resurrection of the person or persons lying in Death Rest during this second Sabbath period. Whoever is being predicted in Death Rest, this same person (or persons) is assumed to be the one (or those) being resurrected afterward.

So who is being symbolized by these Holy Days? Who is to be dead throughout these Sabbaths? And who is to Rise From the Dead subsequently thereafter? There is no more illuminating passage that can shed light on the meaning behind these Holy Days than the following:

1 Cor 15:20, 23 But now Christ has been raised from the dead, the_first fruits_ of those who are asleep. But each in his own order: Christ the first fruits, _after that those who are Christ's_ at His coming...

Here it states the very pattern that the Holy Days sets forth: Christ is first "dead" and then He is "raised from the dead" as "first fruits". Next, everyone else who are "His" are to follow at the coming of the Resurrection. Nearly all of those expected to be Resurrected become "dead" and then they become "raised". So this second set of Sabbaths and Harvest Day is to represent <u>the Death Rest of those of the Resurrected Sainthood.</u> Likewise, <u>the Feast of First Fruits/Weeks/Pentecost is to represent the Resurrection of Whom?:</u>

3rd Decryption Key: Sabbath symbolizes Death Rest

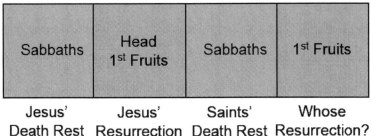

| Sabbaths | Head 1st Fruits | Sabbaths | 1st Fruits |

| Jesus' | Jesus' | Saints' | Whose |
| Death Rest | Resurrection | Death Rest | Resurrection? |

3 Consecutive Sabbaths: Preponderance of Death

Turning now to the study of the Sabbaths of the 7th Month Holy Days, it can be observed that there are 3 consecutive Sabbaths in a row beginning with the first Holy Day of the 7th Month:

7th Month

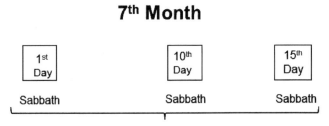

| 1st Day | | 10th Day | 15th Day |
| Sabbath | | Sabbath | Sabbath |

The Fall Holy Days have 3 Sabbaths in a row

As was learned about the multiple Sabbaths of the Spring in being a long period of Death Rest, so too it must be concluded here that there is an abundance of Death expected for what these Days are foretelling. That all 3 of these Sabbaths happen to be the first of 4 Lunar Sabbaths the Law defines, these Sabbaths must therefore represent bleak and darkened Deaths given these do not share a Gospel element with them. Here again is where the Latter Prophets, Jesus' Prophecies and the book of Revelation can all help shed light on what these 3 Days could be symbolizing.

The first big clue would have to be the count of 3 Holy Days. For it is Revelation which breaks down the chronology of Daniel's 70th Week by dividing it into 3! That is, there are to be 1) 7 Brokened Seals, 2) 7 Blown Trumpets and finally 3) 7 Poured Bowls. Across these series of 3, Death is indeed expected to rain down on Earth in hard-to-imagine numbers with few expected to come through on the other side.

Another observation to make is that Jesus declared that the End Times would be like a pregnant woman in labor pangs. In this illustration, each pang would be like a calamity with each succeeding pang bringing greater and more intensifying calamities. They are expected to draw closer and closer together until the calamities come in rapid succession in bringing about a kind of cataclysmic End.

In sifting through the details, there are clues to be found which suggest a gross span of time that is passing for each of these 3 series as they unfold one after another. Beginning with the 7 Brokened Seals it appears as if they consume roughly half of the 7 year period. Next, the 7 Blown Trumpets compress into a shorter span of time, maybe 2/3 of the 3 and a half year period remaining. Finally, the 7 Poured Bowls consume the remaining 1+ final year. In examining the 3 Holy Days in view here, note that the time between the first and second Holy Day is 10 days, then another 4 days between the second and third Holy Day and then the last day assigned as the final sequence.

The first 15 Days of the 7ᵗʰ Month

| 1ˢᵗ Day | ← The Breaking of 7 Seals → | 10ᵗʰ Day | ← The Blowing of → 7 Trumpets | **The Pouring of 7 Bowls** 15ᵗʰ Day |

Throughout this threefold sequence, Revelation predicts Mortal Death will intensify with time as well. For example, the 4ᵗʰ Broken Seal describes a 1/4ᵗʰ of the Human Population succumbing to death. Then, the 6ᵗʰ Blown Trumpet annihilates a 1/3ʳᵈ of the Population. Finally, the Battle of Armageddon comes commensurate with the 7th Poured Bowl and perhaps is to be understood bringing the remaining ~1/2 of the World's Population to death (i.e., 1 - 1/4 - 1/3 = ~1/2), save a few including the Elect of course. Indeed, the Prophet Isaiah predicts that Humanity will become "scarcer than the Gold of Ophir" (Isa13:12). As each of these 3 Holy Days are examined individually, the general span of time for each sequence will shown to be tied to the great major prophetic periods that are to transpire during Daniel's 70th Week.

Yom Teruah's Sabbath: 1/4th of Humanity to Die

Having decoded a great deal about this Day already, what is left to decode is this Day's symbolism of it being a Lunar Sabbath day, the very first Lunar Sabbath to be observed. What the 3rd Decryption Key decodes here is the reality that this Day, and the 3 other Lunar Sabbaths of the 7th Month, are dark and tragic portending Death to the Damned. Having just assigned this Day to be symbolic of the 7 Broken Seals of Revelation, this then means the Lunar Sabbath must represent all the Death that is to come as a result of the Breaking of the Seals. More specifically,

Rev 6:7-8 When the Lamb broke the fourth seal...Authority was given to Death

and Hades over <u>a fourth of the earth</u>, to kill with sword and with famine and with pestilence and by the wild beasts of the earth.

Here is where the book of Revelation begins to predict an ascending cataclysm, starting with the annihilation of 25% of the World's Population! This is a staggering number so great that it has no equal except for the fact that even worse is coming as there are 2 more series yet to unfold. Daniel (12:1) and Jesus (24:21) prophecy that this time will be the single greatest distress to ever come upon the Earth with nothing to compare it with. But the worst is yet to come.

The breaking of the 5th Seal brings even more Death but now to the Saints called the Tribulation Martyrs. These Deaths however are not to be factored in the number of Deaths assigned to Yom Teruah's Sabbath because it lacks Libation Offerings. At the same time however, the Death of the Martyrs should act to stimulate the mind in trying to understand how the Martyrs do actually get accounted for. As was concluded earlier, ALL deceased Saints are accounted for in the symbolism of S1 through S7. What this means is that these Martyrs should be understood accounted for in S7, the last Sabbath accounting for Deceased Saints. Hence, graphically, S7 should certainly be made to overlap the 7th Month 10 Day Holy Period that begins with Yom Teruah and ends with Yom Kippur. Furthermore, the Tribulation Period that Jesus unveils in his Olivet Discourse must thus begin somewhere in this same 10 day Holy Period and last until Yom Kippur.

What the New Moon Libation Offerings account for, as argued in the previous chapter, is all of the Mortal Saints that are depicted in Revelation's prophetic view of Daniel's 70th Week. Clearly, this includes the Martyrs and the 144,000, even though both groups experience entirely different fates. What finally brings this Tribulation Period to an end is essentially the Death of the Last Martyr or Martyrs who are expected to die as a result of this era.

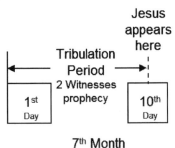

7th Month

Yom Kippur as Sabbath of Sabbaths:
2/3rd of Israel to Die

The next Lunar Sabbath rest day happens to be Yom Kippur. This Day is the most solemn Holy Day of them all. Tradition interprets this Day as a day worthy of fasting and abstaining from all manner of pleasure. The days between Yom Teruah and Yom Kippur are seen as a countdown of sorts, the Days of Awe, a time set aside for repenting and getting right with God before its too late. Shockingly, it would seem as if Tradition has accurately interpreted the nature of this 10 Day Holy Period and the 10th Day of this Holy Period. Given the Day is assigned the symbolism of being the "Sabbath of Sabbaths", what is clearly a Lunar Sabbath at that, this means the Darkest of the Darkest Deaths looms prophetically over this Day:

Lev 23:29,30 If there is any person who will not humble himself on this same day, he shall be cut off from his people. As for any person who does any work on this same day, that person I will destroy from among his people.

While the Atonement Offerings for this Day undoubtedly depict the Elect that Jesus prophesied He is expecting to come and gather together, certainly this means the Dark Sabbath of Yom Kippur symbolizes all those of Israel that Jesus is NOT EXPECTED to gather together:

Zech13:8 "It will come about in all the land," declares the LORD, "That two parts in it will be cut off and perish; but the third will be left in it. I will bring the third part through the fire, refine them as silver is refined, and test them as gold is tested. They will call on My name, and I will answer them; I will say, 'They are My people,' and they will say, 'The LORD is my God.'"

A whopping 2/3rd of Latter Day Israel is expected to be "cut off and perish". This leaves the Remnant to become only 1/3rd of Latter Day Israel! This moment when Jesus gathers the Elect together is to come "immediately after the Tribulation of those days" (Matt24:29). Hence, this is the moment when the Tribulation Period comes to an End and something else begins.

Yom Kippur: Convergence of Prophecy

But what? Christian Eschatology virtually goes over a cliff here when it argues that this occasion is Christ's 2nd Coming! This is absurd, for it completely jettisons the biggest End Times Prophecy of the Latter Prophets, the coming Day of the LORD! Tradition has tragically leapfrogged over the most incredible prophetic chain of events, a Convergence of Prophecy unlike any other moment in Prophetic History.

Where to start reconstructing this Convergence is to first notice that Jesus argues for convergence of 2 Major Prophecies, one new, the other old, in His Olivet Discourse. From His cue other things then start to be added to this skeletal framework from the Latter Prophets and finally Revelation too! The 1st Major Prophetic Event He unveils surrounding this Convergence is entirely new, never predicted before. This would be His prophecy of the "**Tribulation**" (Matt24:21). Now the key phrase Jesus uses to create His Prophetic Convergence is in Matt24:29 when He states "**immediately after the Tribulation**". Here is where Jesus segues into unveiling the 2nd Great Prophetic Event. Continuing in Matt24:29 Jesus states that "**the Sun and Moon will go dark and the Stars will fall from the sky**". This utterance however is not a Prophecy of Jesus but a quotation taken from the Prophet Isaiah in Isaiah 13:10.

In the greater context, the 13th chapter of Isaiah itself is about the Major End Times Prophecy of the coming Day of the LORD and the SIGNS which are to PRECEDE it as Isaiah13:6 & 9 clearly intimate. In other words, this coming Day of the LORD is to be so great and ominous that there will be Divine Signs provided in the Heavens for everyone on Planet Earth to recognize its soon coming!

Yet although the Hebrew Prophets foretell of the Day of the LORD they however fail to explain WHY the Day is to come. Now Jesus fills in that missing piece of information with His new Tribulation Prophecy. The reason why the Day of the LORD is coming is because the Tribulation is to immediately precede it and provoke God's Anger. So what Jesus is really saying is that His Appearing in the Sky is to be a Sign of His own Coming which will COINCIDE with the Signs of the coming Day of the LORD. His Appearing is to be at the Converging Point of the Tribulation Ending and the soon arrival of the Day of the LORD. As part of this convergence there is to be the gathering together of Israel's Elect (Matt24:31).

Olivet Discourse Prophetic Convergence

Tribulation Matt24:21	Signs of coming Day of the LORD Matt24:29 (Isaiah 13:10)	Jesus to Appear Here to be a Sign of His Own Coming (Matt24:30)	Day of the LORD

But there is more! It turns out that there is yet another major Prophecy that is intimately linked to the coming Day of the LORD by the Prophet Malachi! He predicts the return of the Prophet Elijah to Planet Earth BEFORE the coming of the Day of the LORD (Malachi 4:5)! Hence, Elijah's appearing should thus converge upon the Tribulation Period since Jesus predicted the Tribulation also precedes the Day of the LORD!

Olivet Discourse Prophetic Convergence

Tribulation Matt24:21	Signs of coming Day of the LORD Matt24:29 (Isaiah 13:10)	Jesus to Appear Here to be a Sign of His Own Coming (Matt24:30)	Day of the LORD

Elijah to Appear Here Mal4:5	← Malachi's Prophecy to be fulfilled "Before" the coming of the Day of the LORD

What's more is that the book of Revelation adds even more fascinating convergence upon this general prophetic time! Revelation's testimony of the 2 Witnesses is actually unveiling further prophecy regarding Malachi 4:5 which must then segue into the connectedness of Jesus' Prophetic Convergence.

Olivet Discourse Prophetic Convergence

Tribulation Matt24:21	Signs of coming Day of the LORD Matt24:29 (Isaiah 13:10)	Jesus to Appear Here to be a Sign of His Own Coming (Matt24:30)	Day of the LORD

Elijah to Appear Here Mal4:5	← Malachi's Prophecy to be fulfilled "Before" the coming of the Day of the LORD

Testimony of the 2 Witnesses Rev11:3-13	← Revelation's Prophecy adds to Mal4:5

The 2 Witnesses are to prophecy for 1260 days and then be put to death at the hands of the Antichrist. What the testimony is is essentially a "replay" of the lives of John the Baptist and Jesus as portrayed by the Prophets Moses and Elijah! It would appear as if the message is stating that the Church Age on Earth began with the prematurely terminated ministries of John the Baptist and Jesus Christ and it is predicted to end with the completion of the ministries of Moses and Elijah who both had their ministries cut short in earlier times but who are to return and finish them.

If this is an accurate interpretation, that would mean that these 2 Witnesses symbolize the last of the Tribulation Martyrs and that their completed witness indicates the end of the Tribulation Era. And if this is true then that means Matt24:29 is to "immediately follow" after which aligns with the testimony of the breaking of the 6th Seal and then this must mean that Jesus' Appears at this juncture in time and that the Day of the LORD is to soon follow which must then mean that the 7 Blown Trumpets and 7 Poured Bowls of Revelation that follow the 6th Broken Seal must signify the coming Day of the LORD, what is a monumental prophetic chain of events like dominoes falling one by one:

Jesus', Latter Prophets' and John's Great Prophetic Convergence

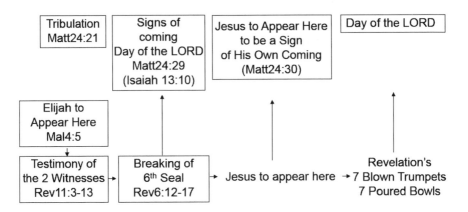

Hence, Yom Kippur is the dividing line between 2 Major Periods of Daniel's 70th Week. Yom Kippur symbolizes the End of the Tribulation Period and the Beginning of the Day of the LORD.

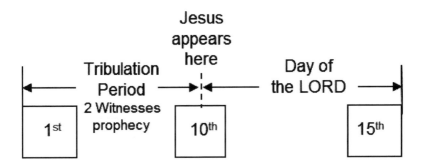

Initial decoded Timeline for Fall Holy Days

Where Revelation predicts this Day is to begin is in the following passage:

Rev 6:17 for the great day of their wrath has come; and who is able to stand?"

Yom Kippur as Sabbath of Sabbaths:
1/3rd of Humanity to Perish

So in recapping Yom Kippur's prophetic symbolism represents the ending of the Tribulation Era and the beginning of the Day of the LORD. Between the 6 Blown Trumpets and the 7 Poured Bowls, there is a total of 13 Divine Judgments predicted to come upon the world throughout the Day of the LORD. The Day goes on to be described by John in Revelation's chapters 8, 9 and 16 in this series of 13 judgments. But perhaps Yom Kippur itself only symbolizes the 6 Blown Trumpets alone, spread out over the 5 days leading up to the 15th Day of the 7th Month. If so, then there is even more Death to be accounted for here. For with the coming of the 6th Blown Trumpet, this brings a further escalation of Death to that of a 1/3rd of all living Humanity:

Rev9:15 And the four angels, who had been prepared for the hour and day and month and year, were released, so that they would kill a third of mankind.

Recall that the last great loss of life came with the 4th Broken Seal which is predicting to bring 1/4th of Humanity to die. So there is an ever increasing amount of Death transpiring between Yom Teruah and Yom Kippur. Adding 1/4th and 1/3rd equates to a little more than half. What then is implied for the 3rd Sabbath of the 7th Month is perhaps the Death of the lesser half of Humanity that remains alive to see Armageddon.

15th Day of 7th Month's Sabbath Rest:
Armageddon Death Rest, ~1/2 of Humanity to Die

Here now is the last of 3 consecutive Sabbath Holy Days, the 15th day of the 7th month, what is the first day of the Feast of Booths. Given that this last Feast symbolizes a long era, the 15th Day itself perhaps symbolizes a much longer period of time than the entire first 14 days of accelerated time. What remains to transpire is the coming of 7 Poured Bowls and all the Death that the ending of Daniel's 70th Week is to bring.

The 7 Poured Bowls will predict a great deal of suffering but Death itself is reserved for the showdown encounter between Jesus and His Heavenly Forces versus Satan and His Army. Satan is to be thrown out of heaven and cast down to earth perhaps as early as the 4th Broken Seal. He then is to gather together all those living mortals still opposing God even after they have suffered unrepentantly through 13 judgments. They will array themselves to face the coming of Jesus. Jesus is predicted to merely open his mouth and perhaps say "It is finished" (as He did upon His Mortal Death) and the whole affair comes to an anti-climactic ending:

Rev 19:17-18 ...to all the birds which fly in midheaven, "Come, assemble for the great supper of God; in order that you may <u>eat the flesh</u> of kings and the <u>flesh</u> of

commanders and the <u>flesh</u> of mighty men and the <u>flesh</u> of horses and of those who sit on them and the <u>flesh</u> of all men, both free men and slaves, and small and great."

Rev 19:21 And the rest were killed with the sword which came from the mouth of Him who sat upon the horse, and all the birds were filled with <u>their flesh</u>.

Here now is the occasion of what must be this Sabbath day's symbolic Death Rest where these bodies are to lay slaughtered from Jesus' mouth. Evidently this 1st day of the Feast of Booths is to be understood equivalent to the "night" portion of the Day of the LORD and how it ends with the Armageddon slaughter. The number of the Slaughter is perhaps to be understood the 1/2 of Humanity that still remains alive at this point.

Booths' 7th Day Sabbath: Gog/Magog Death Rest

Moving on, the next Sabbath is one that the previous chapter pointed out is somewhat of a hidden Holy Day. Nowhere in Scripture is this Holy Day pointed out (but neither is the 7th Day Sabbath of the Feast of Unleavened Bread). It existence comes from the fact that the Feast of Booths is 7 days long. Thus, there is one 7th day Sabbath existing somewhere in this 7 day period. This was first true about the Feast of Unleavened Bread since it is 7 days long too. And it was the Gospel testimony that revealed that on this day is when Jesus' body lay buried in Death Rest. It is this first Sabbath and its interpretation that inspires this very chapter and everything it reveals.

So perhaps this Sabbath has some "hidden" truth to convey. Further still, it most likely implies this day is to have a similar weightiness as the first Sabbath being they are very similar to one another. Notice again that this is a 7th day Sabbath, a day that possesses 2 symbols, a Death Rest and a Gospel element symbolized in its Libation Offerings. The previous 3 Sabbath Days of the 7th Month lacked Libation Offerings. As such it is the only 7th Day Sabbath to be a part of the 7th Month Holy Days.

The previous chapter raised the question as to when this Sabbath should be understood falling during the symbolic Feast of Booths. Recall that it can fall on any one of the seven days of the feast given it "floats" within the lunar schedule. As was pointed out already, there really is only one occasion in Scripture that can qualify in decoding the meaning of this Sabbath's symbolic Death Rest. Given this Holy Day is to be falling somewhere within what the Feast of Booths symbolizes, that is the Messianic/Millennial Kingdom Age, there is only one major incident recorded taking place that matches this. It comes in a close "second" to the epic scale of the Battle of Armageddon in terms of magnitude and death expected. This would be the Gog/Magog Invasion to prophetically materialize when Israel is living peacefully in its land.

Ezekiel is the Prophet who first identifies by name the main perpetrator and leader of the Invasion, "Gog". He also identifies the main tribe of humanity that is to head up this Invasion, "Magog", one of the sons of Japheth, the son of Noah identified in Genesis 10. Here is what Ezekiel predicts will come about:

Ezek 38:8-12 "After many days you will be summoned; in the latter years you will come into the land that is restored from the sword..."And you will go up, you will come like a storm; you will be like a cloud covering the land, you and all your troops, and many peoples with you."... you will devise an evil plan...and say 'I will go up against the land...to capture spoil and to seize plunder...

There will again be a similar outcome as is to prevail at Armageddon. The destruction is to be monumental and its effects are to be felt around the world so that all the nations are aware of the divine power being unleashed in that day. And again, the slaughter of the masses is to be of biblical proportions. Ezekiel has a most appropriate passage for indicating this occasion is yet again to produce a spectacular Death Rest as the Sabbath of the Feast of Booths is to be indicating:

Ezek 39:11 "And it will come about on that day that I shall give Gog <u>a burial ground</u> there in Israel, the valley of those who pass by east of the sea, and it will block off the passers-by. So they will bury Gog there with all his multitude, and they will call {it} the valley of Hamon-gog.

Modern mainline Christian Eschatology again takes an absurd position here arguing that this prophecy is to actually be fulfilled on two separate occasions in order to have it support its views. It believes that one of the occasions is the Latter Day and the other comes where the Apostle John emphatically states it is to come at the end of the Millennial Kingdom. Again, this is an absurd and ridiculous interpretation. There can only be one fulfillment of the Gog/Magog Invasion. Why? Because Ezekiel tells us here that Gog dies and is buried. Gog is a specific person and not a nationality. He is not predicted to rise from the dead in order that he be able to die yet a second time. So it is not possible for Gog to partake in two different failed invasions, only one and that being here at the end of the Messianic Kingdom as John points out in Revelation chapter 20.

The Divine Timing of the Gog/Magog Invasion

It turns out that the Prophet Ezekiel is one of 7 other Latter Prophet writers who will prophecy of this occasion. The Prophets Isaiah, Micah, Obadiah, Nahum, Haggai and Zechariah provide the lesser details while Ezekiel provides the Lion's share. The other writer is the apostle John. He is the one source that unequivocally provides the critical information as to "when" this Invasion is predicted to come. Here is when he communicates the Invasion is to come to pass:

Rev 20:6-8 ...And <u>when the thousand years are completed</u>, Satan will be released from his prison, and will come out to deceive the nations which are in the four corners of the earth, <u>Gog and Magog, to gather them together for the war</u>

John is the one also who communicates the length of the Kingdom to be a 1,000 years, the so called "Millennial Kingdom". Thus, the Gog/Magog Invasion comes at the "end" of the Kingdom Age. Given this is the case, the day to be designated within the Feast of Booths as this Sabbath day should be the 21st day of the 7th month, or the last day of the Feast of Booths:

In the 7ᵗʰ Month

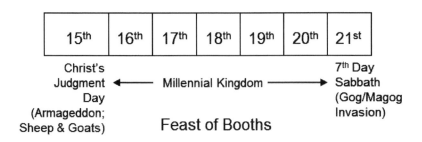

It should be noted that the days of the 16th through the 21st of the 7th month all have Offerings with libations. Hence, the Millennial Kingdom continues to have the Sainthood increase in numbers during this time. Yet, it seems that the last day is a new symbol to watch because the Invasion comes on this day but there is still plenty of time for other things to be taking place on this day if each day is to represent more than a 100 years. So the question is, does the 7th Day Sabbath bring an additional element of meaning with its own libation designated for this day? It would seem that since the first Feast had quite a significant Gospel occasion happening on its 7th Day Sabbath there must also be something similar happening to reckon here. But what could it be? This question happens to be a huge question that eventually needs an answer. This question and a few other critical questions that will remain, after the Holy Days testimony has been dissected to completion, will prompt the study to return to Ezekiel's writings.

The most significant reason why a Holy Days analysis requires a student to return to Ezekiel's testimony is because he has his own Holy Days testimony which needs decoding. But it makes the most sense to first resolve as much as can be understood about the original Holy Days testimony before attempting to do the same for Ezekiel's peculiar Holy Days testimony. Surprisingly or not, Ezekiel's writings have been an historically darkened portion of Scripture from time immemorial. Here light will be shed on this Prophet revealing some very important chronological matters regarding Israel's timely participation in the New Covenant. Needless to say, all signs point to the idea that there lies something hidden here in this 2nd to the last Sabbath of the Holy Days and that it will require moving on to Ezekiel's prophecies to help discover what this happens to be. But before taking up this closing exploration of Ezekiel, the 4th and final Decryption Key of the Gospel will need to be discovered in the next chapter.

The Last Sabbath Holy Day: The 2nd Death "Rest"

It has been well established by now that this last Holy Day symbolizes the Future Eternity, the coming of the New Heavens and Earth. Perhaps the most provocative Lunar Sabbath is this one because of what it implies. In contrasting all the anticipated eternal bliss that is ascribed to this Day, the Day in fact has an equally dark and sobering aspect to it as well as this symbol represents.

But how could it be possible that "Death Rest" be associated with the Future Eternity? Anyone familiar with Scripture's expectation knows that "Death" itself is to be done away, at least for the Saints. But a reader must look closer. This promise is extended to the Nations as a whole yet it must be understood that this promise is extended to the righteous only. That is, for the unrighteous Dead, the coming of this Day means Judgment and not the hope of life. This is the Day the Damned are to be resurrected, what Revelation implies is the "Second Resurrection".

Now John sees a Great White Throne where God Almighty is to sit and judge the Dead (Rev) in this 4th and final Judgment Day. Everyone whose name is not in the "Book of the Lamb" is to be thrown into the "Lake of Fire". When this judgment is completed here is what John records:

Rev 20:14 Then death and Hades were thrown into the lake of fire. This is the <u>second death</u>, the lake of fire.

Notice that "death and Hades" are thrown into the Lake of Fire as if these things are to no longer be what they were all throughout human history. But, then, the Lake of Fire comes to be called the "2nd Death", yet a new term and idea. The great implication made by this unveiled "2nd Death" is there is or was a "1st Death". So what could the "1st Death" be? This death can only be that which was experienced in the Garden of Eden when Adam ate of the forbidden fruit. It was a death that the entire human race subsequently inherited from its Father Adam:

Gen 2:17 "...but from the tree of the knowledge of good and evil you shall not eat, for in the day that you eat from it you shall surely _die_."

Rom 5:12 ...just as through one man sin entered into the world, and <u>death</u> through sin, and so <u>death spread to all men</u>, because all sinned...

How unfortunate it is that institutionalized Christianity created its own extra-biblical terminology for this sinful act known as "The Original Sin", perhaps first coined by Augustine. The more appropriate Scripture based terminology implied by John is that this occasion should be understood the coming of humanity's "1st Death". It is a death that God prepared beforehand to overcome, in the way He designed the Woman. Womankind's Seed must have been made "incorruptible". One possible explanation is that Womankind's equal stature with the Man was "forfeited" when the 1st Woman set in motion Humanity's 1st Death. And perhaps in making Womankind's status to be under the headship of Mankind, God was justified in making Womankind's Seed incorrupt.

211

Hence, the 1st Death is passed down from one generation to the next when a man joins his corrupt seed with a woman's incorrupt seed. This explains how the Holy Seed of God was made permissible to be joined with the Virgin Mary's seed and still remaining incorrupt in the process. This unique life of God joined with Woman created an incorrupt offering for Human Sin as it could be made a vicarious substitutionary sacrifice:

1 John 2:2 He Himself is the propitiation for our sins; and not for ours only, but also for those of the whole world.

Here again institutionalized thinking has erred greatly in arguing that Jesus' mother Mary was uniquely incorrupt herself. This has elevated her to a status of being labeled the "Mother of God". The truth is that all women pass along an incorrupt seed in procreation. In this way, it was God's choice as to which woman would receive the Holy Seed within her womb.

Hence, according to John, the 1st Death has been conquered. However this has now created a new situation whereby the act of the unforgivable sin leads to the 2nd Death:

1 John 5:16 ...There is a sin leading to death

This happens to be the sin of an unrepentant soul. If God offered up His One and Only Son to die for humanity's 1st Death God's only demand for such a price paid is that all who have sinned simply repent and believe in the work of God through Jesus in the Gospel. Otherwise, the 2nd Death awaits all those who reject this repentance. Yes, the Lake of Fire was only intended for the devil and his angels but there will be made room for those of humanity who reject the Gospel.

The most illustrative passage from Scripture that is relevant to the subject at hand is how Isaiah envisions this final death in his very last passage:

Isa 66:24 "Then they shall go forth and look on the <u>corpses</u> of the men who have transgressed against me. For <u>their worm shall not die</u>, and <u>their fire shall not be quenched</u>; and they shall be an abhorrence to all mankind."

How very unusual it is that Isaiah should mention "corpses" and yet discuss how these same men will have a worm that does not die and a fire that is not quenched. It defines a very bizarre "death" where the person and the body are very much alive to sense the worm and the fire but nevertheless is defined as being a corpse. The mind forms a picture by this illustration that a corpse lies down "in rest". That this "corpse" will endure for all eternity is because the unrighteous Dead are to be resurrected into eternal bodies which will sustain eternal punishment. It thus makes sense to conclude that the final Sabbath Holy Day is to indeed represent what John's Revelation calls the "2nd Death" (Rev20:14). This helps explain Isaiah's passage in that this state of death is a spiritual death void of the life of God, not mortal death.

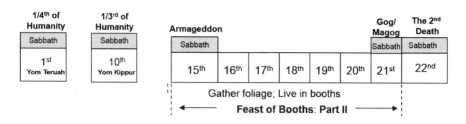

Having now visited all 14 Sabbaths, the following diagram summarizes the basic Death Rest predicted by each one:

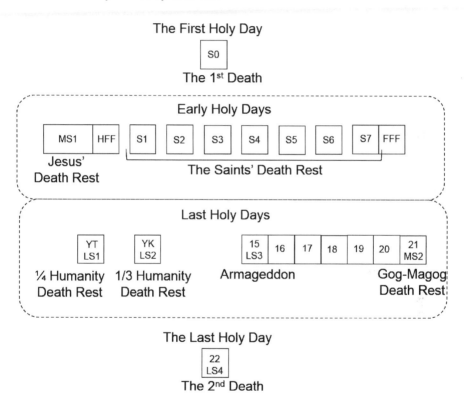

Are the Early and Late Holy Days Correlated?

Now that all the Sabbath Holy Days have been studied it makes sense to review all the Holy Days again to see if and where these Days are to converge upon one another. The biggest clue as to a possible merging of the Spring and Fall Holy Days Paths is to notice that the Feast of Booths testimony splits into two just as the Feast of Unleavened Bread and the 50 Day Mystery Path split in two after Passover.

The Holy Days Code

Because the last 8 Holy Days come to be described in 2 separate testimonies in Leviticus 23, this seems to be patterned after how the Spring creates its 2 Paths. This seems to suggest that perhaps the 2 Paths of Spring are to somehow be joined with the 2 Paths of Fall:

But there is just one problem. There are 2 Holy Days that stand alone before the Feast of Booths. How could it be possible for 2 Paths to continue existing if there is only a single path through these first two Holy Days of the 7th Month? It seems as if there is an impasse here:

If the 2 Paths are to be joined together from beginning to end somehow, this requires that the 2 Paths converge and merge "through" these 2 Holy Days!

In zooming into the intersection or common pathway that is Yom Teruah and Yom Kippur it can be noticed there is a way of partitioning the two Days that create a curious double path through them:

The "Middle" Holy Days Convergence

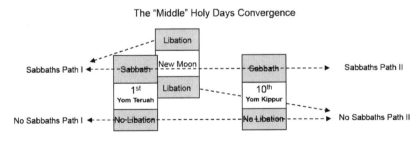

In studying this, it does suggest that the 2 Divine Paths converge through Yom Teruah and Yom Kippur. For instance, both Holy Days are Sabbaths allowing them to become links between Sabbaths Path I and Sabbaths Path II. Yet since both Days have Offerings without Libations, this symbolism allows them to become links between the trend of No Sabbaths Path I with that of the beginning of No Sabbaths Path II. Another interesting observation is that the New Moon Libation Offerings of Yom Teruah "link up" to the Libations at the end of the Sabbaths Path I (Feast of

First Fruits/Weeks/Pentecost). Yom Kippur has only Atonement Offerings which "link up" on one side with Yom Teruah's Atonement Offerings which in turn "links up" to the trend of Atonement Offerings of No Sabbaths Path I. On the other side of Yom Kippur, this Libationless trend abruptly ends too after the 1st Day of Booths. A graphical depiction would look something like the following:

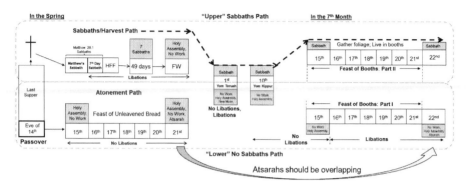

As the diagram points out, the "Upper" Sabbaths Path comes to be formed by threading together the Sabbaths of the Spring Holy Days with the Sabbaths of the Fall Holy Days. As for the "Lower" Path, the Feast of Unleavened Bread represents Israel's Prophetic life from beginning to end. Hence, it must somehow overlap with the Feast of Booths since it represents a part of Israel's prophetic life on a shorter time scale. Recall also that the very last Holy Day shares a unique distinction with the last day of the Feast of Unleavened Bread in that both are given the symbolism of the Hebrew word "Atsarah". Hence, these 2 days, in particular, should be overlapping. And so with this last alteration, the diagram comes to appear as follows:

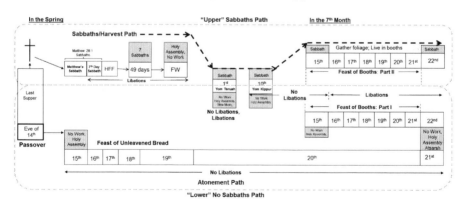

In the previous chapter, a linkage was already suggested with the "No Sabbaths Path I" pathway in that it was overlapping with or contained within itself the 7th Month testimony. Now another observation appears here due to this 3rd Key showing how "Sabbaths Path I" can be made to link up to the 7th Month. It is now understood that the Saints Death Rest is symbolized by S1-S7. This means S7 represents the Death Rest of the very last Deceased Saints. Hence, S7 must be including the Tribulation Martyrs (and possibly the 2 Witnesses). Furthermore, the even greater observation to be made is to realize that there are no other deaths to note for Saints beyond the Tribulation Saints so that makes the Tribulation Saints the last Saints to suffer Mortal Death and so represent the very end of S7 itself!

If this is the case then, Holy Day S7 should align itself with Yom Kippur given this was argued in the last chapter to signify two things: 1) the end of the Tribulation after the Martyrdom and 2) the gathering together of the Elect as Jesus specified in His Olivet Discourse. Thus, the Feast of First Fruits/Weeks/Pentecost should fall somewhere between Yom Kippur and the 1st Day of Booths suggesting the Resurrection comes in this basic general time frame. At the same time, the Feast of First Fruits/Weeks/Pentecost should be understood lasting into the Future Eternity by aligning its end with the other 2 Feasts' End Days. A condensed diagram reflecting these observations along with making the Libation Holy Days shaded is the following:

Domain of the Dead

	Mystery Sabbath	HFF	S1	S2	S3	S4	S5	S6	S7	FFF

P A S S O V E R

NM	YT	YK	15	16	17	18	19	20	21	22
			15	16	17	18	19	20	21	22

15	16	17	18	19	20	21

Domain of the Living

216

Now after the Sabbaths, as it began to dawn toward the first of the Sabbaths, Mary Magdalene and the other Mary came to look at the grave.

Matthew 28:1

Chapter Fourteen

The Resurrection Decryption Key

The testimony of the Last Supper, Crucifixion, and Burial of Jesus have thus far been found possessing a provocative form of decoding for several of the Law's Holy Days symbols as the last three chapters have unveiled. The fourth and final piece of the Gospel testimony is the Resurrection. Not surprisingly, it too brings a unique and final element of decoding for what remains to be unfolded from the Holy Day symbols.

For a thousand years and more ancient Israel and the Jewish People were plagued with having to interpret how to reckon a Holy Day the Law describes in ambiguous terms. For at least a century, tradition had settled on carrying along 2 theories of how to reckon this Holy Day. Oddly enough, every once and awhile the two traditions disagreed over the reckoning of Passover as well. This created the Pharisees' Forbidden Passover Schedule which the Pharisees could not allow to be fulfilled. In an earlier chapter, it was deduced that the Forbidden Schedule came in the year of the Gospel. But the Great Mystery surrounding this ambiguous Holy Day ended forever with the coming of the Resurrection Day testimony. Although the Gospel writers are not unanimous in their reckoning about all the other aspects of the Gospel leading up to this day, they do agree unanimously about this day's accounting.

In chapter 5 the Gospel Schedule was deduced or derived with the help of the 2 Passovers testimony. Liberties were taken there in using information supplied by the Resurrection account to help establish the Schedule without explaining the conclusions needed to make this Schedule. This was done in order to present the Decryption Keys in the chronological order they come to be introduced in the testimony. In reality, the pivotal aspects of the Resurrection account is the singular testimony that first cracks the initial inner workings of the Holy Days Code. Without understanding its meaning, nothing else about the Code can begin to unravel.

It would appear that it was arranged this way to make the Resurrection testimony the main doorway leading into the understanding of the Holy Days Code. So although a great deal of decoding has taken place in the past 3 chapters, the truth is that none of this begins to be noticeable until the Resurrection account cracks the first great Holy Days Mystery. Once this happens this is the great clue that the Holy Days testimony indeed contains a Code behind it.

The actual Resurrection itself is not recorded in Scripture. Instead, eyewitness testimonies of those who first encountered the already resurrected Jesus are recorded. The women who had followed Jesus in His ministry were compelled to return to the tomb with spices to further dress the body but only after complying with the Law's command to observe the Sabbath. Since a biblical day begins at sundown it is clear the women returned to the tomb at daybreak, half way into the day after the Sabbath. Hence, the actual moment of Jesus' Resurrection is unknown. So the next best thing is to simply assume Resurrection Day as being the day eyewitnesses first saw him resurrected.

To anyone reading the Resurrection accounts as the original Greek presents them, they are a very strange reading on the surface. But it turns out that the Gospel writers are drawing from the Law's language for the mystery Holy Days reckoning in order to reveal that the Resurrection had come to coincide with a very special Holy Day, the very first Harvest related Holy Day. Without recognizing this critical association with the Law, the passage becomes indecipherable as nearly all English translations evidence. The message conveyed by it indicates that the day of the Resurrection was prearranged or reserved thousands of years in advance.

Hence, what is being inferred is that the Law's ambiguous testimony of the mystery Holy Day is by design made to yield to a later revelation which would resolve the ambiguity. Thus, this element of the Code is what establishes its impenetrable security in preventing "counterfeit" keys from ever being able to open its contents. At the same time, by a later revelation having the self-evidenced ability to resolve this mystery in its own attestation, this would be the evidence for the validity of the later coming revelation in having the power to unlock the Law's mystery.

What the Gospel comes to supply as an answer to this ambiguity is fascinating in itself. The Sabbath the Gospel writers argue being the Sabbath of Leviticus 23:11 is in fact the Sabbath of the Feast of Unleavened Bread, but with an interesting twist. This Sabbath came back-to-back with the first day of this feast in creating a 2 day "no work" period. Thus, Jesus lay buried for 2+ days not 1. This at the same time provides an answer as to why 2 Passovers are found in the testimony. Why there are 2 Passovers recorded is because of the Law's ambiguity having caused two sects to follow 2 different interpretations. And in the year of the Gospel these interpretations came to observe different days for the Passover. Jesus was then able to observe the 1st Passover and yet become a 2nd Passover the next day, thus maintaining the Law's precedence as well as introduce yet a new thing that does not interfere with the first thing. This testimony is just one of many "proofs" that the Gospel possesses the Keys to unlock the mysteries of the Law and the Prophets.

At the same time, this would raise a monumental flag to the observant reader. Having the very first harvest related Holy Day defined in ambiguous terms only to then have it resolved by way of the Resurrection testimony creates an unmistakable message that the intended 1st Fruits foreseen by this ambiguity is of a human being resurrected from the dead, besides it being the day the Head First Fruits of the Barley Harvest be taken to the High Priest to "wave" before God in the Temple. This is the greatest indication in all of Scripture that the Holy Days testimony contains an imbedded Code filled with encoded symbols needing decoding. It is the single point testimony which is designed to be the Key unlocking the Code's hidden reality. It is supposed to be the greatest clue to the reader to begin a great search for the Gospel's other Decryption Keys that have now been reviewed over the last 3 chapters. Tragically, institutionalized Christianity somehow came under the impression that this "overlapping" of the Gospel with the Passover season was a sign that the Gospel was "replacing" the Passover and not the revelation of Decryption Keys being supplied to the reader to unlock the Holy Days Code.

Unraveling an interdependent message

The way this message comes to be unveiled appears as if to be by design but certainly not something conceivably arranged by the human mind over the course of more than one thousand years of separation. That is, the Law's mystery came to be written at around 1400BC/BCE. A thousand years and more went by without a resolution. Then, the Gospel testimony came to be written in the middle of the 1st Century bringing an astonishing resolution to the riddle. So then who is responsible for having encoded this mystery in the first place and then how was it possible for its compelling decoding to appear much later in time? If the two major groups of followers who hold the two portions of Scripture sacred are hostile to each other, how did this mystery ever find a resolution if either of these 2 parties were responsible?

For what the Law and the Gospel form is a paradoxical like encoded message. Read the Law without the Gospel and there is an unresolved mystery. Read the Gospel without the Law and there is an unresolved mystery. But read the two testimonies together and the two mysteries resolve each other:

The Code's interdependent message between the Law and the Gospel

Encoded Message	Decryption Code
Mystery Holy Day(s): Lev23:11,16	Resurrection Account: Matt 28:1
Resurrection Account: Matt 28:1	Mystery Holy Day(s): Lev23:11,16

The 2 Sabbaths of Matthew 28:1

To begin to resolve the mysteries, the simpler mystery is resolved first and then it can help resolve the more difficult mystery. Matthew 28:1 contains two very crucial time periods that need to be decoded. One period looks back from the timeframe of the Resurrection and the other looks forward from it. Analyzing the two periods from popular English translations will not be helpful. The original Greek must be consulted. The Greek testimony, and an English translation that is true to the original Greek, was supplied earlier and is again given here. The encoding comes in 2 parts and each part testifies to a plurality of Sabbaths:

<u>**Matthew 28:1aa:**</u>

Οψε δε
After but

<u>**Sabbaths Period 1:**</u>

σαββατ<u>ων</u>
Sabbath<u>s</u>

<u>**Matthew 28:1ab**</u>

τη επιφωσκουση   εισ μιαν
as it began to dawn   toward the first of the

<u>**Sabbaths Period 2:**</u>

σαββατ<u>ων</u>
Sabbath<u>s</u>

    The first notable thing to point out is that when a Greek noun is in the genitive (that is possessive form, e.g.: **after** the Sabbath / **of** the Sabbath) the ending of the root noun word having an Omega-Nu ending is the **plural** form of the root. The root here is **sabbat**, or Sabbath, and it is ended with a plural genitive ending. In Matthew 28:1, this occurs twice: one plurality looks back from the Resurrection and the other plurality looks forward from the Resurrection:

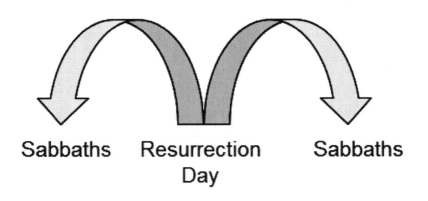

Sabbaths   Resurrection   Sabbaths
Day

Resurrection account forms synthesis w Lev23:16

Synthesis Part I

Leviticus 23:16 & Matthew 28:1ab
... At the dawning of the first of the Sabbaths ...

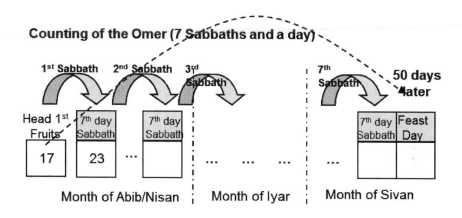

This should be easily recognized as relating to Judaism's so called "Count of the Omer" that was discussed in previous chapters. Recall that Lev 23:16 commands that 7 Sabbaths be counted to establish the coming of the Feast of Weeks. Specifically, from the Day of Head 1st Fruits, the mystery Holy Day, there are to be 7 Sabbaths and a day counted to the coming of the Feast of First Fruits/Weeks/Pentecost. This was something Judaism has long understood to be an important passage of time, something Law abiding Jews would easily have understood from the Gospel accounts and what is being implied here.

Resurrection is fulfillment of the mystery Holy Day

This very same Greek phrase is used by all 4 Gospel writers in unison. (Mark 16:1; Luke 24:1, John 20:1,19). What all 4 writers are communicating is that the Day of Resurrection was in fact the Day of Head 1st Fruits! In other words, the first Harvest related Holy Day was unique in that it began the Count of 7 Sabbaths, a process that these Gospel writers are alluding to when they indicate that this Day was the beginning of a plurality of coming Sabbaths that they were to count leading up to the next Harvest related Holy Day! (To what reads as if to be a cryptic phrase to modern day readers was essentially an encoded message for those Jewish readers of that day. Today, this correlation can be easily missed if a reader is either ignorant of the realities behind Lev23:11&16 and/or is relying upon a translation which hides the

223

true language of the passage.) The authors are all communicating that Jesus' resurrection from the dead answers the mystery behind the Day of Head 1st Fruits. They realized that two things were being made to come together: the mystery Holy Day's true reckoning was to be established by the very day that Jesus first appeared resurrected. In addition, the SYMBOLISM of this mystery Holy Day's harvest theme was to be decoded by the ACTUAL harvesting of Jesus' Body from Death Rest.

Here is where the first "decoding" of the Holy Days Code is made clearly visible for anyone familiar with the Law's mystery Holy Day conundrum. If an argument is to be made that this Holy Day is strictly about the ingathering of the first barley stalks of a given harvest season, this argument fails because its definition of reckoning is never resolved in the Word of God. It is an actual missing piece of information from the Law. When the Gospel testimony finally supplies an answer it is directly assigned to the Resurrection and not to the barley harvest. By having this unique encoding of information in the form of an omission acts as a glaringly indication to the reality of a Code.

This essentially unlocks the first great symbolism of what all the Holy Days share in common in that they all fall within the harvest season. This implies the 7 month Holy Calendar is really about the Schedule of a Divine Harvesting Plan. And of course, it only makes sense if the Code comes to be unlocked at its beginning. In having Jesus' Resurrection be the very first aspect of the Divine Harvest on this Divine Schedule, the rest of the Holy Calendar's Holy Days must also have some tie in to the idea of a human "Harvesting" or "Reaping" from God's Field:

1 Cor 15:20,23 But now Christ has been raised from the dead, the <u>first fruits</u> of those who are asleep...

Resurrection account forms synthesis w Lev23:11

The more difficult mystery to resolve is Matthew's 1st Sabbath period he defines in Matt 28:1. There he describes "Sabbaths" having transpired between the Crucifixion and the Resurrection. The other 3 Gospel writers will not indicate a plurality of Sabbaths, but just that a Sabbath period had passed. But what Matthew is doing is nothing more than quoting Lev23:11's ambiguous phrase of "After the Sabbath" in his own testimony but adding a new interesting twist. He is tying in Lev23:11 to Jesus' Resurrection Day. But it becomes obvious that Matthew has "altered" the phrase taken from Lev 23:11 ever so slightly in making the word Sabbath plural! No doubt this was done for two reasons.

The first reason is that it "duplicates" the plurality of Sabbaths that follow Jesus' Resurrection. Since the meaning of the Sabbaths has been explored already, it can now be recognized that this testimony is creating a pattern of Sabbaths and Harvest, first with the Head First Fruits and then with the Feast of First Fruits/Weeks/Pentecost, to suggest a common thread of decoding which ultimately suggests the Feast of First Fruits/Weeks/Pentecost is also to be interpreted as a day of Resurrection:

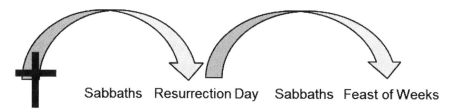

Sabbaths   Resurrection Day   Sabbaths   Feast of Weeks

What Matthew 28:1 is cryptically communicating

The second reason this was most likely done was so as to provide a solution to the confusing testimony the Gospel writers provide leading up to the Resurrection account. By implying that 2 Sabbaths had come back-to-back, one being the 15th day of the 1st month (a "Preparation Day" for the Synoptic Writers) and the second being the 7th day Sabbath, Matthew is conforming with how the Pharisees understood the 15th day of the 1st month. They believed it was to be considered a Sabbath too. Thus Matthew connects his testimony to the Pharisees which then leads to discovering he is describing the Forbidden Passover Schedule.

Synthesis of testimony resolves the mysteries

Other theories have arisen arguing that the 2 Sabbath days were not back-to-back but were separated by a regular day. This would be the idea of the 15th falling on a Thursday, the 16th being the regular day of Friday, and the 17th day falling on the 7th day Sabbath. There are 2 main reasons why this schedule has been proposed. First, Matt12:40 is cited in requiring this length of time in order to account for "3 days and 3 nights". Secondly, there is the argument about the women who return to the tomb. Mark recounts in Mark 16:1 how the women bought spices once the Sabbath was over. The argument is made that this must have been done after the 1st Sabbath was over, that is, on Friday, between Thursday, the 15th day rest day, and Saturday the 7th day Sabbath. How else, it is argued, can the women buy the spices after the Sabbath and yet come to the tomb early in the morning after the same Sabbath is over?

In reviewing this 2nd possible schedule, it is clear that it takes into account some of the testimony. However it does not take into account all of the testimony. That is, Jesus predicted he would also arise on the "3rd day". There is no way this schedule allows this prophecy to be true too because for Jesus to arise on this schedule would require He do so on the "4th day". Secondly, there is an explanation for the spices having been bought after the Sabbath. Many forget the simple fact that a biblical day is over at dusk. Thus, when this Sabbath period was over, it came at dusk. The Jews would have been anxious to open the markets just as the period was ending, at nightfall, in order to begin the new week (e.g., see Amos 8:5) especially if it was longer than a single Sabbath day rest period. Thus the women would have had plenty of time to buy the spices after the Sabbath ended at dusk. They could then return the next morning with the spices in hand. The reason they did not return immediately then is because it was dark. What they wanted to do is return at the earliest moment of daylight after the Sabbath rest and not attempt to work in the dark.

The 3 possible scenarios of the Gospel chronology & their merits

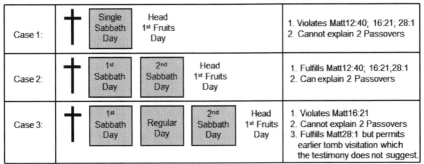

Case 1:	✝	Single Sabbath Day	Head 1st Fruits Day		1. Violates Matt12:40; 16:21; 28:1 2. Cannot explain 2 Passovers
Case 2:	✝	1st Sabbath Day	2nd Sabbath Day	Head 1st Fruits Day	1. Fulfills Matt12:40; 16:21;28:1 2. Can explain 2 Passovers
Case 3:	✝	1st Sabbath Day	Regular Day	2nd Sabbath Day	Head 1st Fruits Day	1. Violates Matt16:21 2. Cannot explain 2 Passovers 3. Fulfills Matt28:1 but permits earlier tomb visitation which the testimony does not suggest.

Furthermore, the no back-to-back Sabbath schedule cannot provide an explanation for why there were 2 Passovers observed in the Gospel testimony. For an explanation to this great mystery the 1st schedule proposed has one. The schedule of the 15th day falling on a Friday and the 16th day falling on a Sabbath does happen to fit all the evidence of testimony. In fact, the testimony allows for this schedule and this schedule alone if there is to be no violation of any aspect of the testimony. Thus, the 15th and 16th days of the 1st month must have been Matthew's "Sabbaths" that the women had waited for to pass before returning to the tomb. This would explain why Matthew can write what he did and yet be compatible with what the other accounts describe. That is to say that back-to-back Sabbaths can be described as either a single period of rest, as Mark and Luke indicate, or be distinguished as 2 separate days as Matthew does to provide the most complete information. Perhaps John's pointing out that the approaching Sabbath coming on the heels of the Crucifixion was a "great" day is his way of saying the same thing.

In short, Matthew is forming two forms of synthesis between Lev 23:11&16 and the Resurrection. Matthew is effectively using the verbiage of Lev 23:11&16 in realizing the correlation it has with Jesus' day of resurrection. It is a message directed to a more traditional Jewish audience whose sensibilities about these kinds of details are peaked. No doubt these sensibilities are what eventually led John to clarify the Synoptic testimony in his own Gospel in pointing out the reality of yet a 2nd Passover.

Synthesis Part II

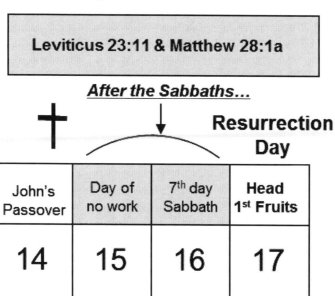

John's Passover	Day of no work	7th day Sabbath	Head 1st Fruits
14	15	16	17

A reckoning of "Passion Week"

In having deduced that the Resurrection Day came on the 1st day of the week on the 17th day of the 1st month, the entire "Passion Week" can be reconstructed:

Sunday	Monday	Tuesday	Wednesday	Thursday	8th day Mary anoints Jesus' feet with perfume	Eve of 9th day Jesus rides on a donkey; the people declare him Messiah
10th day Jesus curses fig tree, throws out moneychangers from temple area	11th day Jesus tested by elders; speaks 8 woes to Israel's leaders Olivet Discourse	12th day Jesus dines at Simon the Leper's house; feet anointed with perfume	Eve of 13th day Pharisees' Passover; Last Supper, Betrayal	Eve of 14th day John's Passover; Jesus crucified and buried	15th day No work day; elders have tomb guarded; 1st burial day	16th day Sabbath Day; 2nd burial day
17th day Jesus' Resurrection on day of Head 1st Fruits; the "3rd" Day					Friday	Saturday

Days in the Month of Abib/Nisan in the year of the Gospel

A reckoning of Jesus' 3 Days and 3 Nights

This is a good place to also address what Jesus meant when he prophesied that he would be "in the heart of the earth for 3 days and 3 nights" (Matt12:40). This was presented earlier in chapter 10 as 1 of 4 mysteries the Gospel testimony contains regarding the reckoning of the Gospel events. Somehow the schedule does not seem to support this statement if one assumes Jesus was referring to his body's Burial Period. But perhaps Jesus was not referring to his body but rather his immaterial being. What if Jesus was referring to his spirit as going to the heart of the earth during his death? The Gospel writers all seem to indicate that Jesus died at around 3PM on Thursday. Hence, Jesus' spirit left his body at this time. If the clock begins to tick here, Day 1 can be defined as the remaining 3 hours left on Thursday prior to sundown:

Thursday 3PM: Jesus dies.
Thursday 3PM to 6PM: Day 1 of Jesus' spirit in the heart of the earth
Thursday 6PM to Friday 6AM: Night 1 of…
Friday 6AM to 6PM: Day 2 of….
Friday 6PM to Saturday 6AM: Night 2 of…
Saturday 6AM to 6PM: Day 3 of…
Saturday 6PM to ???: Night 3 of…

In this interpretation, Night 3 is not to be reckoned a full 12 hour period similarly as Day1 is not either. Hence, Jesus' Resurrection is to be reckoned coming some time between 6PM Saturday and 6AM Sunday. This is the first 12 hour period of the Day of Head 1st Fruits and why readers are to assume this was the general window for when Jesus' actual resurrection took place. By making Day 1 and Night 3 partial in length, this then permits Jesus' other prophecy of being raised on the 3rd Day also valid.

Early Harvest Schedule: Resurrection Harvest

The Resurrection Day falling on the Holy Season's first harvest occasion alludes most readers because the translations hide the mysterious language of the Resurrection account. Traditional thinking stumbles by never coming to the realization that this is supposed to be the evidence that the Holy Days are just beginning to be decoded here. That is, the traditional idea is that the entire Hebrew Scripture is pointing to Jesus and that this is all that its purpose was for. And since Jesus' testimony now exists in its own direct form of the Gospel witness, the Hebrew Scripture's purpose came to an end when this witness was fully written. Thus, the Hebrew Scripture's only remaining function is surmised to be an historical legacy of Jesus' expectation.

But no words can describe the horrific loss that the Christian World created for itself in letting traditional thinking lead the way in this form of thinking. Anyone familiar with the original Passover occasion has to know that Passover represents

Scripture's "Grand Beginning", not its "Grand Ending". So even if hypothetically the Gospel testimony were promoting the idea of "Replacement Theology", the numerous Gospel connections to the Passover should be a sign that a floodgate has been opened, not shuttered. But the evidence is plain to see for those whose eyes can see it that the testimony of 2 Passovers is the first sign that the Divine Plan is introducing a parallel future where two Passovers are to operate and coexist side by side. Now here with the Resurrection account, it reveals its unique status as being the beginning to the unraveling of the secret message imbedded in the Holy Days Code. This is the door that opens for any reader who is wise enough to know there must be a torrent of revelation being unleashed within the context of the Gospel as the last 2 chapters have testified to.

Thus, Jesus' Day of Harvest is to be interpreted the beginning of the Holy Days Harvest, not its End! In order to "decode" the rest of the Holy Days Harvest requires simply understanding the 4th and final Decryption Key or the Resurrection Decryption Key is to reveal that Harvest related encoded symbolisms imply the decoding of the Reaping of Human Souls:

Resurrection Decryption Key:

Harvest Symbolisms = Reaping of Human Soul(s)

In essence then, the Feast of First Fruits/Weeks/Pentecost is merely following the pattern set down by Jesus with a Sabbath Death Rest followed by Resurrection as was reviewed in the last chapter. Since Jesus became the "First Fruits of those who are asleep", this means the remaining Fruits follow after with their own Sabbath Rest followed by their own Resurrection. And as was graphically depicted in the previous chapter, this means all Deceased Saints are to become the First Fruits to follow after Jesus.

4th Decryption Key: Harvest symbolizes Human Reaping

Sabbaths	Head 1st Fruits	Sabbaths	1st Fruits
Jesus' Death Rest	Jesus' Resurrection	Saints' Death Rest	Saints' Resurrection

Continuing down this logical path, the nature of the Offerings by Fire for the Feast of First Fruits/Weeks/Pentecost sheds the needed light on the "make-up" of this Resurrection Sainthood. Recall that there were 3 "Pairs" of Offerings for this 2nd Harvest day: 2 Burnt Offerings, 2 Peace Offerings and 2 Leavened Loaves of Bread.

Hence, there is a Pair of Distinct Saints being identified here. Again, the Apostle Paul has something interesting to say regarding this "duality of the Sainthood":

Eph 2:11-22 ...formerly you, the Gentiles...were...excluded from the commonwealth of Israel...(Christ) Himself is our peace who made both (Israel and the Gentiles) one and broke down the barrier of the dividing wall...you are fellow citizens with the Saints, and are of God's Household...

Thus, the 3 Paired Offerings highlighted in the previous chapter can be construed to signify the Saints of Deceased Israel and the Saints of the Deceased Gentiles. This also explains why there are Peace Offerings to be given as addressed in the above passage. The 2 Loaves of Leavened Bread must signify the redeemed Sinners from both Israel and the Gentiles. Finally, that there are a total of 24 Offerings suspiciously correlates with Revelation's "24 Elders" that are seen before the Throne of God in Heaven as described in the book of Revelation. That is, "12 Elders" are speculated to be synonymous with the Deceased Saints of Israel symbolized by the "12 Tribes of Israel", and the other "12 Elders" are synonymous with the Deceased Saints of the Church also symbolized by the "12 Apostles of the Lamb".

Fall Harvest Unlike the Spring/Summer Harvests

In conclusion, the Spring and Summer Holy Days Harvest is designated by 2 Harvest Days, Head 1st Fruits in the Spring and the Feast of First Fruits/Weeks/Pentecost in the Summer. It is a trivial exercise to identify and locate these Early Harvest Dates. But when turning to the Fall Harvest, the Harvest symbolisms are quite different than those of the Spring and Summer. First of all, there are no specific Days of Harvest to identify and locate. The only symbolisms provided are those that help describe the Feast of Ingathering/Booths.

The suggested idea is that the Feast is to celebrate the final ingathering of crops for the Harvest Season, that is, the Last Fruits (Exo23:16;34:22, Lev23:39). Deut16:13 speaks of the threshing tool in regards to a grain ingathering as well as the winepress in regards to the ingathering of grapes. Hence, the entire 7th Month prior to the Feast of Booths is to be considered the final ingathering period leading up to the Feast of Booths celebration.

Furthermore, in stark contrast to the symbolisms of Sabbaths preceding the Harvest Dates of the Early Harvest, there are no such Sabbaths to recognize in the Fall as has been reviewed in the previous chapter. What is going on here is one more indicator of the reality of the Great Mystery. If the First Fruits Harvest is a "Resurrection" Harvest, no such equivalent thing takes place in the Fall as would be expected since there is only one future Resurrection for the Saints. What that leaves then is that the 7th Month Harvest is not to be identified as being a Final Harvesting of the Righteous Dead but of the Unrighteous Dead as well as a New Harvesting of the Living Remnant!

Hence, no signs of Death are found for the Remnant Harvest. So what kind of signs are there to be found for this new Living Remnant Ingathering? It should not be forgotten that the symbolism of Harvest is not the only one identifying the Resurrection Saints. The other symbolism is the Libation Offerings on the very Harvest Dates themselves. Therefore it makes all the sense in the world to expect that ANY date in the 7th Month that contains a Libation Offering can be considered a Harvest Date. Why? Because when Sabbaths no longer are used to identify Saints the only thing left to identify them with is Libation Offerings. Atonement Offerings certainly identify Saints too but it must be insisted that every and all Saints be first recognized as Saints through a Libation Offering above and beyond what specific Atonement Offerings add to the information being supplied about a certain Saint.

Hence, its time to back away from the details of each Holy Day in order to gain a more broader understanding of what is a string of symbolisms running from beginning to end. Here patterns can be recognized forming that should help explain what is going on on the grander scale. When accounting for all of the Libation Offerings, the striking observation that can be seen is that they all cluster into 3 different places. The first place is all the Libations associated with the First Fruits Ingathering of the Resurrected. Then, in taking the cue of this suggested terminology, one could define the second group as a "Middle Fruits" Libation Offering. Finally, this would make the final string of Libation Offerings as symbolisms for a "Last Fruits" group:

Month	Day	Name of Holy Day(s)	Libation	
1st Month	Twilight of 14th	Eve of Passover	No	
	15th	1st Day of Feast of Unleavened Bread	No	
	16th	2nd Day of Feast of Unleavened Bread	No	
	17th	3rd Day of Feast of Unleavened Bread	No	
	18th	4th Day of Feast of Unleavened Bread	No	
	19th	5th Day of Feast of Unleavened Bread	No	
	20th	6th Day of Feast of Unleavened Bread	No	
	21st	7th Day of Feast of Unleavened Bread	No	
Mystery Month	Mystery Sabbath	(Day before Head 1st Fruits)	Yes	
	Day after Mystery Sabbath	Head 1st Fruits	Yes	
	1st Sabbath after Mystery Sabbath	Countdown to Feast of Weeks: Week#1	Yes	
	2nd Sabbath after Mystery Sabbath	Countdown to Feast of Weeks: Week#2	Yes	
	3rd Sabbath after Mystery Sabbath	Countdown to Feast of Weeks: Week#3	Yes	First Fruits
	4th Sabbath after Mystery Sabbath	Countdown to Feast of Weeks: Week#4	Yes	
	5th Sabbath after Mystery Sabbath	Countdown to Feast of Weeks: Week#5	Yes	
	6th Sabbath after Mystery Sabbath	Countdown to Feast of Weeks: Week#6	Yes	
	7th Sabbath after Mystery Sabbath	Countdown to Feast of Weeks: Week#7	Yes	
	50 days after Head 1st Fruits	1st Fruits (Feast of Weeks/Pentecost)	Yes	
7th Month	1st	Yom Teruah (New Moon)	No (Yes)	Middle Fruits?
	10th	Yom Kippur	No	
	15th	1st Day of Feast of Booths	No	
	16th	2nd Day of Feast of Booths	Yes	
	17th	3rd Day of Feast of Booths	Yes	
	18th	4th Day of Feast of Booths	Yes	
	19th	5th Day of Feast of Booths	Yes	Last Fruits
	20th	6th Day of Feast of Booths	Yes	
	21st	7th Day of Feast of Booths	Yes	
	22nd	Day After the Feast of Booths	Yes	

231

144,000 are the First of the Last Fruits

It has been discussed in an earlier chapter that the Libation Offerings of Yom Teruah perhaps identify both Resurrection Saints as well as Remnant Saints for the reasons cited there. This is what makes the "Middle Fruits" such a provocative and interesting thing. Because the Scripture argues that the Resurrection of the Saints is a onetime event not to be repeated again, this creates an unusual post-Resurrection dilemma. And that is, what is to happen to the mortal Human Race in a post-Resurrection world? Any mortal life conceptually living beyond the Resurrection has no hope of being resurrected after mortal death because the Resurrection is a past fulfilled event. And John's Revelation clearly indicates that the Human Race continues to procreate given the Gog/Magog Invasion materializes long after the Resurrection has taken place. Is the reader to speculate that there are no Mortal Saints existing in the post-Resurrection world? Did not Jesus predict there will be Mortal Sheep entering His Kingdom in Matthew 25? Will not the Messiah convince many of His subjects to become Saints or remain Saints of the Kingdom? Yet, if this is the case, what fate are Mortal Saints to know if there is no Resurrection for them?

The answer that Scripture supplies in a subtle sort of way is that Mortal Saints who exist after the Resurrection are part of a new kind of Harvest, a mortal Harvest or those who become part of a "Mortal Sainthood" as opposed to the Resurrection Sainthood. As part of the transition to a Messianic Age, there is the anticipation that the Messiah will rule over a Mortal Kingdom having Mortal Subjects. A mortal Remnant Israel is expected to enjoy this Kingdom as promised by the Prophets of Old.

1st Resurrection

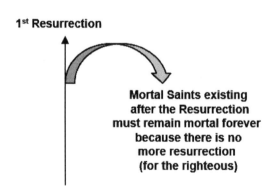

Mortal Saints existing after the Resurrection must remain mortal forever because there is no more resurrection (for the righteous)

As part of the transition, the Remnant called in the Latter Day is to remain Mortal because it must receive its Kingdom as Mortals to fulfill prophecy. However, the Church anticipates being made a part of the Resurrection, what is its ultimate fate. This too creates yet another enormous dilemma given the existence of the Church. Is not the Church its own Kingdom with the Messiah as its King? So how can these two things coexist beginning at some future moment in time? Here is where the reality of the Resurrection is found the second resolving element, after the Rapture, of the transition to a Messianic Age.

Hence, the transitional Latter Day must predict a transition to a Mortal Kingdom of Subjects to receive its Messiah King and its Messianic Kingdom. How the Church fits into this greater Kingdom is that it is portrayed as the Messiah's Resurrected Bride! And so, Scripture is ultimately anticipating Two Righteous Harvests: one of a Mortal make-up, the other Resurrected.

The biggest clue that is provided for the existence of this Second Harvest Group comes in the testimony regarding the 144,000 called of Israel:

Rev 14:3,4 The 144,000 who had been purchased from the earth…from among men as <u>first fruits</u> to God

The expressions "from the earth" and "from among men" contextually indicate that these 144,000 are called as MORTAL first fruits to God. This is why they can be classified here as "first fruits". That is, recall there are already two Harvest Dates designated as First Fruits Ingatherings, Head First Fruits and the Feast of First Fruits/Weeks/Pentecost. So how is it possible that there are still "first fruits" to be designated in this same Harvest? The answer is that these are first fruits of a different "type" of Harvest. Christ is to be understood first fruits from those who are "asleep" (or mortally dead). Here now are new first fruits, those who are mortally still alive! And because they are "first fruits" of this type, many more are expected in a regular ingathering of this same Mortal Harvest! And of course, these would be Israel's entire Remnant anticipated by the Prophets of Old! Furthermore, Revelation 21:3 states in a roundabout way that Mortal Humanity enters the Future Eternity and remains in that condition forever. The Mortal Sainthood is to remain a distinct Harvest Ingathering from that of the Resurrected Sainthood for time without end!

What the testimony of the 144,000 reveals in the book of Revelation is that these are the equivalent of the First Century's Apostles, sent out to preach the Gospel to the whole world. The rest of Israel's Remnant will be called into the Mortal Sainthood by these First Fruit Saints. The Remnant will be guarded by Divine Providence from mortal harm so that they will be able to receive the Messianic Kingdom as Mortal Subjects. But there are more Saints than these expected to heed the call of the 144,000. Gentiles too are expected to receive their message in such large numbers the Scripture argues they will be uncountable! These have been traditionally called the "Tribulation Saints" and are a very unique group of Saints in their own right.

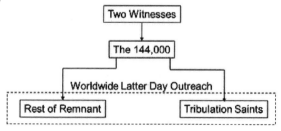

In Rev 7:9 the Martyred Saints of the Latter Day are witnessed holding palm branches in their hands. There is only one real location in the Law that identifies the significance of palm branches and that appears in Leviticus 23:40! There it is learned that Israel was to celebrate the Feast of Booths with palm branches in celebrating the ingathering of the Last Fruits. What this is communicating about the Martyrs is that they are the Last Fruits of their kind!

Altogether then, ***the Latter Day Martyrs are essentially the "Last Fruits of the First Fruits" and the 144,000 are essentially the "First Fruits of the Last Fruits"***! Together, they represent a "Middle Fruits" ingathering, sort of speak. The Martyrs are a part of the First Fruits Resurrection Ingathering while the 144,000 are the First Fruits of a New Remnant Sainthood! Then, at the start of the Millennial Kingdom, Jesus predicts He will judge the surviving Nations in Matthew 25. Those who are granted entrance to the Kingdom are referred to as "Sheep" as they too enter as Mortals making up a Mortal Sainthood. The remaining Fruits of this Remnant Sainthood come in the Final Ingathering Libation Offerings of the Feast of Booths:

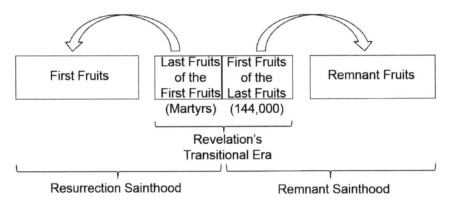

What is fate of the Mortal Race? Atsarah

But this begs one final and important question needing to be asked relating to the Righteous Harvest. If Mortals are expected to come into the Future Eternity as Mortals, what is the ultimate fate of the Mortal Human Race? Is it expected to procreate forever, time without end? Given that there is yet more Holy Days testimony to decode in the writings of Ezekiel, there is still the chance this Prophet will answer this question. And indeed he will with the help of the other Prophets and with the overall testimony of the Holy Days.

The biggest symbolic clue already pointed out in the Law's testimony happens to be what strange testimony is assigned to the last day of the Feast of Unleavened Bread and the very last Holy Day itself. Each of these days are given the symbolism of the Hebrew word "Atsarah". It was conjectured earlier that since both dates are given this symbolism that this must be communicating the 2 dates represent the same time along the Divine Timeline. Being that the last Holy Day must be peering into the furthest point of the Divine Timeline, this must mean that this day represents the Future Eternity. And thus, by default, so must the last day of the Feast of Unleavened Bread be representing the same Future Eternity.

But so far nothing regarding the meaning of Atsarah has been linked to what it might be foretelling about the Future Eternity until now. That is because this final question of the fate of the Mortal Human Race is the last great question that surfaces needing to be addressed. And it would appear that this Hebrew word Atsarah does just that. Atsarah in its most primitive meaning is that of the "closing" of a woman's womb so that she can no longer bear offspring. Hence, it would seem as if procreation is to come to an end in the Future Eternity and that the assigned word of Atsarah to the symbolic day representing the Future Eternity is what is communicating this conclusion to Scripture's Readers. What the Prophets Ezekiel and Isaiah will be shown testifying to in the coming final chapters of this Holy Days Code analysis is that this does not necessarily mean there will be no procreation in the Future Eternity, only that it will end there. In fact, both will argue there will be procreation there. Read on to the finish of this study to learn just exactly what Scripture is predicting as for the fate of the Mortal Human Race in the Future Eternity.

Harvest Plan's Dark Side: The Burning of the Chaff

The previous chapter saw the review of the 7th Month's Sabbaths Holy Days. Within their symbolisms lies the prediction of a sequence, or waves, of Death sweeping over the End Times. Here is where the Divine Harvest Plan can be interpreted as revealing its Dark Side. With the help of the book of Revelation these Sabbaths are given vivid prophecy. The noteworthy occasions are found in 5 places while a 6th occasion is located in Jesus' own prophecies regarding the "Goats" of Matthew 25.

It begins with Revelation's 4th Seal being broken where a Pale Horse and its Rider Death are followed by a 2nd Rider named Hades. These 2 are to bring Death to a quarter of Humanity. Some time later is the blowing of the 6th Trumpet which is to unleash Riders upon 200 million horses bringing Death and Destruction to a third of Humanity. The 3rd occasion is the one direct description of a Dark Harvest symbolism. It is Revelation's testimony of the coming "Wine Press of the Fierce Wrath of God". It is to be reserved for all those who receive the "Mark of the Beast". These are to be gathered up and "thrown into the Wine Press". There they are to be trampled underfoot by the "feet of God" as if He is to crush them like "Grapes" at the War of Armageddon. Blood is to flow like a raging river for a great distance. Birds of Prey are to feast on the bodies of the Dead. Oddly enough, the Antichrist and the False Prophet are not to suffer this fate but are to be preserved "alive". Hence they are sent directly to the Lake of Fire as "mortals" not to await the Resurrection of the Damned. (So, just as there is to be a Mortal Sainthood that is to never see Mortal Death, so there is to be the Mortal Damned who are not to see Mortal Death as well.) Satan too is to be bound and sent to the Abyss where he is to await one final rebellion against God.

As stated earlier, at the start of the Millennial Kingdom Jesus predicts the surviving Nations will be gathered to Him to be judged. Those who are granted entrance into the Kingdom are called "Sheep" but those who are denied entrance are called "Goats". They are predicted to be sent into eternal punishment into the eternal fire. The odd thing here is that these Goats are in their mortal flesh and the passage is suggesting they go into eternal punishment as Mortals as the Antichrist and False Prophet do.

What brings the Messianic Age to its end is Satan being released from captivity. He immediately is to gather a rebellion which provokes the 5th Ingathering of the Damned. The hordes of the unbelieving Mortals of Earth, now numbering on the order as the Sand on the Seashore, come to make war with the Saints of God. And again, these too come to be destroyed en masse, only this time by Fire from Heaven. Finally, Satan is predicted to be thrown into the Lake of Fire forever at this point.

The 6th and final Ingathering of the Damned comes in the form of a Second and final Resurrection from the Dead. In John's visions of the Great White Throne Judgment, the Present Heavens and Earth are expected to vanish in destruction. Then, the Dead of Hades and the Dead of the Sea are to be raised eternal from their place of habitation. Books are to be opened and the Dead are expected to be judged by the things contained in them. Then the Book of the Lamb will be opened and none of the names of the Dead will be shown written in it. Then the Second Death will befall the Damned. That is, these will be thrown into the Lake of Fire where they will suffer eternal punishment for time without end. This is the great burning of the Chaff where an unquenchable fire is to burn as prophesied by John the Baptist.

Synopsis of the Divine Harvest

Altogether then, the Divine Plan's Harvest Ingathering can be consolidated into 4 types of Harvest: 1) The Ingathering of the Immortal Righteous, 2) the Ingathering of the Mortal Righteous, 3) the Disposing of Chaff of the Mortal Unrighteous and 4) the Disposing of Chaff of the Resurrected Unrighteous. These types will be briefly summarized next. Nearly everyone is accounted for here. However because Ezekiel has more to say about the final 2 Holy Days, as the next 3 chapters will divulge, this list will actually have to be appended after that study is completed.

Ingathering of the Immortal Righteous

This Sainthood is of course led by Jesus Christ, the Head First Fruits of the First Fruits Harvest. This group defines the Resurrection Sainthood with Jesus the first to be Resurrected. Since Matthew records (27:52) others being raised with Jesus, they are numbered with him here. Those of His Body that are to be harvested after Him are to be considered part of the "First Resurrection", as defined by the Apostle John. As was learned over the course of the past several chapters, Ancient Israel, the Church, and the Tribulation Saints are to all be included in the coming "First Resurrection" as symbolized by the Feast of First Fruits/Weeks/Pentecost. This list is complete and no more will be added to it. The Holy Days symbolisms accounting for this Harvest are the first two Harvest Dates of the Holy Calendar, Head First Fruits and First Fruits. The 7 Sabbaths between these Dates represent the Death Rest of the Saints. The very Mystery Sabbath symbolizes the Death Rest of Jesus Christ Himself.

Head First Fruits: Jesus Christ Resurrected

Feast of First Fruits: Deceased and Rapture Saints Resurrected
- B.C. Israel
- The Church
- The Tribulation Martyrs

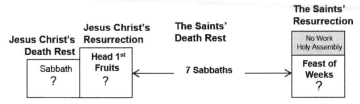

Ingathering of the Mortal Righteous

This chapter has revealed that John's 144,000 Israelites appear to never see death. They are considered the "first fruits" of this assembled Mortal body of harvest. The reader should also assume the rest of Israel's "Remnant" is included here that receives the Messianic Kingdom. These are those that the 144,000 call from their own brethren, which Jesus identified as "the Elect" in his Olivet Discourse. Finally, Jesus' "Sheep", those He is to Judge and will find acceptable to receive the Messianic Kingdom, as explained in Matthew 25, are also to be considered part of this harvest.

First Fruits of the Remnant: The 144,000
Regular Fruits: The Elect
Fruits of the Nations: The Sheep
Millennial Kingdom Fruits: Holy Offspring
Last Fruits: Future Eternity Offspring (Ezekiel's prophecies)

The Disposing of the Chaff of the Mortal Unrighteous

Perhaps the one single Holy Days symbolism that captures this portion of the Harvest Chaff is the 13th Atonement Offering of the 1st Day of Booths. The number 13 is symbolic of an evil element amongst the 12 remaining good. Hence, the first 12 Atonement Offerings represent the good Sheep of Matthew 25. In similar fashion, this 13th Atonement Offering symbolizes evil Mortal Flesh and matches perfectly with Jesus' vision of the Goats of Matthew 25.

Mortal Chaff: Antichrist, False Prophet, Goats

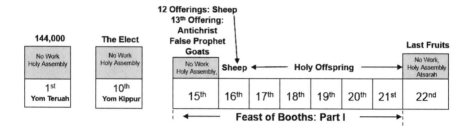

As to the last Holy Day and what Harvest it could be signifying, with its unique Libation Offerings, is something that is beyond the scope of the Law to address and which will be covered in the remainder of this book.

The Disposing of the Chaff of the Immortal Unrighteous

This final Chaff to be disposed of here is all those Damned who will have ever succumbed to Mortal Death. 4 notable occasions of apocalyptic Death are encoded with the symbolism of the Lunar Sabbaths in the 7th Month. All of these Immortal Unrighteous are to then join the Mortal Unrighteous in the Lake of Fire which is also known as the 2nd Death.

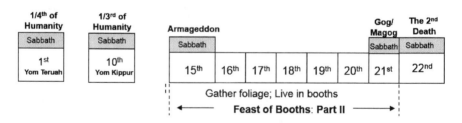

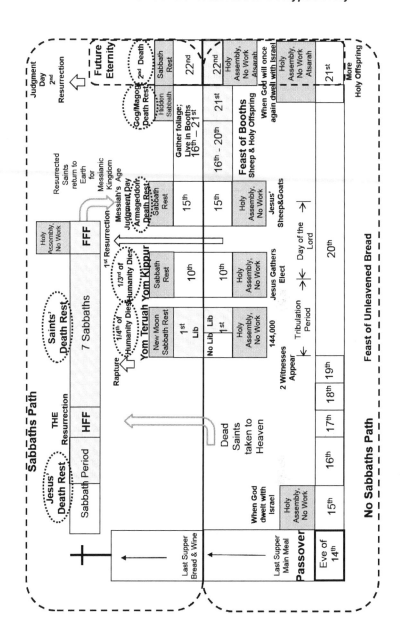

4 glaring problems remain to be solved

The great hidden messages within the Holy Days Code have nearly all been decoded by this point. But there still remains at least 4 issues that need closure:

1. The fulfillment of Jeremiah's New Covenant

To any reader familiar with the Hebrew Scripture, the Prophets arguably foresee two different types of salvation coming to the Nation of Israel. The first is a salvation to a "Remnant" of Israel:

Isa 37:32 "For out of Jerusalem shall go forth a remnant, and out of Mount Zion survivors..."

In this view, only a smaller select group out of the entire Nation is to be saved while all the rest have no such promise given to them. And indeed, the Latter Day picture John paints in his Revelation depicts such a salvation expected to come to Israel at that time.

However, there is yet a 2nd predicted kind of salvation to come to Israel as well. Particularly Jeremiah's prophecy of a coming New Covenant illustrates this kind of salvation better than any other passage:

Jer 31:31,33-34 ...I will make a <u>new covenant</u>...this is the covenant which I will make with <u>the house of Israel</u>...And they shall not teach again, each man his neighbor and each man his brother, saying, 'Know the LORD,' <u>for they shall all know Me, from the least of them to the greatest of them</u>..."

Here it reads that this New Covenant is to come to the "house of Israel" and that the entire house is to "know the LORD" from the least of them to the greatest of them. It is a "universal" salvation expected to come to the Nation. This is a distinct prophecy separate from the ones that predict a Remnant is to be saved. And the Apostle Paul reiterates this basic teaching in his own writings:

Rom 11:25-26 ...a partial hardening has happened to Israel <u>until the fullness of the Gentiles has come in</u>; and thus <u>all Israel</u> will be saved; just as it is written...

What Paul is saying is that God has set aside the fulfillment of Jeremiah's prophecy "until" all the Gentiles who will be accounted as members of God's household are gathered together first. This resonates with Jesus having prophesied that "many who are first will be last, and the last, first." (Matt19:30).

This 2nd passage essentially rules out the idea that early Jewish believers were to be considered the fulfillment of Jeremiah's prophecy. Over the past 2,000 years many Gentiles have been saved so clearly Jeremiah's prophecy must still be future. So another theory that tradition has proposed, having Paul's prophecy in mind, is that Jeremiah's prophecy is to become fulfilled during the cataclysmic years leading up to the Messianic Kingdom. Perhaps John's 144,000 are conjectured being this fulfillment. But even here the question still remains. Does not the book of Revelation suggest that there are still more Gentiles to be saved even during the Messianic Kingdom? If Paul's assertion is to remain true then technically speaking Israel's salvation should be expected to come very late. Institutionalized Christianity has all but ignored Jeremiah's prophecy from its mind since Israel has been considered "replaced" by the Church. Regardless of this position though, the question remains, does the Scripture anywhere predict when Jeremiah's prophecy comes to pass? It happens to be a major missing piece of the Holy Days Code. And given the Code and the Divine Plan regard matters of human harvesting, this is a very relevant date that should be a part of the Holy Days Code. Yet this moment has eluded identity thus far in the Holy Days analysis. This is the first glaring problem that still remains to be solved.

2. The Gospel Connection with the 7th Day Sabbath of Booths

As has been reviewed in the previous chapters, the Feast of Booths has a hidden 7th day Sabbath somewhere within its 7 day schedule. This means it has two symbolisms: a Death Rest symbolism and a Gospel symbolism. It was already argued that the divine slaughter of the rebels of the Gog/Magog Invasion aligns with what Death Rest this Sabbath day is symbolizing. Since John sees this Invasion coming after the 1,000 year Messianic Kingdom, it was conjectured that it makes the most sense to have the last day of the Feast be designated the hidden Sabbath of Booths. But nothing related to the New Covenant has been pointed out here (yet) as being a part of this major event, an event that the prophet Ezekiel, and then later John, foresee coming yet future.

This then is the second glaring problem remaining unsolved. What is the Gospel element of the 7th Day Sabbath of Booths?

3. The Law's place in the Messianic Kingdom and Beyond

The final glaring problem needing resolution is finding the prophetic testimony regarding the fate of the Law in the Divine Plan as it heads into the Future Eternity. Traditional Christianity continues to insist that Israel and the Law no longer have any special place in the Divine Plan. Emphasis comes to be placed on the Gospel salvation alone. Any emerging Remnant of Israel is argued becoming absorbed into the Church as all saved Saints are assumed doing. The Messianic Kingdom appears to be devoid of the Law's observance. Any distinctions made by the Prophets for Israel or the Law are seen as purely temporary and not eternal. So concludes what tradition has argued for thousands of years.

Yet the testimony of the Law clearly records that not only Israel and the Law, but the Land also, are all to be coeternal in relevancy. So the question is, where in Bible Prophecy, beyond the Law's testimony, is the Law corroborated? Where are the symbols to point to that argue for Israel's, the Law's, and the Land's place in the Eternal Kingdom? History seems to have been unable to discover the evidence for these things. So far in this work the Holy Days Code has offered the last day of the Feast of Unleavened Bread as the relevant symbolism indicating the reality of Israel and the Law. But tradition could argue that Rev21:3 is not speaking of a Temple and that God's Presence in the Future Eternity does not require a Temple or the fulfillment of the rest of the Law. Thus, the Law's eternal relevancy stands in the balance. So is there Scripture beyond the Law that can support the revelations of the Law and explain how its place is to be eternally relevant?

4.   The Fate of the Mortal Human Race in the Future Eternity

Finally, the last issue to be resolved is the Libations Offering of the Last Holy Day. Given that all the previous Holy Days were surmised as representing some group of Saints, the same should be true for this last Holy Day. So then what Scripture testimony is there that would unveil who these new Saints are to be emerging in the coming Future Eternity? It would make for an exciting discovery to know that yet more Saints are anticipated coming into existence within the Future Eternity itself!

Ezekiel's Testimony: Resolution of 4 Problems

Although the Law's Holy Days Code has come to be decoded to the extent it has that does not mean the entire Holy Days Code has been investigated. As was pointed out on several occasions already, the Prophet Ezekiel mysteriously supplies his own Holy Days testimony. So it only makes sense that this study now turn there to discover whatever it is that Ezekiel is communicating with his testimony to bring the final and concluding decodings of the Great Holy Days Code.

Over the next 3 chapters, Ezekiel's writing will be examined. And what will be discovered there essentially uproots a great deal of Judeo-Christian tradition. It demolishes theologies and eschatologies that do not make the Law and the Gospel relevant to its teachings. The Moment of Truth has come and the Judeo-Christian World will never be the same if this message can be received. In his path of destruction over modern day teachings, Ezekiel will leave behind new plowed ground in which the Seeds of a New Theology and a New Eschatology will grow into the Truth that has laid waiting to be planted in the Minds of Truth Seekers. But the Walls erected in the minds of readers will need to come down in order for this Truth to be perceived and taken in for all that it communicates.

Recognizing that Ezekiel is a consummate Chronicler will be the sign that his writings are about predicting an orderly future with its important Divine milestones coming in a natural sequence. The first chapter will explore Ezekiel's meticulous chronicling of Israel's fate under the Sinaitic Covenant. One would hope that such an investigation would lead to discovering the Prophet predicting the end of the First Covenant. And indeed Ezekiel does.

Thus, the 2nd chapter will pick up where the 1st chapter ended. As the reader explores the extreme end of the Sinaitic Covenant as described by Ezekiel, it can be discovered that Ezekiel has an entirely new chronology emerging for the New Covenant. Historically, no study of merit has turned up evidence for arguing Ezekiel's final prophecies have anything to do with the New Covenant. But a reader trained by the Holy Days Code can appreciate the subtle findings in Ezekiel that unmistakably reveals Ezekiel is unveiling Israel's New Covenant Kingdom in his last 9 chapters of testimony! What will be discovered is that Jeremiah's New Covenant coming to Israel is what the 7th Day Sabbath of the Feast of Booths is symbolizing! There it will be discovered that the Law has an obvious prominent place in Israel's New Covenant Kingdom, a Kingdom that Ezekiel foresees as never-ending.

Finally, the 3rd and last chapter explores that portion of Ezekiel that appears to append the Law in the Offerings by Fire that the Prophet predicts will be added to Israel's Holy Days observances. In deciphering its meaning, it will reveal how and why the Law can harmoniously coexist with the Gospel. And, after having learned all about the original Holy Days Code, the keen eye will recognize that there is yet another hidden chronology within Ezekiel's Holy Days testimony. Just as the original Holy Days testimony is shown to be a chronology of the Divine Harvest Plan, so too, is it all that surprising that Ezekiel's Holy Days testimony is in fact to be found an appended Harvest Plan? When all is decoded, the chronology will describe important dates surrounding Remnant Israel's New Covenant Kingdom leading all the way into the Future Eternity itself. It will even point out the coming End to the Human Race's days of procreation in a stunning way!

The nations will know that the house of Israel went into exile for their iniquity because they acted treacherously against Me, and I hid My face from them; so I gave them into the hand of their adversaries and all of them fell by the sword...

Ezekiel 39:23

Chapter Fifteen

Ezekiel Chronicles the Sinaitic Covenant

What still remains murky and out of focus is the very end of the Holy Days Code. Recall that it has been argued that the Feast of Unleavened Bread is a symbolic partitioning of, and a chronicling of, Israel's Life. Furthermore, it has been argued that the 7th Month Holy Days testimony is really a "zoomed in" chronicle of the last 2 days of the Feast of Unleavened Bread. So the 7th Month Holy Days symbolize a chronicle of Israel's latter prophetic Life. Yet even this testimony lacks clarity towards the very End.

Now, as Ezekiel is examined, it will be put forth that Ezekiel's Holy Days are really symbolic of a "zoomed in" chronicle of the last 2 Holy Days of the 7th Month:

Ezekiel's Holy Days are a Chronicle within a Chronicle within a Chronicle

Feast of Unleavened Bread: Chronicle of Israel's Prophetic Life

| 15ᵗʰ | 16ᵗʰ | 17ᵗʰ | 18ᵗʰ | 19ᵗʰ | 20ᵗʰ | 21 |

7ᵗʰ Month Holy Days: Chronicle of Israel's Prophetic Remnant

| 1 | 10 | 15 | 16 | 17 | 18 | 19 | 20 | 21 | 22 |

**Ezekiel 45:18-25
Last Chronicle
of the
Holy Days**

Ezekiel's Holy Days chronicle than is really a chronicle within a chronicle (7th Month) within a chronicle (FULB), a most fascinating piece of prophecy. But this innermost chronicle happens to be imbedded under layers of other chronicles that the Prophet is found communicating. In order to properly interpret this Holy Days chronicle, a reader must first carefully unpeel the onion that is Ezekiel's writings, one layer at a time to get to his final layer. At its core, Ezekiel's writings will be shown supplying the finishing touches to the Holy Days testimony and its Code.

So in order to fully expose the very tail end of the Holy Days Code, this book must spend the rest of its pages plowing through all of Ezekiel's onion peels. For those who patiently endure through the details a whole new understanding of Scripture is unveiled. It will send shock waves throughout the Judeo Christian World if the message is ultimately received.

Ezekiel Confounds Traditional Readers

Every book of Scripture is to be considered a necessary component of the greater collective Scripture. Being so, each book needs to make its own unique contribution in setting itself apart from all other books yet binding itself to what all the other books communicate in unison. However, the way tradition has taken to interpreting Ezekiel's writings the Prophet plays no crucial role in Scripture. There has been no real effort to find where this writing's place happens to be in Scripture nor has a unique message been interpreted from it. Traditional interpretation has stumbled so badly over Ezekiel that he is found making no real contribution to institutionalized doctrines and teachings from either side. It is as if his writing could disappear and nothing would change in the traditional perspectives. Because of this Ezekiel remains by far the most elusive enigmatic writer amongst the Hebrew Scripture's writers.

As was touched upon in chapter 9, Judaism and Christendom both have traditional bias against Ezekiel which blinds these institutions to his message. Judaism has been in no historical mood to entertain Jeremiah's revelation of a New Covenant coming to Israel and fails to see a need for alterations to the Law of Moses which Ezekiel communicates. On the other hand Christians cannot perceive how any aspect of the Law could be relevant in a post Cross World. Nor can they fathom New Covenant Prophecy void of a portrayal of a Suffering Messiah as Jeremiah and Ezekiel do.

For Judaism, the Hebrew Scripture does not communicate the reality of a Prophetic Church and hence reject the relevancy of the Church. At the same time, Christians fail to see Israel in John's final vision in his Revelation and so these too have always rejected the idea there is to be a distinguishable Israel apart from the Church in the final analysis of things. But as the remainder of this book will now set out to explore, these 2 traditional viewpoints of Scripture can be shown to be in grave error due to the blindedness that comes from both sides of the debate seeking to isolate the two halves of Scripture from one another.

What is about to be unveiled for the readers to see represents such profound and provocative testimony if only because Ezekiel's writing is nearly 2500 years old and still his message remains as elusive to understand as in the days he first wrote it! The 4 remaining Holy Days testimony difficulties raised in the previous chapter will all be addressed by Ezekiel. That is, the House of Israel is to indeed receive its New Covenant as Jeremiah promised as the next chapter will clearly show when and how. And as for Israel's and the Law's fate, the 2 will become eternal just as the Law and the Prophets foretell. As for the fate of procreation, here again Ezekiel will bring closure on this subject as well in quite provocative fashion when he is found appending the Holy Schedule.

But the mind must be prepared to see these things through the subtle clues being provided. Yet just exactly how subtle can be 71 clues be as Ezekiel will be shown providing? Clearly the minds of countless readers have not been prepared to see these things heretofore. But now, with the help of the understanding of the Law's and the Gospel's Holy Days Code perhaps prepared readers will see the truth in living color for the first time since Ezekiel put pen to paper!

Ezekiel's Onion Peel-Like Layered Testimony

As pointed out earlier, Ezekiel's testimony can be found as if having layers like an onion has peels, one upon another upon another and so on. Each layer must be understood for its form of communication before attempting to peel it away to get to the next layer. Failure to properly understand a given peel and all subsequent layers beneath it are compromised for their understanding too. Therefore, a reader must be prepared to carefully examine each layer of Ezekiel's writings or else risk not being able to go deeper into Ezekiel's inner core layers of revelation. Without doing this, the very end of the Holy Days Code remains hidden.

The Prophet's first and outer most layer is the one that is most important and that should be readily noticeable. In contemplating a simple partitioning of the book it can be suggested the book has 3 main sections and these sections suggest a simple 3 fold chronicle in themselves. Section 1 should be entitled "God in Israel's Midst" up to the end of chapter 12. Section 2 should be entitled "God removed from Israel's Midst" starting from chapter 12 and ending in chapter 42. Finally, Section 3 should be entitled "God in Future Israel's Midst" from chapters 43 onward.

The 2nd and next important layer of Ezekiel's writings are his recordings of the Divine Visitations he had as a Prophet. While in exile in Babylon, Ezekiel informs the reader throughout his writings of what are 13 separate encounters he had. Each of these are carefully chronicled one by one. Hence, on a superficial level, Ezekiel is to be considered not only a Prophet but a Chronicler as well. No other Prophet will record so diligently upon what exact days he received revelation like Ezekiel. Of course, this is a huge sign not to be trivialized away as being a quaint oddity. All such anomalies and idiosyncrasies of Scripture need to be thoroughly investigated as they are used as beacons for the reader. Indeed, Ezekiel's writings contain not only overt chronicles but covert one's as well which altogether are layered in the text.

Ezekiel's 3rd layer of testimony is his contemporary message for the People of Israel of his day and the Nations round about. Abominations are witnessed taking place in and around the Temple and is one major reason cited for God's Plans to vacate His Presence there. What message God has Ezekiel delivering to "all flesh" is the proposition to Live or Die. Those who would be granted Life would be those submitting to the Will of God. Those who would be handed Death would be those refusing to change their ways. God specifically singles out Ezekiel and his fellow exiles as those who would be granted restoration back into the Land but only after the Nation had been purged of its evildoers. In Ezekiel 18 God declares He is not "pleased" with "anyone" who "dies". Nevertheless, Egypt's King and his servants are predicted to go down to the (bottomless) Pit and his Nation was declared never to rise again to the level it would impose its will on other neighboring nations forever thereafter. The city of Tyre however was not to be so fortunate. It was to be leveled, and never to be seen again. Through all of this, Israel and all the Nations were prophesied to come to "know" God under very imposing ways.

Ezekiel's 4th layer of testimony is how it begins to drift far into Israel's prophetic future, what most commentators are unwilling to acknowledge. In 3 discernible Eras being described throughout, Ezekiel envisions Israel as it lives out the predictions of the Sinaitic Covenant's terms and conditions as Moses recorded in the Law. The first Era, what history that has transpired in undeniable fashion, is what has become called Israel's "Diaspora". Ezekiel predicts Israel's Future People would become scattered like Sheep across the whole surface of the earth. There, in Gentile

Lands, Israel's People would live and die and never step foot back in the Land of Israel. The second Era, to follow the first, is the calling of an initial Remnant restored back to the Land. These are to have the Messiah as a Shepherd who is predicted to establish utopian like conditions for the Nation. Mysteriously, however, this Era is not defined as being eternal. Where Ezekiel's visions do take on an eternal perspective is at the very end in what is an anticipation of a yet 3rd eternal Era. It is an Era that is to arise out of what has to be Ezekiel's greatest prophecy he foresees only now Israel is viewed as a collective whole, an entire Nation which is to receive the New Covenant as an everlasting covenant as Jeremiah first envisioned.

This chapter is set aside to examine the first 2 Eras. In the following chapter, the making of the 3rd Era will be studied. What is so mysterious about this last 3rd Era is that its coming is so important yet its time of arrival is enshrouded in mystery. Indeed, Israel receiving its New Covenant, as predicted by Jeremiah the Prophet, remains one of the greatest mysteries of the Bible. Yet Ezekiel has always contained this information ever since it was written! It happens to be the subject of Ezekiel's 5th chronicle what is a most fascinating chronicle unlike all the others.

Look closely and it can be discovered that a repeating theme appears over and over again in the text but then immediately stops. It appears as if to be acting like a series of "stepping stones" in which the reader is to hop from one stone to the next. This series of stepping stones are 71 in all and then they abruptly end as if they are designed to bring the reader to this final destination, like a trail leads to its end.

Where the reader is found at the end of the "chronicle" just so happens to be the unveiling of the general time when Jeremiah's Prophecy of Israel's New Covenant is to be received as an everlasting covenant. From that day onward, the House of Israel is to "know" God and never fall away again. This moment is also to be the moment when God's Divine Glory comes to Israel once again and never leaves it again. This is to be a Harvest Ingathering of both the House of Israel and God-fearing Gentiles from around the World. Provocatively, some 6 other writing Prophets are found embellishing upon Ezekiel's New Covenant testimony making it possible to create a multi-Prophets Chronicle of epic portions.

This happens to be Ezekiel's 6th layer of testimony which includes the unfolding of the Kingdom he envisions, what is Israel's long awaited New Covenant Kingdom. The Kingdom is not Messianic yet nevertheless it will have an eternal Prince and King. There on the Land the Nation is to live forever made up of 3 generations. There is to be a Temple there. God's Divine Glory is to permanently dwell within the Temple there forever. The Levitical Priests are to serve there in the Temple forever. There the Law is to be followed forever along with Ezekiel's 8 additional Offerings he defines as part of an addendum to the Holy Days testimony. In summary, this is to be the place where the House of Israel is to live out its everlasting covenant. What Ezekiel's Holy Days testimony ultimately communicates is the reality of the Grand Mystery of Israel's everlasting life and what the consequences of the Great Mystery imposes on Future Israel.

But there is yet another hidden purpose found for Ezekiel's Holy Days testimony under the surface. It creates Ezekiel's 7th and final layer of testimony, what is his most provocative of all chronicles, hidden and concealed to eyes, until now. All the study and dissection of the Law's Holy Days and everything that the Gospel has come to decode about them, these are the only things that can prepare the reader to see what has to be Ezekiel's Most Secret Chronicle. When making careful observation of Ezekiel's Holy Days testimony, it becomes only too clear and familiar to recognize that Ezekiel is essentially picking up where the Law's Holy Days Chronicle, imbedded in its Holy Days testimony, leaves off! There the Chronicle penetrates into the very Future Eternity and gazes upon what is predicted to take place there, an exclusive Blessing given to the Remnant alone to receive! This last Chronicle of Ezekiel will be studied in the final chapter of this work.

Ezekiel's 7 Onion Peel Chronicles:

1. Ezekiel's 3 Part Chronicle (1:1-48:35)

2. Ezekiel's 13 fold Dated Testimonial (1:1-48:35)

3. Ezekiel's Prophetic Chronicle of His Generation (4:1-33:33)

4. Ezekiel's Chronicle of 4 Future Israels (34:1-37:28)

5. Ezekiel's 70 steps to Jeremiah's New Covenant (5:13-39:28)

6. Ezekiel's New Covenant Kingdom Chronicle (38:1-48:35)

7. Ezekiel's Hidden Holy Days Chronicle (45:18-25)

Although it may appear as if this book is veering off the general path of the topic of the Holy Days Code, ultimately, in the end, all of this "off beaten path" work will pay off in helping to understand the astonishing conclusion to the Holy Days Code.

Ezekiel's Overarching Chronicle

What will be discovered over the next 3 chapters is that Ezekiel's over all message is hinted at by what are the 2 big clues that are clearly noticeable. These clues are to act as guides for the reader in helping decipher Ezekiel's message. Readers who simply pay attention while reading Ezekiel can identify these clues with little difficulty.

The first major clue should necessarily jump out at readers as it is thrust immediately upon them and is so provocatively strange. This would be Ezekiel's witnessing of the Divine Glory in his opening passages. The testimony is so unlike anything else written in Scripture it stands alone without equal. Why such an unusual witness remains somewhat of a mystery as to what it is communicating is simply tragic. This vision is meant to be a deliberate tool designed to make this image of God a lasting and unforgettable one. The shocking introduction can only be meant as a guide to color everything else the reader comes to encounter.

For Jews and Judaism this is a particularly sensitive subject because this was the Law's greatest legacy it manifested for the Nation in its ancient past. No other Nation can boast of having had the one true God dwelling in its midst. And a Great Hope that all observing Jews possess is that one day God is to return to dwell again with Israel, a peculiar message that Ezekiel was given to convey in this most strange and bizarre way.

If Christians want to get an idea of how important this message is for Jews, it parallels exactly the Church's expectation of the 2nd Coming of Christ. That is, God came "once" to Israel but "left" during the Babylonian Captivity. But Ezekiel expects God to "Come Again" a "second time" and to stay forever with the Nation Israel thereafter. Thus, Israel's and the Jews' anticipation of the 2nd Coming of God was predicted of at least 400 years before the Church was given an anticipation for the 2nd Coming of Christ! And not surprisingly, even John's Revelation reminds its readers of this precedent setting anticipation in at least 3 places (1:4, 8 and 4:8).

Ezekiel Theme: Divine Glory's Departure & Return

And so Ezekiel's theme for his witness is simple, to the point, and speaks loud and clear. It comes in two obvious parts. In his first portion of his writing Ezekiel records witnessing God's Glory, a very strange vision the prophet describes. It was to be understood the full expression of the Glory that had been resident in Israel's community there in the Holy Place. This visitation began when Moses first assembled the tabernacle just prior to the first Passover memorial. It remained with the community of Israel and found new residency in Solomon's Temple. This Presence continued leading up to Ezekiel's day. But what Ezekiel is made to see and testify to is the Glory's Departure from the Holy Place. Ezekiel is explained why the Glory was to leave:

Eze8:6...do you see what they are doing, the great abominations which the house of Israel are committing here, so that I would be far from My sanctuary?...

Eze10:18 Then the glory of the LORD departed from the threshold of the temple...

Eze11:23 The glory of the LORD went up from the midst of the City...

To this very day, this condition has never been reversed. Even though a 2nd Temple would come to be built some 70 years after the initial Babylonian exile, the so called "Shekinah Glory" never did return ever again.

But fascinatingly Ezekiel has his second portion of writing revealing when this condition is to come and be reversed forever. Late in his writing, the Prophet sees a vision of God's Glory prophetically returning in a future time coming to dwell within a Temple Ezekiel envisions:

Eze43:4, 7 And the glory of the LORD came into the house...And He said to me, "Son of man, {this is} the place of My throne and the place of the soles of My feet, <u>where I will dwell among the sons of Israel forever...</u>

There simply is no greater thing Ezekiel witnesses than this expectation for the future. That although God had left His place of habitation with Israel at the time of the Nation's exile into Babylon inevitably He was to return and never leave thereafter. What additional things that Ezekiel communicates outside of this must all be seen as collectively supporting and pointing the way to this ultimate destination that is expected to be Israel's eternal future.

So by the time Ezekiel is done writing he will have witnessed the Divine Glory in 2 different settings. The first setting is in Ezekiel's Day as the Divine Glory was leaving Israel's Midst. The second setting is prophetic when Ezekiel envisions the Divine Glory returning to a Future Israel's Midst at some point in the future. From this, Ezekiel's 1st Great Chronicle is established. In more ways than one, Ezekiel's Writing mimics the symbolisms of the Feast of Unleavened Bread and this is not a coincidence.

Feast of Unleavened Bread

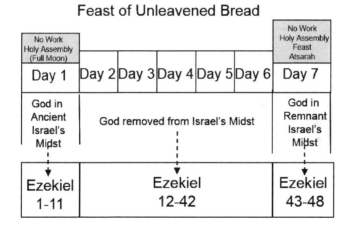

No Work Holy Assembly (Full Moon)						No Work Holy Assembly Feast Atsarah
Day 1	Day 2	Day 3	Day 4	Day 5	Day 6	Day 7
God in Ancient Israel's Midst	God removed from Israel's Midst					God in Remnant Israel's Midst
Ezekiel 1-11	Ezekiel 12-42					Ezekiel 43-48

Ezekiel's 3 Part Chronicle

This so happens to make for a very good explanation for why Ezekiel's Writing is void of the kind of New Covenant revelations most Christians would expect to see. Christians are flabbergasted and dumbfounded by this glaring issue, so much so that they avoid Ezekiel altogether. But just as the Feast of Unleavened Bread symbolizes Israel's entire Mortal Life absent of any Libation Offerings, it turns out that Ezekiel too has no Libation Offerings within his testimony either as was already revealed in chapter 9. Nevertheless, the Messiah is subtly introduced in a moment and then quickly disappears. So too the First fruits testimony comes to overlap the Feast of Unleavened Bread for a moment before it breaks away into its own Path of revelation. As such, Ezekiel's writing is curiously patterned after the Feast of Unleavened Bread.

Ezekiel's Chronicle of 13 Divine Visitations

The second great clue most readers pick up on is Ezekiel's most conspicuous Chronicle he supplies. Indeed, any good commentator will make mention of Ezekiel's chronicling of the Divine Visitations he received. There happen to be 13 such occasions when the Prophet records being visited on a certain date:

Ezekiel's 13 Chronicled Divine Visitations

#	Passage	Year of Ezekiel's exile	Date of Visitation	
1.	1:1	The 5th Year	The 4th Month	The 5th Day
2.	8:1	The 6th Year	The 6th Month	The 5th Day
3.	20:1	The 7th Year	The 5th Month	The 10th Day
4.	24:1	The 9th Year	The 10th Month	The 10th Day
5.	26:1	The 11th Year	The ? Month	The 1st Day
6.	29:1	The 10th Year	The 10th Month	The 12th Day
7.	30:20	The 11th Year	The 1st Month	The 7th Day
8.	31:1	The 11th Year	The 3rd Month	The 1st Day
9.	32:1	(The 11th?) 12th Year	The 12th Month	The 1st Day
10.	32:17	(The 11th?) 12th Year	The 12th Month	The 15th Day
11.	33:21	The 12th Year	The 10th Month	The 5th Day
12.	40:1	The 25th Year	The 1st Month	The 10th Day
13.	29:17	The 27th Year	The 1st Month	The 1st Day

There are several things to note here. At least one date is not in chronological sequence. Ezekiel's last visitation came 27 years into his exile in Babylon yet appears at 29:17. It records Egypt's final prophecy as being Ezekiel's last prophecy received as a Prophet. For this reason it is listed last in the above chronology. Some have noted that it perhaps was originally located at the end of Ezekiel's writing but that it was moved in order to join the prophecies of Egypt together in one place as to make it complete and uninterrupted. Also, visitations 9 and 10 are recorded as having come in the 12th year but variant readings suggest these actually came in the 11th year.

The first visitation came after Ezekiel had been in exile in Babylon for 5 years. This is where Ezekiel came to witness the Divine Glory for the first time. In Ezekiel's 6th year of exile, the 2nd visitation is where Ezekiel will witness God's Glory departing out of Solomon's Temple. The 5th visitation is believed to be the day that Jerusalem came to be broken through by the Babylonians after their long siege against the city, 11 years after Ezekiel went into exile.

Although the month of the year is not indicated, Jeremiah records that Jerusalem's walls were breached in the 4th month while its destruction came in the 5th month. The 11th visitation is prompted when Ezekiel is visited in person by an eyewitness who saw the "taking" of Jerusalem by the Babylonians, this coming nearly a year and a half after the actual day of capture came. The 12th visitation is when Ezekiel received his kingdom vision which came 25 years into his exile. Finally, the 13th visitation came 2 years after his kingdom vision. Here God is recorded declaring that Egypt would be plundered by the Babylonian armies because these same armies had "served" God in having destroyed the city of Tyre without having received due compensation for their hard labor.

Historically, readers have failed to appreciate this peculiar aspect of Ezekiel being a careful date recorder. Nothing in Scripture that is out of the ordinary should be interpreted as being merely a coincidental idiosyncrasy. What it is is Ezekiel's 2nd sign behind that of his peculiar witnessing of the Divine Glory. These are the signs pointing to what greater things Ezekiel conceals within his writing. These easily recognizable elements in his more visible message Ezekiel writes of run parallel with what similar hidden messages Ezekiel develops in between the lines.

It appears to be an innocent form of baiting in enticing the reader to play along in a form of hide-and-seek. That is, Ezekiel provides these 2 readily noticeable elements to suggest these things are part of a greater message which the reader is to seek after and find within the greater text. That is, Ezekiel's visitation accounting is painstakingly detailed as a proper sequential ordering. This suggests that Ezekiel's overall prophetic message is to be interpreted likewise. Furthermore, Ezekiel's entire writing is basically a proper ordering of certain prophetic events which ultimately are to end with the expected 2nd Coming of God.

Sinaitic Covenant to be fulfilled across 4 Eras

It should be considered no coincidence that the terms and conditions of the Sinaitic Covenant itself, dictated in the Law of Moses, sets the prophetic precedent for Israel's future to be divided up into 3 parts. That the Feast of Unleavened Bread's and Ezekiel's composition follows this predicted pattern is simply a testament to the consistency of Scripture. Hence, by natural progression, the New Covenant cannot be expected to appear until AFTER the Sinaitic Covenant is fulfilled first.

This is why Ezekiel's writing can be interpreted as having its early prophecy envisioning the fulfillment of the Sinaitic Covenant whereas its latter prophecy envisions the coming of the New Covenant. Perhaps the summarizing passage of Ezekiel's writing is this one:

Ezek 16:59-60 I will also do with you as you have done... Nevertheless, I will remember My covenant with you in the days of your youth, and I will establish an everlasting covenant with you.

Here it states that God would "do with you as you have done". And what had Israel done? It had forsaken God. So too God was stating he would forsake Israel. This would become part of the fulfillment of the Sinaitic Covenant as its curses would overtake the Nation. But this was not to be for all time because He is to also eventually "remember" the covenant He had made. In that covenant God had promised Israel that he would circumcise the Nation's heart (Deut 30:6). In so doing, this would also "establish an everlasting covenant" with Israel, this being Jeremiah's New Covenant.

So just exactly what did the Law predict for Israel's life under the Sinaitic Covenant? The blessings for obedience are described first in the opening passages of both Leviticus 26 and Deuteronomy 28:

Lev 26:9 'So I will turn toward you and make you fruitful and multiply you, and I will confirm My covenant with you.

Deut 28:2 "And all these blessings shall come upon you and overtake you, if you will obey the LORD your God.

No greater time in Israel's past did its life attain such blessing than during King Solomon's reign. But the Law also predicted curses to come should Israel disobey:

Deut 28:15 "But it shall come about, if you will not obey the LORD your God, to observe to do all His commandments and His statutes with which I charge you today, that all these curses shall come upon you and overtake you.

Again and again Ezekiel, and all the prophets, can be found prophesying of Israel's many future days it would suffer in being scattered for its misdeeds. Ezekiel's readers are even reminded of the occasion when Israel first came under these terms:

Ezek 20:23-24 "Also I swore to them in the wilderness that I would scatter them among the nations and disperse them among the lands, because they had not observed My ordinances, but had rejected My statutes, and had profaned My sabbaths, and their eyes were on the idols of their fathers.

Ezekiel will bring his own predictions of Israel's dispersion in at least 10 different places in his writing: **1)** 5:2, 10, 12; 6:8 **2)** 11:16 **3)** 12:14-15 **4)** 17:21 **5)** 20:34, 41, and **6)** 22:15 **7)** 28:25 **8)** 34:5-6, 12, 21 **9)** 36:19 **10)** 39:23-24. Indeed, the

Nation ultimately suffered the worst the curses would spell out. Historically speaking, the majority of Israel's people would never return after the devastation the Babylonian armies brought to the Land. This large body of Israel's scattered peoples would create the so called "Diaspora" because these people's origins and culture were never lost to assimilation down through history.

But the Law predicted that the Nation would ultimately return to the Land and become blessed at some point:

Deut 30:4 "If your outcasts are at the ends of the earth, from there the LORD your God will gather you, and from there He will bring you back.

So too Ezekiel predicts Israel's regathering, either in the same breath while predicting Israel's dispersion, or in a separate foretelling. In all, there are at least 9 different places predicting this: **1)** 11:17 **2)** 20:34, 41 **3)** 22:19-21 **4)** 28:25 **5)** 34:13 **6)** 36:24 **7)** 37:21 **8)** 38:8, 12 **9)** 39:27-28.

Upon examining Ezekiel's various passages resonating with the Law's prediction of Israel's dispersion and regathering, it becomes evident that Ezekiel is predicting a 4-fold chronology:

1. Ezekiel's vision of his own generation's prophetic fate
   - An unprecedented Babylonian induced dispersion of Israel
   - Judgment to Israel and the Nations round about
   - A partial regathering of a remnant from exile
2. Israel's eventual worldwide dispersion
3. Israel's regathering from its worldwide dispersion in the latter day
4. Israel's final regathering at the furthest point in the future Ezekiel sees

Israel's dispersion was well underway by the time Ezekiel began to write. The Northern Kingdom had been swept away by the Assyrians more than a hundred years before the Babylonian siege. These tribesmen are believed to have been almost entirely assimilated. They have often been referred to as the "10 Lost Tribes of Israel". For the Southern Kingdom there would come 3 general points in time when it would be incrementally taken into Babylonian exile. Throughout this exile Judah's People would remain unassimilated with a small remnant returning and rebuilding after the Babylonian empire fell to the ascending Medo-Persian Empire.

The first exiling occasion was roughly in 606BC/BCE when the prophet Daniel is believed to have been taken (Dan1:1-6). At that time, the sitting king, King Jehoiakim became a vassal to King Nebuchadnezzar of Babylon.

Some 3 years later Jehoiakim would rebel and align himself with Egypt. So a second siege resulted in Jehoiakim being taken captive to Babylon along with Ezekiel and others around 597BC/BCE, Egypt having abandoned Israel. It is interesting to note that the Law had predicted this very thing:

Deut 28:36 "The LORD will bring you and your king, whom you shall set over you, to a nation which neither you nor your fathers have known, and there you shall serve other gods, wood and stone.

Jehoiakim's son Jehoiachin became king but he also rebelled and only after 3 months the city of Jerusalem was again laid siege. Jehoiachin surrendered and Nebuchadnezzar carried yet a 2nd king away along with the vast majority of Israel's people, leaving only the poorest behind. Also, the temple treasures were also carried away to Babylon. Nebuchadnezzar would appoint Jehoiakim's uncle, Mattaniah, as king, renaming him Zedekiah.

Zedekiah would rule for 11 years. But in his 9th year he provoked Nebuchadnezzar to return and lay siege to the city one last time. In and around 586BC/BCE, after the city had been besieged for some 2-3 years, Jerusalem's wall was breached and the city was thoroughly demolished including Solomon's Temple. Zedekiah would attempt to flee but was caught and taken to Babylon after having his eyes gouged out.

Ezekiel's Prophetic Chronicle of His Generation

Ezekiel's ministry would be quite illustrative in being a one man show. He was called to act out various prophecies that were to come to pass upon Israel for all of his fellow exiles to witness there in Babylon. None of what was to come upon Israel was to be seen by the exiles however they did get to witness it all beforehand through the visible witness of Ezekiel. This was all designed to prove to them that Ezekiel was indeed a Prophet of God when all of these things would eventually come to pass (2:5; 33:33).

Judgment of Israel

A huge uninterrupted block of Ezekiel's writings, chapters 4 to 24, is devoted to prophecy of the Israel of Ezekiel's day in condemning it for its evil committed and of predicting of its coming downfall and the downfall of the surrounding Nations.

What was to come upon Israel was not insignificant:

Ezek 5:12 'One third of you will die by plague or be consumed by famine among you, one third will fall by the sword around you, and one third I will scatter to every wind, and I will unsheathe a sword behind them.

Ezek 6:14 "So throughout all their habitations I shall stretch out My hand against them and make the land more desolate and waste than the wilderness toward   Diblah"'"

This general destruction is described as being unprecedented and would never have an equal according to Ezekiel:

Ezek 5:9 'And because of all your abominations, I will do among you what I have not done, and the like of which I will never do again.

Thus, what this exile was to accomplish was to purge Israel of its rebels leaving only those who desired to remain under the covenant:

Ezek 11:21…as for those whose hearts go after their detestable things and abominations, I shall bring their conduct down on their heads," declares the Lord GOD.

Judgment of the Nations

Judgment is also expected to come to the Nations in Ezekiel's day as well. Chapter 25 brings condemnation to Ammon, Edom and Philistia while Chapters 26-28 is directed at Tyre and Chapters 29-32 to Egypt. (Again, 29:17-21 is believed to have been the original last passages of Ezekiel before they were moved to this place by scribes in order to bring all the prophecies of Egypt together in one location.) These prophecies are bold predictions with the fate of Tyre and Egypt having been cited earlier.

(Interestingly enough, Edom is prophesied of again in chapter 35. Hence it would seem the prophecy in the earlier section was predicting Edom's fate in Ezekiel's immediate day and which soon came to pass. Yet the second citation appears to be prophecy yet to be fulfilled in the Latter Day.)

Israel's predicted regathering (70 years later)

Within these passages however, there is a prediction of restoration to Ezekiel and his fellow exiles already in captivity in Babylon. Chapter 11:14-25 is the main, opening prophecy. However, interestingly enough, there are other scattered sections of writings assigned to this same generation in 20:33-44 and then again in 37:22-28.

All throughout Ezekiel there is this repeating prophecy of dispersion and restoration as was pointed out earlier. Yet, in carefully examining each "wave" of these prophecies, there are subtle distinctions to be noticed that evidence what are multiple future occurrences being predicted which cannot be construed as predicting a one time occurrence. For instance, in order to separate prophecy appointed to Ezekiel's generation from any future generation, Ezekiel distinguishes his own generation with the pronoun "you" whereas the pronoun "them" is always used for future generations being foretold by the Prophet. Other clues to notice are descriptions of time where only the last generations Ezekiel foresees are actually predicted eternal longevity while the others are not.

Beginning with his own generation, Ezekiel had been foretold the good news that those exiled with him would be allowed to return and rebuild:

Ezek 11:15,17-20 "Son of man, your brothers, your relatives, your fellow exiles,

and the whole house of Israel, all of them...'Thus says the Lord GOD, "I shall <u>gather you</u> from the peoples and assemble you out of the countries among which <u>you have been scattered</u>, and I shall <u>give you the land of Israel</u>."..."And I shall give them <u>one heart</u>, and shall put a new spirit within them. And I shall take the heart of stone out of their flesh and give them a heart of flesh, that they may <u>walk in My statutes</u> and keep My ordinances, and do them. Then they will be My people, and <u>I shall be their God</u>.

Eze 20:33-37 "As I live," declares the Lord GOD, "surely with a mighty hand and with an outstretched arm and <u>with wrath poured out</u>, I shall be king over you. I will bring you out from the peoples and gather you from the lands where you were scattered, with a mighty hand and with an outstretched arm and <u>with wrath poured out</u>; and <u>I will bring you into the wilderness</u> of the peoples, and there I will enter into judgment with you face to face...I will make you pass under the rod and I will bring you into <u>the bond of the covenant</u>...

Notice that God is to bring Ezekiel's generation under the Sinaitic Covenant. This was expected to take place sometime after the exile was over. The prophet Jeremiah had been told this exile period would last 70 years and then the people would be allowed to return:

Jer 29:10-11 "For thus says the LORD, 'When seventy years have been completed for Babylon, I will visit you and fulfill My good word to you, to bring you back to this place.' For I know the plans that I have for you,' declares the LORD, 'plans for welfare and not for calamity to give you a future and a hope.

Anticipating Israel's worldwide dispersion

An important transition in Ezekiel's writing is in chapter 33 when Ezekiel is informed by an eyewitness that the city of Jerusalem had been taken by the Babylonians in verse 21. Everything that the prophet had warned of leading up to this point had come to pass. Now, with the coming of chapter 34, Ezekiel is made to focus beyond the trouble of that day to what lay in the distant future for Israel. The main subject is God's rebuke of Israel's "shepherds" and how they would historically fail in caring for the flock by being responsible for scattering the flock instead. No doubt this is a prophecy ultimately foreseeing the Religious Establishment of Jesus' day and what outcome they had caused with Jesus' crucifixion which eventually led to the Great Jewish Revolt that catastrophically ended in AD70:

Eze 34:5-6 They were scattered for lack of a shepherd, and they became food for every beast of the field and were scattered. My flock wandered through all the mountains and on every high hill; <u>My flock was scattered over all the surface of the earth</u>, and there was no one to search or seek for them.

Recall Ezekiel had already predicted his own generation would be restored to the Land back in chapters 11 and 20. Hence, Ezekiel is looking prophetically far beyond his immediate generation. The Law's ultimate predictions had made similar visions too:

Deut 28:63-64 "And it shall come about that as the LORD delighted over you to prosper you, and multiply you, so the LORD will delight over you to make you perish and destroy you; and you shall be torn from the land where you are entering to possess it." Moreover, the LORD will scatter you among all peoples, <u>from one end of the earth to the other end of the earth</u>; and there you shall serve other gods, wood and stone, which you or your fathers have not known.

Diaspora Israel vs Latter Day Israel

As the rest of Chapter 34 unfolds, two very fundamentally different Israels are being introduced and foretold of. The first is that of Diaspora Israel, the Israel that came to be scattered into all the world. This phenomenon began as a result of the Babylonian Exile around 586BC but which was catapulted into full blown expression caused by the failed Jewish Revolt beginning in AD66 and ending in AD70. The second Israel unveiled in Chapter 34 is the Israel Ezekiel predicts will eventually be restored back to the Land long after his own generation would live and die and long after Israel would come to be "scattered over all the surface of the earth". This Restoration would necessarily bring an end to the Diaspora and bring about a second Israel, a "Latter Day Israel".

Verses 22-30 summarize these 2 contrasting Israels which is excerpted here:

Eze34:22 I will deliver My Flock...
Eze34:28-29 And they will <u>no longer be a prey to the Nations</u>, and <u>the beasts of the earth will not devour them</u>; but <u>they will live securely</u>...and <u>they will not again be victims of famine in the Land</u>, and <u>they will not endure the insults of the Nations any more</u>.

Diaspora Israel then can be defined as being "God's Flock" that remains undelivered across the surface of the earth. Diaspora Israel is to become prey to the Nations. The Beasts of the earth will devour them. They will not live securely. They will be victims of famine. They will endure the insults of the Nations.

The prophet Hosea certainly seems to have seen this occasion coming too. He foretells that Israel would be "many days" without all the familiar things it needed to be a covenant fulfilling nation:

Hosea 3:4-5 For the sons of Israel will remain for <u>many days</u> <u>without king</u> or prince, <u>without sacrifice</u> or {sacred} pillar, and <u>without ephod</u> or household idols. Afterward the sons of Israel will return and seek the LORD their God and David their king; and they will come trembling to the LORD and to His goodness in the last days.

It was to be a time absent of the Temple and Priesthood and without access to the city of Jerusalem. And indeed, in the year AD70, the temple was destroyed by the

Romans and in less than 50 years, the vast majority of Jews had become scattered into all the world. But then, after thousands of years came to pass, beginning in and around the start of the 20th century, Jews began to miraculously have the opportunity to return to live in the Land of Israel. In 1948, the Nation took on Statehood. In 1967, Israel captured the old city of Jerusalem. At the same time, Israel's countless enemies have waged war militarily and diplomatically to try to remove it without success.

At the present hour, there are as many Jews living in Israel as there are anywhere else in the world. Thus, Diaspora Israel and Latter Day Israel coexist in the current state of affairs. As the Latter Days soon come to unfold, Ezekiel's prophecies surprisingly have no insight on this period of time. Instead, Daniel, Ezekiel's counterpart, was given the vast majority of prophecy into this period of time, now known as Daniel's 70th week.

Speculation as to why Ezekiel provides nothing about the Latter Day is perhaps due to the fact that this era is not considered part of Israel's prophetic life as foreseen by the Feast of Unleavened Bread's symbolisms. Indeed, Ezekiel's prophecies dwell upon matters concerning the first and last days of the Feast of Unleavened Bread apart from the homogenous in-between days. Certainly Ezekiel's Diaspora Israel and Latter Day Israel testimony can be understood as spanning these in-between days.

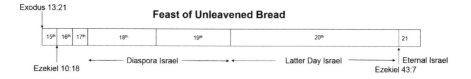

Last Lost Sheep become Latter Day Israel

The passages of 34:10-30 and then again in 36:10-15 make up the predictions for Latter Day Israel. In short, Latter Day Israel is to be the very last "living" generation to suffer as the Diaspora and whom are to be divinely delivered from all the calamities of the Diaspora:

Eze 34:11-12 Behold, I Myself will search for My sheep and seek them out. As a shepherd cares for his herd in the day when he is among his scattered sheep, so I will care for My sheep and will deliver them from all the places to which they were scattered on a cloudy and gloomy day.

The rest of chapter 34 is more predictions regarding Latter Day Israel. As will be shown shortly, a 3rd Israel is to arise apart from Diaspora Israel and Latter Day Israel, as described at the latter end of chapter 37. It is in this last passage where things are finally described as becoming eternal and forever in scope. All passages prior to this one regarding Diaspora Israel and Latter Day Israel do not share such an eternal scope but read more like earlier Israels that are to eventually give way to this final eternal Israel.

This is an oversimplification though. The Great Mystery was argued in earlier chapters to apply to Latter Day Israel too. So what this means is that Ezekiel's final eternal Era for Israel is one that is to replace the finite Eras of Diaspora Israel and Latter Day Israel. What is really being communicated between the lines is that Latter Day Israel is to be considered eternal too but however it will at first exist in a temporary era before it is brought into an eternal era. How Ezekiel subtly communicates this is by the clever words he uses in describing Latter Day Israel. For instance, he uses the phrases "no longer" and "any more" and "not again" in 34:10,22,28,29; 36:12,14,15. In all these passages, the past conditions of Diaspora Israel will be suffered "no longer" by Latter Day Israel and so forth. This allows Ezekiel to reserve the more forceful words like "forever" and "everlasting" to be assigned to the last Era of Israel he will foresee.

Is Ezekiel's Servant David the Messiah?

But there is yet another dimension Ezekiel brings to Latter Day Israel, a Davidic Dimension:

Eze 34:23-25 Then I will set over them one shepherd, <u>My servant David</u>, and he will feed them; he will feed them himself and be their shepherd. [24] And I, the LORD, will be their God, and My servant David will be prince among them; I the LORD have spoken. And I will make <u>a covenant of peace</u> with them…

Here, for the first time, a "covenant of peace" is to be made with Latter Day Israel. This is in fact the New Covenant. (But this is not the moment Ezekiel predicts Jeremiah's Prophecy of the New Covenant comes to be fulfilled. Ezekiel reserves a date yet future from this one in a later passage to make prediction of the timing of when Jeremiah's Prophecy is to be fulfilled. This will be explored in detail in the next chapter.)

An historical debate has raged about whether this passage is referring to the Messiah or not. Given the "covenant of peace" is to come in conjunction with this Davidic Prophecy it certainly appears to be inferring that the Messiah is in view here. The main reason for rejecting such a claim is because Eze45:22 suggests that the "Prince", a title used here in chapter 34:23-24 and then later in chapter 37:24-25, is to offer a sacrifice for himself due to his own sin he commits. In this first location there is no mention of David being a king, which only appears in the 2nd reference.

In the second reference, the Servant David is to become Israel's "Prince" forever (37:25) where no such longevity appears in the earlier passages of 34:23-24. The way in which to resolve this double prophecy is to suggest that the 2 prophecies are indeed not the same prophecy but are foreseeing 2 different Sons of David for two different eras of Israel! The first Servant David of 34:23-24 can be seen as the Shepherd Messiah who tends the Flock during His finite length era of the Messianic/Millennial Kingdom of the Latter Day.

In traditional Christianity's persistent denial of Israel's place in the Messianic Kingdom, its institutionalized thinking has no other choice but to argue that this Prince can be no other person but the Messiah and that Ezekiel's Kingdom itself is merely a foreshadow of the Church's Kingdom. But this theory falls apart when the later references of the Prince describe him as one who will provide a sin offering for himself (45:22; 46:2). This represents a huge problem that makes traditional teaching simply untenable. The Gospel teaches that the Messiah is a sinless offering for sin, a complete incongruence from Ezekiel's Prince.

So what 37:24-25 must then be envisioning is yet a 2nd sinful Servant David, another Son of David, aligning with Eze45:22, coming to shepherd Israel forever thereafter in the last and eternal Era of Israel as its eternal king. This Prince would thus arise after the Millennial Kingdom is over in what will be argued in the next chapter as being the subsequent coming of an eternal era of what is to be Ezekiel's Kingdom he envisions. (Those skeptical of such an interpretation need only be reminded that Daniel, Ezekiel's counterpart, does something strikingly similar. He too envisions 2 Princes in Dan9:25-27. The first Prince in verse 25 is clearly stated as being the Messiah. The second Prince however is none other than the Antichrist himself. Should readers also question how there is be 2 Davidic Kings coexisting together need only contemplate Jesus' title of "King of Kings". This subject is taken up in more detail in the book "Thy Kingdom(s) Come" and at the website thykingdomscome.info.)

The fact that the Messiah is stealthily introduced into Ezekiel's writings is also indicative of the fact that Ezekiel's writings can be considered modelled after the Feast of Unleavened Bread. It is the one Feast which is void of Gospel symbolisms but which coincidentally overlaps Holy Days with the early Mystery First fruit Days. It was also shown in chapter 9 that Ezekiel's testimony of new Offerings by Fire are all exclusively Atonement Offerings having no Libation Offerings. These odd connections collectively suggest Ezekiel is mimicking the symbolisms of the Feast of Unleavened Bread. Thus, Ezekiel's narrative is really all about Israel's Prophetic Life with only subtle clues to a Messianic element.

Ezekiel 37: The 2 Eternal Israels

After having prophesied of Diaspora Israel and Latter Day Israel across chapters 34 and 36, chapter 37 will now bring a final testimony of Israel. In it there will be 2 unveilings of yet another 2 prophetic Israels. What chapters 34 and 36 unveils are the 2 Israels that were predicted to come living under temporary conditions. Now, chapter 37 will unveil those 2 Israels that are expected to come to exist forever.

37:1-14: Dead of Diaspora to be Resurrected

The first half of chapter 37, verses 1-14 regards Ezekiel's famous "Valley of Dry Bones" Vision. Many commentators, including those of traditional Judaism, have insisted that this vision is referring to Latter Day Israel, the Israel that is to be restored to the Land in the Latter Day.

The passage breaks into 2 natural portions: verses 1-10 and 11-14. Traditional explanations want to conclude that each portion is a separate vision and that both are to be seen suggesting what tradition wants to believe. But a simple straight forward reading of the passage reveals that verses 1-10 is the vision while verses 11-14 are the explanation to the vision of 1-10.

The whole point of the vision of 37:1-10 is to describe what the ultimate fate of the vast majority of Diaspora Israel is to become. That is, what is the ultimate fate of those of God's Flock that become scattered over all the earth? What happens to those who become "prey to the Nations" never being given the opportunity to return to the Land? This vision predicts that a great number of Israelites will DIE outside of the Land. And so, what is to happen to them? Is their hope perished? What is their fate? An equivalent situation in the Gospel testimony is the concerns of the believing Thessalonians. They wanted to know what was to happen to those believers who die before the return of Christ (1Thess4:13). Provocatively, the Divine Answer to these two great questions is the same.

With this passage, the Divine Vision is meant to comfort all those of Diaspora Israel wherever they were to find themselves outside of the Land. In effect, God promises to these, His Lost Flock, that they will not perish because they are prophesied here to be Resurrected from the Dead and then to be returned to the Land of Promise:

Ezek 37:12 ..."Thus says the Lord GOD, "Behold, I will open your graves and cause you to come up out of your graves, My people; and I will bring you into the land of Israel."

It is also interesting to note that these People receive God's Spirit just as do all those of Israel who are to be regathered as Ezekiel predicts, yet with something missing. There is no additional statement given that these will walk in God's statutes or who will experience God becoming their God or the making of a covenant with them as the other mentioned Israelites are to experience (see 11:19-20; 36:26-28; 37:23-28). It would seem there is a different standard for these particular People from all the other restored People Ezekiel describes. Here is yet further proof that these passages are not referring to a Mortal restoration of Israel but an Immortal one of the deceased of Diaspora Israel.

37:15-28: The Last and Eternal Israel

What further proof there is to provide in the interpretation just supplied is the second portion of chapter 37. Here again, the same pattern is repeated. There is a vision/parable in verses 16-20 and then there is an explanation to what the vision/parable means in verses 21-28, just like the first portion of chapter 37 is constructed. Here then is a portion of the parable:

Ezek 37:16-18 "And you, son of man, take for yourself one stick and write on it, 'For Judah and for the sons of Israel, his companions'; then take another stick and write on it, 'For Joseph, the stick of Ephraim and all the house of Israel, his

companions.' "Then join them for yourself one to another into one stick, that they may become one in your hand. "And when the sons of your people speak to you saying, 'Will you not declare to us what you mean by these?' say to them:

Here then is a portion of the explanation to the parable:

Ezek 37:21-22 Thus says the Lord GOD, "Behold, I will take the sons of Israel from among the nations where they have gone, and I will gather...and bring them into their own Land...I will make them one nation in the Land...and one king will be king for all of them...they will no longer be divided into two kingdoms...37:24-28: My servant David will be king over them, and they will all have one shepherd; and they will walk in My ordinances and keep My statutes and observe them. 25 They will live on the land that I gave to Jacob My servant, in which your fathers lived; and they will live on it, they, and their sons and their sons' sons, forever; and David My servant will be their prince forever. 26 I will make a covenant of peace with them; it will be an everlasting covenant with them. And I will place them and multiply them, and will set My sanctuary in their midst forever. 27 My dwelling place also will be with them; and I will be their God, and they will be My people. 28 And the nations will know that I am the LORD who sanctifies Israel, when My sanctuary is in their midst forever

Note here for the very first time in Ezekiel the word "forever" is assigned to the Mortal sons of Israel, to the Land they are to "live on", to their Prince, to their New Covenant, and to God's inhabitation with them. It is the Great Mystery in its most greatest form of expression unlike anything else in Scripture. This now does suggest the fulfillment of Jeremiah's Prophecy of the New Covenant has come to Israel in this prophecy. But this passage is given without any context as to what general time it is. Yet it should be noted that the prophecy states that the "ordinances" and "statues" will be observed and that the "sanctuary" God inhabits is to be there too. This is essentially summarizing the things that will be discussed in chapters 40-48. So, this prophecy is a concluding prophecy that the remainder of Ezekiel is to embellish upon there. Ezekiel's 5th and 6th Chronicles studied in the next chapter will explore how and when this whole transformation takes place.

In reflecting upon these last 2 revelations of Israel, Resurrection Israel and Eternal Israel, there is a reason for why they come back-to-back here in chapter 37. It is because these Israels are both necessarily eternal in scope. Resurrected Israel and Eternal Israel together are to be the 2 Israels that coexist together forever in the Future Eternity. Yet the blessing coming to Mortal Israel is necessarily altogether different than the blessing anticipated to come to Resurrected Israel. What is to come to Eternal Israel is what the rest of Ezekiel's writings will explore in detail and what the remainder of this book will explore as well.

Breaking down the 4 sections of Ezekiel's 37ᵗʰ Chapter

Scripture section	General description	Israel in View
Verses 1-10	Vision of Valley of Dry Bones	
Verses 11-14	Meaning of the Vision	**Resurrected Israel**
Verses 15-17	Parable of the Two Sticks	
Verses 18-28	Meaning of the Parable	**Eternal Israel**

As Eze37:21-22 points out, evidently during the Messianic/Millennial Kingdom, Latter Day Israel will morph and become scattered as the Offerings' symbolisms of the Feast of Booths certainly can be shown supporting. And so God anticipates here in chapter 37 needing to gather them up one last time, a regathering that will bring about the formation of Eternal Israel. Given that Ezekiel chapters 38 and 39 loom large immediately after chapter 37's vision of Eternal Israel, it should cause readers to speculate that the Gog/Magog Invasion has some major influence in bringing about the formation of Eternal Israel. But how and why? Again, Ezekiel's 5th major chronicle will divulge these questions in the next chapter.

Ezekiel's Chronicle of 4 Future Israels:
1. Diaspora Israel: 34:5-6,22,28-29
2. Latter Day Israel: 34:11-30; 36:8-12
3. Resurrected Diaspora: 37:1-14
4. Eternal Israel: 37:15 onward

Scripture's 3 Generational House of Israel

Notice that Ezekiel anticipates 3 mortal generations living forever:

Ezek 37:24 My servant David will be king over them...they will have one shepherd...they will walk in My ordinances...They will live on the land that I gave to Jacob My servant...and they will live on it, they, and their sons and their sons' sons, forever...I will make a covenant of peace with them...an everlasting covenant...I will...set My sanctuary in their midst forever.

Isaiah the prophet also predicts something very similar to this regarding the same:

Isa 59:21 "And as for Me, this is My covenant with them," says the LORD: "My Spirit which is upon you, and My words which I have put in your mouth, shall

not depart from <u>your mouth</u>, nor from <u>the mouth of your offspring</u>, nor from <u>the mouth of your offspring's offspring</u>," says the **LORD**, "from now and forever."

So as far as the Scripture is concerned, the House of Israel is to be considered 3 generations of inheritors surrounding the Latter Day blessing. A parallel group of Saints comprised of Gentiles should also be accounted for as well here. These additional generations must thus be added to the previous chapter's list of those to be Harvested:

The initial list of the Ingathering of the Mortal Righteous:

1. The 144,000
2. The Elect
3. Sheep
4. Holy Offspring of the Sheep and Elect
    - Which includes the "House of Israel"

The Final Amendments to the Above List

5. 2nd Generation of Holy Offspring
6. 3rd Generation of Holy Offspring

Therefore Thus says the LORD, "Now I will restore the fortunes of Jacob and have mercy on the whole house of Israel...I will not hide My face from them any longer, for I will pour out My Spirit on the house of Israel," declares the LORD God

Ezekiel 39:25,29

Chapter Sixteen

Ezekiel's New Covenant Chronicles

J eremiah prophesied during the same general time as Ezekiel. He is the first to divulge one of the greatest prophecies of the Hebrew Bible, that of the coming of a New Covenant to Israel, as has been mentioned numerous times already. Yet, at the same time, this prophecy also created one of the greatest Eschatological mysteries of all time. For Jeremiah does not explain exactly WHEN this moment is to prophetically come. And historically, no one to date appears to believe that Scripture supplies an unambiguous answer to this question. And because this has been the situation for such a long time, only speculation has filled in the void left by this universal perception. Many ideas have been floated around but the most popular is the belief that Israel will simply become absorbed as an indistinguishable component of the Church.

Of course, this idea is fueled by Replacement Theology, a cancer that has stricken the Body of Christ for almost as long as it has existed. This has embarrassingly left the Christian Faith, at the very least, in a state of self-inflicted ignorance. But more realistically it has been in a self-inflicted state of error. What this chapter will unveil, in part, is Ezekiel's complimentary Prophecy he supplies to that of Jeremiah's which in fact does establish WHEN Jeremiah's Prophecy is to become fulfilled. Why it has been left hidden is because eyes are not interested in seeing it.

What this revelation represents, in now coming out into the light of day at this juncture in time, can be summed up in one word: DISRUPTIVE. Such revelation will inevitably act as a Wrecking Ball which will swoop down and pulverize everything that gets in its way. Entire theological positions that both institutions have cradled for centuries, and millennia, will be found obviously wrong once this prophecy is comprehended for the first time. By drawing the curtain back and hiding Ezekiel's revelation no more, it will become clear that a new day has dawned, a new source of knowledge has been uncovered for all interested eyes to gaze upon.

A total of at least 7 Chronicles were identified as existing within Ezekiel's writing in the previous chapter. Each one is like an onion peel revelation. Each successive Chronicle needs to be peeled away and studied before attempting to detect the next layer of Chronicles within Ezekiel's body of work. Ezekiel's first 4 Chronicles were reviewed in detail in the previous chapter. This chapter will now take up Ezekiel's 5th Chronicle as well as his 6th Chronicle, what can be considered his New Covenant Chronicles, I and II.

Commentators have long questioned Ezekiel having any revelations indicating a New Covenant. Clearly, eyes have remained blinded to Ezekiel. For anyone who has persisted in taking in what this book has revealed so far, they have already come to see quite a bit. Now those same eyes will come to see yet again another amazing revelation. To discover where Ezekiel predicts the coming of Jeremiah's New Covenant, it starts by noticing that the Prophet begins to form this message early in his writing as if to be leaving a trail of revelation. Over and over, and again and again, throughout his writing, on 71 occasions, it is as if Ezekiel is taking his readers by the hand and leading them along to each of these points along the trail. It stops at a place no one would expect. There at the end of the trail is Ezekiel's unmistakable yet hidden form of communication that makes this Prophet unique in his own most peculiar way. Should a reader question that they've actually arrived at the end of the trail need only observe that the trail disappears beyond this point affirming that indeed the end of the trail is easily identified.

Jeremiah's and Ezekiel's Codes for New Covenant

So why is it that no one seems to be able to see the New Covenant appearing in Ezekiel's writings? The main reason must be because readers are not aware of the various ways in which Scripture identifies or defines or reveals the New Covenant, as if it were being made encoded. Most readers are conditioned to have a very narrow and fairly obvious New Covenant vocabulary. For especially Christians are fixated with the language and textual image of a Suffering Messiah as revealed by Prophets such as Isaiah, Daniel and Zechariah. But Christian beware. This imagery is not the only vocabulary used to describe the New Covenant. Jeremiah himself, the very Prophet who unveils the New Covenant Prophecy, has no images of a Suffering Messiah whatsoever and nor does Ezekiel. So Jeremiah's precedent setting testimony being what it is establishes new ways to speak of the New Covenant that the reader must take in and digest.

Ezekiel's New Covenant Chronicle I: Knowing the LORD

It turns out that there are 2 main ways Jeremiah encodes the New Covenant which Ezekiel will use in the same manner. One of the two encodings will come to be used repeatedly, some 71 times by Ezekiel, in creating his 5th Chronicle. In Jeremiah's famous New Covenant Prophecy the makings for this encoding are to be found:

Jer 31:31-34 "Behold, days are coming," declares the LORD, "when I will make a <u>New Covenant</u> with the house of Israel and with the house of Judah...I will put My Law within them and on their heart I will write it; and I will be their God, and they shall be My People. They shall not teach again, each man his neighbor and each man his brother, saying, <u>'Know the LORD,'</u> <u>for they shall all know Me,</u> from the least of them to the greatest of them," declares the LORD, "for I will forgive their iniquity, and their sin I will remember no more."

The first key idea is that the Law will be written upon the hearts of Israel's People. This first concept will have a strong affinity to the other New Covenant encoding that Jeremiah and Ezekiel use and which will be discussed later. The second key idea is that the New Covenant will cause all of Israel's People to "Know the LORD". The third key idea is that the New Covenant would also cause Israel's

People to receive forgiveness of their sin. Here finally is the ultimate connection to the Gospel of Jesus Christ. It is the second key concept that Ezekiel will use in an encoded sort of way on a repeating basis and which has its origins in the Law:

Exo 6:7 Then I will take you for My people, and I will be your God; and <u>you shall know that I am the LORD</u> your God who brought you out from the under the burdens of the Egyptians.

The phrase "shall know that I am the LORD" is the English translation of the Hebrew encoded expression. To break the original Hebrew down, there are 4 Hebrew words at the heart of this phrase:

1. "yada" (Strong's 3045: "to know")
2. "kee" (Strong's 3588: "that")
3. "anee" (Strong's 589: "I")
4. "Yahweh" (Strong's 3068)

What is found in Ezekiel's 5th Chronology is the repeated use of this encoded message of Exo6:7 which is the basis behind Jeremiah's New Covenant idea of "knowing the LORD". By its use, Ezekiel encrypts the general time of when the New Covenant comes to Israel. The first time he uses this encoding is in his 5th chapter and the last time he uses it is in his 39th chapter. Altogether, he will use the expression 71 times! Here is the very first time the expression appears in Ezekiel's writing:

Eze 5:13 Thus My anger will be spent and I will satisfy My wrath on them, and I will be appeased; then they <u>will know that I, the LORD</u>, have spoken in My zeal when I have spent My wrath upon them.

Notice the expression reads slightly different in Exo6:7. Although the translation in English sometimes reads slightly different than what the Hebrew does, the very Hebrew expression used is the same exact one appearing in 71 separate occasions throughout Ezekiel's writing, starting here with 5:13. But also note in this passage that the context forbids the interpretation that the New Covenant is in view. So the reader must carefully assess whether the encoded expression is in fact communicating a "New Covenant" inspired knowledge of the LORD. And knowing that Jeremiah is specifically foretelling the entire Nation of Israel will come to "know the LORD" this is the big clue for what the reader should be looking for.

In this first passage cited (5:13) the modifier for the phrase is "They". In all, there will be 7 total modifiers used by Ezekiel. These are: "They", "You", "the Nations", "All the trees of the field", "All flesh", "All the inhabitants of Egypt", and "the House of Israel". Here is a list of all 71 citations where this encoded expression appears:

Ezekiel 's New Covenant Chronology I
70 steps to the New Covenant

#	Verse	Modifier	Used
1	5:13	They	1
2	6:7	You	1
3	6:10	They	2
4	6:13	You	2
5	6:14	They	3
6	7:4	You	3
7	7:9	You	4
8	7:27	They	4
9	11:10	You	5
10	11:12	You	6
11	12:15	They	5
12	12:16	They	6
13	12:20	You	7
14	13:9	You	8
15	13:14	You	9
16	13:21	You	10
17	13:23	You	11
18	14:8	You	12
19	15:7	You	13
20	17:21	You	14
21	17:24	Trees	1
22	20:12	They	7
23	20:20	You	15
24	20:26	They	8
25	20:38	You	16
26	20:42	You	17
27	20:44	You	18
28	21:5	All flesh	1
29	22:16	You	19
30	22:22	You	20
31	23:49	You	21
32	24:24	You	22
33	24:27	They	9
34	25:5	You	23
35	25:7	You	24
36	25:11	They	10
37	25:17	They	11
38	26:6	They	12
39	28:22	They	13
40	28:23	They	14
41	28:24	They	15
42	28:26	They	16
43	29:6	Egyptians	1
44	29:9	They	17
45	29:16	They	18
46	29:21	They	19
47	30:8	They	20
48	30:19	They	21
49	30:25	They	22
50	30:26	They	23
51	32:15	They	24
52	33:29	They	25
53	34:27	They	26
54	34:30	They	27
55	35:4	You	25
56	35:9	You	26
57	35:12	You	27
58	35:15	You	28
59	36:11	They	28
60	36:23	The Nations	1
61	36:36	The Nations	2
62	36:38	They	29
63	37:6	You	29
64	37:13	You	30
65	37:14	You	31
66	37:28	The Nations	3
67	38:23	They	30

272

Ezekiel's modifiers to the expression: "will know that I (am) the LORD"

Modifier	Number of times used
1. They	32 (e.g., see 5:13)
2. You	31 (e.g., see 6:7)
3. The Nations	4 (e.g., see 36:23)
4. All the trees of the field	1 (see 17:24)
5. All flesh	1 (see 21:5)
6. All the inhabitants of Egypt	1 (see 29:6)
7. The House of Israel	**1 (see 39:22)**

It may be tempting to believe the passage containing the modifier "All flesh" could perhaps be the one predicting the coming New Covenant but in fact this passage is nothing but very bad news so it cannot be the passage the reader is looking for. What happens to be the all-important modifier is none other than the last one that appears, that being the "House of Israel". And notice it only appears once, as should be expected, since Jeremiah's Prophecy is only predicting a single occasion and not multiple occasions.

So when and where does the modifier "House of Israel" appear being used with the expression "will know that I am the LORD"? That is, where does Ezekiel announce that "the House of Israel will know that I (am) the LORD", thus evidencing the coming of the New Covenant to the House of Israel? It comes at a single location, on the 70th occasion out of the 71 occasions where the expression "will know that I (am) the LORD" appears in Ezekiel's writing!

It is as if Ezekiel is creating a trail for which the reader is to follow to its end. That is, on the final 2 locations of where the expression "will know that I (am) the LORD" is used, this happens to be the prophetic moment anticipating when the New Covenant is to descend upon Israel. It is suddenly unveiled as coming to Israel, an unmistakable prophecy any informed and observant reader can detect:

Eze 39:21-22, 28-29 "And I shall set My glory among the nations; and all the nations will see My judgment which I have executed, and My hand which I have laid on them." And the <u>house of Israel</u> <u>*will know that I (am) the LORD*</u> (70th occasion) **their God <u>from that day onward</u>. ..."Then they <u>*will know that I (am)*</u> <u>*the LORD*</u>** (71st and last occasion) **their God because I made them go into exile among the nations, and then gathered them {again} to their own land; and I will leave none of them there any longer..."And <u>I will not hide My face from them</u> <u>any longer</u>, for <u>I shall have poured out My Spirit on the house of Israel</u>,"** declares the Lord GOD.

Here the "House of Israel" is to be understood the entire Nation existing in the prophetic day Ezekiel foresees. Note also the expression "**from that day onward**". This indicates the idea of finality as if the New Covenant comes here and remains forever thereafter. Finally, the expression "**I shall have poured out My**

Spirit on the House of Israel" is given as the final indication of the coming of the New Covenant, what is the evidence of the coming everlasting covenant, and also the covenant of peace, the indwelling of the Spirit of God within the entire House of Israel. A spiritual outpouring is to come upon the entire mortal assembly of Israel of that day.

So what occasion then is the context of Ezekiel's 39th chapter predicting is to be the moment when Jeremiah's Prophecy is to come?

Ezekiel's New Covenant Chronicle II

It now becomes apparent at this juncture that yet another chronology has already begun to form that is Ezekiel's last overt one to account for. Recall that in Ezekiel's chapter 37, Resurrected Israel and Eternal Israel were prophetically unveiled but with little context of when these Israels appear. As for the timing of the Resurrection, as indicated by Ezekiel coming somewhere in between Latter Day Israel and Eternal Israel, this has already been clearly established in the Holy Days Code examined thus far in earlier chapters and is consistent with Ezekiel's timing.

But in regards to Eternal Israel and of its formation in the overall timeline, this is where the reader can only conjecture it is late in the Holy Schedule but exactly where in time, chapter 37 provides no useful clues. With the coming of chapters 38 and 39 though, Ezekiel's emerging 6th Chronology will provide all the needed clues to identify the timing of Israel's coming New Covenant.

This chronology noticeably begins in Eze38:2,8:

Eze38:2,8 "Son of man, set your face toward Gog of the land of Magog...After many days...in the latter years you (Gog) will come into the land that is restored from the sword, whose inhabitants have been gathered from many nations to the mountains of Israel which had been a continual waste...they are all living securely, all of them.

It should be fairly apparent that the Israel in view here is Latter Day Israel. The Land of Israel had been a continual waste until this Israel is expected to return to the Land and restore it. This again is the idea that the last generation of Diaspora Israel will become transformed into Latter Day Israel. The reader must also assume that the reason Israel is living securely is because this is the time when the Shepherd Messiah is tending to the Flock.

Gog/Magog Invasion & a Final Ingathering

The monumental occasion that follows is that Gog is prophesied to come up against Israel to plunder it. Because the Land of Israel is to become like "Eden" (36:35) and be as the "navel of the world" (38:12) in the "latter years", the mortal Gentile hordes will see it as plunder to be taken. But God is to intervene and destroy Gog and the hordes of Gentiles with him. This is so that God will be sanctified amongst the Nations when He acts and this will then cause a great awakening of the whole House of Israel and fulfill Jeremiah's New Covenant Prophecy. It is not only expected to be a Harvest Ingathering of Israel but also of all Nations from around the world as other Prophets are found providing details only hinted at by Ezekiel:

Eze38:10; 39:4,6 "...you will devise an evil plan...and you will come up against My people Israel...so that the nations may Know Me when I am sanctified through you before their eyes, O Gog...You will fall on the mountains of Israel...I will give you as food to every bird and beast of the field...And I will send fire upon Magog...and they will know that I am the LORD"

Eze 39:21-22 "And I shall set My glory among the nations; and all the nations will see My judgment which I have executed, and My hand which I have laid on them."

So when is this Invasion coming in the general timeline of biblical prophecy? It is an unknown thing within the Hebrew Scripture. But with the help of the Apostle John the Gog/Magog Invasion is revealed to be ultimately instigated by Satan (the Divine Hooks into Gog's Jaw Eze38:4) when he is to be released from the Abyss after having been bound there for a 1,000 years during which time the Millennial Kingdom transpires.

It is within this context that the House of Israel is to receive its New Covenant! That is, just as the Messianic Kingdom comes to a close by having Satan unbound from the Abyss to end it, this is the general timing of the coming of the New Covenant to Israel. But why here, so late in time, at the end of the Messianic Kingdom? Eschatology has unjustifiably argued from time immemorial that the Gog/Magog War belongs as part of Latter Day Prophecy even though it is in direct defiance of John's clear revelation it comes 1,000 years later.

This is just one of several places where tradition continues to oppose and run counter to clear biblical teachings in order to perpetuate the heresy of Replacement Theology. This timeless rigidity to prejudice explains why the Scripture remains a virtual interpretive jungle. But Ezekiel is not alone in testifying to this condemnation:

Eze 38:17 "Are you the one of whom I spoke in former days through My servant_s_ the prophet_s_ of Israel, who prophesied in those days for many years that I would bring you against them?

Given Ezekiel reveals in 38:17 he is not the only one predicting the Gog/Magog Invasion, it so happens that the other inferred Prophets do actually offer further proof that John has always been consistent with the Latter Prophets in seeing Israel's late Salvation. Having two or more witnesses is the Scripture's rule for establishing testimony and so it should be expected that there be other witnesses to what Ezekiel teaches other than himself. This helps to reinforce Ezekiel's message and makes it simply more difficult for skeptics and detractors to deny a literal reading of Ezekiel's New Covenant and Kingdom visions and as to their time of arrival.

In all, there are perhaps 6 other Prophets foreseeing surprising developments as a result of the foiled Gog/Magog War: Isaiah, Micah, Nahum, Obadiah, Haggai and Zechariah. Isaiah especially supplies the critical clues as to why here, at this late moment in time. He prophecies in 66:16-21 that as a result of having witnessed this cataclysmic event, the Nations will respond en masse and receive salvation and gather themselves up and come to Jerusalem to worship God there. In effect, it is to represent the event that brings about a final sudden Harvest Ingathering of all Nations. Zechariah chapter 12 also predicts the same cataclysmic event but then foretells in sequence that the Messiah will be finally revealed to Israel here at this time and the whole Nation will mourn in repentance as a result!

So how does this explain why Israel's conversion is to come so late? The Apostle Paul teaches of the mystery of Israel's "partial hardening" in that it will be in place until the "fullness of the Gentiles has come in" (Rom11:25). Hence, a great consequential result of the Gog/Magog Invasion is the bringing of this fullness! Hence, this final overt chronicle Ezekiel supplies, starting in chapter 38, is really a New Covenant Chronicle. Thus, Ezekiel's closing passages are meant as commentary on what the New Covenant is to bring to Israel in the form of a restored Kingdom after the last call is made with the Gentiles as part of the foiled Gog/Magog Invasion.

Fall Out of Foiled Gog/Magog War: Mystery Era

As Ezekiel's 6th Chronicle continues, the foiled Invasion is predicted to leave behind a great mass of weapons. He states that Israel's inhabitants will gather them together and use them for fire for 7 years instead of gathering wood (Ezekiel 39:9). Furthermore, due to the human carnage left by the foiled War, Ezekiel also predicts that there will be 7 months of work to see to the proper burial of all the dead so that the Land may be "cleansed" (Eze39:12-16). These 2 events are important details that should not be overlooked.

This is because many Eschatologists like to argue that John's description of the Gog/Magog War is really a 2nd War not related to Ezekiel's prophecy. This is impossible though since Gog dies and is buried in Ezekiel's prophecy! How can he then live mortally again to be destroyed yet a 2nd time? It makes no sense whatsoever. Furthermore, this untenable argument proceeds to believe that the War is immediately followed by the present Heaven and Earth being destroyed and the Great White Throne Judgment set up as envisioned by John (see Rev20:7-15).

But it is clear that there is at least 7 years of time passing after the foiled Gog/Magog War and hence at least that amount of time must pass before an "End of the World" event could take place due to the weapons being burned for that length of time. But really, any amount of time is possible passing beyond this 7 year period before this "End" takes place." Hence, it must be concluded that John's vision in Revelation is simply silent about this "Mystery Era" after the foiled Gog/Magog War. But this is not the first time Scripture is silent about something. Indeed, the Hebrew Bible itself is silent about the "Church Era" that has lasted now for nearly 2,000 years!

And so it would seem the two Scriptures have jurisdiction over their own Dominions and which do not necessarily require acknowledging matters strictly confined in the other's. Historically, Judaism has been in a state of denial about the Kingdom of Heaven but let it be recorded here that Christianity too has been in denial about the coming Kingdom of Earth for just as long. Thus, the Scripture reveals the

Sovereign Will of God despite what its two groups of followers continue to believe in defiance of what this Will is revealed to be in a straight forward reading of it.

Ezekiel's Kingdom: When, Where, How, Why?

The problem Sinaitic Israel was found having was that it was powerless to fulfill the Law and God had to eventually leave His place of habitation with the Nation. But this problem is permanently solved in the future day when the House of Israel receives the New Covenant. Every heart will have the Law written upon it and the Spirit of God will dwell within every Israelite to supply the power to fulfill the Law in mortal flesh forever. Hence, the Divine Glory is to return with this occasion and never be compelled to ever leave again. But in order for this to be possible, Ezekiel is making the case that a Temple must be built, Priests must be called and the provisions for maintaining a cleanly holiness must be resumed if God is to Come Again. Only the incremental alterations to the Law Ezekiel records will be the difference between what the Sinaitic Covenant provisions were and what the New Covenant provisions are to be.

When Ezekiel receives his vision, the entire Kingdom is seen in its completion. There is no explanation for how the Kingdom came into existence. This is one reason why so many readers do not want to believe this vision chronologically follows the Gog/Magog Invasion. It appears as if to be a separate and standalone revelation not tied to anything. But Ezekiel consistently maintains a chronological presentation all throughout his many chronicles. So why should it be that Ezekiel violate his work as a Chronicler in misleading his readers about this most important reckoning of this event? It makes no sense and goes counter to logic. Yet there is one small detail that also suggests a post Gog/Magog timing for Ezekiel's Kingdom when Ezekiel records the thoughts of the Invaders. In 38:11, their plan to take plunder for themselves is perceived as if to be an easy task because the cities are without walls and gates. Yet Ezekiel's Prophetic City has walls and gates. So whatever condition Jerusalem is found to be in at the time of the Invasion it should not be interpreted the same as for which Ezekiel envisions as conditions for the Kingdom.

Another explanation to provide is that the reader is being asked to put the pieces of the puzzle together. God turns His face toward the House of Israel only after it receives the New Covenant. For the reader who can come to discover this most important revelation of Ezekiel's, the pieces begin to fall into place rather easily from there. Besides, having a Temple during the Millennial Kingdom only to have it remain empty of God's Glory until it ends seems inappropriate.

Israel's King David was told by his prophet Nathan that David's own offspring would one day build a Temple (2 Sam7:13). David's immediate son, King Solomon, appeared to fulfill this. But because his kingdom was not eternal he became only a symbolic fulfillment. The prophet Zechariah also states something similar, that the Messianic figure, "The Branch", would be the one to build the Temple (Zech6:12). But Isaiah and Zechariah both also suggest that the Nations come and participate in the general rebuilding of Israel and the Temple in the Latter Day (Isa 60:10; 61:5; Zech 6:15). Again, multiple Prophets together help fill what missing gap of revelation Ezekiel leaves out between the end of chapter 39 and the rest of his writing.

In putting these pieces of the puzzle together, it would seem that the Harvest of the Final Ingathering seek to pay homage to God and flock to Jerusalem to serve in whatever capacity they can. Since Ezekiel's description of the Kingdom is detailed enough to make a blueprint from it, the instructions for what is expected to be built has been prepared thousands of years in advance. In understanding that perhaps everyone participates in seeing to this Kingdom being built, it should be interpreted a byproduct of all the Saints' labor, from the Messiah to the lowliest of Saints. Put under this light how could any reader ever conceive of such a Kingdom not being made eternal? What reason would there be to destroy it? It is to be understood an eternal memento of the Present Creation, the only thing to be built from this Present Creation evidently to be saved for all eternity!

Ezekiel's Kingdom to start out in Present Creation

When a reader comes to the end of Ezekiel's writing, it is as if what is being described is to be understood an eternal Kingdom. But there is at least one thing that forbids the reader to conclude that this Kingdom is in the Future Eternity:

Ezek 44:25 And they shall not go to a dead person to defile {themselves;}

Predicted future priests are instructed that they are not to expose themselves to a corpse just as the Law set the precedent for this idea. And so human death is being communicated here as if to be a possibility, and so it is communicated Ezekiel's vision is still in the Present Creation at the time it is to become fulfilled. So the reader is left in somewhat of a quandary in understanding how the Kingdom is to be everlasting in nature as it sits in the final hours of the Present Creation. The final question left for Ezekiel's readers then is how does Ezekiel's Kingdom, existing in the Present Creation, become made an everlasting thing if it is an integral part of the existing Earth that is to come to be replaced with a New Earth?

One popular theory goes that Ezekiel's Temple is to exist during the Messianic Kingdom but then ultimately disappear. The reason again is because John in his Revelation does not appear to be acknowledging there is to be one in the Future Eternity. But the argument can be made that John does not acknowledge there is to be a Temple during the Millennial Kingdom either. But Ezekiel reveals why a Temple is needed in the post-Gog/Magog time frame. The fundamental purpose of a Temple on earth is so that God's Glory can dwell with a mortal Israel.

Since God is expected to turn His face toward Israel after the Gog/Magog Invasion according to Ezekiel, and since this does not take place until the Millennial Kingdom is over according to John, then a Temple is needed after the Millennial Kingdom, not before it. There simply is no practical purpose for a Temple before the Invasion because God would not be resident in it. Furthermore, the Messianic Age is exactly that, Messianic. The Messiah is to rule and reign and Zechariah clearly teaches that the 2nd Person comes in the name of the 1st Person. And even further, the Resurrected Saints are pointed out as acting as "priests" in this Age in Rev20:6. If a Temple were in place during this Age, there would be a theological jurisdictional conflict of dominions as Hebrews 8:4 points out. Hence, the Temple is not to have a place in the Messianic Age.

And so the two sides of the debate are in no position to grasp the message of Ezekiel. Only those who are interested in the truth are capable to. And a great deal more truth will be left to be pondered by the time this work is fully revealed. Hopefully there will be those who seek the truth. The fact of the matter is that careful examination of Ezekiel's Holy Days' testimony explains to the reader why a Temple must still exist even in a post-Cross world in the way the testimony subtly acknowledges the Gospel's predicted influence it would bring. No, the prophet Ezekiel perhaps was not aware of the Gospel overtones of his writing which is why it must be considered divinely inspired. What makes Ezekiel's writing so provocative is that his Kingdom vision is being described as if the Gospel is active and in place and the reality of this is what is overshadowing the writing. One form of proof of this will be provided shortly. Hence, the methods of communication in this writing are unique and mind numbing in that respect.

The reason why a Temple is required in a post-Cross world happens to be the same reason why a Temple was needed for Sinaitic Israel and why a Temple is found existing in Heaven (as Hebrews and Revelation clearly communicate). It is a simple idea. The Divine Glory cannot dwell with Mortal Humanity without provisions being made to allow for it. (Thus, the idea of a Temple in Heaven is suggesting the simple idea that Mortal Flesh, or its equivalent, must be residing in Heaven). The fallen Adamic flesh is corrupted and atonement must be made for it, what is a repeated teaching all throughout the book of Leviticus (and again in Ezekiel). An argument might be made that Jesus' sacrifice should remove this corruption. But in reading the fine print. Christ's sacrifice secures the coming Resurrection and New Creation that is to come. It was not meant to "cleanse the flesh", something that mere animal sacrifices have been set aside to do (Heb9:13).

And so this again addresses the nature of the Great Mystery. As long as any of Adam's offspring remain in a mortal state such a person remains corrupted. Even after mortal death, the book of Revelation argues corruption persists when it is read that "white robes" are required for the dead Tribulation Saints to wear in order they be allowed to serve in the Temple as Rev7:14-15 describes. (A more thorough study of this subject can be found at www.alphakaiomega.info.) Only in the Resurrection is the corruption of Adam's flesh removed for the one receiving it once and for all as Paul points out in 1Cor15:52-53. And because the Remnant and the House of Israel will never replace their Adamic flesh with a Resurrected body, the corruption of their Adamic flesh will be eternal right along with their mortal condition.

What Ezekiel subtly communicates with his testimony corroborates these simple ideas. This also explains why the Law speaks in terms of having everlasting relevancy. It is written in such a way that it always anticipates mortal Israel will be in need of its provisions. This then is also assuming the Divine Glory is to one day make a permanent residence with mortal Israel, the only major reason why "cleansing of the flesh" is necessary. Here too Ezekiel confirms this 2nd Coming of God in his own unique way unlike any other prophet.

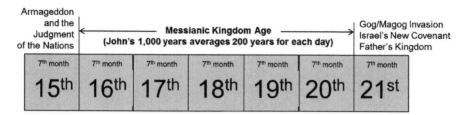

Symbolisms for the Feast of Booths

Ezekiel's "New Covenant" Kingdom

Because Ezekiel's final chapters follow immediately after chapter 39 this implies that Ezekiel's vision is in fact the blueprints for Israel's New Covenant Kingdom. From time immemorial traditions from both sides of the fence have downplayed the significance of Ezekiel's Kingdom. Indeed, it is a conundrum of conundrums for all sides of the debate. Judaism can hardly be expected to embrace it because what it finds objectionable about it is what makes it a New Covenant Kingdom. Judaism has never believed the Sinaitic Covenant is a finite covenant and so gives no heed to Jeremiah's prophecy. So too, traditional Christianity wants nothing to do with Ezekiel's Kingdom if it is interpreted a post-Cross Kingdom because it attests to too much Law keeping. So the best way it can come to accommodate Ezekiel's Kingdom is to interpret it symbolically, figuratively of the Gospel (or as a temporary existence in the Millennial Kingdom). And for the few who do believe Ezekiel's Kingdom could be literal, it certainly is not to be interpreted an Eternal Kingdom.

A 2nd Gospel encoding: Circumcision of the Heart

As was posited earlier, there is yet a second form of encoding that is used by Jeremiah and Ezekiel to communicate the reality of the New Covenant. This second encoding is the expression "Circumcision of the Heart". In Ezekiel, this second encoding appears within Ezekiel's Kingdom Vision which starts in chapter 40 to be reviewed shortly. This is yet a second proof that the Kingdom is indeed to be understood a New Covenant Kingdom as did the first encoding communicate as part of Ezekiel's 5th Chronicle.

As it turns out, this idea or concept is again first developed within the Law of Moses as was the first encoding. The first place it appears it is in the negative form in Lev26:41 where the "uncircumcised heart" is mentioned. Then in Deut10:16 God commands that each person "Circumcise their heart". But then, later in Deut30:6, it is prophetically predicted that "God would circumcise the hearts of Israel's People" on some future day. This then must be inferring the same occasion as Jer31:31-34 when the New Covenant is to come to Israel. And given it is predicted there that God is to "write the Law" upon the hearts of Israel's People, this "circumcision" must then also be a part of the same working of God upon human hearts. (To be thorough, the

Hebrew Bible also talks about lips, Exo6:12,30 and ears, Jer6:10, being uncircumcised.)

As for Jeremiah, he is a second source who reiterates Deut10:16 in Jer4:4. Then he speaks of uncircumcision in Jer9:25-26. Ezekiel is yet a third witness in Eze44:7 and Eze44:9 (speaking "uncircumcision"). A fourth and fifth source are in the Greek Bible: Stephen in Acts 7:51 (uncircumcision) and the Apostle Paul in Rom2:29 and Col2:11, where finally circumcision of the heart is directly revealed to be a work of the Gospel through Christ.

Ezekiel joins together the Law with the Gospel

Amongst all of these passages however, Eze44:9 has to be understood standing alone and apart in a most provocative and revelatory way that does not appear anywhere else in the Hebrew Bible. The passage is quite subtle and yet telling if an observer can carefully dissect the passage into its principle parts:

Eze44:9 Thus says the Lord GOD, "<u>No</u> foreigner <u>uncircumcised in heart</u> and <u>uncircumcised in flesh</u>...shall enter My sanctuary

There are several shocking things to be revealed here. The first thing to notice is that the passage is given in a double negative format, "No" and "uncircumcised". What this means is that if a reader merges the double negative statements to then make an equivalent positive statement the same information can be communicated another way:

"A foreigner circumcised in heart and circumcised in flesh...shall/may enter My sanctuary".

The first thing here to recognize is that the New Covenant Gospel (circumcision of the heart) and the Law (circumcision of the flesh) are both represented here. This is what makes the passage unique, unlike any other in the Hebrew Bible. In essence, it is predicting the time in the future, in Ezekiel's Kingdom, where the Law and the Gospel will be coexisting together! Ezekiel is effectively bringing together the two passages of Deut30:6 (circumcision of the heart) and Jer31:33 (writing the Law upon the heart) and making a combined revelation.

That is, Eze44:9 puts these ideas of the Gospel and the Law together in a very interesting way in suggesting that "circumcision of" and "writing of the Law upon" the heart happen together. But should a reader more narrowly interpret Jer31:33's "Law" as being a "spiritual Law", Ezekiel corrects such a view when he conveys there will be fulfillment of a physical commandment of the Law in the coming Kingdom to order to imply there will be a future fulfillment of the Law in general.

But now look closer and an even greater revelation is unfolded to the reader. Not only will the Law be administered in that prophetic day but Eze44:9 suggests that "foreigners who will be among the Sons of Israel" will observe the Law along with the Sons of Israel! A second witness that can be cited here to affirm these basic conclusions would have to be Isaiah 66:21 where Isaiah prophecies that Gentiles will also be made "Priests" and "Levites". Nearly 700 years later, the book of Revelation would essentially corroborate Ezekiel in a similar testimony too (12:17; 14:12). As is clear, Eze44:9 appears inside of Ezekiel's Kingdom prophecies. So reiterating again here, Ezekiel's Kingdom must be properly interpreted as being a New Covenant Kingdom because Israel's Priests are predicted to be circumcised in the heart and in the flesh, otherwise they are not allowed in God's Sanctuary.

So to recap what has been unveiled in this chapter thus far, Ezekiel's Kingdom is in fact a New Covenant Kingdom. It is to appear soon after the foiled Gog/Magog War which brings about Israel's New Covenant. This immediately follows the Messianic Kingdom which is ended by the release of Satan from being bound in the Abyss to instigate Gog to invade. Seven facets of Ezekiel's Kingdom will be reviewed here based on Ezekiel's latter portions of his writing:

1. The Everlasting People of 3 Generations:

Ezek 37:21-25 "Behold, I will take the sons of Israel from among the nations where they have gone, and I will gather them from every side and bring them into their own land…they will be My people, and I will be their God. "And they shall live on the land…in which your fathers lived; and they will live on it, <u>they</u>, and <u>their sons</u>, and <u>their sons' sons</u>, forever…

Eternal Israel was explored in great detail in the previous chapter. More will be unveiled regarding how the 3 Generations are to be distinguished between one another in the next chapter.

2. The Everlasting (sinful) King:

Ezek 37:24-25 "And My servant David will be king over them, and they will all have one shepherd…and David My servant shall be their prince forever.

Ezek 45:22 "And on that day the prince shall provide for himself and all the people of the land a bull for a sin offering.

Traditional Christianity argues vehemently that Prince David is the Messiah. But Ezekiel provides 2 references for the servant David, in chapter 34 and chapter 37. Thus, the first reference is arguably Messianic while the second reference must yet be another "son of David" in view who is wholly human and needing cleansing from sin. Recall 2Sam 7:14 has Nathan communicating the same in regard to "iniquity" committed by David's descendant. The king for Israel's Eternal Kingdom cannot be the Messiah of Israel if the Messiah is without sin. Hence, the House of Israel has another descendant of David who will be its king. Since Jesus is declared "King of kings" then this allows for one son of David to be king of Israel while the second Son is to become King over this king and all other (Gentile) kings.

3. The City:

Ezek 40:2 In the visions of God He brought me into the land of Israel, and set me on a very high mountain; and on it to the south {there was} a structure like <u>a</u> <u>city</u>.

Ezek 48:35 "{The city shall be} 18,000 {cubits} round about; and the name of the city from {that} day {shall be,} 'The LORD is there.'"

Isaiah predicts that Jerusalem will ultimately receive a new name by God in his 62nd chapter. Here too Ezekiel seems to imply the same. Ezekiel is made to sit on a "very high mountain" to the north where he saw the City to the south built upon it. The City up to this point has suffered through several earthquakes: John's Revelation predicts 1/10th of Jerusalem is to "fall" in the earthquake of Rev 11:13 and then again is to become split in 3 parts in another in 16:18. Zechariah predicts that Jerusalem's landscape is to be radically altered due to an earthquake that the Messiah is to create upon his feet touching the Mount of Olives. Perhaps this is the same moment as Rev 11:13. But there may be even more alterations from the fallout of the Gog/Magog Invasion as well.

Many speculate that the Messiah will see to the rebuilding of Jerusalem and Israel throughout the Millennial Kingdom but the Scripture seems to be predicting this is all to take place after the Gog/Magog Invasion. For example, Isaiah chapters 60-62 could be argued what is all to take place after the Messianic Kingdom is over. Rather, the Messianic Kingdom is written as being a restorative spiritual era where prisoners are released from darkness, where righteous judgment will prevail, and where peace will ensue as a result. That is, Isaiah (2:2-4) and Micah (4:1-3) both predict virtually the same prophecy that there will be no more wars after the Kingdom is established. So how then can this be speaking of a Kingdom prior to the Gog/Magog War?

4. God's Eternal Habitation in the Temple:

Ezek 43:10 "As for you, son of man, describe <u>the temple</u> to the house of Israel, that they may be ashamed of their iniquities; and let them measure the plan.

Ezek 43:7 And He said to me, "Son of man, {this is} the place of My throne and the place of the soles of My feet, where I will dwell among the sons of Israel forever.

That a Temple is to exist in this City forever with God dwelling in it implies that mortals will reside in it forever. Flowing out from the threshold of the Temple and the Throne of God is to be a river that is to be an eternal form of sustenance that will cause fish to thrive in it and for plants to grow and for fruit bearing trees to flourish upon its shores. It is to sustain mortal human life forever. Sickness will either be prevented or cured in the ingestion of the leaves from the trees. Should anyone refuse to eat of it these will necessarily ultimately perish in the Present Creation era. The big question this raises is how Ezekiel's Physical Kingdom is to survive the destruction of Earth. This will be addressed in the next chapter.

5. The Priesthood:

Ezek 40:46 ...the chamber which faces toward the north is for the priests who keep charge of the altar. These are the sons of Zadok, who from the sons of Levi come near to the LORD to minister to Him."

The necessary requirement for these Priests is again that they be circumcised both in heart and flesh according to Ezekiel. Some of these are to even be Gentiles who will be made as Levites as Isaiah 66:21 foretells as does Eze44:9 in a roundabout way. Another odd thing to draw out of Ezekiel's testimony (e.g., Ezekiel chapter 44) is that the Prophet appears to predict that Priests who will have served in a mortal capacity in Israel's ancient past are to somehow be found serving in Ezekiel's Kingdom! Similarly, Ezekiel himself (the "you" throughout chapters 40-48) appears to be commissioned to take part in administering matters surrounding the establishment of this Kingdom when it appears. The only conclusion one can draw is that it is predicting that Ezekiel and other deceased Priests will be resurrected and come to work alongside mortal Priests in Ezekiel's future Kingdom (Ezekiel chapter 44). Since Ezekiel clearly teaches of Resurrection in chapter 37 contrary to what tradition teaches, the context allows for this to be the most viable interpretation. If eyes are open while reading Ezekiel there is a great deal more to see and ponder.

6. The Land:

Ezek 47:13-29 Thus says the Lord GOD, "This {shall be} the boundary by which you shall divide the land for an inheritance among the twelve tribes of Israel..."This is the land which you shall divide by lot to the tribes of Israel for an inheritance, and these are their {several} portions," declares the Lord GOD.

Abraham was promised that the Land which he saw with his own eyes would become an eternal possession to he and his descendants (Gen 13:15). Here Ezekiel has the Land divided up as an inheritance for all 12 tribes. The Priests are to receive no inheritance except the perimeter around the Temple. How this becomes an eternal possession has always been a mystery which the next chapter will resolve.

7. The Altered Law:

Ezek 37:24 and they will walk in My ordinances, and keep My statutes, and observe them.

Ezek 45:17 "And it shall be the prince's part {to provide} the...sin offering, the grain offering, the burnt offering, and the peace offerings, to make atonement for the house of Israel."

Last but not least to be mentioned here is Ezekiel's new ordinances he appends to the Law's. These are to be interpreted as three fold in nature and eternal in scope: 1. Additions to the Law, 2. Alterations to the Law, and 3. One single Deletion to the Law. These 3 groups of ordinances together acknowledge the reality of the Gospel having already transpired and provides basic supplemental Offerings for the increased population that Israel will be made up of when Mortal Death ceases to exist. The Law is designed to offer atonement for a mortal population. But in that day there is expected to be an Eternal Israel, a much larger body of mortals who will never succumb to death and not the scenario that the Law first made provision for. Hence, the new atonement offerings are designed to compensate for the consequences of the Great Mystery!

Consecration of New (Eternal) Altar

In completing this chapter, it will now return to finish off Ezekiel's 6th Chronology also known as Ezekiel's New Covenant Chronicle II. Where it was last left at was with the narrative explaining that future Israel is to gather the weapons left by Gog and burn them for 7 years as fuel while also cleansing the Land of the deceased for 6 months. It is at this juncture where a reader is left to contemplate where the next chronological development is to be found in Ezekiel's last chapters he supplies. This moment should perhaps be considered described in the latter verses of chapter 43.

After all the building and craftsmanship has been completed surrounding the Temple, there are to be initial Offerings provided in order to cleanse the "Altar of Sacrifice". This Alter is of some significance given it is to be used forever thereafter for all the Offerings spelled out in the Law and in Ezekiel's testimony. The "offspring of Zadok" are to be the Priests designated for this duty. Zadok was David's High Priest. Evidently, the other Levitical Priests defiled themselves in their duties and are to be forbidden from this service as cited earlier. Clearly, Eze 44:9 states that no one will conduct these services unless they are upholders of the Law and the Gospel together.

So, before this New Covenant Kingdom can get underway, all these provisions need to be in place. Once this moment arrives now something provocative happens in the testimony if a reader is keen to see it. For Ezekiel will now lead into his Holy Days testimony.

Ezekiel's Appended Holy Days Testimony

Starting in 45:17, the reader is informed that the Law's Holy Days Offerings as well as Ezekiel's later defined new Offerings, coming on new dates of the calendar, will become administered thereafter, time without end. As pointed out on numerous occasions already, noticeably missing from Ezekiel's new Offerings are any signs of Libations (one of the greatest hints in the Hebrew Scripture suggesting the existence of some kind of Code behind the Holy Days testimony). Ezekiel's appended Holy

Days Offerings have been studied in an earlier chapter and will be followed throughout the remainder of this, Ezekiel's 6th Chronicle, and also again for his 7th Chronicle examined in the last chapter.

What the reader needs to come to realize at this juncture is that something mysteriously similar takes place as what occurs in the Law's Holy Days testimony. The great hint in the Law's Holy Days was that the very first Holy Day to observe was really the very end of a Day, the only Holy Day of its kind. This is to help lead the reader into grasping the idea that this sliver of time was essentially to be symbolic of the very event of Passover itself. Thus, the Divine Schedule began with the occasion of Passover and each subsequent Holy Day is representing yet future Events beyond the Passover of such Divine significance that it was made as part of the Holy Days. These Holy Days were to be observed each year in anticipation of what each of these Days are prophetically anticipating. If and when these Prophetic Moments came to pass from the reference point of the observer they would transform from being prophetic to becoming memorials looking back at what they ultimately signified.

So how can a similar pattern be recognized here with Ezekiel's additional Holy Days? Well, what is the first Holy Day on the schedule? This would be identified in 45:18:

Eze45:18 ...In the <u>first month</u>, on the <u>first day of the month</u>, you shall take a young bull without blemish and cleanse the sanctuary.

The biggest clue happens to be that this is the Divine New Year's Day! Recall that the first Holy Day of the Law is the eve of the 14th Day. Now, Ezekiel is informed that the 1st Day of the 1st Month is to be a brand new Offering Day. So at this point the reader has to be cognizant of the fact that the Priests will have to first initially cleanse the Altar so that these and all future Offerings can be administered there. Hence, it has to be believed that after the cleansing of the Altar takes place time will pass awaiting the arrival of this New Year's Day so that Ezekiel's very first Offering can be administered for the very first time. Once this very first cleansing of the Temple takes place this will create the very first time when conditions are met to allow for God's Second Coming! It will be the first occasion when it will be permissible for God's Glory to fill the Temple and indeed Ezekiel's final vision of the Second Coming of God will then be realized!

New Year's Day Brings the Divine Glory!

In other words, the reader must try to figure out just exactly when God's Glory is to come to the Eternal Temple as Ezekiel sees this event as a prophetic vision of the future in 43:5. The most important thing is that the Altar must first be cleansed in order that an Offering can be made which can then cleanse the Sanctuary so as to allow God's Glory to enter there! And since this cleansing first appears on New Year's Day this means the very first time this cleansing takes place the Glory of God will soon thereafter enter the Temple!

So this very first time this Offering is performed coincides with the very Day God's Glory is to enter the Temple. Hence, the New Year's Day Offering will from then on be made a "memorial" for this Grand 2nd Coming of God! This will essentially "demarcate" the coming of the "New Covenant Kingdom"!

But wait. There are more new Offerings beyond this one. There is yet another Cleansing Offering exactly like this first one just 7 days later! How very odd to have the same Offering performed just 7 days later. (Doesn't make much sense at all except that the 1st Month now matches up with the 7th Month as was shown in chapter 9.) But wait! It must be symbolic of what the next great occasion is to be as part of Ezekiel's new Appended Holy Schedule and so on and so on.

Hence, this happens to be the subtle beginning of Ezekiel's 7th and final Chronology he communicates! The next chapter will pick up from New Year's Day and present a conjecture as to what Ezekiel's Holy Schedule is predicting beyond the coming of Israel's New Covenant Kingdom on the Divine New Year's Day. Here is where Ezekiel's Holy Days testimony will be found crossing over into the Future Eternity where it will divulge something very fascinating about what is to take place in the Future Eternity!

Ezekiel's New Covenant Chronology II

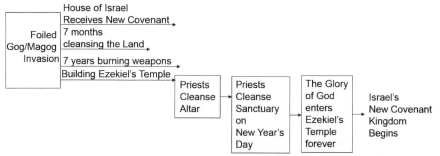

So since Ezekiel adds new Holy Days, this represents yet a 3rd timeline of Holy Days testimony. The Feast of Unleavened Bread became the first timeline symbolizing Israel's prophetic life. The 7th Month Holy Days became the second timeline symbolizing Israel's prophetic Latter Days. Now Ezekiel's new Holy Days becomes the third timeline symbolizing Israel's eternal New Covenant Kingdom. How these timelines are made to converge upon one another is to first recognize that the foiled Gog-Magog War/Invasion aligns with the last day of the Feast of Booths, what happens to be the 7th day Sabbath of this Feast. Its symbolic Death Rest is fulfilled in Gog and the Magogites while the Gospel symbolism is fulfilled by Israel receiving its New Covenant. Recall also that the very last Holy Day symbolizes the Future Eternity. Since the last day of the Feast of Unleavened Bread symbolizes God's dwelling with Remnant Israel, this day starts with the Divine New Year's Day occurring sometime after Gog/Magog but before the coming of the Future Eternity. The start of this same day happens to be the moment God comes to dwell in Ezekiel's Temple on New Year's Day. A possible timeline diagram for these 3 converging timelines is shown below:

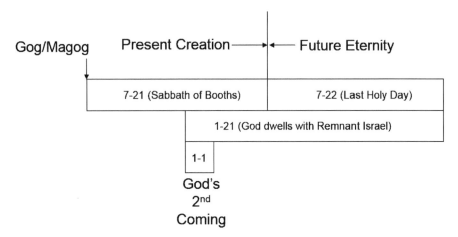

Who is assigned to the last Holy Days Libations?

Part of the Great Mystery that surfaces here is that the last Holy Day is assigned Libation Offerings. What this essentially symbolizes is that new Saints are to appear in the timeframe that this Day represents. Recall that this last Holy Day is symbolizing the Future Eternity! Shockingly, this must be communicating the idea that procreation continues on even into the Future Eternity! So the huge question becomes just exactly what Saints are being accounted for by these Last Libation Offerings and when exactly does procreation come to an end?

It was indicated earlier that Eternal Israel is to be composed of 3 generations. So how are these 3 generations to be accounted for and which of these generations are to appear in the Future Eternity? This is where Ezekiel's new Offerings will be argued answering these questions as will be explored in the next and last chapter.

In the first month, on the fourteenth day of the month, you shall have the Passover, a feast of 7 days; unleavened bread shall be eaten.

Ezekiel 45:2

Chapter Seventeen

Ezekiel Appends the Holy Schedule

How to unravel the hidden meaning behind Ezekiel's Holy Days testimony is to assume that the Prophet is simply continuing on with what the Law purposed in its Holy Days testimony. What the Law is ultimately communicating through its Holy Days is a hidden chronological harvest schedule of the Scripture's Divine Plan as the previous chapters have revealed. But this Schedule becomes somewhat sketchy as it comes to a close. So one could speculate that Ezekiel's Holy Days testimony is meant to particularly focus on the very end of the schedule. Indeed, Ezekiel will actually be shown appending the Schedule.

Ezekiel's witness begins and ends by seeing the Divine Glory. But he also reveals himself to be a prolific chronicler from beginning to end. Put these two central themes together and what lay hidden underneath his contemporary witness is a chronicling of the 2nd Coming of God. This coming of God signifies Israel receiving its New Covenant and this coming late in the Nation's prophetic life. Six out of Ezekiel's Seven Chronicles have been peeled back and studied in previous chapters in what is preparation for the student to understand his final chronicle. Now the moment has arrived to expose Ezekiel's inner most onion peel revelation, what is his 7th and last Chronicle.

Ezekiel's 7th and Final Chronicle

1st Day of the 1st Month:
Israel's New Covenant Begins in LORD's Kingdom

No greater hint is needed to get this idea off the ground than the one offered in Ezekiel's very first Holy Day as was studied in the last chapter. In Eze 45:18, Ezekiel's first Holy Day is one that is entirely new. Its location on the Divine Calendar is a big clue in helping to unravel the meaning of all of Ezekiel's Holy Days testimony. It so happens to fall on the 1st day of the 1st month, the Divine Calendar's New Year's Day. It is as if this day had been reserved specifically for this moment from the very beginning. It is as if to be saying "this is the real beginning" that God had planned long ago. And so, what is to take place on this New Year's Day? Ezekiel records this day is to be reserved for "cleansing the sanctuary".

On the surface, this does not read like much of anything spectacular. But look closer and it reveals something astonishing. First of all, in order to cleanse the Sanctuary, the Sanctuary needs to be built first! And time must be allotted to allow for it being built. And as was reviewed earlier Zechariah hints to the idea that all the nations participate in helping build this Temple. This building project must commence sometime after the foiled Gog/Magog Invasion. So how much time should be considered for how long the Temple takes to be built? There really is no way of knowing. Once it is built though then the Divine Plan's New Covenant chronology begins here with this New Year's Day. As part of this New Beginning, the Sanctuary comes to be cleansed on this day. So why is this such a big deal? Well, this moment represents the first time conditions will be met for allowing the 2nd Coming of God to His Sanctuary since Ezekiel first saw God leaving Solomon's Temple some time around 586BC.

Zechariah reveals the following about the general time frame:

Zech 14:16-17 Then it will come about that any who are left of all the nations that went against Jerusalem (i.e., Gog/Magog) will go up from year to year to worship the King, the LORD of hosts, and to celebrate the Feast of Booths. And it will be that whichever of the families of the earth does not go up to Jerusalem to worship the King, the LORD of hosts, there will be no rain on them.

Jesus must have been referring to this period as His "Father's Kingdom" (Matt26:29). Hence, these prophecies cannot commence until after God's 2nd Coming takes place as foreseen by Ezekiel. How long the "LORD of hosts" is to rule as King in this Present Creation is unknown. What is clear is that the last day of the Feast of Booths, the 21st day of the 7th month, symbolically represents the length of this Kingdom and certainly explains why the Nations are commanded to celebrate this Feast at that time.

Timeline constructed from testimony of: Ezekiel, Zechariah and John

7th day of the 1st Month:
End of the LORD's Kingdom and Present Creation

With the coming of the 7th day of the 1st month, Ezekiel spells out the date for the next Holy Day Offering. It is to be yet another Sin Offering to again cleanse the Sanctuary. This time it is be as a result of anyone committing sin "naïvely" (45:20). This terminology is first introduced in the Law (e.g., Lev4:2). The Law further explains there is no cleansing for sins committed knowingly in defiance (Num15:30-31).

What is odd is that this comes only 7 days after the same Offering was first given. But here again is further evidence that there is a hidden chronology being conveyed by this testimony. Seven Days represents a most important time period as all those familiar with the Holy Days knows. It represents the fullness of something. Hence, these first 7 days must be symbolic of the Father's Kingdom Era, the Mystery

Era. Those sins which will be committed unintentionally will be forgiven during the Father's Kingdom. Those committed intentionally will not be. Zechariah has already alluded to the idea that there will be Gentiles who will not obey in not coming up to Jerusalem. These will be left to live in drought. Yet because the entire House of Israel has received the New Covenant along with many Gentiles too and all are led by the Spirit of God, the only possible intentional sinning will come by way of those of the Nations who become new rebels in this new era.

If the Present Creation is to perish, What then is to happen to Ezekiel's Kingdom?

By all indications, when the Mystery Era is completed this must signify the end of the 21st Day of the 7th Month. Recall that this marks the end of the "Feast of Booths". Note that there is no gap of time between the 21st Day and the 22nd Day, the very last Holy Day. So this would appear as if things are not to be interrupted or suspended as the 21st Day comes to an end and the 22nd Day begins. Indeed, Ezekiel's Kingdom is described as eternal.

Yet the description of the Feast of Booths is that Israel is to live in Booths in remembering the Nation's wilderness stay between Egypt and the Promised Land was a temporary one. So effectively what this symbolism is communicating is that whatever is in place at the close of the Present Creation it is to be understood "temporary housing", or, in other words, a finite situation. Whatever appears on the "other side", as being a part of the Future Eternity, this then is what is to be understood the "permanent housing" that takes the place of the "temporary housing".

What monumental prophecy exists between the Present Creation and the New Creation is of course the predicted destruction of the Present Creation. Perhaps it is the Psalmist who is the first to break the news that the Present Creation has a limited life span:

Ps 102:25-26 "Of old You founded the earth; and the heavens are the work of Your hands. "Even they will perish, but You endure; and all of them will wear out like a garment; like clothing You will change them, and they will be changed.

The Apostle Peter then comes to shed more light on the same subject:

2 Pet 3:10 But the day of the Lord will come like a thief, in which the heavens will pass away with a roar and the elements will be destroyed with intense heat, and the earth and its works will be burned up.

Strangely, the apostle Peter describes the ending of this Present Creation as if to be like a "thief". This is a very good clue to suggest that the Mystery Era is meant to be an unknown period of time. No doubt it is to catch many unawares of its ending with the destruction of the Present Creation much like how Noah's Flood caught Noah's generation by surprise.

While the Present Creation awaits a destructive judgment than, the Prophet Isaiah reveals what is to take its place:

Isa 65:17 "For behold, I create new heavens and a new earth; and the former things shall not be remembered or come to mind.

The Apostle John describes his vision of this epic transition in his own peculiar way when he records that he saw the heavens and earth had "fled away" from the sight of the One sitting on the Great White Throne in Rev20:11. For John, this "in between" occasion, between the destruction of the Present Creation and the creation of the New Creation, he declares is to be the coming Judgment Day. This is the day when all the remaining Dead are to be resurrected into what John calls the "2nd Resurrection". These Dead are to be judged and then thrown into the Lake of Fire. Only after this does John then see an equivalent vision of Isaiah's prophetic New Heavens and Earth.

The paradoxical question that confronts every reader when studying this transition is: if the Present Creation is to be destroyed how then is there to be a continuation of certain things which are necessarily integral to the Present Creation but which are prophesied to become eternal? Beginning with Abraham, he was promised that the Land he saw with his eyes would become he and his descendants' possession forever (Gen13:15). And what is to become of Ezekiel's Kingdom, a place where God is to dwell with Israel forever (Eze37:28)? And what is to become of Edom, a place where God promises "smoke will go up forever", a place which is to be given to the pelicans, hedgehogs, owls, ravens, jackals, ostriches, desert creatures, wolves, hairy goats, night monsters, tree snakes, and hawks forever according to the prophet Isaiah (Is34:5-17)? What is to become of all these "eternal" things which are to first exist in the Present Creation?

It is as if the Scripture is necessarily leaving it to the reader to figure out how eternal things of the Present Creation are to somehow survive in becoming part of eternal things reserved for the Future Eternity.

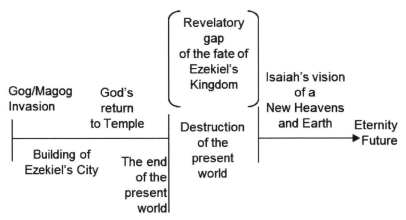

Scripture students must "fill in" the revelatory gap

If these things are possible to be revoked than so can anything else that God has promised in His Word. So a reader must either believe that everything that God has promised to be everlasting stands or none of its stands. There is no middle ground to find on the issue. The Scripture leaves no wiggle room for compromise. Clearly Scripture is leaving it up to the reader to "fill in the gap" between where Ezekiel's Kingdom's existence resides at the end of the Present Creation and what must happen between then and the creation of the New Heavens and Earth. So what must be the answer to this dilemma?

If Ezekiel's Kingdom must be preserved, Where is it to be preserved?

Scripture's Dilemma regarding Ezekiel's Prophecies:

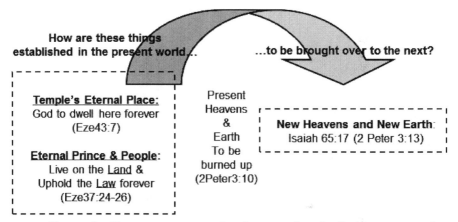

How are these things established in the present world... ...to be brought over to the next?

Temple's Eternal Place:
God to dwell here forever
(Eze43:7)

Eternal Prince & People:
Live on the Land &
Uphold the Law forever
(Eze37:24-26)

Present Heavens & Earth To be burned up (2Peter3:10)

New Heavens and New Earth:
Isaiah 65:17 (2 Peter 3:13)

If even the Heavens are expected to burn up, then for Scripture to remain true there is only one place Ezekiel's Kingdom can go and that is in the Highest Heavens where God dwells. Only there can Ezekiel's Kingdom escape destruction. There is simply no other alternative:

Scripture's Only Possible Resolution:

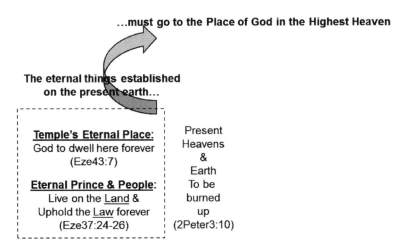

...**must go to the Place of God in the Highest Heaven**

The eternal things established on the present earth...

Temple's Eternal Place:
God to dwell here forever
(Eze43:7)

Eternal Prince & People:
Live on the <u>Land</u> &
Uphold the <u>Law</u> forever
(Eze37:24-26)

Present
Heavens
&
Earth
To be
burned
up
(2Peter3:10)

From the 8th day to the 13th day of the 1st month: The Creation of the New Heavens and Earth

The next Holy Day Ezekiel will reckon is the 14th Day, the preparation day for the Passover! So there happens to be 6 days that are to transpire since the last Holy Day on the 7th Day and then 6 days pass before Passover. So what do these 6 days represent? Recall that the opening passages of Genesis record that God created the present Heavens and Earth in 6 days. Thus, these 6 days must be reserved for God to create the New Heavens and a New Earth!

Isa 65:17 "For behold, I create new heavens and a new earth; and the former things shall not be remembered or come to mind.

The 1st Month

7th Day	8th Day	9th Day	10th Day	11th Day	12th Day	13th Day	14th Day

|←——— **6 Days of creation for New Heavens and New Earth?** ———→|

During this time it is also suggestive that Ezekiel's City may receive some further work done to it by God himself as the prophet Isaiah seems to indicate:

Isa 54:11-12 "O afflicted one, storm-tossed, and not comforted, behold, I will set

your stones in antimony, and your foundations I will lay in sapphires. "Moreover, I will make your battlements of rubies, and your gates of crystal, and your entire wall of precious stones.

Perhaps the reader is to understand that while God creates the New Heavens and Earth He is at the same time judging the Unrighteous Dead! Ezekiel's Kingdom too must also be safeguarded along with all the Saints. But not only that, the Beast and False Prophet were thrown into the Lake of Fire at the end of the Battle of Armageddon (Rev19:20). Hence, God must also preserve the Lake of Fire. The Place of the Dead however undoubtedly is destroyed and all of its inhabitants are resurrected in the 2nd Resurrection after which they are taken to the presence of God to be judged according to John.

And if Ezekiel's Kingdom is to be guarded by God, Where is its permanent home to be? And how does it get there?

The eternal Earthly things taken to the Place of God in the Highest Heaven must...

...be brought down to the...

New Earth: Isaiah 65:17 (2 Peter 3:13)

Isaiah's Testimony of the Coming Eternity

So if the 22nd day of the 7th month is to symbolize the Future Eternity what can be gleaned from the rest of the Scripture testimony to shed light on it more? The prophet Isaiah closes his writing in Isaiah 66 verses 22, 23 and 24 with the most illuminating perspective of the eternal state that the Word of God provides. As was reviewed in the previous chapter, Isaiah acknowledges that some of the Gentiles will be called to be as Levitical priests in verse 21 out of the Gog/Magog Invasion.

Starting in verse 22 it is declared that the New Heavens and the New Earth will endure just as the offspring and name of the Saintly Remnant are expected to endure likewise. No doubt this infers both Israel and the Gentiles that were just mentioned in verses 20 and 21. The clue of the New Creation is what tells the reader that these final passages all refer to its age. So it is especially interesting to note the word "offspring" here. This will turn out to be a provocative subject as Ezekiel's Holy Days testimony comes to be interpreted. Verse 23 then states that on every New Moon and on every Sabbath, all "flesh" is to come and bow down to God. Here is yet more definitive proof indicating the Law is alive and well in the eternal state. And again, "flesh" is indicated coming to worship God as if inferring mortal flesh.

Finally, in verse 24 this Saintly clan is to readily have access to look upon what is essentially the "Damned", those that "transgressed" against God. These Damned are to have a worm that never dies and a fire that is never quenched. The worm is no doubt in reference to the idea that these will be eternally tormented with the error of their ways as they self-reflect. That the fire is never quenched infers that God's anger against them never subsides. Is the Lake of Fire Edom which is to also be brought into the New Creation? (Isa34:10;Rev14:10-11)

In closing, the Future Eternity is a place where the Righteous and the Unrighteous coexist together but in polar extremes from one another. By all accounts, the reader is left interpreting the New World as being populated with mortal Saints that "endure" just as the New World is to "endure" and interestingly, "offspring" are a new detail to this subject of mortal life in eternity.

14th day of 1st month: Unveiling the New Creation

On Ezekiel's next Holy Day, the 14th Day of the 1st Month appears to be symbolizing the time when the New Creation is completed and comes to be unveiled. This is the first Day of the New Creation! The oddity that Ezekiel brings here is that the entire 14th Day becomes a full reckoned Holy Day. The Law only reckons the very end of the 14th Day as Passover. Ezekiel now calls this the 7 day Feast of "Passover"! He further states that "unleavened bread shall be eaten" as if to say nothing is really changing except that the 14th Day is now a full-fledged Holy Day and that Passover is the theme of the feast. It now also matches the 7 day Feast of Booths with its appended 8th day as if filling in missing pieces of the Law. Why the end of the 14th Day is not made the beginning here is because a new appended Schedule is being created having new Holy Days and new purposes for existing Holy Days. Why existing Holy Days are being used is because it can bring together old symbolisms (Passover) with new symbolisms (New Creation) to create a hidden message of how the New Creation is purchased with the blood of the Passover.

The first Day of the New Creation is reckoned a Day for cleansing corrupt Mortal Flesh. Ezekiel divulges that the Prince of Israel is going to offer yet another Sin Offering, this time for himself and all the People. Hence the Prince cannot be the Messiah. All the Mortal Flesh that is to be brought into the New Creation will need to be cleansed. Hence, physical cleansing is revealed as remaining necessary throughout the Future Eternity because Mortal Flesh is to survive throughout this same period. But the source for Spiritual cleansing that Ezekiel stealthfully confesses in Eze44:9 is a hidden message being linked to Passover.

Ezekiel's Feast Offerings:
2nd & 3rd Gen to be harvested in Future Eternity!

Here, for the first time, a consecutive number of Holy Days, 7, are accounted for in Ezekiel's Holy Days testimony. 7 consecutive Holy Days having all Atonement Offerings is not a new idea. It happens to match up exactly with the original Feast of Unleavened Bread Offerings. The Law's symbolism assigns this to be prophetic of Israel's Mortal Life which its Atonement Offerings are designated for. So it should be speculated here that Ezekiel is reusing the same Holy Days as if he were appending another group of Saints over and above what the original Holy Days symbolize. This new group is to emerge throughout the Era defined by the 7 consecutive Holy Days. This Era again is inside the Future Eternity. The Atonement for these Saints are provided for by Ezekiel's appended Offerings over and above the original Offerings for the same Holy Days period. The only viable explanation for what this 1st feast's 2nd set of Offerings symbolize is that some new element of the Remnant is expected to emerge inside the Future Eternity. There is no other possibility. And again, the last Holy Day Offerings of the 22nd are Libations. So this too emphasizes that new Saints are expected to appear in the Future Eternity.

So now the question becomes exactly who is to be understood being symbolized here? Before attempting to answer that, it first helps to recognize also that Ezekiel's final Holy Days Offerings are also appended over and above the Feast of Booths! Notice that the middle Feast of First Fruits Ezekiel skips over along with all the other Holy Days. In other words, he jumps immediately to the next 7 congruent Holy Days found in the original Holy Days Schedule. But here Ezekiel's Offerings are the same as those prescribed for the first feast. Thus, at this point there are 2 additional 7 Day Supplemental groups of Atonement Offerings to understand. And so there is yet a 2nd group of Saints being identified appearing during a 2nd Era symbolized by a 2nd period of 7 consecutive Days 6 months after the first group. Hence, there are 2 groups appearing one after the other separated by 6 months. With this knowledge, it is appropriate here to re-quote both Isaiah and Ezekiel in light of these absolutely astounding revelations from Ezekiel's Extended Holy Days Code:

Isa 59:21 "And as for Me, this is My covenant with them," says the LORD: "My Spirit which is upon you, and My words which I have put in your mouth, shall not depart from <u>your mouth</u>, nor from <u>the mouth of your offspring</u>, nor from <u>the mouth of your offspring's offspring</u>," says the LORD, "from now and forever."

Ezek 37:25 "And they shall live on the land that I gave to Jacob My servant, in

which your fathers lived; and they will live on it, <u>they</u>, and <u>their sons</u>, and <u>their sons' sons</u>, <u>forever</u>...

      This should be all the hints that an inquisitive reader needs to analyze in order to solve this riddle. For perhaps the final 2 Prophetic Generations of the Remnant out of the 3 that are prophesied making up Eternal Israel are being accounted for in Ezekiel's appended Schedule. The very 1st Generation is perhaps then being accounted for by all those who are harvested within the Present Creation! Hence, the Mortal populace of the Remnant that was brought into the Future Eternity is what the 1st Generation is defined as being in the accounting of God! This then leaves the 2 additional Generations to be accounted for inside the Future Eternity. The 2nd Generation is assigned to the First Feast's supplemental Offerings while the 3rd Generation is assigned to the Last Feast's supplemental Offerings! And so, after these 2 additional Generations come into existence, procreation comes to a halt.

Symbolism for Ezekiel's Feast Offerings of the 1st Month

15th Day	16th Day	17th Day	18th Day	19th Day	20th Day	21st Day

**The 2nd Generation of the Remnant
to be harvested inside the Future Eternity**

Symbolism for Ezekiel's Feast Offerings of the 7th Month

15th Day	16th Day	17th Day	18th Day	19th Day	20th Day	21st Day

**The 3rd Generation of the Remnant
to be harvested after the 2nd Generation**

The Ending to the Holy Days Code

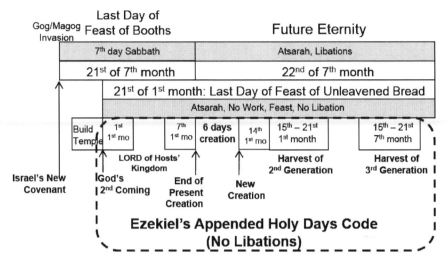

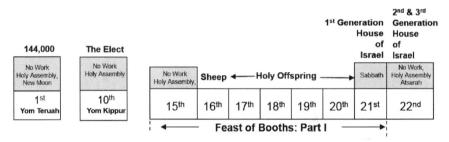

As can be noted, there is nothing here that takes away what the Gospel testimony communicates for those things promised for the Church. Everything is carefully laid out and room is left for the Heavenly Realm to be allowed to blaze its own trail, along its own path, which the Holy Days First Fruits testimony predict it does. That the Testimony of Jesus does not also bring these particular facets of Ezekiel's revelations to light is really not something of its concern. Each realm has its own place. Nevertheless, it has already been shown that the House of Israel is to receive its New Covenant and be given eternal mortal life because of it. But because John teaches that the 1st Resurrection ends at the beginning of the Messianic Kingdom Age, every Saint that emerges from then on must remain mortal forever. There can be no death to a mortal Saint beyond the 1st Resurrection. Hence, the Law's purpose remains intact being that it applies to someone as long as they live. If God is to dwell within mortal Israel's community than the atoning Offerings must remain being given for as long as mortal Israel survives. Since mortal Israel is predicted to live forever than so too the atoning Offerings need to be sustained forever as well.

Ezekiel also adds Atonement Offerings for the Sabbath, the New Moon and every Day. It is not difficult to understand why more atonement offerings will be necessary. Given that the Great Mystery means there will be many, many mortal lives living in the Future Eternity this simply suggests that the Law does not account for this increase with its own atonement offerings. Hence, Ezekiel's additional Daily, Weekly and Monthly Offerings anticipate an increased mortal population to atone for.

It is important to point out that Ezekiel records the East Gate of the Temple is to remain closed for the 6 days of work but then opened on the Sabbaths and New Moon days to allow the House of Israel to worship there. On the Law's harvest Holy Days, the Temple's North and South Gates are to be opened to allow for greater numbers of people to traffic through the Temple complex. Could it be possible that all the Saints, mortal and immortal, are all expected to come to pass through and worship here on the respective Holy Days since these very Days represent the entire Harvest Ingathering of the Divine Plan? It certainly is an intriguing prospect.

Readers may be questioning the validity of this interpretation of what Ezekiel's Holy Days testimony symbolizes since the traditional Christian view is that the Apostle John does not see Ezekiel's Kingdom in his visions of the Future Eternity in the book of Revelation. But the book entitled "Alpha Kai Omega: Expositing Scripture's Climatic Ending" reviews the book of Revelation in its entirety and shows that indeed John does corroborate Ezekiel's visions (see also the Website alphakaiomega.info). What this can only mean is that reader's eyes from time immemorial have been made blinded by Replacement Theology, so much so they cannot even see Ezekiel's Kingdom when John clearly presents it!

(This book has been made into a Website at theholydayscode.info. Most of the pages have a password in order to access them. This password is: **leviticus23:11kaimatthew28:1.**)